Barn 14 – Meg's Meadows

Also by the author

~ * ~

Call Me Lydia
Maple Dale
Favored to Win
Maple Dale Revisited
The Frog, the Wizard, and the Shrew
Ellie's Crows
Hannah's Home
A Thoroughbred's Dream
Odds on Favorite

Barn 14 - Meg's Meadows

Book Three of the Winning Odds Series

MaryAnn Myers

Sunrise Horse Farm
11872 Chillicothe Road
Chesterland, Ohio 44026
440-729-0930
www.sunrisehorsefarm.com

First Edition
10 9 8 7 6 5 4 3 2 1

This is a work of fiction. Names, characters, places, and incidents either are the products of the author's imagination or are used fictitiously, and any resemblance to actual persons, living or dead, events, or locales is entirely coincidental.

1. Fiction 2.Horses 3. Love Story 4. Thoroughbreds 5.Sports

Formatted to save paper

Barn 14 – Meg's Meadows is the long-awaited continuance of Favored to Win & Odds on Favorite of the Winning Odds Series.

Welcome back to Nottingham Downs!

Chapter One

Ben Miller took the news rather well, considering. At his age something like this was bound to happen sooner or later. Dawn looked at the doctor. "Are you recommending surgery?"

"Yes. The quicker the better."

"Can we put this off until the end of the month?" Ben asked. There was too much going on: The construction for the old-timers' retirement home, the Burgundy Blue Stake, the HBPA banquet, the ongoing debate over slots....

"No. This can't wait. Not if you to want to keep your eyesight." The doctor made notations on Ben's chart. "Both cataracts need to be removed."

"At the same time?"

"No. Six weeks apart. We'll do your right eye first. It's the most severe." The doctor glanced back from the door. "Look at the bright side. At least it's not glaucoma."

Dawn hooked her arm around Ben's as they left the building and walked to his truck. "It's not the end of the world, Ben," she said.

"That's easy for you to say. You're not the one that's old and feeble. Here, do you want to drive?" He offered her his keys.

She refused them and walked around to the passenger side. "The doctor didn't say you couldn't drive."

"Not yet. Just wait."

Dawn climbed into the cab of Ben's truck and smiled. "Are we done feeling sorry for ourselves?"

"Just about." He reached for the "Overnight" he'd picked up earlier today at the racetrack guard shack and scanned the list of horses in the fifth race. "I can read fine," he insisted, adjusting his glasses up and down. "I tell you, I can read perfectly."

~ * ~

Tom walked down the corridor to the cashier's desk, paid the boy's bail, and stood waiting. The longer he waited, the angrier he became. "This is the last time, Junior," he said, when the boy finally showed. "I should've let your sorry ass rot in jail."

Junior, Douglas Rupert Jr. to be exact was as the saying goes, "Trouble."

"Get in the truck."

Junior climbed in and stared out the side window. "You gonna tell my dad?"

Tom started the truck and looked at him. "Did you just hear yourself? Listen to you. You're eighteen years old, a grown man. Did you get dropped on your head or something when you were a baby? What the hell is wrong with you?"

Junior held his hand up, a bandaged hand no less. "I didn't start that fight. I'm going on record as saying that."

Tom shook his head. "Yeah, well I'm going on record as saying you're a piece of shit."

Junior looked at him. "My mom says you were just like me at my age."

"Oh really? Just shut up. Okay? Just shut up." Tom rammed the truck into gear and pulled out onto the highway. "Where do you want to go, home or the racetrack?"

Junior hesitated.

"Well?" Tom asked. "What's it going to be? What's your problem?"

"Um…I'm kinda hungry."

"Aw, Jesus," Tom said. By the time they stopped at McDonald's to get Junior something to eat it was after one before they pulled into the horsemen's entrance at Nottingham Downs.

The guard motioned for Tom to stop. "Did you hear?"

"Hear what?"

"Ferguson went skinny dipping in the infield pond?"

"What?"

"In broad daylight and drunk as a skunk! Nigh on to half an hour; kept yelling for everyone to either leave him alone or throw him a bar of soap."

Junior laughed.

Even Tom had to chuckle, though from racetrack management's perspective it was hardly funny. "How'd they get him out?" Ferguson was no small man. "Never mind. I don't want to know." He had more important things on his mind.

Ben looked up from his desk when Tom walked into the tack room with Junior in tow. He stared at the young man's battered face. "Your father's looking for you."

"Lucy too," Dawn said, appearing in the door behind them. "She's been down here twice."

"Don't tell her you saw me."

Dawn looked at him and cringed.

"Please…" Junior pleaded.

Dawn shook her head. "You can't keep avoiding her."

"I can for a little while," Junior insisted.

Tom reached for his chaps. He had three horses to pony this afternoon. "Remind me again why we hired you."

Junior looked at him, two black eyes, cuts, scrapes, bruises, three stitches in his chin and all. "Because I'm the best damned exercise boy on God's green earth."

"And the biggest bullshitter too," Tom said, laughing.

"Not when it comes to riding," Junior said.

Tom looked at him. "If you're not careful that's going to be your only claim to fame. Nothing else. Do you actually want to go through life a piece of shit? Because let me tell you, that's where you're headed."

Ben motioned for them to either shut up or leave.

Tom left. Junior left. Dawn left. Ben called after her. "Where are *you* going?"

Dawn laughed. "I'll be right back."

This morning had uncovered quite a few concerns. One of them Dawn couldn't help worrying about as she walked over to the grandstand to talk to Wendy. Given the volatile turn of events with the *Morning Banter*, a local newspaper taking exception to just about everything concerning Nottingham Downs lately, now this….

Wendy looked up from her desk and shook her head. "Are these people serious? Do they actually think we rig the races?"

Dawn sat down. "Apparently so."

"How are we going to respond? What do you want to do?"

Dawn stared out the large plate-glass windows overlooking the racetrack. "Is ignoring them an option?"

"Not really. Not with that open-letter challenge. It would be like admitting guilt. I wish Richard was here."

Richard Spears, Nottingham Downs' General Manager was on medical leave and not expected to return for weeks. Contrary to what the *Morning Banter* printed last month, he was not in rehab for alcohol abuse. He was recovering from complications brought on by gallbladder surgery.

"What does Ben think?"

Dawn sighed. "He thinks I should write an op-ed."

"An op-ed?" Wendy smiled.

"Yep, that's what he said." The Ben Miller of old wouldn't even have known what an op-ed piece was, but since this ongoing battle with the *Banter*, he was up on all kinds of journalistic terms.

"What do you think? Are you going to write one?"

"I don't know. I'm afraid it'll just open up a can of worms."

Both women paused. "Well, you know what Richard would say? The best defense...."

"Is a good offense." Dawn nodded. "I know."

"Do you want some coffee?"

Dawn shook her head. She and Wendy were the best of friends. Even long before Wendy and Tom were married, the two women had become as close as sisters. Both lived in houses on Ben's farm and ate dinners most every evening together. They were like family. Tom and Wendy were known as Uncle Tom and Aunt Wendy to Dawn and Randy's children, D.R. and Maeve. Wendy and Dawn were like daughters to Ben. Tom and Randy were like his sons. They were all in this together.

The first race was about to run. Dawn glanced down at the crowd and smiled at the sight of the people standing in line for a hotdog. It had been Tom's idea to build an outdoor hotdog stand and it was a hit.

"Make it the best one we've got where you can get just about everything you want on it." The consensus was to draw the line at anchovies. But when it came to onions, cucumbers, dill pickles, chili, relish, sauerkraut, mustard, ketchup, cheese, jalapenos, olives, coleslaw, you name it, they had it. Inside the grandstand, only the standard hotdogs were available. People flocked to the stand outside, the specialty being the Daily Double Ultimate Hog Dog grilled over an open fire and served up all day. Rumor had it business men from near and far would dash in for lunch and a daily wager and could be back to work in a little under an hour. The perfect lunch break and that was the best part. It brought in more racetrack fans and had them outside watching live horseracing.

"I'll see you later," Dawn said, waving over her shoulder.

Wendy smiled. "Let me know what you want to do."

Dawn's hands-on involvement in the daily operation of the racetrack the past couple of years was reassuring to everyone involved, albeit annoying at times like this if you asked Dawn. The *Morning Banter* had become a thorn in their collective sides.

Wendy stood looking out the window and watched Tom for a moment. He was "parked" over to the side of the paddock with all the other pony boys and girls. When Red; Tom's pony, pinned his ears and nipped at the pony standing next to him, she smiled. This was just Red. She recalled riding him on the farm one day scared to death no matter how much Tom assured her the horse would be the perfect gentleman. And he was. Yet, on the racetrack he could be so tenacious.

"He has to be," Tom said. "It's what makes him a great pony."

Tom glanced up and the two of them smiled at one another. She didn't always know when Tom had a horse to pony in a race, but whenever she was in her office, she always looked before the start of a race just in case. She asked him once if he was ever going to retire from ponying horses.

"No, I'm going to be just like Mim. I'll build a ramp so I can mount and off I'll go."

Wendy recalled the day she first met Mim. The old woman chewed her out. She couldn't recall exactly what Mim was scolding her for, but surely it had to be about the backside and something she felt needed changed for the betterment of the horsemen.

Tom motioned to the starting gate and he and Wendy focused their attention on the race. The four horse was acting up in the gate. Wendy glanced at the tote board. The horse was 5-2. The favorite. He reared. He stomped. He fidgeted. He settled.

"And they're off!"

When the phone rang, Wendy turned away reluctantly. "Nottingham Downs."

"Mrs. Girard?"

"Yes," Wendy said, "speaking."

"This is Metropolitan General Hospital. Your son Matthew has been in an automobile accident."

Wendy stared. "Is he okay?"

The man hesitated. "You're going to want to get here as soon as possible."

Wendy was a good hour away and that's if there was no traffic, no construction. She grabbed her purse and cellphone, scribbled a note to leave on her desk and hurried to her car. Matthew was her oldest, due to graduate this year and get his BA in computer science. He was a kind, sweet boy, a man actually. He was twenty-two years old.

Was? Wendy barreled down the highway with tears streaming down her face. "Don't let him die, Al," she said, talking out loud to Matthew's father; her first husband now deceased. "Don't let him die." She swerved to miss a truck turning in front of her. "Oh my God!" She just missed it. "Oh my God, oh my God, oh my God. Please, God!"

She drew a deep breath at the light, tried composing herself. "You're going to want to get here as soon as possible." The man's voice echoed in her mind, in her heart. "As soon as possible. As soon as possible."

The light turned green. When her cellphone rang, she glanced at the caller ID. Metropolitan Hospital. "Oh my God, no." She pulled off to the side of the road. "Yes?"

"Mrs. Girard?"

"Yes."

"We want you to know that we are life-flighting your son Matthew to the Edgewater Trauma Center."

Life-flight. Life-flight. Edgewater Trauma Center. "That means he's still alive," Wendy whispered. "That means he's still alive."

"Mrs. Girard?"

"Yes. Yes, I'll be there." Her voice caught in her throat. "I'm on my way."

"Do you know where Edgewater is located?"

"No," she said, "but I'll find it."

"Mrs. Girard, your son Gordon is with him."

"Oh my God. Gordon? Don't tell me he was hurt too?"

"No, he's fine. He just arrived."

Arrived? "I don't understand." Arrived from where?

"I'm sorry. I don't have details."

Wendy swallowed hard and pushed her hair off her face. "Can I have the address please?"

The woman relayed the address. Wendy punched it into her GPS and glanced over her shoulder, made a U-Turn across a four-lane highway and headed for the Edgewater Trauma Center. Her estimated time of arrival was thirty-three minutes. She had already been on the road over three-quarters of an hour.

She thought about her Grandma June, how she lay on a gurney the last hour of her life outside the door of a MRI room while the entire family paced the floor upstairs around her empty hospital bed. "Grandma, help him," she said. "Help me get to him. I don't want him to go alone. Help me get to both of them."

A flash of light caught her eye. "Oh no! No!"

The police car siren blasted.

"No! This can't be happening! Oh God, why?"

She pulled over. The police cruiser pulled in behind her. Before the officer could even get close she had her door open, crying and trying to explain. The man stepped back, his hand on his revolver.

"It's my son. Help me. I need help. You don't understand. They're taking him to Edgewater and I have to get there. My grandmother died alone."

"Ma'am, calm down. Ma'am, just calm down."

"Here's my license. Here's my purse. Please just let me go. I have to go."

The office took her license. "What's your son's name?"

"Matthew." She wiped her eyes, sobbing. "Matthew Morrison."

Just as the officer received confirmation of the information, Wendy heard the sound of a helicopter and looked up at the sky. "Oh my God! Matthew."

The officer took her by the arm and led her to the police cruiser. "I'll take you there. Be careful, watch your head. I'll get you there in no time. Don't worry."

Wendy stared out the window, her face pressed against the pane trying to follow the helicopter. It was right in front of them, then overhead, behind them, and then it was gone. She turned frantically, trying to see out the back window.

"We're only a few minutes away," the officer said, siren blaring. "Try and relax. Your son is going to a good hospital. It's the best in the area. They'll take good care of him there."

They sped by cars, slowed only through intersections, and drove up the ramp to the Edgewater Trauma Center at a blistering speed. The officer killed the siren. At the top of the ramp sat a helicopter, propellers still turning, engine idling.

Wendy sat paralyzed with fear as the helicopter door was opened. An attendant stepped out, then a young man. "Gordon." The name of her youngest son escaped her lips. "That's my son," she said. "My sons." Gordon stepped back out of the way as the emergency room attendant climbed up into the helicopter.

"Ma'am," the officer said, door open and at her side. He offered her a hand.

"Those are my sons," she said. She could see Matthew lying on the gurney, not moving, lifeless amidst a barrage of tubes and wires. No one knew her sons better than her. She'd practically raised them by herself. Their father had died so young. It was just the three of them for the longest time.

"Don't, Al. Don't take him," she whispered.

Gordon looked up as the officer led Wendy to the landing pad. "Mom?" His eyes welled up with tears. "It's bad, Mom. It's bad."

Wendy reached for his hand and gripped it tight, both trembling. She looked in at Matthew, so still, so close and yet so distant. The officer helped steady her. She looked at the helicopter paramedic. He shook his head. "We're losing him," he said.

"No…" Wendy cried. "No…. No…." She reached in to touch him. "Matthew, come on. Come on, Son. Come on." She rubbed his arm, the way she always did when either of her sons weren't feeling well. "I love you, Matthew…don't go." Gordon put his arms around her.

"Don't go, Matthew. Don't go…."

The paramedic studied the dials and motioned for her to keep talking.

"Matthew. Listen to me. It's Mom. Listen to me. You have a long life ahead of you. You can do this, Son. You can stay."

Gordon stood at her side. "Come on, Matthew, damn it. Come on."

The paramedic nodded again.

Wendy rubbed Matthew's arm over and over. "Son!" She glanced at the heart monitor. It was moving faster and faster. "Son!"

The paramedic glanced at the emergency attendant. "All right, let's do this." The officer tugged Wendy back out of the way. She looked at the paramedic. He smiled. Not a great big smile, but a smile nonetheless. "Walk alongside and keep talking," he said. "Both of you."

Chapter Two

Joe Feigler tracked Tom down at the barn, "Here." He handed Tom the note, out of breath and holding his side. "Wendy left this for you."

Tom glanced at it and looked up at him. "When? When did this happen?"

"What's going on?" Ben asked, from the tack room.

Tom turned. "Matthew's been in a car accident."

"Is he okay?"

"I don't think so." Tom grabbed his cellphone out of his pocket and dialed Wendy's number. No answer. "I better go. Get someone to cover for me," he told Joe. "I've got one in the fifth for Burton."

Joe nodded and just then Tom's cellphone rang. He looked at the ID.

"Wendy?"

"It's Gordon. Mom's with Matthew."

"How is he?" Tom stared at the note.

"He's uh…." Gordon cleared his throat. "He wasn't good when he got here, but he seems to be doing a little better. They say his heart is beating more regular now."

"Good, that's good." Tom motioned to Ben. "What happened?"

"He was driving and…" Gordon hesitated. "Texting me about his exam."

"Fuck," Tom said, staring down at the ground and shaking his head. "How many times have I said…?"

"I know. I know." Gordon cleared his throat again.

"How's your mom?"

"She's okay. She's okay, I think. We're waiting to hear about the brain scan."

When Ben said something, Tom turned. "Is he conscious?" Ben asked.

Tom stared at him. "Gordon, is he conscious?"

"No. He's been out the whole time."

Tom shook his head. "I'm on my way. Tell your mom."

"We're at Edgewater. They life-flighted him here." Gordon's voice cracked. "Tom, he died on the way. His heart stopped beating."

"What?"

Gordon tried speaking and couldn't. Tom turned away at the sound of the young man crying. "I'll be there." He hung up and looked at Ben and Joe. "Check with Freda about Burton. I'll call you, Ben. Tell Dawn. Okay?"

Ben nodded. Joe nodded.

"If Freda can't do it, get Junior." Tom glanced back. "He can use Red. Get him to run stalls too. Don't you be doing them, old man. You hear me?"

Ben waved for him to go. Edgewater Trauma Center was about a fifteen-minute drive from the racetrack this time of day when there was little traffic. It took longer to find a parking space once Tom arrived. As he walked to the entrance, he looked for Wendy's car, for Gordon's. There was a hearse parked close by.

He entered through the sliding door and walked to the desk. A young woman looked up at him. "Matthew Morrison," he said.

"Are you related?"

"Yes," he said. "Stepfather."

She pointed. "Room four, on the left."

Tom slowed his pace as he approached the room. He'd never referred to himself as the boys' father before, a stepfather. Gordon looked up when he entered the room. Tom put his arm around him, gave him a pat. Wendy had her back to them. She turned. Tom motioned for her to not get up. She was sitting at Matthew's side. The boy was pale, tubes everywhere, beeping machines, a crease in his young brow.

Tom walked to his other side, trembling. How was it that in less than two years, this family had come to mean so much to him? This *was* his family. He smoothed Matthew's hair back, hair so long, and always Tom teasing about his needing to get it cut.

"Men don't wear ponytails," he would say.

"Oh yes they do," Matthew insisted. "Real men anyway."

Tom gazed at Matthew, as much a son to him as if he'd…. "Dear God," he whispered. "Save my boy."

Wendy, Tom, and Gordon turned when a man wearing scrubs entered the room. "Hello, family. I'm Dr. Hanover."

Tom shook his hand. Gordon shook his hand. Wendy could only nod, frightened by the look in the doctor's eyes.

"I'm not going to sugarcoat this. It's going to be touch and go for the next couple of days. This young man suffered a severe blow to the back of his head." He scanned the chart in his hands up close, looked at it hard for a few seconds and then tucked it under his arm. "That is the major concern and also the amount of time his heart stopped. Fortunately he was on oxygen at the time."

Wendy looked at Matthew. She looked at Gordon. She looked at Tom.

"We're going to keep him sedated, at least for a little while," Dr. Hanover said. "If he wakes too soon he's going to be extremely uncomfortable. I don't want to have to introduce pain killers just yet, not until we see how much inflammation we're going to encounter."

"Is he going to make it?" Tom asked.

"He has a good chance. A lot will depend on how determined he is, what type of personality he has, what's going on in that head of his at the moment."

"There's probably a lot going on in there," Gordon said affectionately. "My brother's a geek."

"Oh gee, so was I," Dr. Hanover said. He looked at Matthew. He just looked at him.

Tom watched the man, wondering, what was he observing? What was he seeing?

The doctor sighed. "We want to do everything we can to make sure the same Matthew comes out of this. That's why we're being so careful."

Wendy, Tom, and Gordon let the weight of that settle over them.

"I'll check back in with you in a few hours." Dr. Hanover started out the door and looked back. "Be careful what you say around him. I have a feeling he's listening."

Wendy smiled, holding onto hope. "Thank you, Doctor."

~ * ~

The Stewards lodged an inquiry after the finish of the seventh race. In question: whether or not the five horse; on the lead and lugging out on the rail, impeded the three horse that ended up running second. This was the first time since Ben and Dawn took ownership of Nottingham Downs that there was absolutely no one in the General Offices during race time. Richard was gone. Wendy was gone. Tom was gone. Dawn was gone. Technically, even Ben was gone. He was over at the barn on the backside running stalls. Given the circumstances, no one actually needed to be in the General Offices. The inquiry was the Stewards' concern. But the fact that not one person of ownership or management authority was present, upset the racing secretary Joe Feigler to no end.

If it weren't for the "nursing home" upstairs, he probably wouldn't have minded so much. As it was, he couldn't help but worry. What if something happened to one of the old-timers? What if something happened to Mim? He paced back and forth in front of the window overlooking the track and was startled when he heard a noise behind him.

"Excuse me," he said, taken aback. He didn't know this person, let alone the young woman's appearance, flaming red spiked hair and dressed like a pixie. "What can I do for you?"

"I'm here to deliver a telegram."

"A telegram? How did you get through security?"

The young woman hesitated. "I came in the back way."

Joe stared. "The back way?" Just then the phone rang and he picked it up. "Nottingham Downs."

"Is this Richard Spears?"

"No. Can I take a message?" As Joe reached for a pen and notepad, the young woman disappeared. He dropped the phone and hurried out into the hall. "Miss?" He glanced in one direction then the other. She'd vanished completely. He hurried back in and picked up the phone only to find that the caller had hung up. He sat down in Richard's chair and sighed. "Hell of a job I'm doing."

He closed his eyes and rubbed his forehead. He'd had an argument with his wife Lucille that morning. She said she hated him. She'd said that before. The menopause. He told her one day he was going to believe her. She said that day had better be today.

"Yes, dear."

He reluctantly opened his eyes and glanced out the window. The official sign had posted. The five horse was taken down and placed second. The three horse entered the winner's circle.

"Joe!" Someone yelled to him from the Secretary's office. "Come here a minute."

"I'll be right there." A message on Richard's desk caught his attention. He checked the doorway and picked up the note. "More bad news," it read. "Call me. Tee."

"Who the hell is Tee? What kind of bad news? We don't need more bad news."

"Joe!"

"I'm coming!" He put the note down and straightened it the way it lay, walked away, and then came back and straightened it again just to be safe.

~ * ~

Dawn and Randy walked down the hospital corridor to Matthew's room. It was at the far end of the hall on the left. The drapes were pulled shut, the room rather dark. "He's sleeping," Wendy whispered, motioning to a monitor. "Somehow they can tell."

When Matthew furrowed his brow, perhaps hearing his mother speak from a sleepy distance, Randy smiled and nodded. It was just a little over twenty-four hours since Matthew's accident and already the young man appeared to be stabilized. Randy scanned the monitors. Heart rate good. EEG good. Matthew's blood pressure was a little high but under the circumstances that was likely normal. Randy glanced at the catheter bag hanging low on the side of the bed rail. Urine clear.

At one point Randy had thought about going into Internal Medicine. Cardiology interested him a great deal, but with growing up on a working farm and his inherent love of animals it was little more than a fleeting thought. He was destined to become a veterinarian.

"Ben was here earlier," Wendy said softly.

Dawn gave her a hug. "How are you doing?"

"Okay. I'm hopeful. Tom was here all night."

"He said to tell you him and Gordon picked up your car and that he'll be here later."

Wendy nodded. "He's bringing me things so I can wash up. I don't want to leave until…."

Dawn held her tight. "He's going to be fine. Shhh, don't cry."

Wendy wiped her eyes. Randy stepped back out of the way when a nurse entered the room. She made some notations on Matthew's chart and smiled. "I can tell this boy is loved."

"Definitely," Wendy said, wiping her eyes again.

"Wish we could IV him some latte," Randy said. "That'd move him right up, Matthew style."

They all chuckled.

"Perhaps tomorrow," the nurse said, leaving.

The plan was to wean the young man off sedation gradually. Everything depended on tomorrow. Randy looked at Wendy. "Why don't you go take a break."

Wendy hesitated, shrugging as she looked at Dawn.

"Go on. You two go. I'll sit with him," Randy said.

Wendy looked at her son. "If I only knew what he was thinking…."

Randy smiled. "I think he's thinking you need to listen to *the doctor*," he said, meaning him.

Wendy laughed. "Fine, we'll go. You have my cell number, right?"

"Yep," Randy nodded. "Go on, go."

Wendy and Dawn walked down the corridor, arm in arm. "What a difference a day makes," Wendy said, as they boarded the elevator. "I still don't know what happened, not really. If he comes out of this…."

"When," Dawn said, "Not if."

Wendy nodded. "When. He's probably going to lose his license. They'll need to get another car too." The two of them stepped off the elevator and followed the signs to the cafeteria. "It's not as if they really need a car with them both living in that ridiculous frat house right across the street from the campus entrance," Wendy added, thinking out loud.

Both women laughed. The house was indeed a dump. Not having a car would hurt Gordon the most. The majority of his classes were to the south side of the mile-long campus. "They have a shuttle but really they'll need another car soon. I'm not sure how this works. If the accident is his fault, what's covered?"

"Everything," Dawn said. "That's what you have insurance for."

"You're right. I'm repeating myself. I'm not thinking straight. Everything's going to be all right."

Upstairs, Randy was assuring Matthew of the same thing. "Everything's going to be all right." He studied the young man's face. Matthew reminded him a little of him at this age, all except for the long hair. He sighed and then glanced around the room. There was a *Time* magazine on the windowsill. He walked over, started leafing through it, then settled down in the chair next to Matthew and started reading softly. "This is interesting. You'll like this. It's an article on the molecular structure of snails."

He propped his feet on the bed rail and turned the page. "The female is in a perpetual state of estrus and can produce young throughout her entire lifetime. The male on the other hand is subject to periods of infertility."

The actual article he was reading was about natural gas fracking; a drilling practice Matthew vehemently opposed. There was no way Randy was going to read that one and chance Matthew comprehending from deep inside the fog and getting riled up.

"Read me a story, Daddy," Randy could hear Maeve and D.R. say. How many times? Probably a hundred. Randy had making up stories down pat.

"Now the youngsters in the snail family never go far." He chuckled to himself. "That's because the mother snails have radar in their antennae and can summon them back with an annoying vibrating sound that only their own young can hear. And the snail is wired so that they can't refuse."

Wendy and Dawn stood quietly in the doorway, listening.

"It's in the molecules of their DNA. Just like people there are no two snail DNA alike. Male snail DNA has an extra chromosome that enables them to roam further than the females but they find when they are in foreign territory they start to get a stomach ache."

When Dawn and Wendy laughed, Randy turned and smiled. "He's doing fine. He's liking this." He motioned to the monitors and then quietly turned another page. "So the snails all stay close to home and live happily ever after."

Chapter Three

Ben made himself a mayonnaise and cheese sandwich, poured a cup of coffee, and walked out onto his farmhouse porch to sit for a while. It wasn't often he fixed himself something to eat anymore, not with all the "lady folk" here fussing over him all the time. He drew a breath and sighed. Speaking of lady folk....

Brenda came tooling down the drive on the ATV. "Any word?"

"No. Last I heard he was doing okay though, so hopefully when they wake him up tomorrow he'll be on the mend."

As he took a sip of his coffee, Brenda narrowed her eyes. "That's not high-test, is it?"

Ben shook his head. "Don't you have some work to do?"

"Listen, just because Wendy isn't here doesn't mean I'm not watching you."

"Yep." Ben took another sip. "Fat chance this old man can make his own decisions, particularly when it comes to what he eats and drinks."

"Oh, don't start," Brenda said, smiling. "If we didn't love you...."

"Yeah, I know. Yadda yadda yadda. And if it weren't for all of you loving me I'd be eating pork hocks swimming in grease and washing it down with expresso so strong you could stand a fork in it."

Brenda laughed. "It's *espresso*, Ben, not expresso. And trust me, you wouldn't like it."

They both turned, puzzled when they saw Wendy's car turn off the road into the driveway. As it got closer, they could see it was Gordon driving. The young man parked over by the main barn and walked up to the house. Brenda studied his eyes. He looked like he'd aged ten years in a day.

"Have you been to the hospital?" Ben asked.

He shook his head and walked past them. "No, I don't want to go. I can't stand seeing him like that." The screen door banged shut behind him.

"Should we go talk to him?" Brenda asked.

Ben stared over his shoulder in the wake of the young man's path. "There's nothing we can say that'll help. He needs to deal with this his own way."

Brenda nodded. They all knew Gordon well. He kept things to himself, dealt with things by himself. Matthew on the other hand was an open book and wanted to debate issues to death. What if? Why not? That's not right? What the hell? That was his favorite expression, "What the hell?"

Brenda drove on. Ben used to love mayonnaise and cheese sandwiches and wondered why this one didn't taste as good as he remembered. Where were the dogs when he needed them? He scanned the pastures and damned his failing eyesight. Was that them up on the hill by Randy's parents Liz and Randy Sr.'s ranch house? Probably not. If that were them, they'd be moving. Must be trees, he thought. "No, can't be. There never used to be any trees there."

"You talking to me, Ben?" Gordon asked from inside the house.

"No, I'm talking to myself. It's what old men do when they can't see."

After a good long silence, Gordon commented. "Wonder if Matthew will live to be an old man?"

"If the Lord's willing," Ben said.

Gordon scoffed. "I hate when people say things like that."

"Yeah, me too," Ben said, and here came the dogs, all six of them; five Labradors and a Standard Poodle. He fed them the rest of his sandwich, each got a tiny piece. Then he shooed them off the porch. Rotty, the Standard Poodle refused to leave and whined at the door for Wendy. "Go on. She'll be home later."

"Who?" Gordon asked.

"Your mom. Rotty's looking for her."

Gordon appeared in the doorway and just stood there for a moment, looking down at Rotty and then all the other dogs. He just stood there, and Ben just sat there, a minute, maybe two. "They say he might not even be okay even if he does wake up, you know."

Ben looked at him. "The odds are in his favor. He's young. He's healthy."

Gordon nodded, but only slightly. "He aced his exam. I checked with the Prof."

Ben smiled, and again, Gordon just stood there and Ben just sat there.

"I don't know what to do," Gordon finally said.

"Me neither," Ben said. "If I were a younger man, I think I'd go clean some stalls or move some hay or something. I'd be staying busy."

Gordon looked at him.

"George and Glenda could probably use some help. They're going to be bringing in the mares soon."

Gordon nodded and walked outside and down the steps. About halfway to the barn he glanced back. "Thanks, Gramps."

Ben chuckled. D.R. and Maeve called him Grandpa all the time. So did Linda Dillon's little girl Maria. But this was the first time Gordon had ever referred to him as Gramps.

"If George and Glenda are done, see if Dusty needs some help."

"Sure thing, Gramps." The young man walked on, smiling.

Ben was smiling too. But then he thought about Matthew, how close he and Gordon were, and how devastated Gordon would be if Matthew didn't recover or was impaired in some way. "I don't understand life, Meg," he said, talking to his dead wife, the love of his life. "Why do things like this have to happen?"

Talking to her wasn't new. He'd actually never stopped talking to her after she passed. He looked around the farm and could see her everywhere. He thought about how she loved to hang sheets on the clothesline. He thought about how often she used to scrub the porch, how she would plant petunias each year, all different colors, how she'd bury crushed eggshells in the rose beds.

He stared out over the north pasture to T-Bone's place. The six-bedroom farmhouse was currently being refurbished and turned into an "old-folks home" for Mim and the other old-timers. Sometimes he swore he could see old T-Bone out in the garden, but the man had passed away last year in his sleep. Turnip greens were his favorite thing to eat, to grow. Who'd have ever thought they'd grow back wild this spring?

Ben decided to take a walk, to take his own advice. Keep busy. Walk, walk, walk. One foot in front of the other. From a distance, George, Brenda, Gordon, and Dusty watched.

"Where's he going?" Brenda asked.

Ben wasn't one to walk anywhere except back and forth to the racetrack and the grandstand. Meg was the one that loved to walk for the sheer joy of walking. Ben would look down the shedrow, wondering where she'd gone, and here she'd come. "Where were you?"

"Just walking."

He'd always ask and that's what she'd always say. She was actually the healthier-conscious of the two. That's what made it so ironic that she passed before him. He'd have gladly given up his life for her. He told her that as she lay dying. Some people say things like that in times of sorrow, but he meant it.

"Is he walking to T-Bone's?" Brenda asked.

Sure enough, when Ben got to the end of the driveway he took a breather and then turned left and kept on walking. The dogs were scouring the front pasture and decided to join him, all frolicking and barking. Rotty was the biggest barker, albeit it a high-pitched yap.

"Quit," Ben told them.

"Should I go see…?" Brenda said.

When Gordon shook his head, Brenda smiled.

Ben waved at a passing truck. The driver, a distant neighbor, waved back. Ben continued walking along, just him and the dogs. Gimpy licked his hand. Sloopy nipped at his feet. Dawber jumped on Piccolo. Piccolo jumped on Runt. Rotty just kept yapping.

T-Bone's house was over a hundred years old. Its age was its saving grace in turning it into the old-folks home. After months of fighting with zoning, Dawn's Uncle Matt's people found a loophole. It would require fudging a few things, Matt had said. "What do you want to do?"

Ben didn't have to think twice. "These people need a home. I'll change my name if I have to, to get this done."

Ben recalled the first time he'd met T-Bone. "What, were we in our twenties, Meg? Thirties?"

~ 29 ~

"You were thirty-two and I had just turned thirty," he could hear her say.

T-Bone had been a good neighbor. He could be a little cranky and definitely territorial, but a fairly reasonable man. Ben remembered the time Beau Born's sire Native Beau got out of his paddock and bred one of T-Bone's Morgan mares. "I outta sue you," T-Bone said, leading a rather docile after-glowing Native Beau home by way of this very road and up Ben's driveway.

"Oh yeah? Well, you're just lucky I don't charge you a stud fee."

The two men didn't speak for months after that. It was the wives that smoothed things over and the foal was so pretty. "Beau's Tryst" they called it.

Ben glanced ahead and kept walking. By now the dogs had settled down and were intent on leading the way. Over the years there had been a lot of shared dinners at T-Bone's place. The dogs probably had hopes of some table scraps. They seemed to have picked up their pace.

"Either that," Ben said, "or I'm slowing down."

He thought about all the bickering among the families of the soon-to-be residents of this old-folks home. Not one of the old-timers had assets, but some had pensions. Most received monthly Social Security checks and were on Medicare. One had no benefits at all. It didn't matter to the old-timers one bit who was going to be paying how much or how little, but their sons and daughters and even some of the grandchildren sure had plenty to say.

"My mom should not have to share a room with someone who is paying less."

"My grandfather should have more care than the rest since he's paying more."

"I don't like this arrangement. My dad is going to need more care eventually. This is not a good idea. I think you're doing this just for the money."

"The money?"

Ben climbed the front steps to T-Bone's old house, sat down, and wiped his brow. The dogs milled all around him. If he had a favorite, it was probably Sloopy. He had the kindest eyes and eyebrows that were always twitching one way or the other. He had a look of wisdom about him. Ben patted them all on their heads and gazed at the farm he'd just left behind. It seemed counties away. An odd thought crossed his mind. Would he end up here someday too, needing rails on the walls to get from one room to the next, a bed with rails on both sides?

"Meg?"

Nothing. Normally she would respond. He looked at Sloopy. "What do *you* think?"

Sloopy wagged his tail.

The Amish builders had left hours ago and yet the scent of fresh-cut pine boards lingered in the air. When Ben had enough of a rest, he rose and walked inside T-Bone's front door. It was currently unlocked, but according to the offspring of the soon-to-be residents, they needed "security." Ben had lived a lifetime without security. He'd lived a lifetime with very little fear.

"Don't worry," Dawn had insisted. "We'll take care of it."

The living room of the house was plenty big enough to accommodate eight residents. There were plans for a large screen television between the two front windows. There would be a table for playing cards. A table for a jigsaw puzzle. It would be nice, Ben thought.

What else could they do? They only had a short time to finish. They were targeting a deadline of mid-month to get them out of the executive offices at the racetrack and in the meantime keep Social Services at bay. Ben smiled, remembering the night Tom picked them all up from the nursing home where they were about to be evicted. He said their eyes all lit up at the sight of the horse van there to transport them. They loved being at the racetrack.

Ben sighed. It's certainly where he'd like to be if he were them. And if not there, then here would be almost just as good. They could see all the barns and the ones that still got around good could take walks. The new pasture for the yearlings was practically in the back yard. They could enjoy the horses romping and playing, grazing, watch them lying down in the tall grass. They could hear Beau Born when he let out that stallion whinny of his.

Ben chuckled. "I'll have to warn them about that."

T-Bone's kitchen was being brought up to code. Another day or two, it would probably be completed. The bathrooms were already finished. More rails to hold onto, high seats. The women had to have their bathroom, the men, theirs. The ramps for wheelchair access were being built and would be installed last. Everything seemed to be in order.

Ben walked out onto the back porch and smiled at the sight of all the dogs waiting for him. Piccolo had a turnip he'd obviously just dug up and was alternately chewing hard on it and tossing it into the air. Runt crouched nearby, ready to pounce on him. The rest....

Ben noticed something moving way off the distance by the main barn at his farm. Was that Randy's truck? He squinted. "What's he doing home so early?" Surely if something was wrong with one of the horses, Brenda or George would have let him know.

Or would they, he wondered. "I don't like people protecting me." The dogs all wagged their tails in apparent agreement. "Guess it's time to head back." He gave thought to trekking down through the pastures, but the hill up the other side might prove too much of a challenge. He took the road instead, took his time, and was halfway down his driveway when Tom pulled in.

"What's going on, old man? You lost?"

Ben laughed. "Nah, I took a walk. How's the boy?"

"Still sleeping. You want a ride?"

Ben hesitated, thinking. He didn't have that much farther to walk to the house, but the barn was a good distance further. "Nah, that's okay."

"All right. I'm gonna go take a nap. I'll see you later," Tom said. The dogs followed his truck, barking and frolicking. Ben walked on, thinking. If it weren't for Matthew lying in a state of limbo at the hospital, this would be just a routine day at the farm.

Randy, George, Glenda, Dusty, and Gordon stood talking in the main aisle of the barn, and turned as Ben approached. A routine day? Not if you asked them. "What's going on, Ben?" George asked.

"I don't know. I was just about to ask you the same thing." They were all standing in front of All Together's stall. "What's going on?"

George looked in at the mare and sighed. "I think she's horsin'."

"What?" Ben turned to Randy.

"She could have slipped the foal." Randy said. "I don't want to palpate her for fear of bringing something on if she is still in foal."

The mare walked around her stall, squatted and passed some fluid. It was too thick for urine, but.... "Let me do some blood work first and rule out an infection. We'll go from there." Randy walked to his truck to get the items needed to draw blood.

"When did she start this?" Ben asked.

"Just a little while ago," George said.

"When was someone going to tell me?"

~ 33 ~

George just looked at him a moment. He'd been Ben's farm manager for years. Ben was involved in the day- to-day operation of the farm, but not on a hour-to-hour, minute-to-minute basis. "I don't know, maybe when I had something to tell you. What's going on with you, Ben?"

"Me...?"

"Yeah, you. If All Together slipped her foal, it's nobody's fault."

"I didn't say it was anybody's fault." Ben looked at each one of them. This was his family; these were his friends. "I don't want to have surgery on my eyes," he said.

"Is that what this is all about?" Dusty asked.

Ben shrugged and looked at Gordon. "I want the best for your brother." He shook his head. "It's not fair. He's too young to be going through this. Never mind, I...." He turned and started to walk away, but then stopped, because they were all following him.

"Ben, we're in this together. Okay?" Brenda said.

He nodded. "I'm going to ride into the hospital. Anyone want to go?"

Gordon hesitated and then nodded. "I'll drive," he said.

Ben gave him a look.

"Fine, I don't care. You drive." Gordon climbed into the passenger side of Ben's truck and whipped out his cellphone. They rode most of the way to the hospital in silence, Gordon texting and Ben deep in thought. The ride up in the hospital elevator was quiet, the walk down the corridor to Matthew's room, quiet.

"I'm going to go to the men's room," Gordon said, just shy of Matthew's room.

"All right, I'll wait for you," Ben said.

"You don't have to," Gordon replied.

"Go." Ben motioned to the men's room door. "Go on. Go."

Gordon went into the men's room, bent over the sink for a moment, and studied his reflection in the mirror. There was so much of his brother in him. He splashed cold water on his face again and again. When he lifted his head, he looked for a paper towel. There was none, just a hot air dryer. He wiped his face on his shirt sleeves, dried his hands on his jeans, and smoothed his hair back.

Ben observed him keenly when he emerged and the two of them walked into Matthew's room together. Wendy looked up from keeping vigil at Matthew's bedside and smiled.

"Hey, Son," she said. "Ben."

Gordon stared at his brother, monitors beeping, oxygen machine hissing.

"How is he?" Ben asked.

Wendy looked at both of her sons before answering. "Um, I think he's doing okay. All his vitals are good. He's still sleeping according to all indications."

"Sleeping?" Gordon said. "Mom, come on."

"Gordon, listen to me. I'm not going to lie to you. I'm scared too. But they can tell somehow by the brain activity. He's sleeping. He's not in a coma or anything."

"Then why won't he wake up? Hey, Matthew, wake up."

Wendy smiled a sad smile. "He's sedated, but he probably hears you. Remember what the doctor said?"

Gordon looked at his brother. "Don't let them cut his hair."

"Why would they cut his hair?" Wendy said.

"I don't know. Just don't. Make them leave it alone."

Wendy sighed. "If I recall correctly, you were the last one that cut his hair."

Gordon looked at her and laughed, remembering. "I was like what, five or six at the time?"

Wendy laughed softly, then got choked up and had to dab discreetly at her eyes.

Ben looked at Matthew and then Gordon. "Are you going to tell him about his test?"

Gordon hesitated. "You tell him."

"What?" Wendy said.

Ben sat down in the chair next to her. "Gordon says Matthew did well on his college test."

Matthew furrowed his brow.

Gordon looked at him. "Your psych test. Prof says you aced it."

Matthew furrowed his brow again.

"He said he might have to start using a new learning curve." All three studied Matthew's expression. "Was that a smile?"

Wendy shrugged and shook her head. "I don't know. Let's let him rest."

Another furrow appeared on Matthew's brow.

"Rest, Son."

Chapter Four

Dusty drove back to the racetrack to check on the twelve horses in the ReHoming barn and stopped to talk to the guard at the stable entrance. "Anything new?"

"No, it's quiet tonight."

"Good."

"All except for…." He motioned to the first barn. "That boy's trouble. I wonder what he's up to?"

Dusty laughed. Junior Rupert was standing next to his pimped-out pickup truck parked near the second barn, simultaneously talking on his cellphone and filling his jaw with chewing tobacco. The second barn was the Guciano barn. He was probably hanging out waiting for Guciano's daughter Lucy.

Junior nodded in Dusty's direction and a couple of minutes later as Dusty was watering the horses, the young man walked over to talk to him. "Hey!"

Dusty smiled. Junior could be a royal pain in the butt, but overall he was also an okay kid as far as Dusty was concerned. "What's up?"

"Nothing. They have a colicky horse."

"Their vet come?"

"Yeah."

Dusty glanced at the purple bruise on Junior's jaw. The stitches looked tight, swelling all around them. "When do you get them out?" He motioned.

"I'm supposed to go tomorrow. I can't afford it though." He spit into the ditch outside the barn. "I'm going to have Lucy cut them out."

Dusty nodded. Many of the backside employees were without hospitalization. Nottingham Downs management, essentially Ben, Dawn, Tom, Wendy, Richard, and Dusty, were working on trying to get an affordable plan for everyone, but so far none of the insurance companies' quotes were "affordable." The cost wasn't the only snag. The tendency of many backside workers to be transient presented additional problems. Hospitalization required a waiting period. Some had to have entrance physicals; some plans wanted drug testing, some….

"Do you have twenty dollars you can lend me?" Junior asked.

"For what?" Dusty walked on to the next stall. This large chestnut gelding was the newest horse to the barn. Hopefully, they'd find a home for him soon.

"I want to take Lucy out for something to eat."

"With twenty dollars?"

Junior smiled. "It's a start."

Dusty handed him the hose, took out his wallet, gave him a twenty and a five-dollar bill. Junior thanked him and proceeded to water the next horse and the horse after that. When he got to the last stall, one being currently occupied by Disco Dan, he spit over his shoulder into the shedrow and shook his head. "I told that ass-wipe Donovan he wasn't right. But would he listen to me? No, two-minute lick him. Asshole." He reached up and pet the horse on the neck. "I'm sorry, old buddy."

The horse was sore and done up in all fours. The main concern was his right front. The x-rays were inconclusive. Randy planned to x-ray him again tomorrow. They were all hoping for the best, but it didn't look good for this horse. Not that Junior was privy to this information.

"Tell Ben I'll be by early in the morning if he needs me," Junior said.

Dusty watched him and Lucy pile into Junior's pick-up truck and drive off. Then he sat down on the bench outside the tack room/medicine room. Once a horse arrived at this barn there was no more need of tack, at least not here at the racetrack. The purpose was to give them an evaluation and rest, and to ultimately decide the horse's fate and future prospects. Dusty had been the racetrack liaison person for several years now. He enjoyed the job and relished the responsibility. He was a dedicated steward to the horses. He was Ben and Tom's right-hand man. He lived on Ben's farm in the renovated loft above the mares in the foaling barn. It was fairly primitive lodging with a small kitchen, bathroom, and living room bedroom combination, and was solar heated; a system he designed and built himself.

When the horse in the third stall stuck her head out and nickered, Dusty stood and walked down to talk to her. She was a pretty little filly, little being a characteristic that would likely be held against her when it came to finding her a home. She didn't stand more than 15 hands at best, probably didn't weigh eight-hundred pounds, and that was with her being fit and in good flesh. He smoothed her mane and cooed to her, "Hey, Bonnie Bee." She pricked her ears.

What was it that her trainer had said? "She ran her race every time. She could just never catch up. Still, she'd come back so proud."

"That's because you have spirit," Dusty said. She was a three-year old, unraced at two, and as sweet as could be. Over the past two and a half years, thanks to the self-sacrificing help of Veronica and Karen from the Shifting Gears Thoroughbred Rescue and the relentless, tireless help of everyone else involved, they'd successfully ReHomed one hundred and twelve Thoroughbreds. The filly rubbed her head against his arm. "Don't worry," Dusty assured her. "We'll find you a good home too. I promise."

~ * ~

It took hours for Dawn to finally get D.R. and Maeve settled down and tucked into bed. She left their doors open and looked back in at both of them, saddened by their broken hearts, saddened at the thought of what Wendy must be going through, saddened at the prospects. She said a silent prayer for Matthew.

They all were praying, even little Maeve. "Please, God, make Matthew all bedder."

"Amen," D.R. said, with a quivering bottom lip.

"Shhh…." Dawn said softly. "Go to sleep."

As she walked down the hall to the living room, she wiped tears from her eyes and saw Randy's truck lights in the driveway. He opened the truck door but remained seated and she could see he was on his cellphone. When he leaned his head back, she could almost hear him sigh.

He shut the door and put the truck in reverse. A second later the house phone rang.

"I'll be right back," he said.

"Why? What's going on?"

He'd stopped in the driveway to swing around and pull out and smiled at the sight of her standing in the bay window. "Have I told you lately how much I love you?"

"Yes," she said.

"I won't be long."

"Randy…?" She hesitated. "Do you think Matthew's going to be okay?"

"Yes, of course he'll be okay," he said, but didn't sound so convincing. "I'll see you in a little while."

Dawn walked to the couch, lay down, head on the armrest, and hugged a throw pillow to her chest. Years ago, and even younger than Matthew, she too lay in a hospital bed clinging to life for hours, days, a week. She remembered vividly the anguish in her father's and mother's eyes as she struggled to wake, to stay awake, to fight back, to live.

"Mommy?"

Dawn wiped her eyes and smiled, put on a happy face.

"We can't fall asleep," D.R. said, standing there holding his little sister's hand. "We're scared."

Dawn made room for them and tucked them in close.

"Where's Daddy?" Maeve said, sniffling. "I want Daddy."

"Daddy's working, sweetheart. He'll be home soon. Shhh…don't cry."

"Why are you crying, Mommy?" D.R. asked.

"Oh, I don't know. Sometimes Mommies just cry."

"Are you sad?"

"No. Yes. I guess."

"Don't cry, Mommy," Maeve said, hugging her mommy tight. "Don't cry. Iddle be all wight."

The children's nanny Carol came down the hall and assessed the situation at a glance. Once she retired to her "room" for the evening, it was rare to see her in the main part of the house. Dawn was very conscious of Carol's tendency to work-work-work and unless there was an emergency, insisted that Carol's down time actually be down time.

Carol had gone to her room hours ago, her room being a rather spacious bedroom, living room, efficiency kitchen, bathroom, and a balcony overlooking the yearling pasture. She had just seen Randy drive away. That man, in her opinion was the one who worked way too many hours. He was such a good man, a good father, a good husband. In all her years as the children's nanny, she never once heard him raise his voice to the children or to Dawn either for that matter. She often told Liz and Randy Sr. that they had certainly raised him right. "He's such a gentleman."

"Who wants hot chocolate?" Carol asked, heading for the kitchen.

"Me, me, me," D.R., Maeve, and Dawn, chorused.

~ * ~

Randy pulled up the driveway of Devonshire Equestrian Club and parked near the main entrance. This was one of the few barns Randy knew of that had a night guard on duty. But ever since that four-hundred-thousand-dollar mare was stolen last year....

The guard opened the door and stepped back for Randy to enter. "Hey, Barney," Randy said. His calling the man Barney, as in Barney Fife of the old Andy Griffith show was a standard joke between the two of them. The man's actual name was Sal. Randy produced his ID. Sal looked at it and handed it back. After Randy signed the in-and-out log, he was then allowed through another door. This was the only entrance into the barn area after 8:00 in the evening until 5:00 in the morning seven days a week. The farm owner had gone a little overboard with security after the mare theft in his efforts to keep the horse owners, trainers, and upscale students happy. The entire barn, front to back, inside and out, was riddled with surveillance cameras, in addition to the ones at the entrance and Sal's work space. Even though Sal knew Randy and Randy knew him – in fact Randy had vouched for him to get the job - if Sal didn't ask for the ID each time, it would be just cause for immediate termination. For what they were paying him, as Sal said, "No way I'm messing this up."

Randy checked the huge floor map of stalls which listed all the horses by name in case the mare had been moved to an exam stall, then took a left. Within days after the night when the infamous mare was stolen, Randy had a sit-down talk with Dave, the owner of the facility.

"Listen, you can't lock the stall doors and you can't lock the barn doors. It's not only ridiculous: it's highly dangerous."

"No, what's dangerous is one empty stall in a barn getting sixty-two hundred dollars a month board per horse. My clients pay for the best and I give them the best."

Randy sighed. "Weren't you the one that told me it ended up being the woman's husband?"

"Ex-husband," Dave said. "And that was classified information in case you don't remember."

Randy shook his head. "Why not just put up a 10 foot-high chain-link fence around the entire barn area, barbed-wire across the top, and…."

"Wow, that's a great idea."

Randy was being facetious with that suggestion, but if that's what it would take to get the man to give up the idea of locking each stall and every entrance, he was all for it. In his opinion, the horses' lives would be in double jeopardy in the event of fire or a roof collapse. When that tornado touched down late last summer and hit the main barn at the Fairways, if it weren't for the fact that they could open all the stalls and chase the horses outside quickly, they likely would have lost all of the horses not to mention human lives. The barn had collapsed in on itself just minutes after the last horse ran out and all the people behind him.

Randy's client was a pretty Arabian show mare with a tendency to get cast; stuck up against the wall when rolling, in spite of her fourteen-by-fourteen-foot penthouse-sized stall. Chances are this time she would be fine too, but Randy had to be the one to say so. A decision like that could not be left up to the owner, trainer, groom, or handler. The insurance policy on this mare specified any suspicion of....

The mare's groom stood up as Randy approached the stall, put down the magazine he'd been reading, and shook Randy's hand. "I don't know what I'm going to do with her."

Randy smiled. "Well, aside from having Dave install a pendulum swing hoist that'll bob up and down on a bungee cord so she can eat her grain and hay and drink water whenever she wants...."

The man's eyes lit up. "Do they make such a thing?"

"No. At least not that I know of," Randy said. "And *do not* suggest one to Dave."

Both men laughed.

"Well, so what's the story?" Randy reached for the clipboard form he would have to fill out and sign. "How long was she down this time?"

"Not long. I'd say less than a minute. I heard her hitting the wall and thought she might be just striking. I was in the tack room and had just walked away."

Randy made a few notations. "I'll tell you, every time I see this mare she all but takes my breath away."

The man nodded. "I know what you mean."

Randy examined the horse from head to toe. No cuts, no signs of tenderness or soreness, no signs of anything out of the ordinary. "Oh no. What's that?"

"What?" the groom asked.

Randy smiled. "Just kidding."

The man laughed. "Don't do that to me."

Randy finished filling out the paperwork, took another look in at the mare, shook his head at her sheer beauty, and bid her groom good-night. Sal opened one door for him. Randy glanced at his watch, recorded the time and signed out, and had a second door opened for him.

"Don't call me, I'll call you," Randy said.

Sal laughed.

As Randy climbed into the truck, his cellphone rang. It was Dawn. "I'm on my way home," Randy said. "Any word about Matthew?"

"No. But your mom and dad are home. They just pulled in. You might want to help them unpack. You know your dad."

"Thanks, Hon. I will. I'll see you in a little bit."

Randy's mother and father had just begun unloading the luggage when Randy pulled up their drive. His mom waved. "Oh good, you can help your dad. He hurt his back."

"My back is fine," Randy Sr. said. "God bless it, I wish you'd stop saying that."

Randy gave his mom a hug. "Please tell me I'm not going to grow up and be just as cranky as him."

His mom laughed. Even his dad laughed.

Randy reached past his father and pulled out two of the larger suitcases. "So what happened to your back?"

"He was playing horseshoes."

Randy looked at his father. "That's it? Playing horseshoes?"

His dad smiled. "It was a tight game. I had to give it my all."

"So let me get this straight. You didn't hurt your back? Your back is just sore?"

"Yes. Tell your mother that."

Randy winked at his mom. "There is a difference you know, Mom."

"Yes. But he's going to have to be more careful from now on to not overdo. We're not getting any younger."

"But you're getting prettier." Randy planted a kiss on her cheek. "Every day. It's good to have you home. Both of you," he added, nudging his dad out of the way. "How's Cindy?"

"She's good. Her doctor thinks she's through the worst of it." His sister Cindy was three months pregnant and had gotten off to a rocky start. She took a fall in the tub just a little over six weeks into the pregnancy which bought on spotting and concern. "She's starting to get a little tummy. They know it's a girl."

"Ah, now why did you tell me that? There goes my track record for guessing." Randy put their bags down and went back out to get the rest. Three loads and they were all in. "I'll see you tomorrow."

"Keep us posted on Matthew, okay?" Liz said.

Randy nodded. "Put some heat on your back, Dad, not ice. Okay?"

His father nodded.

Randy's parents were originally going to stay another week with Cindy and her husband Marvin. Because of Matthew's accident, they had decided to return early. They wanted to be here at home if they were needed. Home. Liz waved to Randy and closed the door. It felt good to be home. It would feel even better when Cindy and Marvin moved closer.

The young couple had placed a bid on a house about four miles from here, for when she and Randy set up practice together. But with Cindy's precarious condition, they pulled the bid and decided it would be best to wait until after the baby was born to even start thinking about moving. Phase one of that plan, Liz and Randy Sr. selling their farm and building a ranch here on Ben's property had been completed a little over a year ago. Their farm sold right off within a week. They broke ground here on the new house and were completely moved in less than seven months later.

Randy heard the dogs barking when he got out of his truck at home and turned toward the direction of the sound. Ben's truck had just pulled into the drive, and not far behind, Dusty's. He walked down to see what was going on.

Gordon got out of the truck and smacked Randy on the arm in passing. Randy looked at Ben and Dusty. "Where have you guys been?" It was fairly commonplace to run into one another on the way out in the morning, but usually not at night.

"I was at the hospital."

"Any change?"

"No."

"Is Tom there?"

"Yeah."

They both looked at Dusty. "What about you?" Randy asked. "Anything I need to know?"

"No, I was just checking on the horses. They're fine, all except for Disco Dan. He's restless."

"I don't blame him. I would be too," Randy said. After another set of x-rays, they would make a decision tomorrow. The three of them said good night and walked toward their respective homes. "My mom and dad are back," Randy said, a short distance away. "Everything's fine."

Dusty and Ben waved. Good news for a change.

Chapter Five

Every horse in the Miller barn was scheduled to go to the racetrack. Tom had spent the night at the hospital with Wendy and Matthew, but arrived at Nottingham Downs at his usual time in the morning. Dawn arrived shortly after that and then Ben. Tom had coffee brewing, had fed the horses, and was tacking Red.

"No news," he said. "They're cutting back on the sedative and think around noon he should start coming out of it providing all goes well."

Dusty arrived a few minutes later and then here came Junior. Tom walked past the young man without so much as a glance.

"Who do you want me to get on first?" Junior asked.

"Do you know how to read? Go read the training chart?" Tom said.

Junior looked at him. "What the fuck's wrong with you? The training chart doesn't tell me who goes first?" The boy made the mistake of absentmindedly pulling out his cellphone at that precise moment and Tom grabbed it out of his hand.

"Do you know what you could do with this?"

Ben stepped in. "Tom, enough."

"Do we need him?" Tom said. "Do we really need him?"

When Junior reached for his phone, Tom slipped it into his shirt pocket. 'I'll give it back to you when you're done. How's that?"

"How's you go fuck yourself! Give me my phone, dammit!"

Tom held both arms out, challenging him. "Come on, go ahead. I'd like nothing more than to kick your sorry ass all the way down the shedrow."

"And scare the horses," Dawn said, getting between them. "I don't think so. Give me his phone. Now! I mean it, Tom! Give me the phone."

Tom hesitated, looking from her to Junior, then Ben, then Dusty. "Tom," Dawn repeated. "Give-me-the-phone."

Ben looked up from his desk when Tom finally handed the phone to Dawn and shook his head. "Get Whinny out first."

Dawn gave Junior his phone. "Put it away," she said, in the same tone she'd just used on Tom. "Put-it-a-way."

Junior tucked his phone into his pocket and walked into the tack room to get the exercise saddle and Whinny's bridle. Dawn did the mare's legs up in felt bandages for galloping and brushed her off. Whinny, a five-year old mare whose registered name was Winning Beau, was probably going to be retired to breeding after this year. Sired by Beau Born, she was a sweet mare and had done really well for Dawn and Ben. A little headstrong in the morning when going to the track, she always had to be ponied.

Tom mounted Red outside and sat waiting for Whinny and Junior. Dawn gave Junior a leg-up and led the mare around the shedrow. Ben walked out to talk to Tom.

"Listen," he said. "I never had any children, so I'm no expert on this. But if you keep telling that boy he's a piece of shit, then that's what he's going to turn out to be."

"I'm not his dad."

"He looks up to you. We all know what his dad's like. Cut the kid some slack. Okay?"

"What are you, Dr. Phil now all of a sudden?"

Ben smiled. "Do unto others as you would have them do unto you."

Tom laughed. "Oh, now you're going to throw the Bible at me. That's low."

"Whatever it takes," Ben said, backing up as Dawn led Whinny and Junior out from under the shedrow. The boy winced as he snapped his helmet strap. His jaw was still sore. Whinny bucked and squealed. Tom looped the lead through the D-ring on her bridle. Ben followed along behind them at a safe distance. Another buck. Another squeal.

"Hey, Tom," Brubaker said in passing.

Tom nodded.

Junior stood in his stirrups to balance them, adjusted his helmet, and stroked Whinny's neck. "Good girl, good girl."

The mare pricked her ears back and forth.

"That's a good girl."

Tom ignored them both. Horses and ponies and grooms and trainers were coming and going to the racetrack all around them. Red was all business, glowering at the ponies, shrugging off Whinny, head down and all puffed up. A loose horse ran off the racetrack.

"Be tied on," Tom said.

"I'm always tied on," Junior said.

"Loose horse," Tom yelled, glancing over his shoulder.

Ben stepped back against the side of one of the barns. Just about everyone on foot did. Whinny started bucking even more. Bucking, squealing, and trying to rear. Tom tapped her on the top of her head and she shied, but came back down on all fours.

"Loose horse!" Several people shouted. "Loose horse!"

"Whoa! Whoa!" Buck Davidson attempted to stop the horse and it almost bowled him over. He ducked out of the way just in time. "Whoa! Whoa!"

The horse's reins were flapping, stirrups…snap snap flap flap!

Whinny tried rearing again. Tom brought her back down.

"Whoa, whoa… That a boy! Whoa, whoa…." Digger almost got hold of the loose horse's rein, but the horse made a sudden turn and headed back in the opposite direction, straight toward Whinny. She squealed, she bucked, she snorted, gnashed at the bit, squealed and bucked some more. And all the while Junior just grinned. He was in the saddle, up out of the saddle, sitting back down, up, down. Whinny kicked out with both hinds legs. The horse stopped just shy of her and one of Nelson's grooms grabbed hold of its rein. Caught!

Trainers, jockeys, owners, grooms, exercise riders, all calmed their own horses. Normalcy quickly returned. Tom glanced at Junior, just a glance, no compliment per se, but for an understanding in their eyes. Junior was good. He knew it and Tom knew it.

"Yep, Lucy is a lucky lady," the boy said. "A ride like that puts a big smile on her face every time."

Tom shook his head and sighed. This kid was surely a punishment from God for all those years of his being just like Junior - or worse. They jogged onto the racetrack at the gap by the track kitchen amidst heavy horse traffic. Whinny kicked out again and again. "Heads up!" Tom warned everyone in striking distance. "Heads up!"

Customarily when entering the racetrack, horses were walked or trotted on the outside rail for a short distance in the opposite direction of the horses training and then turned around to either gallop or pony. In theory, this strategy kept a horse from walking onto the racetrack and galloping right off.

Tom turned Whinny and Junior around just this side of the grandstand and kept a good hold of Whinny until Junior gave him the nod. Ben stood in the relatively-new Ginny stand built up by the kitchen. There were times his legs bothered him and he'd stand outside and spare himself climbing up the steps inside. Today he walked right up without even thinking about it. He smiled at Junior as the boy and Whinny galloped past. The mare had her head tucked, a good hold of the bit, and was wide-eyed and aggressive. When she approached another horse, she'd pin her ears. Her ears were pinned at the wire in every win picture they had of her.

Ben had mixed feelings about retiring Whinny this year. She was still competitive, running allowance races, and sound. But she was also a phenomenal broodmare prospect. She was slated to be bred to Robo Racer her first heat cycle in February next year. Ben had always wanted to have a foal sired by a Seattle Slew stallion.

"Hey, Ben," Bill Squire said. A fellow trainer, owner, and HBPA official, when Ben and Dawn first bought the racetrack, Bill was one of the few trainers that didn't turn tail early on. Not that he was totally supportive. In fact, he was rather skeptical overall. But he took a wait-and-see attitude, and so far so good. "Joe's running around the Secretary's office like a chicken with his head cut off."

"What about?" Ben asked, only half-listening. Joe was always running around like a chicken with his head cut off as far as Ben was concerned. He'd been that way for years. Apparently it was just his way.

"He says no one's running the racetrack."

Ben looked at him.

"He says he's been left to do it all."

"I see," Ben said. "You think he's fishing for a raise?"

Bill laughed. Ben laughed too. By this time Whinny and Junior were galloping down the stretch and Tom was positioned on the backstretch to help pull her up and lead them back to the barn.

Bill's horse passed in front of the Ginny stand. A big dark brown gelding with a white blaze. Ben nodded to Johnny, the jockey riding him. Johnny held up his hand. Five more and he'd be down to the Miller barn to work Bo-T.

Whinny galloped out strong. Ben watched her pull up, patted Bill on the back in passing and walked down the steps and out to the rail. When Tom was close enough to see him, Ben motioned he was going over to the grandstand to the Secretary's office.

Joe Feigler looked up when Ben entered the room and shook his head. "We have problems."

"Oh?" Ben said. Surely Joe wasn't going to discuss this in front of the two trainers standing at the counter.

"First," Joe said.

"I'll be right back." Ben headed toward the men's room as a decoy. Oh, the games he's had to learn to play these past few years. He didn't like playing games. But as Richard pointed out, sometimes you have to put your personal feelings aside "For the good of the herd."

Ben chuckled to himself remembering the day Richard said that. "What do you know about the good of the herd?"

"Not much," Richard had replied. "But I know you do and that's my point."

Ben looked forward to Richard's return. As he walked down the hall to the men's room, he took out his cellphone and speed-dialed Joe, another skill he'd honed the past couple of years.

"Yes, Ben?"

"Meet me in the lower office."

"When?"

"Now."

Joe Feigler was there in a flash. "What's the matter? What's going on?"

"Sit down," Ben said.

"Why?"

Ben looked at the man. "Okay, then stand."

Joe sat down on the edge of the seat across from Ben's desk. Both the lower and upper offices had desks for all three of them, Ben, Richard, and Wendy. Ben preferred the lower office. He could see the racetrack from the grandstand-sized window and….

"Ben?"

"Right," Ben said, with a sigh. "I hear tell you're feeling a little overworked."

"I didn't say that. Who said that?"

Ben sat back, studying the man for a moment.

"If anybody said that, they're lying. I never said that."

"Calm down, Joe, okay. Let's just relax."

There was a knock on the open door and in walked Linda Dillon.

"What are you doing home?" Ben said, smiling.

"Didn't you hear?"

"Hear what?"

"They closed down Erie."

"You're kidding?"

"No." She sat down next to Joe. "Hi."

Joe nodded. Everyone on the backside of the racetrack was aware of how "tight" Linda had gotten with ownership-management. Word was she was practically like family.

"Does this mean you're looking for a job," Ben said. "Joe here could use some help, at least for a few days till Wendy gets back."

"Where is Wendy?" Linda asked.

Ben glanced at Joe before answering. "Her son's in the hospital. We'll know more today."

"Matthew or Gordon?" Linda asked.

"Matthew. I'll keep you posted. Where's uh....?"

"At the farm."

"All right," Ben said, standing. "I've got to get out to the track. Meanwhile, see what you can do to help Joe."

"I don't need any help," Joe said, in a rather indignant tone.

"Well, I do. Fill in wherever you can," Ben told Linda. "Entries, the phone in here, wherever. I gotta go." It was a long walk to the gap by the Ginny stand. Ben was a little winded by the time he got there, but not nearly as much as he thought he would be considering he'd rushed. He looked down the road between the barns, looked long and hard, squinting, and finally here came Tom and Red, leading Bo-T, Johnny on board.

Ben climbed the stairs to the Ginny stand and sat down next to Amadou.

"Mornin', Mon!"

"Morning." Ben nodded.

"What you know?"

"Not much," Ben said. "How about you?" Bo-T walked onto the track as if he owned it, and in a way he did. He still held the track record for 6 ½ furlongs and probably would have won the Ohio Derby last year had Ben not had to scratch him the morning of the race due to a stall injury.

Amadou pointed. "Your horse, Mon. He no fear."

"No, no fear."

Johnny adjusted his goggles and looked at Ben. Ben motioned for him to take it easy.

"He give heart."

Ben agreed. Bo-T literally put his head in the air and sniffed as a filly passed by close on the rail. "Oh, for a

~ 54 ~

crystal ball," Ben said. Bo-T being a four-year-old was still considered a colt, but had stallion written all over him from the time he was a yearling.

"Too much testosterone," Randy always said of him practically from the time he was born. "Way too much."

Ben wasn't interested in having two stallions standing at stud on his farm. Beau Born was plenty enough. He'd had offers on the colt, but as Dawn flatly stated, "Bo-T is not for sale." Ben sighed. Bo-T was now giving thought to trying to mount Red.

Amadou pointed and laughed a deep laugh. "Ah! Bad boy, bad boy, what you gonna do!"

Ben nodded.

"Far be it for me to argue," Ben had said to Dawn. "Who knows how much longer I'll be on this earth."

Dawn laughed at that. "You're going to live forever. And he's still not for sale." At this point in time, he had her half-talked into leasing him to Breezeway Farm. "He'll get a shot at some really nice old mares and a few young ones."

"We'll see," Dawn said.

"It's either that or the alternative," Randy had teased. "When it comes time to bring him home for good, he's not going to be happy with all those mares around. If you want to turn him into a pasture buddy for Poncho and Biscuit, I have the technology."

Leasing him for stud was a good option.

"And may Beau Born live forever," Ben said.

"What?" Amadou asked.

"Nothing. I was just thinking out loud. I just don't want any more heartache. Some things I'd rather not live long enough to see."

"I know the saying," Amadou said. "I do not believe in it. No, Mon.."

Ben shook his head. Even from this far away, he could see Bo-T fighting Johnny, fighting Tom. "Just a little more. Just a little more. All right."

"You got him?" Tom asked Johnny, glancing over his shoulder. It was all clear, no horses coming, not that they'd catch up anyway, he thought. "You ready?"

When Johnny nodded and Tom let them go, Bo-T took off as if he'd been shot out of a cannon. Ben lost sight of him until the horse was coming down the stretch. Ben always had a horse worked an eighth of a mile past the wire; his old-school rule of not wanting a horse to get in the habit of pulling up at the wire. Ben picked up the clocker's phone hung on the wall of the Ginny stand.

"48 and 2/5ths, Ben."

"Thank you."

Ben waited until Tom helped Johnny pull up Bo-T and headed toward the barn. When he glanced ahead, it puzzled him to see Dawn. He hadn't seen her at first, and then there she was standing practically in front of him.

"Matthew's coming out of it."

"It's too early. Is he okay?"

Dawn hesitated, glancing over his shoulder at Tom as he approached with Bo-T. "They don't know. Wendy needs him there."

Tom saw the look in her eyes, dismounted and handed Red to Ben, Bo-T to Dawn. Johnny had dismounted at the gap to get on another horse right away.

"Is he awake?"

Dawn nodded.

"You got him?" Tom asked, of Bo-T.

"Yes," Dawn said. "Go."

Tom didn't even stop to take off his chaps and arrived at the hospital in less than twenty minutes. Gordon was standing by his mother's side, both looking down at

Matthew. Two nurses hovered over their patient. Monitors were beeping, the breathing machine hissing.

"What's going on?" Tom asked.

"Something's not right," Wendy whispered, not wanting Matthew to hear. "Something's...."

"No," Matthew said. "No."

"No what, Son?" Wendy asked instinctively. "No what?"

"No."

The nurses looked at her, glanced over their shoulders watching for the doctor, looked at Wendy again, and stood waiting, ready to administer more sedation.

"No."

"What's happening?" Tom asked the nurses.

Both shook their heads, watching the monitors, watching Matthew, another glance of concern at Wendy, another glance at the door.

Tom stepped forward. "Matthew," he said. "Calm down, Son. Calm down." When he touched Matthew's arm, Matthew jerked and then started trembling.

"Maybe don't touch him," one of the nurses said.

"No," Tom said.

"No," Matthew said.

Tom gripped Matthew's hand.

Matthew jerked again.

"I got you," Tom said. "You're not going to fall. I got you."

Matthew moved his hand and clasped Tom's.

"That's right, see? I got you."

Wendy edged up close, touched Matthew's arm, and nudged the nurse out of the way. She touched Matthew's face. "It's all right, Son. It's all right."

"Matt, come on," Gordon said. "Stop being so dramatic. Wake up. We're all here."

Matthew laughed. It sounded like a cough. He laughed again.

"He's tripping. You're tripping, Matt."

Matthew tried to open his eyes and then jerked again, gripping Tom's hand even tighter, tried opening his eyes again. Dr. Hanover entered the room, assessed the situation, and wrote up orders for two medications, STAT.

"What's happening?" Wendy asked.

"Well, either this young man is trying to swim up river or he's having a reaction to one of the meds. The nurse returned quickly, injected the meds into the IV and everyone stood waiting. Matthew's brow relaxed and he stopped trying to open his eyes but still held on to Tom's hand.

"Is that going to knock him out?" Tom asked.

"It shouldn't." Dr. Hanover checked the machines for Matthew's vitals, and just then, Matthew opened his eyes; both of them and without struggle.

"Matthew? Son?" Wendy said.

"Matt?" Gordon said.

Matthew looked from one to the other and then at Tom. "Why are you holding my hand?" he asked.

"Because you were falling," Tom said. "I know the feeling."

"Thank you," Matthew said. "I think I was. Where am I?"

Wendy started crying, not silent tears, sobs, and Dr. Hanover put his hand on her shoulder. "It's all right. It's all right. If you could all just give me some room, I need to examine my patient." He smiled reassuringly at Wendy and they all stepped back, nurses too, all except for Tom, standing on the other side of the bed.

"Are you all right?" Tom asked.

"I think so," Matthew said.

"Okay. Then I'm going to let go of your hand."

Matthew smiled. "Good. You were starting to worry me."

The doctor chuckled along with everyone else. "Okay, Matthew. Since you don't know where you are or how you got here, I have a few questions for you." He examined Matthew's eyes, shining a tiny flashlight in one then the other. "What's the single most important issue facing the world today."

"Global warming," Matthew said, to everyone's delight, especially Gordon's.

"Geek."

Tom put his arms around Wendy and held her close. "Shhh….it's okay," She nodded, her face against his shoulder, eyes on her sons. "It's okay."

Dr. Hanover leaned close to Matthew. "I want you to close your right eye, Matthew."

Matthew closed his right eye.

"Now your left one."

Matthew closed his left eye, but slower than the right one, and not closed completely. "All right, all right. That's to be expected. It'll come. See if you can lift your right arm?"

Matthew lifted his right arm.

"Left."

Matthew hesitated, or so it seemed. The room fell silent. It was as if no one was even breathing. "That's all right. Try again."

"Mom," Matthew said, when his left arm wouldn't move.

"It's nothing to be alarmed about," Dr. Hanover said. "It'll come. Try just moving your little finger."

Matthew stared at his left hand, tried moving his little finger, tried willing his little finger to move, try harder – try harder. It moved. Not a lot, but a little.

"All right, that's good. Now let's check out your legs."

Wendy clung to Tom.

"Right leg first. Good. Good. Left leg."

Matthew looked at his brother, wide-eyed and pale as a ghost. "Did it move?" He didn't want to look himself. "I can't feel it."

"It moved a little. Come on, let's try harder," Dr. Hanover said. "This is to be expected. Nothing to panic about."

Matthew tried harder and leaned his head back when he looked and could see his left leg just laying there.

"Can you wiggle your toes?"

Matthew glanced down and saw his toes wiggling.

"Well, that's encouraging," Dr. Hanover said. "Do it again."

Matthew wiggled his toes again, both feet this time, something he wasn't exactly trying to do, but that had just happened. He looked at the doctor, searched the doctor's eyes. The doctor seemed to know and smiled. "The body is an amazing phenomenon. I, for one, believe the day will come when we will be able to grow new appendages. In the meantime," he said, "what's going on has a lot to do with swelling and pressure on some of your cranial nerves."

Matthew found comfort in that, as did his family.

"It may not come as quickly as you would like, but, it'll come. And you will almost be as good as new."

"Almost?"

"The perfect part and how you deal with it will be up to you."

~ * ~

Miguel was the eldest of the old-timers currently living in the executive offices upstairs at Nottingham Downs. Everyone clearly understood it was only to be a temporary situation, but as soon as zoning got wind of it, plans to "house" them elsewhere had to be moved up. Sadder yet, none of the residents wanted to move. They loved it at the racetrack. The racetrack had been their life. This was the perfect place to live out their years if you asked them.

Ben always made a point of checking up on them every day. They were all friends of his. He enjoyed visiting them and they looked forward to seeing him. Originally there were seven of them with nowhere else to go. Now that Mim had decided to join the pack, there were eight. Well-known for her sharp tongue, Mim had a crusty exterior, a no-nonsense attitude, and a heart as good as gold.

When Linda Dillon looked up from Wendy's desk, phone pressed to her shoulder as she scribbled a message on a pad, there stood Miguel and Mim. She hadn't seen them for years, but would know them anywhere, particularly Mim. She and the old woman had never gotten along.

She motioned she'd only be a second, finished taking the message, and hung up the phone. She didn't know what to say, what to do. She'd heard they were living upstairs. "Hello," she said, for lack of anything better. It seemed silly to say something like "What can I do for you?" She only just a few minutes ago had gotten comfortable with answering the phones.

"Miguel. Mim."

"Humph. If it isn't Linda Dillon. What are you doing here?" Mim asked. She never liked this girl, didn't like how she treated her ponies, didn't like the way she dressed. Why wear jeans that tight? She didn't like the girl period.

"I'm answering the phones and helping out. Everyone's at the hospital."

"Why?" Miguel asked.

"Well…." Linda hesitated. It was probably none of their business, but with the way Mim was looking at her, the way Mim always looked at her, she felt compelled to answer. "Wendy's son Matthew was in a car accident."

Both of the old-timers looked suddenly stricken, blood draining from their faces.

"But he's going to be all right," Linda quickly added. "I just heard from them and he's awake and alert." Wendy's words exactly. "Here, sit down." She jumped up and guided them both to a chair. "Can I get you some coffee? It's decaf. Apparently that's all they have around here."

"Do you have whiskey?" Miguel asked.

"No, I don't think so."

Miguel laughed. "I kidding, Momacita."

Linda looked at him. Does Momacita mean he knows I'm a mother? Or? "Cream and sugar?"

Mim and Miguel nodded.

"I'll be right back." She hurried out for the cream and sugar, got a little sidetracked when she ran into Bob Messer, who gave her some hell for something years ago, and returned a few minutes later to find Mim on the phone.

"Yes, yes, I'll let him know you called. Nice talking to you, Mr. Jackson."

Linda fixed their coffee and handed it to them. "So what can I do for you?" she asked, adding, "Not that I'm sure I can do anything. Is everything okay?"

"Everything's fine," Mim said, sipping her coffee. "What are you doing here?"

"Well." Linda sat down behind Wendy's desk and paused. "I don't know if you heard about Erie."

"Yes," Mim said. "I saw it on Facebook. It's not a done deal. What are you doing, giving up on them?"

Linda just looked at her. Facebook? She couldn't even imagine Mim on a computer, let alone Facebook. "Do you Twitter too?"

Mim smiled.

Linda stared. Mim, smiling? Smiling at her? She wondered if the old woman was getting senile. "Mim, do you remember me?"

"You'd be pretty hard to forget."

Linda laughed. It was obviously sarcasm, but she'd said it in such a Mim-way. "Well, so what I'm doing here is answering the phone and I'm supposed to be helping Joe out, not that he'll let me."

"He's a paranoid schizophrenic," Mim said. "He can't even trust himself to help."

Linda laughed. That was certainly an interesting observation. "Well, I'd offer you some snacks, but…."

"There be chocolate in top drawer." Miguel motioned.

Linda leaned back and checked. Sure enough. When she started to pass them to Miguel, Mim shook her head. "I wouldn't do that if I were you."

"It's okay. I'm sure Wendy wouldn't mind."

"Probably not. But Miguel's a diabetic. We both are."

"Oh my!" She'd just fed them both sugar. She flashed Miguel a stern look and put the candy away. Joe started into the office just then and promptly turned on his heels.

"Do you need anything?" Linda called after him.

Nothing. No reply.

"Fucker," Linda said, under her breath.

Mim took another sip of coffee. "I knew your father."

Linda nodded. "Yes, I know."

"He and I are the same age. I was sorry to hear of his passing."

"Yeah, well I wasn't," Linda said.

Mim looked at her. "There's dietetic candy in the bottom drawer."

Linda leaned down, searched, and brought out a box of sugar-free dark chocolates. When Mim and Miguel helped themselves, she took a bite of one and made a face. She looked around for the waste basket, grabbed a tissue, and not so discreetly spit it out. "Oh my God! That's awful!"

Mim agreed. "Yes, but it's amazing what you can get used to when you have to." She and Miguel finished their chocolates, downed the rest of their coffee, and stood to leave.

"Can I give someone a message for you? Wendy? Ben?"

"No, that's okay," Mim said. "I'm sure we'll see 'em later."

Linda walked them to the door, why, she had no idea, and watched as they boarded the elevator. Mim hailed her cane in salute fashion just before the door closed. Linda walked to the water fountain down the hall, rinsed her mouth of the god-awful sickening-sweet chocolate taste and decided to see if she was needed in the Secretary's office.

Joe looked up and gave her a disgruntled look. "How are entries?" she asked, ignoring his attitude. "You need some help?"

"No," Joe said.

"Hey, Linda," Brubaker said, third in the line four deep to enter. "You working here?"

"For the moment," she said.

"Good." He stepped ahead of the line and bellied up to the booth next to Joe's. "'Cause I'm in a hurry."

~ * ~

Tom returned to the barn a little after one and was surprised to see Red tacked up and tied outside. Had he been out there all morning? He looked for Ben, looked for Dawn, and found Junior instead.

"Good. You're back," the boy said. "Billings said you were ponying for him in the second. I figured to cover for you. I just tacked up. Red's ready to go."

"Where's Ben?"

"Up at the kitchen."

"Where's Dawn?"

"She went home. Ben told her he'd feed." Junior looked at him. "You okay?"

"I'm fine. Don't you worry about me." Tom walked into the tack room and checked the training chart. None of the horses were crossed off for the day, so apparently they all got to the track.

"You want to do Billings or you want me to?"

"I'll get him," Tom said, looking hard at the young man. "Thank you."

"No problem." Junior waved over his shoulder. "By the way, there was some girl here dressed like a pumpkin. Cute little shit too."

"What do you mean a pumpkin?"

"A costume. A pumpkin costume. I guess she must have been going to some kind of party. I'd fuckin' party her, that's for sure!"

Tom sat down on the cot in the tack room and raked his fingers through his hair wondering how on earth anyone ever put up with him at Junior's age. Better yet, how is it that Ben had stood by him all these years? When Dusty walked into the tack room, Tom looked up.

"How's Matthew?"

"Well, he seems to be holding his own. He's got some paralysis, but I guess that's to be expected and will hopefully go away once the swelling goes down." Tom stood and reached for his helmet hung on a hook. "How's Disco Dan?"

Dusty sighed, a sigh that said it all.

Tom shook his head. "That's a shame. He was such a nice horse."

They'd set criteria early on for the horses in the Nottingham Downs ReHab and ReHome program where anything and everything possible would be done if the horse could be saved, even the ones that might end up only being a pasture mate. But the horse would have to have a good chance at a relatively pain-free life in the long run. This was the deciding factor for Disco Dan. His injury was too extreme. The horse already had arthritis in that joint, so even if the now-confirmed fracture healed, which was highly unlikely given the extent of the break, it was most likely he would always be in pain and considerably more as he aged.

"Is he gone?"

"Yes." Dusty had stroked the horse's neck, talked to the horse, cradled his head as he took his last breath.

Even when they all knew it was best for the horse, it still hurt to let them go. Tom patted Dusty on the back as he walked out of the tack room. Red nickered as Tom approached. He had a blade of straw in his mane. Tom picked it out and mounted, checked the girth, and headed down between the barns. Off in the distance beyond the guard shack, the truck hauling Disco Dan's remains pulled out onto the highway.

Chapter Six

Randy's mother Liz and Dawn prepared the dinner meal for everyone while Carol entertained D.R., Maeve, and Linda's little daughter Maria. Wendy had called from the hospital earlier and said she would be coming home after Matthew ate. The doctor ordered a soft diet, even though Matthew insisted he wanted a cheeseburger and fries.

"Maybe tomorrow," Dr. Hanover said.

Liz tasted the spaghetti sauce, added a little more salt, and then a wee bit more. She was looking forward to putting up her own tomatoes from the garden. Store-bought canned sauce just didn't have the same rich tomato taste. When she'd once mentioned teaching Dawn how to make sauce, Randy laughed. "You've got to be kidding," he said, and then high-tailed it out of the kitchen fast when Dawn chased after him with a wooden spoon.

"So what's Linda going to do?" Liz asked.

"I don't know," Dawn said, slicing cucumbers for the salad. "She's helping out in the office today, but...."

Joe Feigler was correct in his assessment that Linda had become family to Ben and Dawn, to all of them. They loved her and she loved them. They loved little Maria. Whenever the two were in town, Maria and Maeve were inseparable.

Randy Sr. came into the kitchen and helped himself to some cucumber slices, some red pepper, and a green onion. "Do we have any dip?"

Liz frowned. "Don't you think you should wait for dinner?"

"No, Mother, I don't." He searched in the refrigerator for ranch dressing. "I'm a retired man and I'm going to eat whenever I want. This'll do. What time is dinner anyway?"

"In about an hour."

"Oh." He put the ranch dressing back, ate the veggies plain, and headed out the door. "I'm going to go check on the mare."

He was referring to All Together and the fact that her blood work results indicated she was most likely still pregnant. "If you top off her water bucket, record it,"

Dawn said. They were keeping tabs on her fluid intake. He nodded and then waved to George outside.

George waved back. When Randy Sr. and Liz first moved here and built their ranch house, George admittedly got a little annoyed with Randy Sr. being constantly underfoot. He felt as if the man was not only watching his every move but was also trying to tell him how to do his job. He went to Randy, the man's son, with his concerns.

Randy laughed. "Are you kidding me? He's a farmer! That's what farmers do! They'll sit at the local diner and debate the circumference of a blade of grass for hours on end just for the hell of it! And don't ever expect them to agree on anything!"

From that moment on, George stopped taking things so personally and actually started enjoying having Randy Sr. around. He was a wealth of information and there wasn't anything the man couldn't fix.

Randy Sr. climbed onto the back of George's tractor and rode along with him to the barn. All six dogs ran alongside. The broodmare, All Together, was standing in her stall munching hay. It had been over six weeks since her last foal was weaned. All three of her foals had been sired by Beau Born, as was the foal she was hopefully carrying now.

She'd drunk half a bucket of water since checked last. George filled it back up and Randy Sr. made note on the stall chart. "So what does Randy think is going on with her?"

"He says she could possibly have some bladder irritation."

"Pressure from the foal?"

"He says it could be."

"So what's the plan?"

"Well, he's taking a wait and see approach. All her blood work came back good. She's eating, drinking a fair amount of water." George glanced at the chart. "Though not as much as usual."

Randy Sr. stood looking in at her. "Gosh, she's a pretty mare. I like gray horses; I always have."

George nodded. "Me too. I used to bet all the gray horses at the trotters. It could be just me, but it seems there's a lot more gray Standardbreds than Thoroughbreds."

"Did you work with trotters?"

"Oh yeah, for years. Glenda too."

"Speaking of which...."

Glenda pulled into the drive and stopped close to the barn. "I'm taking the pies up to the house. Then I'll go take care of the yearlings." The dogs took off after her. Randy Sr. helped George hay and water the other broodmares and from there they rode the tractor down to the stallion barn. Upon their arrival Beau Born bellowed his wild stallion mating call and they laughed and shook their heads. He was always on the lookout for a rogue mare coming to pay a visit.

"I hear him sometimes at night," Randy Sr. said.

"Me too," George and Glenda's house was even further than Randy's parents' home. It was a quarter of a mile the other side of T-Bone's place. "If there's no wind and the night is perfectly still, I swear I can hear him taking a piss. I know it's him because of his big groan at the end."

Randy Sr. laughed. "He is proud of his plumbing, isn't it?"

"Oh yeah."

Beau nipped at George and playfully tossed his head. Beau stood 16.3 hands high and probably weighed somewhere around 1250 pounds. Bright-penny chestnut, he had a white snip, wild and crazy mane and forelock, thick jowls, and a thick stud neck. When he raised his head, he looked ten feet tall.

Randy Sr. peered into the next stall as he filled the mare's water bucket. Hurry Sandy was Beau's pasture mate, a barren mare with a no-muss, no-fuss attitude. She wasn't much to look at but was really kind and gentle with people, especially children whom she apparently adored. Even when they didn't bring her carrots, she was still happy to see them. It's Beau that she gave a hard time to, in spite of him dwarfing her in size. She was alpha mare and took her job seriously.

"It's amazing," Randy Sr. said. "And he listens."

George laughed. "Don't we all?"

"Yes. It's the safest way."

"All kidding aside, it works out good for Beau," George said. "It's not often stallions are allowed to graze with mares. She's made him a kinder breeder. Because of her, he respects the mares. He's got one thing on his mind when it comes to breeding and that's getting the job done, but he's kinda sweet about it. I took care of a stallion a few years back that liked to almost kill the mares. We had to muzzle him and everything."

Ben pulled up the driveway and parked in his usual space by the main barn. Tom pulled in right behind him. As both got out and walked toward the stallion barn, Linda pulled in and drove past them, holding up a bag for all of them to see. East Coast Original Ice Cream to go with the pies. Dinner and dessert: covered.

Randy arrived home next and, following him, Wendy and Gordon. Gordon walked to Randy Sr. and Liz's house while Wendy washed up. She welcomed the time alone to gather herself. "Everything's going to be all right," she kept saying. "Matthew's going to be just fine."

There was lots of hugging and kissing when she arrived. She hadn't seen Liz and Randy Sr. for weeks and Linda and little Maria for months. There were also tears shed. Tom put his arm around her. "You okay?"

She nodded, wiping her eyes. "I'm fine."

Everyone sat down to eat.

The little ones were dotted throughout. Maria sat between her mother and Tom, Maeve between Dawn and Liz, and D.R. between his two "Grandpas" Ben and Randy Sr. He'd turned into a finicky eater and ate best when not sitting next to Dawn or Carol.

"I've been thinking," Ben said, when they had all gotten their plates full and the passing of dishes had ceased. "We need to come up with a name for T-Bone's place."

"Whatever it is," Dawn said, "It can't sound like a nursing home. Uncle Matt ran into a brick wall with zoning."

"I don't like those people," Ben said. "How can they stop a person from putting up a sign on their own property?"

"Well...." Dawn looked at Wendy, both she and Ben trying to get her engaged in the conversation to take her mind of Matthew, even if just for a few minutes.

Wendy hesitated. "They can't stop you from putting it on the house."

"They can't?" Ben asked.

"No. Matt said you can make the sign as big as you want."

"All right, I'm okay with that. So what are we going to call it?" He motioned for Gordon to pass him the grated cheese. "Are you hogging that all to yourself?"

Gordon chuckled.

Ben shook a whole bunch of cheese on his spaghetti, dared anyone to say a word with a glance, and then passed it back. "Well?"

No one had any suggestions. Either that or they were too busy eating, even the children. Tom laughed at Maria imitating him twirling his spaghetti. "You got it, little one," he said. "Look at you go." Everyone at the table chuckled. She was so proud when she got it all in her mouth. So cute.

"What's wrong with just calling it T-Bone's Place?" Gordon asked. "I kinda like that. I like thinking about the old man every time someone says his name. And it is going to be for old people." Everyone looked at him. Gordon and Matthew had spent the past two summers at T-Bone's place and had grown to really care about the old man, cranky, opinionated, and all. "I think he'd like that."

Brenda agreed. Dawn agreed. Randy nodded. They all agreed.

"Well then," Ben said. "Can I see a show of hands?" They'd gotten into this formality at dinners when deciding anything important or equally unimportant for that matter. Everyone raised their hands, even Maeve, D.R. and Maria. "Okay, T-Bone's Place it is."

They all went back to eating. "How's come you don't have a farm name, Ben?" Linda asked.

Ben paused. "Meg and I were thinking about one but then she took ill, and...."

"What was it?" Dawn asked.

"Well, mind you, we had the horses, but we weren't breeding to any outside mares until then, so...."

Everyone looked at him.

"But now with Beau, I probably should think of something else, I just can't seem to bring myself to...."

"What was the name?" Dawn asked.

Ben looked at her and hesitated.

"It's all right," she said, reaching over and squeezing his hand. His eyes had instantly filled with tears. One look and so did D.R.'s.

"Grandpa," D.R. said. "What's the matter, Grandpa?"

Maeve and Maria looked at him with the same sudden concern in their eyes for their "Grandpa."

'It's okay," Ben said. "I'm okay." He paused and drew a deep breath, looking from one child to the next and then the adults. "We were going to call it Meg's Meadows. Meg loved the Meadows."

"It's perfect," Linda said. "She's everywhere here."

They all nodded in agreement. "Let's see a show of hands," Randy said.

Everyone raised their hands, the little ones too.

Ben smiled. "Then 'Meg's Meadows' it is."

They all sighed collectively and went back to eating.

"Can we make a real big sign?" Ben asked.

Wendy nodded. "Yep, and you can put that one right out front."

Having communal meals just about every evening here at the farm started by accident. Someone was trying to cheer someone up, they all put together a meal, and it became a habit they all enjoyed. When T-Bone would join them, he'd always bring beef jerky. No matter the menu, beef jerky was his contribution. The old man died at home in the middle of the night, the way he always said he wanted to go. He hated the thought of going to an old folks' home, said he'd jump off a bridge first, so it was rather ironic that his old homestead was being turned into a haven for the old-timers from the racetrack.

"So, Linda," Glenda said. "Do you think you'll move back home for good?"

"I don't know," Linda said. "They paid really well at Erie."

"So you're saying you don't think we pay well?" Tom joked. "Who told you that?"

"Plus you know just about everybody here," George said.

"I know, and I think that's the biggest problem. I didn't have any of that at Erie. I liked myself there. I had no past. It's hard to leave the past behind when you see it in everyone else's eyes."

They all just looked at her. She'd grown so much the past couple of years and they were all so proud of her.

"That and the health care in Canada is great. Maria gets all her shots and...."

"I don't want shots," Maria said, bottom lip pouting. "I don't want shots."

"No-no-no, that's not what Mommy's saying."

They all chuckled at the look of instant relief on Maria's face.

"It's just a big decision," Linda said. "I appreciate you letting me work today, and I'll do everything I can to help. Joe's a trip, by the way. I don't recall him being so paranoid."

"I'm a little concerned about him," Ben said. Understood at the table was that nothing said ever left the table. They could all speak freely and not fear it might be repeated elsewhere. "I mean he's always been a little odd, but he seems to be even odder lately."

"He told me that a pixie came to see him today."

"A pixie?" Tom said.

"Yep, that's what he said."

"Yeah, well Junior said a pumpkin visited him this afternoon."

"A pumpkin?"

"That's what he said."

"You know, I thought I saw someone dressed like Dorothy from the Wizard of Oz the other morning," Dusty said.

Everyone looked at one another.

"Where? At the office or on the backside?" Randy asked.

"The backside."

"Was it someone you know?" Ben asked.

"No." Dusty shook his head. "I figured it was some owner's kid, just dressing funny. I really didn't think twice about it till you two mentioned the pixie and the pumpkin."

When Wendy's cellphone rang, they all fell silent. She looked at caller ID. "It's the hospital. Hello."

"Hey, Mom, it's Matthew."

"It's Matthew. Are you okay?"

"I'm fine. I just remembered something. I was in a car accident."

"Yes, Son, you were."

"I don't remember what happened, but I remember the sound of breaking glass. I didn't hit anyone, did I?"

"No." She looked around the room, implying everything was okay. "Fortunately you just hit a pole."

"Ah, I see. Good."

"Did you remember my cellphone number?"

Matthew hesitated. "No, but you wrote it on the blackboard."

"Oh that's right, I did." Wendy smiled.

"The nurse dialed it for me. I'm going to take a nap now. Bye."

"Bye, Son." She hung up the call and glanced at everyone and shrugged. "Apparently he remembers being in an accident. He says he remembers the sound of breaking glass, but that's all. That's good, right?"

"Yes," Randy said. "I'm assuming his memory will come back a little at a time."

"When I see him tomorrow I think I'll tell him he blew a date with Rosie Davidson at the Beer Brew," Gordon said.

"Who?"

"Just kidding, Mom. Trust me, you don't want to know. Remember that song about the cocktail waitress in a Dolly Parton wig."

"Vaguely."

"That's her."

They all laughed, finished dinner, and had pie and ice cream. It had been a long day for everyone. They were all tired and they were all feeling relatively happy, hopeful for tomorrow. It was decided Linda and Maria would stay with Randy's parents. Everyone else walked out into the night together.

"I think I forgot to check the mail," Ben said, walking past his house.

"I'll go check it," Tom said.

"Why? I can walk."

"Fine. Knock yourself out," Tom said, his arm around Wendy, her head resting on his shoulder.

"Hey, Gramps," Gordon called after him. "You want me to walk with you?"

"No." Ben laughed.

"Fine." Gordon went on into the house. "Don't say I didn't offer."

Chapter Seven

Tom made a point of going over to the Secretary's office early in the morning even before entries were being taken and took Joe aside. "Are you okay?" he asked the man.

"Yes! Why would you ask? Is this because of Linda?"

"No," Tom said. "This is because of you. You're like a loose horse. What's the hell's wrong with you?"

"I've got too much to do," Joe said. "I don't know if I'm coming or going."

Tom pointed to the general office and followed the man inside. "Listen, if you need some time off…."

"Oh, is that what this is about? You want me to leave?"

"No, I want you to get a grip! Look at you! Look at your eyes!"

Linda walked into the Secretary's office, heard their raised voices and headed down the hall in a hurry. "Hey, hey, Guys! What the hell's going on?"

"Why didn't you say you wanted my job, Linda? I asked you and you said no. What, were you lying to me?"

"Uh, no."

"Come on, we're going upstairs," Tom said.

"For what?"

"I'm going to have Vicky check you out."

"Vicky? There's nothing wrong with me."

Vicky was the live-in formerly-retired nurse on the floor with the old-timers. "Let's have *her* tell me that. Linda, watch the desk."

"Oh great," Linda said, walking back down the hall.

Joe yelled after her. "I hate your guts, Dillon! You hear me?"

"Yeah, I hear you. You're not real high on my list either."

Tom nudged Joe toward the elevator. "Come on, let's go."

"This is ridiculous!" Joe said, as the two of them boarded.

"I agree," Tom said.

"Are you making fun of me now?"

"Not at all. I'm wishing you'd shut the fuck up though. I'm trying to say a prayer for you."

"I don't need your prayers."

"All right, then I'll pray for me. 'Cause if you don't shut up, I'm going to knock you senseless and need some forgiving."

The elevator doors opened and the two of them stepped out into the lobby of the executive offices. A fleeting thought crossed Tom's mind. This was where he'd first laid eyes on his wife Wendy who'd seemed pretty much like a real bitch back then. Joe followed Tom down the hall. Vicky, the old-timer's nurse had just administered an insulin injection to Mim.

"Morning, gentlemen," Vicky said.

Tom smiled. "Good morning."

"What can I do for you?"

Joe took on an entirely different demeanor in front of Mim. He just stood there.

"Are you all right, Joe?" Mim asked.

"I'm fine," he said, repeating himself. "I'm fine."

"Can you check him out?" Tom suggested.

"Okay." Vicky must have sensed something going on with Joe too, as she immediately had him sit down and wrapped his arm with a blood-pressure sleeve.

"I am fine, I'm telling you. Just fine."

"I'm sure you are," Vicky said. "You sound fine. Let's just check it out for the heck of it."

Joe's blood pressure was 192 over 100. Vicky looked at Tom.

"What? What is it?" Joe asked.

Vicky just sat there for a second, mulling over what to do. "Well, your blood pressure is not bad, but I'll need to take it again in a few minutes. My machine has been acting up."

Mim looked at him.

"What? What's wrong?" Joe asked.

"Nothing," Mim said. "I was just thinking about the day you had me fill a race with that really nice mare of mine."

Tom looked at her. "Is this a happy story? Otherwise…." He didn't want to go down a negative road with Joe's blood pressure so high.

"A happy story. She ended up winning. I'd have never entered her in that race though. I thought nice as she was, she'd be a little out-classed. She win easy. I don't know if I ever thanked you for that, Joe."

"You did, Mim. Thank you. I had a hunch she'd run big. That and I needed at least one more horse to make the race go."

"I think I remember that horse," Tom said. "What was her name? Divvits? Doggone? Dippity?"

"Denise Deville," Mim said.

"Yeah, that's her." Tom smiled. "What did you ever do with her?"

"She's a broodmare. Her first foal is a yearling."

"Who'd they breed her to?"

"That Native Challenger stud at Reese's."

"Ah, the competition," Tom said.

"Beau wasn't proven then."

During this exchange, Joe just sat listening and then felt the sleeve on his arm taking another blood pressure reading.

145 over 82. Vicky let out a sigh of relief, as did Tom, looking over her shoulder. She removed the sleeve.

"Well?" Joe asked.

She read him the numbers and added a caveat. "This pressure is not too bad, but it's still a little high. What blood medication do you take?" As a veteran nurse, she knew from experience just how to ask a question. Asked if he took blood pressure medication, he'd probably say no. Joe told her the drug name and dose.

"Okay." She listened to his heart with her stethoscope. "It sounds good." She listened to his lungs. "Take a deep breath. Another. Another. Good." She took his pulse. She took his temperature. She looked at his eyes. "How old are you, Joe?"

"Fifty-two."

She nodded. "Mind if I take your blood pressure one more time?"

"No." Joe was feeling rather calm.

This time it was 138 over 79. "I think you're good to go."

Tom looked at her. "He's fine?

Vicky nodded.

"I told you," Joe said.

"As a professional, I must caution you to follow the advice of your doctor and seek medical attention if you find yourself not feeling well."

Joe and Tom and Mim looked at her.

"Sorry, I'm required to say that, and I have thus said it. Now go on, get out of here. I have work to do."

On the way down in the elevator, Joe fidgeted. "I can't lose my job, Tom. My wife would kick me out on the street."

"Nobody's after your job. That's what I keep trying to tell you."

"Then what is Linda doing here?"

"Helping out. For all practical purposes, Erie closed. You're not the only one with problems, Joe."

"I'm sorry," Joe said. "Truly." He looked at Tom. "I am."

As Tom walked back to the barn, his cellphone rang. It was Wendy. "I just had the scare of my life," she said, out of breath.

"What happened?"

"I just got to the hospital and Matthew wasn't in his room. Apparently he took it upon himself to get out of bed and go take a shower."

"What about all those electrodes?"

"As soon as they removed them he left the room. He took the IV with him and off he went. I can't believe he did that. The nurses were frantic."

Tom couldn't help but smile. "Didn't they look for him in the bathroom?"

"No. At first they just assumed someone had come to take him for a test. But then when I arrived and...."

"Is he okay?"

"He's fine. He's back in bed. All squeaky clean he says." Wendy chuckled. "I don't know what I'm going to do with him."

Dusty was paged over the backside loudspeaker to barn seventeen. Tom gave thought to heading in that direction, but had too many things of his own to attend to. "What time are you planning on coming in?" he asked Wendy.

"Just as soon as I talk to Dr. Hanover. They say he makes his rounds around 9:00."

"Okay, I'll see you then." Tom waved to Pastor Mitchell. "Morning!"

Pastor Mitchell waved back. "It's a glorious day, Tom!"

"I couldn't agree with you more."

Ben glanced up from his desk in the tack room when he saw Tom walking down the shedrow. "Everything okay?"

"Yep, fine."

"Good. I think I just saw Winnie the Pooh."

Tom laughed. "Seriously?"

"From a distance and blind as a bat, yes. After all these years with D.R. and Maeve, I'd know him anywhere."

"Wonder what the hell that's all about?" Tom reached past Ben for his chaps. "By the way, I just talked to Wendy. It seems Matthew took it upon himself to go take a shower without letting the nurses know."

Ben smiled. "If they don't watch him, he'll probably up and check himself out. Frankly, I don't blame him. I don't like hospitals." He glanced at the calendar. His cataract surgery was scheduled for the following Monday. His pre-op appointment was this Friday at 1:00. They had horses in today, Saturday, and Sunday.

Dawn came around the corner leading "Born All Together" nicknamed Batgirl, a five-year old allowance mare sired by Beau Born out of All Together. Dawn had her tacked and ready for Johnny who was due any minute.

"Did you line up company for her, old man?" Tom asked.

"Yes."

"Who?"

"She's going to work with Shaolin, Marvin Talbot's big mare."

"All right. That should be fun. She run big last time out." Tom put on his chaps, grabbed his helmet, and went out and mounted Red, standing obediently next to the barn. "Here he comes," he yelled to Dawn. "Bring her out."

Batgirl was a kind and sensible mare. Very little rattled her, but she had a tendency to want to run off. Just having Tom and Red at her side apparently meant a world of difference, as Tom rarely had to muscle her to keep her in line.

Marvin Talbot's mare Shaolin jogged onto the racetrack, also with a pony, and bucked and squealed. Both mares hadn't run in over two weeks, hence the work "in company" scheduled this morning going three-eighths of a mile. It was still relatively early, but there was a lot of activity on the track. The two mares were ponied toward the grandstand and when there was a clearing in the training activity, they were turned and allowed to canter.

"This should be fun," Jim, the other veteran pony boy said.

Tom laughed. The plan was to breeze the horses 3/8ths of a mile from the ¼ pole to the 7/8th pole past the wire. They'd be good and warmed up before the start and they were in Ben's words, "Not to set the world on fire." The two mares picked up their pace down the backstretch, both jockeys doing their part to keep them under wraps. As they approached the clubhouse turn, Tom and Jim started edging the mares down closer to the rail. One more horse galloping down on the rail to go and they'd have clear sailing.

"You got her?" Tom asked.

"You got her?" Jim asked.

Both jocks nodded, both grinning. Next to an actual horse race, this was about as good as it gets for everyone involved. Tom and Jim turned the mares loose. They both dropped down onto the rail and took off. Tom and Jim cantered to the outside rail out of the way of other horses training and turned around and started jogging back to where they would help pull the mares up. Tom stretched as tall as he could to see over the tote board. The mares were head to head, both on the same lead, matching stride for stride.

"Katy bar the door," Tom said. "I'm glad they're not running against each other Sunday."

"What are you guessing?" Jim asked, when the mares passed the 7/8ths pole and the jocks stood up on them.

"Thirty five and change," Tom said.

Ben watched the mares gallop out in front of him and heard the "clocker's" phone ringing. He picked it up. "That wasn't a work. That was just a breeze," Ben said.

"Right," the clocker replied. "Thirty five and three."

"Thank you." He relayed the information to Marvin and patted the man on the back. "You've got a nice mare there. Don't forget Beau Born when it comes time for breeding her."

"I won't." Marvin smiled. "Thanks, Ben"

Ben looked at him.

"For everything," Marvin said. "For what you're doing for the track, the soft whips, the ReHoming project, all of it. I just want to thank you."

Ben nodded. "You're welcome."

The next horse to track for the Miller barn was B-Bo. Native Born Beau. "Two miles," Ben told Junior. Dawn gave the boy a leg-up. "Don't let him get lazy."

B-Bo cared more about eating than anything else. A five-year old also this year, he'd developed a habit of daydreaming and shuffling along. As was the routine, Dawn preferred to stay back at the barn and would do stalls, bath the horses, hang them on the walking machine, and get the next one ready. She liked the routine and didn't like any disruption. She gave Batgirl a drink of water and a bath.

When Randy stopped by to check in with her, she handed him Batgirl's lead shank, wiped the mare down and put a cooler on her. "Did you ever have a feeling that someone was watching you?" she asked.

"Yes, all the time," Randy said, "And I tell them I'm married."

Dawn laughed. "I'm serious." She took the lead shank, gave the mare another drink and led her to the walking machine. Whinny was due to come off. She hung one horse on, took the other one off, and led Whinny down the shedrow and into her stall. Randy stopped to look in at Bo-T.

Randy wasn't one to pick a favorite horse, but if pushed, it would have to be Bo-T. "How's the man?" he asked, patting the big colt on the neck. "How's the man?"

Bo-T nickered. Dawn brought Randy up to date on Matthew. Randy left, Dawn did B-Bo's stall, and had just finished dumping the last muck basket load when she thought she saw someone duck around the other side. "Hello!" She walked around to get a better look, but no one was there. Then here came B-Bo back. She walked down to the end of the barn to take him from Tom.

"How'd he go?"

"Good. He went good. I'll be right back. I'll meet you at the wash rack." B-Bo could practically be ground-tied. That's how quiet he was. He stood for his bath like a perfect gentleman. He would even lower his head to get his face rinsed.

"You're such a sweetie," Dawn said. Then out of the corner of her eye, she thought she saw someone peeking at her from around the edge of the barn. "Hey!" she said, and backed up. But once again, whoever it was, had vanished. "I think I'm losing my marbles, B-Bo! Yes, there they go."

The horse pushed up against her with his soaking-wet muzzle. "Thank you for caring," Dawn said. Tom showed up to help scrape him off, wiped the horse's face with a towel, and they all headed back to the barn. "I'm think I'm seeing things," Dawn told him.

"Like what?"

"People looking at me."

Tom glanced at her. "I can see why. You're quite a sight."

Dawn laughed.

"Give me the horse. I don't want to be seen with you."

Dawn handed him B-Bo and ducked into the ladies room. She checked her appearance in the mirror, looked perfectly normal for already having given three horses baths, and smoothed her hair back. Bright red auburn, thick and long, the way Randy liked it; she always wore it braided in the morning. She tucked some stray hairs back into the braid, dried her arms and face with a paper towel, and heard someone cough in one of the toilet stalls. A tiny restroom by any standards, as she was leaving, she noticed the woman's shiny bright red boots under the stall door.

She walked outside, chuckling to herself. The boots looked like something Dorothy in the Wizard of Oz would wear. Click, click. There's no place like home. There's no place like home.

Tom had B-Bo on the walking machine and Batgirl back in her stall. Morning Dew was next, the three-year-old filly sired by Beau Born and a half-sister to Whinny. Junior showed up in time to help tack her. Dawn gave him a leg-up, off they went, and she cleaned her stall, filled her haynet, scrubbed her water bucket, filled it back up, and stopped the walking machine to offer B-Bo another drink. He smacked his lips in the water but was done drinking. She took his cooler off and turned the walking machine back on to let him walk a few minutes longer.

Tom had gone to pony a horse for another trainer and returned just as Junior came back with Morning Dew. "Ben said to tell you he's walking over to the Secretary's office."

Dawn held Morning Dew while Junior untacked her. Bo-T was next. Junior went into the tack room, hung the bridle on the tack hook, reached for Bo-T's bridle, and walked down the shedrow to the colt's stall. "Hey, Big Man!"

Bo-T was just about everyone's favorite. A gorgeous, flashy chestnut just like his sire Beau Born, Bo-T broke the track record as a first-time starter two years ago, and the track record still held. He was the "Big Horse" in the barn. Dawn came back from the wash rack with Morning Dew, gave her another drink, hung her on the walking machine, put B-Bo into his stall, and came down the shedrow just in time to give Junior a leg-up and lead him and Bo-T out to Tom.

When Morning Dew bucked and kicked on the walking machine, Bo-T ducked back to whinny at her. Junior thumped his sides and Tom pulled him forward. Junior stood in his stirrups, nodding along and singing a tune. Tom looked at him. "He's in tomorrow, remember."

"I remember."

"Yeah? Well, just don't forget."

Junior sat down in the saddle and sighed. Ben got back to the Ginny stand from the Secretary's office just as Tom was leading Bo-T out onto the racetrack. Ben wanted the horse to just stay loose, nothing more than a light gallop. Junior touched the rim of his helmet.

Ben smiled at him and then shook his head at Tom's sour expression. Meanwhile, Wee Born was also scheduled to gallop. Dawn did her legs up in running bandages, brushed her off and did Bo-T's stall, his water bucket, and hay net. She turned off the walking machine, offered Morning Dew another drink. The filly drank a little and then a little more.

"Good girl."

Walking machine back on, Dawn stood watching Morning Dew for a moment, and then started rolling bandages. When she was done with each set of wraps and bandages, she placed them neatly in front of the respective stalls where the horses couldn't reach them, and walked down to tack Wee Born. She was leading Wee Born, tacked, around the shedrow when Tom and Bo-T arrived back at the barn. Junior dismounted. Dawn gave him a leg-up on Wee Born and took Bo-T from Tom. Just like clockwork. Dawn untacked Bo-T, gave him a drink of water, and headed over to the wash rack. She glanced at her watch; nine o'clock and one to go. Alley Beau.

Chapter Eight

Wendy sat at Matthew's side waiting for Dr. Hanover to arrive with an update on her son's condition. The head nurse on the floor said that she thought the plan was to discharge him today or tomorrow. It would all depend on the results from the latest MRI taken earlier in the morning. Matthew was sitting up in bed with headphones on listening to music.

Gordon was texting his friends. He tapped Matthew's arm. "Jeeter found your cellphone."

Matthew pulled off the headphones. "Seriously? Where?"

Gordon texted Jeeter and got an instant message back. "On a porch near the accident. Here." He showed Matthew a picture of it.

Matthew tilted his head and squinted. The picture was fuzzy. "Is it toast?"

"Oh yeah."

Wendy stared out the window. She hated just the mention of the accident. Such a close call, was all she could think about, and so hard to believe. She turned when Dr. Hanover entered the room. Both boys looked up. Matthew turned off the music and removed the headphones. Gordon turned his cellphone off.

"Good morning." The doctor glanced at Matthew's chart. "According to this, your MRI looks pretty good."

"Pretty good?" Matthew said. "What's that mean?"

"It means there's still a little swelling."

"When can I get out of here?" Matthew asked, either oblivious or ignoring the implication.

"Well, I'd like to keep you around for at least another day or so. I think you're on the way to recovery, but…."

"I need to get back to school," Matthew said. He glanced at his mother and Gordon. "I was hoping to get out of here today. I get around good. I went and showered."

"So I heard."

"Well, then what's the problem?"

The doctor looked at Matthew thoughtfully and sat down on the edge of the bed with a sigh. "I don't want to alarm you, Matthew. But this injury is not going to go away overnight. Is it going to haunt you? For a little while at least, yes."

"What do you mean? I can walk and talk and…."

"You're still experiencing headaches."

"Not really, no. All right, yes. Maybe a little."

"So what do you think that means?" Dr. Hanover asked, "Aside from the fact that you're not well yet?"

"It means the food here is bad." Matthew smiled, perhaps thinking he could charm his way out of the situation. "That I miss my friends. That I miss school."

"Have you tried doing any reading?"

"No." Matthew motioned he'd been watching television. "We don't have cable at the frat house."

"We're lucky we have plumbing there," Gordon added.

The doctor nodded and glanced around for a magazine, picked one up off the side table and handed it to Matthew.

The young man looked at him and then opened it to page one and stared.

"That'll go away in time," Dr. Hanover said. "But you're going to need some rest. Not necessarily bed rest."

"What?" Wendy asked, studying her son's puzzled expression.

"The letters jump. Some are disappearing, missing." Matthew moved the magazine away and then closer, changed the angle of his head, closed one eye and then the other. "Doubling."

Wendy looked at the doctor. Gordon looked at the doctor. Matthew looked at the doctor.

"This is what I was talking about with the 'almost perfect' part. I believe you are going to make an almost perfect recovery. It just might be slightly different than what you expect and it is going to take a while."

"How long?"

"With rest? Maybe a couple of weeks. Maybe a couple of months."

"What do you mean, rest? No school?"

Wendy's heart ached for her son. He lived for school. He'd been talking about grad school. He loved research. Studying. She couldn't see him just resting, not even a day, let alone weeks or months.

"Let's not forget," Dr. Hanover said. "A little less than two days ago we weren't sure you were even going to make it. The blow you suffered to your head is why you need rest. You're going to need some controlled physical therapy too. You cannot overdo. Are you listening?"

"Yes," Matthew said, trying to read the magazine again.

The doctor took it from him. "Matthew, you have your whole life ahead of you. How you proceed at this point is key. You need to heal. More importantly, you need to let your body heal itself and that's going to take time."

~ * ~

Dawn sat in Wendy's office and listened to the whole story. "The hardest part was when he was told he couldn't drive. I reminded him that he probably was going to lose his license anyway, but...."

"Well, I'm sure that didn't cheer him up," Dawn said, smiling supportively.

"I thought being a mom was going to get easier when they got older. You should have seen the fit he threw when the nurse mentioned in-house rehab."

"Do you mean a facility where he would stay?"

"Yes, she had a list of them. The one they recommend is where a lot of athletes go to recover from 'debilitating' sports injuries. He said, 'Oh, just what I need, to sit around with a bunch of jocks. It'll be just like being back in high school. Let's bench-press the nerd.'"

Dawn chuckled.

"I had no idea he'd ever had issues in high school."

"What did Gordon say?"

"For a while he didn't say anything. Then he tried cheering Matthew up, but by then, his silence had spoken volumes. As Tom would say, they don't bullshit one another."

"No, that's for sure. And they're so close."

They both turned when there was a tap on the open door and were startled. There stood a young woman, a girl actually - she couldn't have been more than seventeen or eighteen, dressed as a witch. A witch.

"Can I help you?" Wendy asked.

"Are you Dawn Iredale?"

"No," Dawn said. "I'm Dawn. What can I do for you?"

"I have a telegram for you." As she started toward Dawn, Joe Feigler rushed in behind her.

"Miss? Miss? Miss? I'm talking to you, Miss?"

The girl turned and in a panic, hurled something at Dawn in a bottle. It hit her in the chest and splashed bright red all over her.

"Shut the door," Dawn shouted. "Shut the door!" It was blood.

Joe shut the door, blocking the girl inside.

"Wendy, call Security!" Dawn said. "No, wait! Don't!"

The young girl had started to cry.

"Where did you get this?"

"It's blood on your hands!"

"Blood on my hands?"

"I read your articles. I know you're lying! These horses are treated horribly here."

"I'm calling Security," Joe said.

"No. Sit down," Dawn told the girl. "What's your name?"

"How did you get in here?" Joe asked. "You're that pixie from the other day, aren't you? Do you have identification on you?"

The girl shook her head defiantly.

"You don't work for a telegraph company, do you?" Joe said. "Do you?"

"This is a personal assault, Dawn. You have to call Security," Wendy said, hovering somewhere between shock and exhaustion. Was this a dream? "Dawn?"

Dawn saw the possible headlines tomorrow flash through her mind. A front page photo. "Call Uncle Matt," she said. "Tell him to...."

"Who's Uncle Matt?" the girl asked, defiant and yet looking about as innocent as a teenage witch could look, and scared.

"What did you hope to accomplish by doing this?" Dawn asked.

"To make you think."

Dawn looked at her. "To make me think?"

"I want to know how she got in here," Joe said. "There's no way she can get in here unnoticed. Not unless...."

All three of them looked at the girl. Was she familiar? Had they seen her on the backside before? Dawn stood, trying to decide what to do. She reached for the Kleenex and started wiping the blood from her shirt. "I guess we're going to have to call the police. Races don't start for an hour. Let's get this over with."

"No, don't!" the girl said. "I'm sorry! Let me go and you'll never see me again! I promise!"

"And I'm supposed to take the word of a young woman who threw a bottle of blood at me."

"It's not blood! It's glycerin and red dye!"

Dawn sniffed the tissue. No smell. Certainly not blood.

Dawn, Wendy, and Joe looked at one another.

"You can't let her go," Joe said. "We have to have her arrested."

"For what crime?" Dawn asked. "Although, this was one of my favorite shirts."

"Assault."

"What horses are being mistreated?" Dawn asked.

"All of them. I've seen how they're treated."

"Here? On this racetrack?" Dawn gave up trying to wipe off her shirt and threw the tissue in the waste basket.

"Yes, here."

Dawn looked at her. "So you work here?" When the girl refused to answer, Dawn looked at Joe. "Let's have her fingerprinted then let her go. If she's been licensed here, Uncle Matt can have them matched up. Have Security escort her out."

"What about my car?"

"Oh, your car," Dawn said. "Well, that's possible identification. Maybe we should just keep you here until closing and when your car is the last one left in the parking lot…." Dawn glanced down at the girl's red boots. "Wait a minute. Were you stalking me over at the barn?"

"Stalking you? I wasn't *stalking* you."

Dawn stood shaking her head. Tom opened the door and started in the room. Joe practically slammed the door on him. "What the hell?" Tom said, nudging Joe out of the way. "What's going on? What happened to you?" he asked Dawn, about the stain on her shirt. He looked at the girl. "Who are you?"

"She attacked Dawn," Joe said.

"Attacked her?"

Joe motioned to the glass bottle on the floor. "It was full of stuff that looked like blood. We're trying to decide what to do with her."

"Well shit, let's have her arrested," Tom said. "That'll make for some excitement. Maybe she's armed. Are you armed, you little witch?"

The girl shook her head.

Tom walked over and using a pen from the desk, picked up the bottle by the spout, held it up close to his nose and sniffed it. "Glycerin…?"

The girl looked away. Then here came Ben, and right behind him, Dusty. It was not unusual for them all to gather in the office. The only thing unusual at the moment was the young girl dressed as a witch.

"I know you," Dusty said. "Where do I know you from?" He looked long and hard at the girl when brought up to date. "Were you trying to hurt Dawn?"

"No, I'm just trying to raise awareness."

"Oh, Jesus," Tom said. "Are you from ….?"

"I am from nowhere."

They all laughed. It wasn't really all that funny, but with the girl sitting there in the witch costume and looking so serious, they couldn't help themselves.

"You're all sick," the girl said. "I'm leaving."

"No, you're not," Dawn said.

"You can't hold me against my will."

"Oh really. We could hold you here forever. You don't even exist," Dawn said. "You're just a witch from nowhere. Where did you park your broom? Or do you even have one?"

The young girl looked defiantly at her. "Go ahead and make fun of me. I don't care."

"I'm not making fun of you," Dawn said. "I'm trying to make sense of all of this. Joe, go get the fingerprinting pad. And not a word of this to anyone, do you understand?"

Joe nodded and left the room.

Tom looked at Wendy. "How's Matthew? When's he getting released?"

"Tomorrow."

"That's good news."

"Yes and no. I'll tell you more later."

Joe returned with the fingerprint pad and ID form. If the girl thought Dawn was bluffing, she had another thing coming. When that sunk in, she fessed up. "My name is Hillary Walker."

"Who do you work for?"

"I don't. Not on the racetrack at least. I work at Casey Costumes. I'm in high school."

"How did you get on the backside? How did you get in the offices?"

"I worked here one day. That's how I got my groom's license."

Dawn looked at Joe. He nodded, left the room, and returned in a flash. "Yep, it's her. She worked for Garrison."

"I only worked for him that one day. He's mean to his horses."

"Yes, he is," Dusty said. "That's why he's not here anymore."

"He's not here anymore?"

Dawn reached for the girl's groom's license printout, complete with photo. "Is this still your home phone number?"

The girl shrugged.

Dawn sighed. Enough. "Let her go."

"You sure?" Joe asked.

"Yes. I've got enough right here to track her all the way back to her great grandmother. Let her go. Hillary," she said. "Tell your mom I'm coming to see her."

"My mom?" The girl sat back down.

"Yes, now go on. Go home. Get out of here."

The girl stood up and walked past all of them and looked back at the door. "Would it help if I said I'm sorry?"

"No," Dawn said. "Now go on, leave before I call the police, and don't ever step a foot on this racetrack again." She looked at Joe. "Have Security escort her to her car, accompany them and get me the make, model, and license number."

~ * ~

Dawn washed up at the ladies room by their barn and changed shirts. She always kept extra shirts and jeans at the track just in case, which normally was when one of the horses had gotten her soaking wet or muddy. She unbraided and re-braided her hair without looking in the mirror. She never looked in the mirror when braiding her hair.

"Why not, Mommy?" Maeve had asked.

"Because I can't see back the back of my head," she said. "Can you see the back of your head? Try."

She loved Maeve's little giggle in response, turning round and round.

Dawn sighed. How would she feel about Maeve doing something like this Hillary just did? The girl clearly had her reasons and maybe even good intentions. Still….

Someone tapped on the door. "Dawn, you okay?"

Recognizing Tom's voice, Dawn opened the door and smiled. "Yes."

"Just making sure," he said."I know she was just a little shit and you could handle her and all, but…."

Dawn laughed. She didn't have a violent aggressive bone in her body and they both knew that. "I kind of feel sorry for her. It was an act of desperation and she'd obviously been planning it for days."

Tom put his arm around her as they walked to the barn. "Apparently. She was all those characters. Joe said she had all the costumes in the back seat of her car. This world is full of whackos."

"I don't know that she was a whacko," Dawn said. "Though that was my favorite shirt."

"Can you get another one made just like it?" Tom teased.

"Yes, I plan to," Dawn said, glancing at the stained shirt in her hand. "Several of them." She wasn't kidding.

Tom smiled. "I have to tell you, Dawn. Whenever you do the Fioritto thing, and mind you, it ain't often, it scares the hell out of me. I forget how much power you have. To me, you're just Dawn."

"I am just Dawn. And I luv you and you luv me…." The two of them started singing, announcing their arrival at the barn.

Ben looked up from his desk. "I can't see crap," he said. "What's this say?"

Dawn looked at the note in his hand. "It's from Dusty." She started laughing. "It says, 'Oh no, that little filly got on a van somehow and is headed for Meg's Meadows. I don't know how it happened.'"

Chapter Nine

Alley Beau, the three-year-old filly out of All Together sired by Beau Born was in the fifth race today. This would be only her third lifetime start. She'd run fourth in her first race, had a win in her second race after getting left in the gate, and was favored to win today. She hadn't raced as a two-year old, was "a little squirrely" as Tom would say, and had wide eyes and big ears.

"Lord help us if she ever grows into those ears," Ben said, the day she was born. As a yearling, she stood close to 16 hands. She was 16.3 as a two-year old, and stood today at better than 17.2, taller than both her sire and dam. She was bay; the first bay born of or sired by either horse, and gangly.

At the call for the fourth race, Dawn did up Alley's legs in Vetwrap, applied rundown patches on the backs of each wrapped fetlock, and wiped her shiny coat with a grooming towel. Tom was ponying a horse in the fourth, so the plan was for Dawn to meet him up at the gap. Timed perfectly, he'd be coming back off the track with the horse in that race right as Dawn arrived with Alley. If the wind was just right and there was very little traffic or activity on the road between the barns, a person could hear the bell ring on the starting gate. Dawn listened, heard it, put Alley's bridle on, tied her tongue, and looped her halter and lead shank around her arm. In the past, they had always come back to the barn after the race for the halter and shank if they placed, but with the new ruling by the Stewards, everyone had to bring their halters and lead shanks to the paddock with them.

She walked Alley a lap around the shedrow, then out the barn and up the road to the track. Tom was waiting for her at the gap. "The horse got claimed," he said. "Jackson's pissed. If he keeps spouting off, I'm going to yellow card him."

He was joking. But in all seriousness, both he and Dawn knew what it was like to have a horse claimed from them and you actually did feel like screaming. Claiming races were designed to help keep racing honest. That was Horseracing101. Still….

Alley was not in a claiming race. Tom put the lead on her and Dawn followed him and Red and Alley to the paddock. Jackson was still screaming at the trainer who had claimed his horse. "Damn you, Hannity! Damn you!" He looked at Tom venting his frustration. "Damn him, Tom! He knows how much I love that horse!"

"I know." Tom shook his head at Hannity. "What the fuck is wrong with you? That's the man's one and only horse."

"He shouldn't have run him claiming then."

"You know what? No, never mind. Never mind," Tom said, trying to stay calm himself. The sight of Jackson following the horse he loved, now going to a different stable, different owner, different trainer was heartbreaking, particularly with the way he was clutching the horse's empty bridle. The man had tears in his eyes and the horse kept looking back at him.

"Damn!" Tom said.

At the entrance to the paddock, Tom dismounted Red and ground-tied him. Ben was waiting for them in the Number 6 stall. "Where you been, old man?" Tom asked.

Ben shook his head. "Everywhere. You wouldn't believe."

Dawn led Alley in past them. She stood quietly to be saddled, her ears like radar turning this way and that, eyes big and watching everyone. Jockey Jenny Grimm approached them with a big smile on her face. Tom put his arm around her and pointed up to the General Offices window. Wendy looked down at them and laughed, waved.

Ben patted the filly on the neck. "Just let her run her race," he told Jenny.

"Roger," Jenny said. She'd been the filly's regular jock since day one.

"Riders up!"

Tom walked out ahead of them. Dawn gave Jenny a leg-up, and led the mare out onto the racetrack to the sound of the bugle. Tom loved that sound. The fans loved that sound. The man had been their regular bugler for a couple of years now, ever since they bought the racetrack and got rid of the cheesy piped-in bugle music.

The filly looked at the fans. She'd become a crowd favorite because of her size and her wide eyes. She had a way of looking as if she were posing for a photo with each step, and had a real long lanky stride.

"Poetry in motion," an article in *Blood Horse* called her.

"We love you, Alley!" two little girls called out.

Alley nodded her head up and down as if in appreciation.

"We love you!!"

It was an eight-horse field of three-year old allowance fillies, non-winners of two, going six furlongs. Alley

Beau's odds were 5-2. When the post parade turned at the end of the grandstand the horses and their ponies fanned out and broke into a trot and then a canter to warm up.

"Ladies and gentlemen," track announcer Bud Gipson said. "This field of three-year old distaffers will be going to the gate in less than six minutes. Do not get shut out."

Dawn went into the Secretary's office to check in with Linda.

"All's well," Linda said. "All except for...." She angled a glance toward Joe and whispered, "He is an idiot."

"Now, now. He has some good qualities I'm sure."

"Well, then he must be hiding them," Linda said.

Dawn smiled. "I'll see you later." She went back outside and down to the rail, where Ben always stood with Dusty to watch the races. Dusty wasn't there. "Where is he?"

"He just called from the farm. He'll be back."

"What's his plan with that horse?"

"I don't know." Ben shook his head and sighed. "I think he wants to keep her."

Dawn looked across the racetrack to the starting gate. The horses were being loaded. "He can turn her out with Biscuit and Poncho."

"Don't encourage him," Ben said.

"They're at the post!" Bud Gipson announced.

Dawn's heart took a leap. There was a time not all that long ago, when she couldn't watch their horses race without getting a stomach ache. She used to live in the ladies room for hours prior to post time.

"And they're off! Taking the early lead is Pining Plum. Miss Twister is a close second. You've Got Mojo is laying third. Three lengths back is Tippy Toes. Dab Blast It is closing ground along with My Names Appy and three lengths back is Alley Beau."

~ 101 ~

Dawn glanced up at the General Offices window. Wendy was watching the race through her binoculars.

"Approaching the clubhouse turn, Miss Twister is challenging the leader. You've Got Mojo is making a move. Tippy Toes has dropped down on the rail. Dab Blast It is making a bid for third….and trailing the field is Alley Beau."

Dawn looked at Ben. Ben looked at Dawn. "Don't panic," he said.

"At the head of the stretch and down on the rail it is Tippy Toes charging to the lead. Miss Twister and You've Got Mojo are vying for second. Dab Blast It has dropped back. Pining Plum is no longer a factor. And here comes Alley Beau."

"Come on, Alley!" Dawn said. "Come on, girl."

Ben squinted at the fractions and smiled. From his vantage point, even with the fast pace, Alley had reached her stride and the race was over.

"Closing with a rush on the outside, hand-ridden, is Alley Beau. It's Alley Beau! It's Alley Beau! It's Alley Beau at the wire by three."

"Yes!" Dawn gave Ben a hug and waved up at Wendy. Wendy waved back. Instinctively, Dawn glanced toward the track kitchen to look for Randy's truck, an old habit from when he always made a point of watching the race when one of their horses was running. But gone was that luxury for him anymore. He was just too busy.

~ * ~

The celebration at The Rib restaurant was big and loud. Everyone involved was there but Matthew and Gordon. Since the young men were usually at school an hour away, their absence wasn't totally alien to the festivities. Gordon had driven his mother's car back to school and would return tomorrow for Matthew's discharge and transfer from the hospital.

"Hear! Hear!" Tom said, seated next to Wendy. "To Alley Beau!"

George and Glenda, Ben, Dawn and Randy, D.R., Maeve, Carol, Linda and Maria, and Dusty, Tom and Wendy, Randy Sr. and Liz, all raised their glasses.

"Salud!"

"She came back good, huh?" George said. Alley Beau was *his* favorite.

"Hell! She was just getting going!" Tom said. "She didn't want pulled up."

"I told you she's going to be a router," Dusty insisted.

Ben smiled. How many times had they sat at this very table over the years? How many times had they celebrated, agonized, made decisions.

"She's a big Cadillac made for cruising," Dusty said. "Who knows how far she'll run."

Ben laughed. "There were times I couldn't see her keeping her long legs untangled. Remember how rubbery-legged she was as a baby." He imitated her jelly-legging it. "I had my doubts."

"Not me. Never," George said.

Randy smiled. It had been a long day. He was exhausted and could barely keep his eyes open. He took a long swallow of his ice cold beer.

"Daddy!" Maeve tugged at his arm. "I dressed myself all by myself today."

Randy chuckled and kissed the top of her head. "I can see that. You look so pretty!"

"Me too," Maria said.

"And you look so pretty too!"

Both girls were dressed in pink from head to toe and had big pink ribbons in their hair. "What about you, little man?" Randy asked D.R.

"Daddy!" D.R. scolded. "I always dress myself." Jeans and flannel shirt just like his daddy. "You know that."

Randy laughed. "Ah, I forgot." He ruffled D.R's carrot-top hair and smiled when his son combed it back in place just like Uncle Tom's.

Here came the salads, hot rolls, cold butter and homemade jam. "Everyone decide what they want?" Two servers stood ready to take their orders. It was a long drawn-out process. Once that was done and everyone started eating their salads, talk went back to "the kids."

D.R. learned how to spell encyclopedia today. Maeve and Maria learned how to stand on their heads and say the Pledge of Allegiance. "...to the flag, one nation, under Gods, for which it stands, Americas for all."

"I like that," Ben said. They all agreed. "So, Dusty, what do you plan to do with that little filly?"

"Well." Dusty slathered his roll with butter and motioned for the jam. "I haven't thought very far ahead on that. I don't think it's going to be easy finding her a home, even if she is relatively sound. I'm thinking maybe I could turn her out in T-Bone's old field for a while."

"Why not turn her out with Biscuit and Poncho," Dawn said, discreetly ignoring the rather imploring look she just got from Ben. Biscuit and Poncho were Linda Dillon's old ponies. Dawn bought them from her when Ben had kicked Linda off the racetrack and she left town. It was because of that turn of events, they'd all become friends.

"What's the filly's name?" Linda asked. "They might know her."

Everyone laughed.

"Her name's Bonnie Bee." Dusty piled jam onto his buttered roll. D.R. imitated him, piling his just the same way. "I just don't want to get attached to her," Dusty said.

"You mean, anymore than you already have?" Tom asked.

Dusty smiled. "She's such a cute little thing and she tries so hard to do everything right."

"I hear you," Ben said. "But there's going to come a day when you will all realize you can't fall in love with them. You just can't."

"Oh, not this again," Glenda said, chuckling. "This is a business, this is a business…."

"And you have to think like a business person," Dawn added.

"Or else," George said, pointing a finger.

"It's a business, you hear me," Tom said."It's a tough business and you have to make tough business decisions, because that's the business."

They all laughed, Ben included. "I don't want you all going around with your head in the clouds and your feet too high off the ground."

Maria and Maeve lifted their feet in the air.

They all laughed again and from across the room, the people at several tables nearby laughed along with them. This restaurant was a regular hangout for racetrackers. It was close to the track. The food was delicious, hardy, affordable, and the portions were generous.

Randy put his arm around Dawn and kissed her on the cheek. She smiled. "What's that for?"

"I don't know. I was just thinking about that day you told me to bug off here."

"Bug off?" She laughed.

"Yeah, or something like that, and you did that Fioritto thing."

Dawn laughed again. "That's the second time I've heard that today. What is a Fioritto thing? I don't know what you're all talking about."

"It's a look," Tom said. "A look that makes people say, "Oh shit!'"

Maeve and Maria sat up straight in their chairs.

"Tom!" Carol said.

"Sorry, kids. My badd!"

The girls giggled.

"I heard from Cindy today," Liz said. "She had another day of Saltines and ginger ale."

"How well I remember that," Linda said absentmindedly as she cut up the tomato on Maria's salad. "Day after day after day."

They all looked at her. Linda had been pregnant and alone. Maria's father was long gone, a fleeting moment in her life. She'd ponied and exercised horses through her fifth month. Talk on the racetrack back then was she was trying to make weight and give riding another try. That's how skinny she'd gotten. She had Maria in the off season and no one knew. Some thought she'd gone to Florida for the winter. Some thought she'd gone out West.

Linda raised her eyes, saw everyone looking at her, and sighed. "But it was all worthwhile. Cindy will forget all about it when the baby's born."

They nodded, all looking at little Maria.

"Eat, eat!" Mama Leone, the third-generation owner said appearing at their table. "Food come out soon!"

"Yes, Ma'am!"

The table fell quiet as they munched and ate. No one dare argue with Mamma Leone. As the main course was brought to the table, Randy got a phone call. He cupped his hand over his ear and listened, then got up and walked out to the foyer.

Dawn glanced up as he returned. "Emergency?"

He nodded. "I gotta go."

"Do you need help?" Tom asked.

"No, I'm fine." He lifted his Porterhouse steak with his fork, positioned it in his napkin to take with him, baked potato in another napkin and gave Dawn a kiss. "This shouldn't take long. I'll see you at home. Good night, everybody."

"He needs help," Randy Sr. said. "He's wearing himself out."

Dawn sighed. "I know. But he won't listen to me."

"Can't he hire another vet?" Liz asked.

"A good-looking one my age," Linda said.

They all laughed and then fell quiet again, but for the business of chewing, eating, and cutting up meat.

"Pass me the A1, please."

"Can I have the Tabasco?"

"More tea?"

"Yes, please."

"Mommy?" D.R. said.

"Yes."

"I don't like peas."

"Since when?"

"Since today," D.R. replied, entertaining everyone with a most serious expression on his face as he moved them all around his plate. "I don't think I'll ever like them again."

~ * ~

Dawn stopped at Ben's farmhouse on the way to work in the morning to have coffee with Wendy and wished her luck today with Matthew's transfer to rehab. "He left me another message this morning," Wendy said. "He's still insisting he's not going."

"It doesn't appear that he has a choice," Dawn said. "Does he? Can he just come home?"

"No. They say he needs physical therapy and a controlled environment because of the damage to his eyes."

Ben and Tom had left for the track already and it was just the two of them. Wendy poured them both a second cup. "In a way, I almost wish T-Bone's Place was done already. Maybe he could have just gone there."

They were all nervous about the old-timers coming to live at T-Bone's. Having them at the racetrack was a huge responsibility let alone having them practically in the front yard. Early on when discussing the possibility of having T-Bone's house turned into their permanent home, everyone involved admitted to having fears of one of the residents falling, emergency vehicles at night, deaths, funerals.

"Well, that's just a simple fact of life," Mim had said in typical Mim fashion. "We're all going to die sooner or later. It's going to happen wherever we end up. You want us to sign something that says you're not responsible for us falling over and hitting our heads or dying of old age or living past a hundred?"

Wendy and Dawn looked at one another across the kitchen table, so many things on both of their minds. "Are we ready for this?"

"I think so," Wendy said. "At least as far as T-Bone's Place goes. Everything's moving right along. Vicky wants to try and do the cooking herself. I have a feeling she's going to wear herself out."

Chef Diamond Lou at the racetrack was "orchestrating" the meals for the old-timers now. Not that he had been on board at the beginning. "I can't serve without seasoning! It's a travesty. Who say old people don't like spice?"

"It's hard on their digestion, Diamond," Wendy insisted.

"Fine. No problemo. I give them parsley each meal to fix digestion."

He and the old-timers and Vicky had worked it out. They now ate healthy favorites and gourmet meals each day and had come to some indisputable conclusions as to which spices and herbs worked and which unfortunately did not. Parsley accompanied each meal and was never not eaten. Chef Diamond Lou drizzled agave juice on it and served it fresh at breakfast, lunch, and dinner.

"What time's Ben's appointment today?"

"Noon. High noon he says." Dawn finished her coffee and stood up to leave. "Good luck today."

"You too," Wendy said. "You're going with him, right?"

"Yes."

When Dawn arrived at the racetrack, she was surprised to find the young girl from yesterday standing outside the guard shack with a woman whose appearance and stern posture, strongly suggested she was Hillary's mother. Dawn parked her car and walked toward them. Jason, the stable guard stepped outside to greet her. "They're here to see you." The girl avoided looking at her.

"Good morning," Dawn said. "What can I do for you?"

"I'm Janet Walker," the woman said. "This is my daughter, Hillary. I understand you have already met."

"Yes," Dawn said. "We met yesterday."

"Well, we're here to apologize."

Dawn looked at the girl. "I believe she apologized yesterday."

"Yes, but she didn't mean it," her mother insisted. "Did you, Hillary?"

The girl looked at Dawn. "No, but...."

"Well, I appreciate you both coming by," Dawn said. "I was going to make a trip over to see you later today and now I don't have to. Thank you for saving me the time."

"I love horses," the girl said. "I hate what happens to them at the track."

Her mother sighed.

Dawn looked at the girl. "Hillary, you're mistaken. I don't know where you got the impression that bad things happen to all the horses at the racetrack. Bad things happen to horses everywhere. I hate that too. But here... here at Nottingham Downs, we're making a difference. We're doing something about it. I think it's great that you love horses. So do I. But you can't go around judging people and places as if we're all the same."

"I tell her that all the time," her mother said. "I don't know what to do anymore. If it's not horses, it's the puppy mills, the cattle feedlots, the sheep herders."

Dawn looked at her. "The sheep herders?"

The woman shrugged. "I don't know. Something about the sheep."

"What's with the sheep?" Dawn asked the girl.

"Duh! They take the babies away."

Dawn stared. "Seriously? Why?"

"I don't know. So they can make some rare expensive cheese with the milk."

"What do they do with the lambs?"

The girl looked at her. "Easter dinner."

"Oh, that's sad," Dawn said, the guard Jason still standing at her side.

"We'd like to replace your shirt," the mother said, reaching into her purse for her wallet. "Rest assured, you *will* pay me this back, Hillary."

"I don't want your money," Dawn said. "Thank you anyway."

The woman looked ready to cry. "Please...I need to do something."

Dawn glanced at the first barn, where Dusty stood looking at her. He called to her. "Is everything okay?"

"Yes." She looked at the mom and then the girl. "Are you off school today?"

The mom nodded. The girl just looked at her.

~ 110 ~

"Dusty, could you use some help this morning?"

"Doing what?" he said.

"Stalls?"

"Sure."

"There you go," Dawn said, nodding in Dusty's direction and then looking at the mom. "Can you pick her up in a couple of hours? A couple of hours' work and we'll call it square. How's that?"

Even as the mom was nodding in agreement, the girl was shaking her head. "I can't work on this racetrack. I told you I know what goes on here."

"Yes, I know, and you're wrong" Dawn said. "Dusty, would you please come here a minute."

Dusty walked over.

"Hillary's going to help you out this morning."

"Okay," he said.

"Hillary," Dawn said. "Dusty is our liaison person at Nottingham Downs. It's his job to make sure all of the horses here are treated well. He takes his job seriously."

"I'll bet," the girl said, staring off in the opposite direction.

"You'll be working with some of the horses that are retired and going to be ReHomed."

The girl turned.

"Let's go," Dusty said. "Do you know anything about horses?"

"Yes. Obviously."

"Good," Dusty said, walking back to the barn with the girl trailing behind. "I don't have all day to babysit you."

Dawn looked at the girl's mother and glanced at her watch. "She'll be fine. Don't worry. Why don't you pick her up around ten o'clock?"

"Does she have a license?" Jason asked.

"Yes, I have a copy of it right here." Dawn reached into her purse and showed it to the guard. "Go ahead," she told the girl's mother. "We're all set."

~ * ~

It was a light training morning for the Miller barn with Alley having run yesterday, two horses in tomorrow and two to be entered for Sunday. Tom came and went, ponying horses for a few other trainers. In between, he helped Dawn with stalls and doing the horses up. The blacksmith was due around ten-thirty. No one was scheduled to be shod today. Brownie was just going to check the horses running this weekend to make sure all was well. Johnny came and went. Jenny Grimm came by to check in on Alley Beau. Junior came and went. Randy stopped by. Juan stopped by.

Ben walked over to the Secretary's office around nine o'clock to check in with Linda and Joe. Wendy wouldn't be in the office until later in the afternoon after she got Matthew settled in at the rehab facility. Ben didn't envy Wendy. Matthew could be pretty headstrong and entirely way too independent.

Linda looked up from taking an entry and smiled. Joe had one trainer in line. She had three. Ben jokingly tried nudging two of them out of the way and they laughed. He got behind the one in Joe's line.

"What can I do for you, Mr. Miller," Joe asked, when it was Ben's turn.

"Well, I don't know, Mr. Feigler," Ben said. "Let me think."

Joe smiled. "Did you hear Erie might be back in business?"

"No, I didn't," Ben said. He glanced at Linda who smiled and crossed her fingers. "Good! That's good news." Ben placed his entries for Bo-T and Wee Born on Sunday and then took the elevator upstairs to check on the old-timers. Every one of them, including the nurse Vicky was sitting in front of the big grandstand window watching the morning training activity.

"Buenos dias," Miguel said.

"Buenos dias." Ben pulled up a chair and sat down beside him. "How is everybody?"

"Good, good, fine, fine," they all said, eyes glued to the racetrack.

Ben watched along with them for a moment. "Who is that?" he asked, pointing to a large black horse being galloped.

"Rider or horse?" Mim asked.

Ben chuckled. "Horse."

"That's Spring Bucket Bob."

"I thought so."

"That's Junior Rupert galloping him," Jack said.

All the old-timers nodded, agreeing.

"I never liked that boy," Steven said. "Was always late, could never get his ass out of bed."

'He's a lot better now," Jeannie said. "I hear he's going to be a father."

"What?" Ben said.

"Guciano's girl Lucy."

"Ah, Jesus," Ben said.

"How's the house coming?" Bill asked.

"It's coming along nice," Ben said.

"I'm going to miss this place," Jack said.

Clint nodded. "Me too."

"I wish you could stay," Ben said. "Hell, I'm thinking I wish I could stay. It's awful nice up here."

Frank looked at him. "Is there any way we could come every once in a while?"

"Of course. Wendy's working on it."

"You know that, you old fool," Jeannie said.

"All right, so I forgot. Shoot me."

"I'll do worse than that."

They all laughed.

Ben stood up to leave. "I'll see you all later."

Vicky followed him to the elevator. "Are you okay?" she asked.

"Yeah, I'm fine." He tipped his hat back and scratched his forehead. "I have that pre-op stuff today for my cataract surgery."

"You'll do fine. That procedure is so routine now it's nothing."

Ben nodded and boarded the elevator. "Looks like about a week till you guys are moving home."

"Home," Vicky said. "That has such a nice sound to it."

Ben rode down to the first floor and when the doors opened did a double take. "Richard? Richard, what are you doing here?"

"I'm just here to visit," the man said, shaking Ben's hand.

"How are you feeling?"

"Great! I'll be back to work before you know it."

"Now don't you be rushing yourself. All right?"

Richard nodded and walked down the hall into his office and sat down in his chair. "God, I love this place," he said. "Who'd have ever thought?"

There was a time when he hated coming to work and didn't much like Ben or Tom or Dawn either for that matter. They all got along famously now. He looked out the window at the horses training on the track and smiled. As Nottingham Downs General Manager, he didn't have a plush top floor executive office with his own private bathroom anymore, perks that seemed extremely important to him not too long ago. He loved his job and no longer cared about such things. Sharing combined offices with Ben and Wendy had turned out to be the best thing that ever happened to him, and his marriage.

He touched his side where his gallbladder used to be. He wasn't missing it at all or the pain that had accompanied it either for that matter. What a horrible week. Now if only the infection would clear up. He leaned back in his chair and sighed. A memo lying on his desk caught his eye. He reached for the notepad and sat pondering the message.

"More bad news. Call me. Tee."

He stared. It was dated weeks ago. Too late.

~ * ~

Wendy sat with her hands in her lap. Just days after fearing for her son Matthew's life, she was giving thought to pushing him off a cliff. Gordon could be difficult but Matthew was impossible.

"Matthew."

"Mom, please. This has nothing to do with you. Look at this place. Come on, it's no better than a hospital. In fact it's worse. It stinks! God, what is that smell?"

The physical therapist stood at Wendy's side. "It's probably from the wing next to us. I've been here so long I don't even smell it anymore. You'll get used to it."

"I don't think so," Matthew said. "I'm not going to be here that long. In fact, I'm not staying. I don't need a hospital bed. I thought this was a therapy place for athletes. I can't see an athlete sleeping on that bed. It's a hospital bed."

"What difference does it make, Matthew?" Wendy asked. "A bed is a bed. You're supposed to be getting rest. What would you rather have? A futon?"

"Yes!"

Wendy laughed. "Come on, Son. I know this isn't easy, but at least give it a try."

Matthew looked around the room. "All right. So where's my TV?"

"There's one down the hall in the social room," the therapist said. "If you'll just let me get through my list of assessment questions, I'll show you where it's at."

"You're going to show me?" Matthew said. "You mean you don't think I can find my way down the hall?"

"That's not what she meant and you know it, Matthew. Don't be rude," Wendy said.

"Fine." Matthew motioned for the therapist to get on with her list of questions.

"Are you having any trouble holding your urine?"

Gordon laughed at the expression on his brother's face.

"Holding my urine?"

"I'm sorry, Mr. Morrison. But these questions are important to your course of therapy."

"All right," Matthew said. "Let me ask you a question. What kind of therapy am I going to be doing?"

"Well," the woman said, visibly unnerved. "You'll obviously be doing some physical therapy. You'll be doing some stretching exercises, lifting some light weights."

"Uh, that's good," Gordon said, "'Cause light weights is about all he ever could handle."

His mother gave him a look. "Gordon, be quiet. I said enough. Okay?"

"So where is this physical therapy room? Let me go look at it."

"Just a moment. Let me finish with your evaluation and I'll get someone to accompany you."

"Accompany me? You mean I can't walk down there by myself?"

"No. Not until after we observe you for a few days and complete our evaluation."

Matthew looked at his mother. "This is ridiculous."

"You'll also be doing occupational therapy. This will help you with any difficulties you might have dressing yourself, showering, shaving."

"Holding my urine," Matthew said, cupping his hands.

Gordon laughed.

"Go out in the hall," Wendy said. "Go on! You're not helping."

"Mom, there's nothing wrong with him. His eyes are a little funny. He'll get over it. He doesn't belong here."

Wendy drew a breath and sighed. "Matthew, please. Can you just try it for a few days? You have another MRI scheduled on Monday. We can see how the results are then and go from there." Perhaps it was the tears Wendy was trying to hold back that swayed Matthew. Perhaps it was fatigue catching up to him from the ordeal of getting brought over here in an ambulance against his wishes. Suddenly, he just sat down on the bed, punched the two pillows, and leaned his head back. "No problem with the urine. What's the next question?"

"Have you had a bowel movement today?"

Matthew closed his eyes and started laughing.

"Do I take that as a yes or a no?" the therapist asked.

~ * ~

Dawn walked down to the ReHab and ReHome barn a little before ten o'clock to check on Hillary. She was brushing the horse in the third stall. She looked at Dawn. "Do you know what these little scars are from all up and down the front of her legs? Pin-firing!"

"Yes, I know," Dawn said.

"They take a little soldering iron kind of thing and go up and down in lines and...."

Dawn held up her hands. "Do you know what they do to women having babies by caesarian? They cut their stomachs open. Come on, Hillary, the medical profession

~ 117 ~

is full of unpleasant procedures. It's a way of fusing a shin buck. The shin away from sheath covering the.... "

"You sound like a vet," Hillary said, back to brushing the horse.

"No, but I am married to one," Dawn said.

Hillary looked at her in mock pity.

"Gelding horses is not pretty either."

"Why are you doing this? Why are you giving me shit?"

"Why are you brushing the horse?" Dawn asked.

"Dusty said I could. She likes it."

"Most racehorses do. They get groomed a lot, you know."

The girl shrugged and wouldn't look at her.

"You get more bees with honey, Hillary. If you want to do something for animals and pets, you need to go about it in a sensible way."

Dusty walked down the shedrow. "Your mom's here."

"How'd she do?" Dawn asked, noticing how hesitant the girl was to leave the stall.

"I need to finish her mane. Can you tell my mom I'll be right there?"

Dusty looked at her.

"Please," she said.

"Sure." Dusty walked away.

"Do you think I could ever come back?"

"What? To this horrible place?" Dawn asked.

"Well, this part wasn't so horrible. Dusty was nice, and he obviously cares about the horses like you said."

Dawn told her she'd think about it, waited for the girl to finish brushing the horse's mane, and walked with her to the stable gate where her mother stood talking to Dusty.

"Thank you," Janet Walker said. "Thank you, I appreciate this. You ready?"

"I guess," Hillary said, already walking toward their car. She looked back at Dawn. "You'll let me know, right?"

"Yes."

~ * ~

Ben sat in the pre-op waiting room along with five other patients anxious for their names to be called. Finally, "Ben Miller."

"Yes." He stood and followed the woman down the hall.

"Have a seat, please."

Ben sat down.

"I see your surgery is scheduled for nine o'clock on Monday. You are the second surgery scheduled for Dr. Branower that morning, so barring any complications, your surgery should be right on schedule."

"Complications?"

She glanced at him and then took his blood pressure, which was a little high. She took his temperature, listened to his pulse and listened to his heart. "Deep breaths, please."

Ben tried reading a chart on the wall. Best he could make out it was either about what to do if someone was choking or someone was having a heart attack. There were lots of purple people in the illustrations.

"Okay, I think you're all set." She handed him a printed sheet of instructions. "Don't eat or drink anything after midnight Sunday. No gum, no mints. You can brush your teeth and rinse, but don't swallow."

Ben looked at her.

"I know," she said. "Sounds ridiculous but some people do. Continue with your regular medication. Did you start the eye drops this morning?"

"Yes."

"Good. Continue all the way through Monday morning. You do not have to bring them with you. Do you take insulin or oral medications for diabetes?"

"No."

"Okay. The rest is explained here. Is transport picking you up?"

"Transport?"

"The ambulance service. Are you in a facility or living at home?" She didn't wait for an answer. "You'll want someone to drive you here and take you home. You will receive detailed post-operative instructions after your surgery. Have a nice day."

Ben walked down the hall thinking about his wife Meg. Whenever he was in a hospital, he thought about her. He wished he didn't have those memories of her, but.... He stopped at the patient information desk to ask if Matthew was still a patient here.

The receptionist looked for his name, shook her head, and he walked on outside. "I don't want to die here," Meg had said. "Please, Ben, take me home." She passed two days later, cradled in his arms in their bed of forty-two years.

Chapter Ten

When the phone rang in the middle of the night, Tom grabbed it. "Yes? Yes," he said, softly. "Yes. I'll be right there." He pulled on his jeans and reached for his shirt.

"What's going on?" Wendy asked, glancing at the bedside clock. It was two thirty-five.

"Nothing, I uh…just need to help Randy. I'm going to meet him at the uh…uh the farm down the road. Go to sleep. I'll be back."

As he drove down the road, he berated himself. I should have known. What kind of father am I? Not a very good one, he thought. He parked just outside the front door at the rehab facility and walked inside. A rather frantic Nursing Director was waiting just inside the reception area wringing her hands. "This has never happened before, not even with the Alzheimer's patients. He apparently just up and walked out. We've searched everywhere."

Tom stood staring down the hall.

"I thought of calling the police, but...."

"No, that's okay," Tom said. "When did you see him last?"

"Well, see, that's just it. We don't know. Second shift is gone."

"I understand," Tom said, trying to think. What would Matthew do? Where would he go? He didn't have any money, no cellphone. He didn't even have any clothes. "And you're sure you've searched everywhere?"

"Yes."

"All right." Tom looked out the lobby glass doors, thinking Matthew probably didn't even have shoes. "No one could have taken him back to the hospital, right?"

"No."

Tom nodded. He didn't think so. Just then he saw the dash light go off and on in his truck. At first he thought he probably hadn't shut the door totally but on second thought. "Excuse me," he said, and walked outside. He opened the driver's door and there sat his stepson: Wendy's first born, in the passenger seat.

"What the hell took you so long?" Matthew said. "I've been freezing my ass off out here. I was ready to start walking."

Tom smiled, a myriad of emotions washing over him, pride being the strongest. "That would have been quite a sight." Mathew was wrapped in sheets, had washcloths taped to his feet, and had a towel draped over his head. His long hair spilled down the sides of his face. "You okay?"

Matthew looked at him and nodded. "I want to go home."

"To school? You can't. Your eyes…."

"No, I want to go to the farm. Take me home, Tom. Please."

"All right." Tom looked at him and nodded. "Let me go tell them what's going on."

The Nursing Director was hovering just inside the lobby door. "I'm going to take him home," Tom said. "Do I need to sign anything?"

"Yes," she replied, but couldn't decide what. "Here." She handed him a blank piece of paper. "Write…." She paused, looking out at Matthew all hunkered down in the passenger seat of the truck. "Write being discharged into parent's care, state that you will check in with his doctor in the morning, date it, and sign your name."

"Okay." Tom wrote down the required details, signed, dated it, and then turned to leave. "Thank you. We'll drop off the sheets."

The woman nodded and locked the door after him. Tom climbed in behind the wheel and looked at Matthew and sighed. For some reason he thought about the last time he bailed Junior Rupert out of jail.

"You hungry?" Tom asked.

"I'm starved," Matthew said. "I'd kill for a cheeseburger."

Tom put the truck into gear and headed for the all-night drive-thru burger joint by the racetrack. When he pulled up to the cubbyhole window, the man looked warily at Matthew sitting there in the truck all wrapped in white. "He's fine," Tom said. "He thinks he's Jesus."

~ * ~

Randy turned into the driveway at the farm a little after four in the morning, parked next to the house, and here came the dogs. He opened the door and all six jumped into and over his lap and crammed themselves into the passenger seat and on the floor, wagging their tails and panting. "Good boys, good boys," Randy said, patting them all on their heads, scratching their ears, scratching under their chins.

When Dawn woke an hour later, had breakfast, and walked outside to leave for the racetrack, she found him sound asleep in his truck, head resting on Dawber's shoulder and all the dogs sardined around one another next to him. Runt was stretched out on his lap with a leg slung over the steering wheel.

Piccolo picked up his head and seeing Dawn, starting barking happily. Randy opened his eyes, all the dogs stirring now, and yawned. "What time is it?" he asked.

"A little after five," she said, kissing him. "Why don't you go inside and get some sleep."

"I would," he said, yawning again and leaning back so all the dogs could jump down out of the truck. "I have a...." Another yawn. "I have something I have to do right at seven. I can't remember. What the heck was it? Oh yeah, now I remember, a scope. I didn't want to wake you."

Dawn glanced at Ben's farmhouse. The upstairs light wasn't on, which was odd. Tom was always awake this time of morning. "All right, I'll see you at the track. I love you," she said.

"I love you better," he replied, playfully grabbing at her behind and missing it. "What races are you in?"

"The second and the seventh."

"I'll see you later."

As Dawn drove past Ben's farmhouse, the upstairs light came on. It wasn't often she beat Tom to the racetrack. It was going to be fun razzing him, she thought, and smiled. She waved to Ben; standing at the window by the kitchen sink. He usually always left right behind her. She pulled out onto the road and did a little beep on her horn as she passed George and Glenda's, another morning habit. They relied on her to wake them up.

"I think I'll pick up some donuts," she said to herself. "I haven't done that in a while. Some custard ones. It's going to be a good day."

~ * ~

Wendy rolled over in bed and looked at Tom. He was standing by the dresser putting his wallet into his jeans. She glanced at the clock. "What time did you get back?"

"Oh," he said. "Not long after I left. You were sound asleep."

She smiled and burrowed down into the sheets and blankets. "I'll see you later."

Tom stood at the door.

"What?" she said, when he just stood there.

"Uh…." He scratched the side of his face. "I don't want you coming downstairs and getting freaked out, but…."

"But what? What's going on?"

Tom hesitated.

"Is it Matthew? Is he okay?"

"Oh, he's okay all right. He's downstairs."

"What?" Wendy sat up in bed. "What?"

"He walked out of the rehab place last night and I went and got him."

"He can't do that," Wendy said, trying to untangle herself from the covers and get out of bed.

Tom put a hand on her shoulder. "Listen, he's probably sleeping. There's no sense you going downstairs and waking him. Go back to sleep."

"Oh yeah, right. That's just what I'll do. I'll go back to sleep." She pushed his hand away, put her feet on the floor and started pacing. "Why would he do something like that?"

"I don't know. He's your son."

"He's not my son, not anymore. He's been your son for about a year now. He doesn't listen to me."

"He's a grown man," Tom said. "He's not your little boy anymore."

Wendy stopped pacing to glare at him. "I'm not talking to you. You hear me? I'm not talking to you."

"I hear you. I gotta go. If he's sleeping, let him sleep."

Wendy raked her hands through her hair and put her hands on her hips. "Go! I thought you said you had to go!"

"You're so cute. Look at you," Tom said.

"I said go!"

Ben looked up from eating his oatmeal as Tom came down the stairs and tipped a sideward glance. Matthew was all curled in the crook of the L-shape part of the couch, sleeping like a baby. Ben held his hands out in question.

"I'll tell you at the track," Tom whispered. "He's fine."

Ben nodded and looked at the boy.

Tom glanced back at the stairs. Wendy had tiptoed down and was peeking at her son. She shook her head and tiptoed back up. Tom left and Ben left shortly thereafter. The plan was for Wendy to borrow Glenda's car for the day. Gordon still had his mom's car and would be home in the evening.

Wendy showered, dried her hair, got dressed and came down the stairs as quietly as she could. Matthew was sitting up, headphones on and watching television. She walked over and turned it off.

"Now don't you be upsetting me, Mom," he said, removing the headphones.

"Me? Upset you?"

Wendy picked up the empty bowl and glass on the coffee table in front of him. "What's this?" She took them to the sink to rinse them.

"Oatmeal and juice," Matthew said. "Ben left it for me."

She rinsed the glass and bowl for an eternity. "Matthew," she said, finally turning off the faucet and facing him.

"Mom, don't. It's a done deal."

"So what? I'm just supposed to go to work and not worry?"

"Yes. George is here. Glenda's here. Liz and Senior are here. Carol's here. What can go wrong?"

"I don't know. They can come in here and find you unconscious, maybe dead."

"Well, that would be a downer now wouldn't it?" Matthew got up and started down the hall.

"Where are you going? What are you doing?"

"I'm going to go to the bathroom," Matthew said in slow motion. "It's what I do when I have to go pee."

In spite of herself Wendy laughed. "Matthew…?"

"I'm fine, Mom. I'm fine. Okay? I'm fine."

~ * ~

Tom showed up at the barn with a dozen donuts also. He figured since he was already late he might as well come bearing gifts. Dawn had the horses fed, the coffee made, and was sitting at Ben's desk reading the racing form when they arrived,

"I'm replaced already," Ben said. "Look at that."

"Did you check the horses' feed tubs?" Tom asked, with his mouth full.

"No, Tom, I didn't."

He laughed, spraying powdered sugar everywhere. "What about Alley? She eat up?"

"I don't know. I didn't check for that either."

Tom grinned. "Just keeping you on your toes."

Dawn got up so Ben could sit down and in came Junior. "Who made the donuts?" He helped himself to one and a cup of coffee. Ben looked up at him.

"What?"

Ben motioned for him to shut the door and waited. "There's a rumor going around. Is it true?"

Junior hesitated. "About Lucy?"

Tom glanced from one to the other. "What about her?"

Junior sat down on the cot next to Dawn. "She's in foal."

Tom stood looking down at him.

"She doesn't know for sure."

"What are you going to do?"

"I don't know. I don't know what to do. What if it's not my kid?"

"Not your kid?" Tom said. "Weren't you the one bragging all over the racetrack a couple of months ago about how you popped her cherry? What the fuck is wrong with you?"

"Tom…." Dawn said.

"What? Don't Tom me. Junior needs to grow up and act like a man for once in his life."

Junior looked up at him. "I've only been a man about a year and a half now. What about you? You've been a man all your life! Look how long it took you to grow up."

"Enough," Ben said. "God, I'm so tired of you two and your constant bickering."

There was a knock on the door. Tom opened it and let Dusty in.

"What's going on?"

"Oh, you haven't heard?" Junior said.

"I heard. There's not much I don't know on this racetrack, Junior." Dusty looked into both boxes of donuts, helped himself to a creampuff, and poured himself a cup of coffee.

"Well, then maybe you can tell us who the father is," Tom said.

"Who?" Dusty looked at Tom. "There's no question about who the father is."

"Oh yeah," Tom said, reaching past Junior for Red's saddle and bridle. "Well, tell that to this piece of shit."

"I swear, Tom, if you say that one more time," Junior said.

"What are you going to do, Big Man? What are you going to do?"

Dawn put up her hands. "Frankly, I'm tired of this too. Junior, Lucy's young and she's going to need pre-natal care."

Tom turned.

"No, Tom," Dawn said. "I'm talking now. This is about Junior and Lucy. This isn't about you."

"Fine," Tom said, slinging his saddle over his shoulder and kicking the tack room door open. "Go ahead and hold his hand. That'll make him grow up."

Dusty closed the door behind him and turned to Junior. "Are you scared, Junior? Is that what this is all about?"

Junior hesitated and then leaned back and sighed. "I don't even like kids. What am I going to do with a kid?"

Dawn looked at him. "You'll learn. Nature has a way of taking over."

Junior shrugged. "But Lucy and I don't even get along half the time, Dawn. It ain't like with you and Randy."

Ben looked at him. "Oh? Do you think they always got along?"

Dawn laughed. "Don't remind me."

Chapter Eleven

Randy walked down Ralph Symchek's shedrow with diagnostic instruments and supplies in hand. He was scheduled to scope the horse prior to galloping and again afterwards. This horse was the pride of the Symchek barn, a big, strapping, full-of-himself four-year old with potential as an Ohio Bred sire. Randy hoped he didn't have bad news for the owner when it was all said and done.

"Well, let's see what we've got."

The horse had thrown a bad race last time out. The jockey said he'd sounded like "a freight train" during the stretch run and pulled up so abruptly going into the turn he almost fell down. There was no temperature upon examination after the race, no signs of illness, no signs of internal bleeding, no lameness. Additionally, the horses showed no evidence of illness, lameness or distress the following morning, afternoon, or evening.

"This'll tell us everything, right?"

"Well, if we're lucky, it'll give us an idea." Randy gently slid the endoscope up the horse's nose, a rather gentle procedure given the size of a horse's nostrils, unlike humans.

Dusty walked down the shedrow, nodded to Ralph and stood at Randy's side. Randy glanced at him. "What's up, big guy?"

Dusty chuckled. Compared to Randy's height of six-foot-four, he was not a big guy. "How's it going?"

"So far so good."

The backside p.a. system sounded. "Dr. Iredell, you're needed at barn six immediately. Dr. Iredell you're needed at barn six immediately."

Randy never even blinked.

"You want me to go tell them you'll be right there?" Dusty asked.

"Yes." Randy nodded. "Thank you. Ralph, now take a look here."

Ralph shook his head, his hand pressed instantly over his stomach. "No, that's okay."

"All right," Randy eased the endoscope out gently. "Everything looks good. We'll see how it looks when he gets back."

The horse in barn six was showing signs of colic. Randy examined the horse thoroughly, listened, observed. The trainer, Dave Johnson, watched. "What do you think?"

"We'll see," Randy said.

The man walked down to tack one of his other horses as Dusty held the colicky horse for Randy. "Doc Jake would be proud of you, you know that. When did you start being so wise?"

Randy yawned. "I don't know. I guess when I started having to be."

Dusty smiled when Randy yawned again. "You need a vacation. You and Dawn need to go away for a while."

"Right. But now's not the time."

"Then you need an assistant. Hell, you've got me yawning and I sleep like a baby every night. Why not hire someone to help?"

"Nah, I don't want to go there," Randy said. "They're all girls and I'm too good-looking."

Dusty laughed.

Randy had been partners with another veterinarian for several years but the man fell in love with the owner of a

~ 130 ~

ship-in stakes horse, and that was that. Within a year, the two got married and his partner up and moved to Kentucky. His departure spurred Randy's sister Cindy's plan to go back to school for a year and a half of specialized large animal classes to add to her small animal veterinarian degree and move here. Even when she found out she was pregnant it still seemed like it would work out. The baby would be born in the down season at the track. But now with her experiencing complications....

"Wonder if there is such a thing as a rent-a-vet somewhere?" Randy said.

"You could probably get an intern," Dusty replied.

Randy shook his head. "I don't have time to break 'em in."

"Why don't we just look? What can it hurt? Wendy could probably find you someone in a day."

Randy eased his arm out of the horse's rectum, dropped some hard balls of manure to the ground, and took off his plastic sleeve glove. "All right. Find me someone that knows racehorses and we'll give it a shot. But make sure they know it's only temporary."

~ * ~

Matthew walked out onto the front porch of Ben's farmhouse, bare-chested, barefoot, and in ratty jeans. He stood tall and stretched his arms over his head.

"Hey!" Glenda yelled to him from the barn.

"Hey!" He waved back.

"You okay?"

"Yep! I feel great!" Well, maybe not great, he said to himself.

"You need anything?"

"No. Thank you!" He went back inside to spare her any more concern and poured himself a cup of cold coffee. Since it didn't have any caffeine in it he figured he'd be safe, but less than fifteen minutes later he started to get a headache. He put on a shirt and shoes and walked out to the main barn. He liked doing stalls and thought about it, but didn't want to chance the headache getting worse. It felt like pressure on the back of his head.

Glenda looked at him. "How's the seeing thing going?"

"Okay, I guess. It's like it comes and goes."

Glenda studied his eyes. "Liz made blueberry muffins. She was going to bring you down some when you woke up."

"I'm up," Matthew said, smiling.

Glenda nodded. "You certainly are." She liked Matthew. Who didn't? He was a kind boy, always said what was on his mind, handsome in a hippy-throwback kind of way, gorgeous long dark hair and big blue eyes. "Do you want me to go up and get you some?"

"No, I'll walk up."

"You can take the four-wheeler."

Matthew looked at it. As a rule, it was his favorite mode of transportation. It could be a little jarring though, especially over the gravel. "I'll walk. I think I need the exercise."

Glenda watched him start off and when he was out of hearing distance, phoned George and then Liz and Senior. "He's not looking so good, but he's moving."

George kept an eye on him from the stallion barn and Liz pretended to be surprised to see him when Matthew appeared outside her porch screen door. "Come in! Come on in!"

Matthew sat down at the kitchen table, a little dizzy, a little blind. "Is that Matthew?" Senior said, from the bathroom, shaving.

"Yep, it's me."

Liz put the platter of blueberry muffins down in front of him. "What would you like to drink? You want some coffee?"

"No, I don't think so. Can I just have some water? Maybe some warm water?" He was afraid cold water might make his head hurt worse, brain freeze. That's what it feels like, he decided, brain freeze.

Liz observed him for a moment. He wolfed down one muffin and then another.

"Well, there's nothing wrong with your appetite," Senior said, walking into the kitchen drying his face with a towel.

"What? Did you want me to save you some?" Matthew asked.

Senior sat down next to him, smiling, thanked Liz for the cup of coffee she placed in front of him and reached for a muffin. "Tom says you'll be needing to check in with your doctor today. I'll be driving you."

Matthew looked at him. "Do I have to have an appointment?"

"No, it's all taken care of." He'd expected Matthew to balk at going, give him a hard time. He sipped his coffee and glanced at the boy. "Whenever you're ready."

~ * ~

When Dawn was paged to the guard shack she had a feeling it was going to be that little girl Hillary, and sure enough. "My teacher says I can shadow you every morning."

"Actually, I don't need a shadow, Hillary. I have two of them at home."

"Please," the girl said.

Dawn looked at her. "Does your mother know you're here?"

"Yes." She motioned over her shoulder to where her mother sat in her car waiting.

Dawn sighed. Of all the days. She had so much to do and coddling an angry young girl was not one of them. She waved to the mother. "Ten o'clock, okay?"

"Okay. Thank you."

The girl walked along with Dawn. "What do you want me to do? Do you want me to help Dusty again?"

"Let me check with him. Three of the horses went out yesterday. He might be done already this morning."

Hillary stared longingly at the ReHome barn as they passed. "Not Whippet?"

"Yes, Whippet. Is that why you wanted to be here? Do you want to leave now? Call your Mom."

"No, I just...." The girl followed Dawn down to the Miller barn and into the tack room. Ben looked up.

"We have her until ten. What can she do?"

Ben shrugged. Everything was done. Even the shedrow was already raked.

Randy pulled up next to the barn, sat talking on the phone for a minute and got out and walked into the tack room. "You guys need me for anything?"

Dawn shook her head. Ben shook his head.

Randy helped himself to a couple of donuts.

"So this is your husband?" Hillary asked. "He looks so much older than you."

"Well, thank you," Randy said.

Dawn chuckled. "Randy, this is Hillary, Miss Personality."

Randy glanced at the girl. "I figured as much."

"So where are you going?" Dawn asked.

"Shifting Gears. I'll be right back."

"Why don't you take Hillary with you?"

"No thank you."

The girl made a face at him. "I don't want to go. What's Shifting Gears anyway?"

"It's a rescue farm," Dawn said, looking at the girl. "And the two women who run it will eat you up and spit you out if you even think of giving them a hard time. Got it?"

Hillary held up her hands. "Ooh, I'm scared."

"You should be," Randy said, motioning for her to go on around to the passenger side of the truck. The seat was full of papers, supplies and clipboards. "Throw them in the back" He looked at Dawn and lowered his voice. "You sure this is a good idea?"

"It beats her shadowing me. Besides, yes, I think a trip to Shifting Gears is precisely what she needs."

Veronica and Karen, co-owners of the Thoroughbred Rescue Farm were expecting Randy and had the horse to be treated standing in the crossties. The five-year-old gelding had been neglected for months by its previous owner to the point of near death. Since he'd come to Shifting Gears, one day he would appear slightly better, and the next, worse. He was scheduled to get his weekly vitamin injection and was one of the quietest Thoroughbreds the two women had ever had at the farm. There was no way of knowing what his temperament was like when he was racing or if he was always this quiet. Hopefully time would tell.

Hillary was silent the whole way there, not giving Randy the satisfaction of showing any interest whatsoever. When they pulled in the drive, she sat up a little straighter, perhaps in anticipation, perhaps in dread. Randy glanced at her.

"What?"

"Nothing."

He got out of the truck. So did she. On the way into the barn, he figured he'd better warn her. "'Most of the horses here at the moment are well on their way to recovery.

This particular horse, though, is still not out of the woods by any means."

"So?"

"So, I'm just letting you know."

Veronica and Karen met them just inside the aisle way of the main barn, having heard Randy's truck pull in. "Hey, Randy!"

"Morning, ladies!"

The two women smiled and then looked at the girl. "Who's this?" Veronica, always the worrier, asked.

"This is bad-ass Hillary," Randy said.

"Oh?" Karen said. "Because…?"

"I'm not sure," Randy said. "Hillary, this is Veronica and this is Karen, two angels from heaven."

Hillary stared. They just looked like two old farmer ladies to her. Randy followed the women down to the crossties with Hillary trailing along behind him and looking all around.

"How's the guy doing?"

"Okay. About the same," Karen said, glancing over her shoulder at the girl.

When Randy stopped near the horse in crossties, Hillary had been gawking around so much she practically ran into him. Randy took out a syringe and stepped toward the horse, patting him gently on his skeletal neck. "Hey, pretty guy."

Because of Randy's size and the fact that Hillary hadn't exactly been paying attention to where they were going, when Randy stepped closer to the horse to administer the vitamin injection, Hillary gasped, her knees buckled, and she fell to the floor.

"Oh my God," she said, tears springing to her eyes. "Oh my God." The horse looked down at her with the utmost curiosity. "What happened to him? Who did this?"

Karen and Veronica helped her back to her feet. "Who did this?"

"I prefer not to know," Karen said. "And we don't ever let Veronica know. It would not be wise."

Hillary stepped toward the horse warily as if she were afraid of frightening the animal and touched his face gently with a trembling hand. "Oh, you poor horse. You poor horse."

Randy observed her reaction. "We've been trying to convince him that he is looking good, so…."

"Oh! I'm sorry. You do look good. I'm so sorry." She stroked the horse's face softly. "You're beautiful. You're beautiful." She pressed her face against his nose, hot tears streaming down her face. "So beautiful." She looked at Randy. "Is he?" She looked at Karen and Veronica. "Is he…?"

"Is he going to be all right?" Tears welled up in Veronica's eyes. "Is that what you want to know?"

Hillary nodded, wiping her eyes and looking up at the horse. Veronica and Karen steadied the girl when it appeared as if she was going to collapse again. "Randy, you should have warned her."

"I did."

"Here, come sit down," Veronica said.

"I can't." Hillary gasped for breath. "He needs my energy."

Randy looked at the two women, all three exchanging worried expressions.

"It's all right," the girl said softly to the horse. "It's all right."

Randy stepped back. The horse seemed to be responding to her. The girl cupped his muzzle and breathed into his nose. She focused on his eyes. She touched his ears. "Foregone," she said. "Yes, Foregone."

Karen and Veronica looked at one another and then at Randy.

"I promise," the girl said. "Yes, I promise." She stepped back and nodded. "I promise."

"Promise what?" Veronica asked.

"To be by his side no matter what. I promised." She touched her chest, drew a deep breath and sighed. "I never break a promise. Can I come see him every day?"

Veronica and Karen looked at Randy. He shrugged. What did he know?

The girl shivered and then shook her arms and hands, drew another deep breath and put her head down and fluffed her hair, wiped her chest off, her legs, moved her feet.

"Well, we'd better get going," Randy said.

Hillary nodded and looked at the two women. "You will let me come back, won't you?"

They both hesitated and then looked at the horse, more alive than he'd been for weeks. "Of course," Karen said, with Veronica agreeing. "Of course."

The girl reverted back to her crabby self in the truck, staring out the window and refusing to talk. Finally, she said to Randy, "So now you know why I can't stand to see an animal suffer. I don't just see it; I feel it."

"How did you know he's a Foregone offspring?"

The girl looked at him. "Easy. He told me."

Chapter Twelve

George stood watching All Together in the paddock. The mare was looking longingly at the pasture, probably wondering why she wasn't allowed to fun free. She kicked and bucked and trotted up and down the fence line.

Glenda walked up next to him. "How's she doing?"

George motioned. "She wants out."

The mare stood at the gate, whinnied loud and long and then started trotting again. "She keeps this up, I'm going to have to bring her in."

"When will Randy know?"

"Sometime today," George said. "Wait, did you just see that?"

Glenda shook her head.

"Watch. The foal just kicked. Look, on the right side."

Glenda stared, saw it, and smacked George on the arm. "Yes!"

The foal kicked again and adding evidence, All Together kicked at her belly in response or retaliation, one of the two. George phoned Randy immediately.

"You sure?" Randy said.

"Yep. Oh, it just kicked again."

"All right!" Randy said. "Good news!"

"Can I turn her out?"

"Yeah, go ahead. Just keep an eye on her."

Glenda slipped between the fence rails and walked down and opened the gate to the pasture. All Together took off running down to where her regular pasture mate stood grazing. The two mares nipped and played halter tag for a moment or two and then both grazed, muzzles inches apart. These two mares had been together for five years now.

"They aren't just friends, they're family," Glenda liked saying. "A lot like the rest of us here at the farm."

It went without saying they'd keep an eye on the mare and would search the pasture when they brought her in - necessary procedures with mares in foal, particularly with one having shown signs of possibly being in heat or having an infection. Randy had sent off additional blood work. The results were due back later today.

Randy had matured into a hands-on practitioner. What the man saw when examining a horse was equally as important to him as the clinical aspects. George and Dusty had talked quite often about it and with Senior too. What Dusty liked best was Randy's pragmatism, and his ability to take a wait-and-see approach and not rush into a diagnosis or prognosis.

He told Randy that once and Randy laughed. "I don't like being wrong. I'd much rather wait a little bit and be right." He'd learned that from Doc Jake early on, but it wasn't until Doc Jake passed away and Randy was on his own that he started putting it into practice. Always when confronted with a difficult case or a life or death decision or something way out of the ordinary, he would ask himself, "What would Doc Jake do?" Then one day, without asking himself anything, he just started reacting on his own.

"Dawn said she found him asleep in his truck again this morning," Glenda said. "He's exhausted."

"I know." George nodded. "Dusty called. He said Wendy's going to try and get him some temporary help."

"Will Randy agree to that?"

"Dusty said he did. We'll see."

They were all concerned about the amount of hours Randy put in and feared he was just going to up and collapse one day. Randy laughed when they told him that, said they were worrying for nothing.

George and Glenda watched All Together and Scarlet graze a little while longer, then went back to cleaning stalls; Glenda in the main barn, George in the stallion barn. The two-year olds on the farm wouldn't start training for another month or so and were all turned out. The yearlings and weanlings were on pasture twenty-four hours a day and had big run-in sheds to get out of the weather. In addition, the weanlings had a boss mare no longer being bred, turned out with them. Dusty's new little horse Bonnie Bee was in the pasture with Poncho and Biscuit and as content as could be. There were horses to care for everywhere. There was mowing to do, and the garden to harvest and weed. There was maintenance on the barns and fences. Glenda and George were never bored and had never been happier.

~ * ~

Liz walked over to Dawn and Randy's house to check in on Carol and the children. They were playing Come and Get Me, a modern variation of Hide and Go Seek that Carol invented for her own grandchildren who she rarely saw anymore. One of her daughters lived in Alaska, the other New Mexico. The children loved the game. They didn't really have to hide. They just had to go somewhere and call out for someone to come tag them.

Grandma Liz had brought them blueberry muffins. They each had one and then ran off to the playroom to watch *Barney* on video. The two women sat down in the dining room for a cup of herbal tea, Carol's special blend of dried flowers, lemon, and honey. It went wonderfully with the blueberry muffins.

"Everything going on and I feel so useless," Liz said. "At least when I was back home, I had outside chores to do. I don't know anything about horses. I need to find something to do or everyone's going to be visiting me at a funny farm."

Carol smiled. "That's how I felt. That's why I'm here."

"I mean, I'm worried about Cindy. I'm worried about Matthew."

"Are they back?"

"Not yet."

"And when we were working on the house getting all set up, that kept me busy. But it's all done now. All the curtains are made. I finished the last pair just before we went down to Cindy's."

"I hear you."

The two women were about the same age and had a lot of the same interests, though Carol was more of an indoor person. Liz missed the outdoors. "There's just nothing for me to do."

"Have you thought about helping Glenda with the garden?"

"I wouldn't want to intrude. See, and that's just it. I'm thinking I'd like to put in a garden of our own next year but I don't want to offend her since she grows enough for everyone."

Carol sipped her tea. "Would you like to spend more time with the children?"

"No, not really. I mean I love them. I love them dearly and I don't want to sound selfish, but I don't know how to be me anymore. I need to be me," Liz said.

Carol smiled. She hadn't actually feared Liz was hinting at wanting to take over the children's care, but the fact that she didn't came as a relief. Her job as nanny to the children was her livelihood, her home, her life. Period. What on earth would I do without this family? Her daughters wouldn't want her. They would probably consider her a burden. She would have nothing to offer them. "I think I know how you feel or at least how I would feel."

"I honestly hoped when Randy and Cindy opened the new vet hospital that I maybe could volunteer as their receptionist. Frankly, if I don't do something, Senior's going to drive me crazy. He's constantly underfoot. Do you know just this morning he tried to tell me how to make the bed."

Carol laughed.

"I'm serious! He said I tucked the sheets too tight. I said why didn't you ever say anything before and he said he'd just now noticed. I tell you, Carol, he's driving me crazy. I think he's feeling much the same way I am. We need something to do."

The two women drank their tea, quiet for a moment. Too quiet. "I'd better go check on them," Carol said, and was back a few minutes later. "A new episode of *Barney*. Go figure. They're mesmerized."

Liz finished her tea, bid Carol good-bye and walked out to visit with Glenda as she worked in the garden. "Any word?" Glenda asked.

"No." Liz turned over a bucket and sat down. "Senior's not one to call. We'll have to wait till they get home." She watched how Glenda pulled the weeds straight up and out. If asked, she'd tell her that technique only works for young weeds. The more-established ones need to be gripped and tugged sideways. She'd have less break-off that way. And oh, the way she was tilling the dirt so close to the plants. Liz's eyes widened. Do you know you're killing important microbes, she desperately wanted to say. Don't till so close to the plant, please. Paleeze....

Glenda looked up at her. Was there something on the woman's mind? "You okay, Liz?"

"Yes. I'm just about as useless as tits on a boar hog though."

Glenda laughed.

"Pig farmer humor," Liz said, laughing with her. "But honestly, I'm going stir crazy. I really am. I'm actually thinking about applying for a job somewhere. Senior would have a fit though."

Glenda smiled. "Senior is a little old-fashioned, isn't he? Though seriously, if George told me to stop working and just do nothing, I just might like it for a little while at least."

"For a little while is the definitive part. Forever? No."

Both women smiled and fell silent, one weeding, one observing. "So what would you be doing if you were back home on the farm?" Glenda asked.

"Oh, probably be out weeding the garden. Our growing season back home is a little later than here, but I always had weeding to do."

"Sounds like you really miss it?"

"I do," Liz said, absentmindedly reaching down and plucking a weed.

Glenda reached for it, looked at the snarly root, intact, and tossed it into the bucket.

"It's a grip-and-pull-toward-you motion," Liz said.

Glenda handed her the till handle, watched how Liz made a large circle around each single plant and kept a wide berth of the rows of plants. "Do you want some gloves? I have an extra pair in the bucket over there."

"No, I like the feel of the earth. Thank you. Baking soda cleans them right up." The women worked together, both using their shirt sleeves to wipe their brow and stood back to admire their handiwork. "Thank you," Liz said. "I actually feel like I need a nap. Isn't that great? Wonder what I can do tomorrow?"

Glenda smiled, and then she and Liz turned at the sound of Senior's truck pulling in off the road. Both wiped their hands in preparation for the news. "Well?" Liz asked, when they parked and he and Matthew got out.

Matthew shrugged. "The doctor was not happy."

"To say the least," Senior said.

"But, he said as long as I 'behave' myself I can stay here at the farm."

"So, that's good news. Right?" Glenda asked.

Matthew shrugged again. "He thinks it might be months for my eyesight to heal."

"The doctor says there is no way of knowing how long," Senior said.

Matthew stood a moment staring off. "He also said it could be permanent."

"There's no way of knowing that either," Senior said.

"So," Matthew said. "It's a waiting game."

~ * ~

Randy pulled up next to the Miller barn and Hillary got out and walked around the front of the truck without so much as a wave or a good-bye. Randy shook his head, got out, and went looking for Dawn. She was in the feed room, quietly mixing feed for this evening. The two horses in today were in the "drawing" phase of racing. No hay. The last thing anyone would want was for them to hear her preparing dinner.

"Your indentured servant is back," Randy said, about half a second before Hillary appeared at his side.

"Oh, there you are," the girl said to Dawn. "What are you doing?"

"Starting the oats for dinner," Dawn said. "Shhhh...."

Ben was old school about drawing a horse before a race and also about cooking oats every day. "Cooked oats are easier for the horse to digest," he insisted. When the oats were ready, he would add other grains he felt the individual horses needed.

Hillary pushed past Randy, and not so politely. "What's this?" she asked, looking into the flaxseed bin.

Dawn motioned for her to lower her voice.

"Why?" the girl whispered. "Can't we just shut the door?"

"No, they'll know," Dawn said quietly.

"I'm leaving," Randy said. "By the way, just so you know, Miss Personality is welcome back at Shifting Gears."

"Oh?" Dawn asked.

"Apparently," Randy said softly, "she has quite a gift with horses."

The girl looked at him.

"I'll try to get up for the races. I can't promise anything though." He gave Dawn a kiss, crossed his fingers in a hex sign when stepping past the girl, and walked to his truck, smiling. He'd heard about people with a gift for sensing what animals feel. He didn't doubt there was at least something to it. He wondered if the "sensitive" ones were all this miserable. He gave that second thought. How would you not be, considering....

Dawn explained all the different grains to the girl, explained why this horse got more barley than the others, why another horse didn't get as much flax seed. Why all of them got just a little bran. Why the added supplement of iron and vitamins. "When the cooked oats are done at afternoon feed time, we scoop the hot oats into the feed tubs, mix it up and the horses love it." She nudged Hillary out of the feed room when she was done mixing the feed and tiptoed out behind her.

"So what's this about a gift?" Dawn asked, walking down the shedrow to Alley Beau's stall to groom her and do her legs. The girl shrugged. Evidently she didn't want to talk about it. Dawn grabbed Alley's bandages and wraps and grooming bucket and ducked under the mare's stall webbing. The girl stood in front of the stall, not talking, just standing there.

Dawn glanced at her watch. It wasn't even nine-thirty yet. The girl stepped closer to the inside wall when a horse being hot-walked was led by. Dawn studied the young girl's expression. It was hard telling what she was thinking.

"Dawn!' Tom called.

"I'm with Alley," she said.

He walked down the shedrow with Red following along behind him. He looked at Hillary. "You still here?"

"Her mom's picking her up in about a half hour," Dawn said.

He glanced at the girl and then looked at her again. "What?" She was studying Red for some reason.

"He's tired," she said.

"I know that. We both are. We ponied six this morning. He'll get a rest."

The girl stroked Red's neck, traced the huge scar from when he was a foal. Tom watched her. Dawn watched her. Red watched her. "He loves you, you know."

Tom looked at Dawn.

"Randy says she has a gift," Dawn said.

"What kind of gift?"

"I think you're seeing it," Dawn said.

"So you know what they think?" Tom asked.

The girl shrugged. "Sometimes."

"Would you know if they were going to run good? If they're going to win?"

Hillary shook her head in disgust. "I sense what they are feeling at the moment. Duh! Horses don't know their future. They live in the now."

"Oh," Tom said.

The girl looked at him. "Idiot!"

Tom laughed. "Bitch!"

Hillary couldn't help herself and laughed as well. Tom handed her Red's reins. "Eighth stall, untack him and don't baby him. We have two horses in today and he'd better be tied on."

Dawn looked at him as the girl led Red down the shedrow.

"What? You gonna try and tell me how to talk to women?"

Dawn smiled. "I wouldn't think of it."

"Good. So where's Ben?"

"He walked over to see the old-timers. He's really getting nervous about his surgery. He says he doesn't like the odds."

Tom glanced in Red's stall as he passed and kept right on walking. He smiled. The girl didn't see him. Apparently her sensory perception applied only to animals. She'd taken Red's saddle off and was removing his bridle ever so gently and Red had smitten written all over his face.

Chapter Thirteen

Ben checked in with Wendy on his way to see the old-timers. She was on the phone and motioned she was up to her eyeballs in work. He waved and boarded the elevator. He felt it was good for her to be busy. It would help her keep her mind off Matthew. As always, the old-timers and Vicky were happy to see him. Training hours were just about over so the track was practically empty. There were just a few horses galloping. Ben sat down between Clint and Jeannie and looked around at the motley crew. Truth be known, he thought, I'm older than several of you. I lose my eyesight, then what? Jack was practically blind and Frank had thick glasses like Coke-bottle bottoms.

"What's the matter with you, Ben?" Jeannie asked.

"Oh, nothing."

"Good. There's nothing the matter with me either. Not unless you have about an hour or two to listen."

Ben laughed.

Mim watched the last horse gallop and yawned. "This is exhausting business."

Everyone laughed.

"Well, what's the update?" Vicky asked, joining them. It was snack time. She passed around a plate of cheese and crackers.

"Everything's moving along," Ben said, helping himself to some.

"We're still looking at next week?"

"Yep."

They all sat gazing out at the racetrack. The old-timers liked watching the water truck and tractors groom the track surface. "It's like the Indy 500 sometimes," Steven said, pointing to the two graders. "My money's on the truck on the inside."

Everyone chuckled.

"Pastor Mitchell says he'll still come see us," Jack said. "Course not every day and probably in the evening."

Ben nodded. The old-timers enjoyed Pastor Mitchell's visits. It was one of the highlights of their day even when he came up during race times. Pastor Mitchell liked watching the races too. "Now you know we're going to have the races televised for you. I know it won't be the same, but it'll be in real time."

"Real time?" Several of them asked.

"Yes, that's what Wendy said." Ben smiled. "I think it means it won't be as fast as live, but pretty darn close."

"Good. If a horse breaks down, then don't play it," Jeannie said.

"Okay, I'll see if we can do that."

The two grading tractors were bumper to bumper, nose to nose. "See, I told you the one on the inside would win," Steven said. It rumbled under the wire a good half length in front of the other one.

"And the crowd go crazy!" Miguel said, waving his hands.

They all laughed and then fell quiet. "No doubt about it, we're going to miss this every day, Ben," Frank said. "But we're going to like being out at your farm too."

"Thank you," Ben said. "It's going to be good having you there."

~ * ~

Wendy hung up one line and switched to another. "Nottingham Downs, Assistant Manager Wendy Girard speaking."

"Ms. Girard, this is Dan Gotbert from Social and Family Services."

"Yes?" The man's name didn't sound familiar.

"We have received a complaint from the family of a Mim Freemont alleging that she is living in a non-residential zoned facility, more precisely, your racetrack."

Wendy hesitated. "Excuse me."

"I believe you heard me and I see by my notes that there have been other complaints."

"Could you hold on just a second, please? I have another phone call I have to take or perhaps you would like me to call you back."

"No, that's okay. I'll hold. I see here according to the file no one returns phone calls from Nottingham Downs."

Wendy put the man on hold and phoned Dawn. "They're back; Social and Family Services. Apparently Mim's daughter is complaining. Can you get ahold of your Uncle Matt and see if he can buy us some more time?"

"I'll give him a call and let you know."

Wendy got back on the line with the man. "I'm sorry, Mr. Goth...?"

"Gotbert."

"Yes, Mr. Gotbert, I'm sorry. Now where were we?"

"We were at the point where I was about to inform you that I will be coming to Nottingham Downs tomorrow to investigate this allegation."

"Tomorrow? During racing? That would be rather difficult."

"Difficult how?"

"Well, we prefer to address non-horseracing business on our dark days, which are Mondays and Tuesdays. Let me look at my appointment schedule."

"An appointment won't be necessary. My plan is to just stop by." Click

When Tom met up with Ben in the hall and the two entered the office together, Wendy gave them the news.

"Did you call Dawn?" Tom asked.

"Yes. Any word about Matthew? I miss his not having a cellphone."

"I don't," Tom said, referring to the reason for Matthew's car accident. "No, I haven't heard anything."

Ben sat down at his desk. "You know, I'm amazed how much Social Services cares now, and yet they were ready to put these people out on the street."

"It's the family members. They're so afraid someone is out to take their money?"

Tom's phone rang. It was from Ben's home phone. He showed it to Wendy and answered. "Hello."

"Hey, Tom, it's Matthew."

"How are you doing? How did it go today?"

Wendy and Ben looked on.

"Okay. Do you want the good news or the bad news?"

"Both."

Wendy held out her hands. "How is he?"

Tom covered the receiver. "He sounds fine, just a minute."

"Dr. Hanover says I can stay at the farm, but it might be for a while. My sight may or may not clear up."

"He said that?"

"Yes. Senior was there too. He asked all kinds of questions."

"So what are you supposed to be doing?"

"Nothing. Nothing that requires any amount of eye-hand coordination that is. He said it might initiate an anxiety effect."

"What's that mean?"

"I don't know. Ask Senior."

"All right. Go get some rest or something."

"I'm going to take a nap."

"Okay. I'll tell your mom." Tom hung up and gave Wendy a slightly more upbeat version of the news. "The doctor says he can stay at the farm to recuperate and to not overdo till his eyes clear up."

"That's it?"

"Well, he says to talk to Senior, that he asked lots of questions."

Ben nodded. "I think resting on the farm for a while will be good for the boy." He couldn't help but think about his own eyesight. He glanced around at the items on his desk. They were all slightly blurry even with his glasses on.

Wendy's cellphone rang. "It's Dawn," she said. "Hello."

"Okay, Uncle Matt's going to see what he can do, but he says they're already on to him, so he might only be able to buy us another day or so. He says he can only step on so many toes when it comes to things like this."

Wendy looked at Ben. "Can they work around the clock on T-Bone's Place?"

"Amish? I don't think so. They won't be there at all tomorrow."

Wendy sighed. "Thanks, Dawn. Keep me posted." She relayed the message. "Uncle Matt might only be able to buy us a day or two."

"I can't believe the Family Services guy would come out here on a Sunday," Tom said.

"Me neither. I think he's gunning for us. He sounded like he's taking this personally. Keep in mind, Uncle Matt has stalled this three times already. The guy's suspicious."

"Well, I'm headed back over to the barn. You coming, old man?"

"Yeah," Ben said, rising from his chair. "I might need you to show me the way."

Tom laughed and looked at Wendy. "See you later."

~ * ~

Dawn walked with Hillary to the stable gate, much to the girl's chagrin. "I'm not a child, you know."

"I know, but I want to talk to your mom."

"I wouldn't mention my gift. It freaks her out. Ever since I told her our cat Cicely was going to die that day, she doesn't want to hear it."

"All right." Dawn smiled at Hillary's mother sitting there waiting in her car. "By the way, why aren't you driving yourself? I thought you had a car."

"I do. I'm grounded."

Dawn chuckled. "That's what's you get for being bad."

"Very funny." The girl walked around her mother's car and got in the passenger's seat.

"Did she give you any trouble?"

"Actually no, she was a big help. I wanted to mention something to you though. There's a Thoroughbred rescue place about fifteen minutes from here called Shifting Gears. They could use some free help and Hillary would not only be getting her shadow hours in, she'd be doing some community service."

The woman looked hesitant. "I'll give it some thought."

"She could probably make her own hours. It's a good place."

"I'll think about it."

Dawn nodded and stepped back. When the woman turned her car around, Hillary looked at her. She just looked at her and then at the last minute, just before they pulled out onto the highway, the girl gave her a thumbs up.

Dawn smiled and walked back to the barn. With a little luck, she'd have some time to start the newspaper article that was overdue. Ben looked up from his desk. "Have you always been that tall?"

"Yes." Dawn laughed. "You're going to be fine, Ben. Stop worrying."

"I'm not worrying," he said. "Not really. Well, I guess I am. I just want to make sure I remember things the way they are."

Dawn pretended to be shrinking.

"Very funny."

Dawn put her arm around his shoulder, recalling the morning Ben had a stroke in this very tack room and how she feared he would die. "You're going to be fine, Ben."

"And if I'm not, what kind of life am I going to have?"

"A good life," Dawn said. "Just like now."

He glanced up at her. "Well, I can't deny that I'm thinking today and tomorrow might be my last days doing what I love here. I feel so sorry for those old-timers and I'm this close to being one of 'em."

Chapter Fourteen

With Batgirl in the second race today and B-Bo the seventh, Dawn had about a half an hour before she had to put the first one in the ice tub. "I'm going up to the kitchen? You want anything?" she called to Tom. "Where are you?"

"Taking a piss," he called back from one of the stalls. "Can't a man have a little privacy?"

Dawn laughed.

"Bring me a Cheese Mac."

Dawn was headed for a Cheese Mac too. It was a favorite of just about everyone on the backside. Homemade macaroni and cheese, baked to perfection, topped with bacon.

"Single or double?"

"Double."

"Ginger ale?"

"Yep."

Tom went for ice while she was gone and came back with two bucket loads. Originally he was supposed to pony a horse for another trainer in between their horses' races and hadn't planned to be at the barn when it came time to ice B-Bo. Dawn said she'd be fine by herself or she could get Junior to help her. Tom had changed his mind since, unnerved with Hillary saying Red was tired, and got another pony boy for the other trainer's horse. When Dawn returned, the two of them put Batgirl in the ice tub and settled down in front of her stall on folding chairs to eat their lunch.

"That's really freaky about that girl sensing things with horses," Tom said, with his mouth full.

"I know. It sure explains why she's so unhappy."

"So what, she's going to volunteer out at Shifting Gears?"

"I hope so."

"God forbid one of those horses die when she's there."

"I know. I thought about that too."

"They almost lost that Foregone horse twice now."

Dawn nodded. "Randy said she knew it had a Foregone bloodline."

"Really?"

"Apparently the horse told her somehow."

Tom stared. "Well, I'd be pretty proud of that too if I was him, but that's some scary shit, her being able to do that."

Dawn agreed.

"So what's Linda going to do about Erie? Did she say?"

"No. I wish she'd stay here, but she does like it up there and if they're going to open again…."

"She's really good at the Secretary's office."

"That's what Ben said. Wendy too."

Tom sighed. Wendy…. "There's a possibility Matthew's sight might not return totally."

"Oh no, you're kidding," Dawn said, sadly. "Are you sure?"

Tom nodded, gathered up their containers and tossed them into the trash. "Senior said the doctor gave it to Matthew straight."

"Did his leaving rehab last night make it worse?"

"No, apparently not. The doctor didn't even examine him today. The damage stems from the accident. How he heals will be how he heals I guess."

~ * ~

Dusty had a mid-day routine where he would walk up and down every shedrow without exception. Sometimes he would change his course; sometimes he would even go back through a few barns. He didn't want anyone expecting him at a certain time and would always stop and talk to trainers and grooms along the way. Often he'd run into Pastor Mitchell, the man making his rounds, and the two would stop and chat for a while. Dusty had been at Nottingham Downs for over forty years. He'd seen it all. He'd done it all. Pastor Mitchell too.

"Did you hear about Lucy Guciano?"

Pastor Mitchell nodded. "I just sat both of them down and talked to them this morning. It seems neither of them told their parents and both sides heard through other sources."

"I'll bet that went over well."

"No," Pastor Mitchell said. "It didn't."

Dusty patted the man on the back and walked on. He'd made it a point to check on Jackson's horse ever since it was claimed. Hannity was a little annoyed each time Dusty stopped, but he'd been civil, until today.

"I don't think you have a right to come messin' in my business every day," he told Dusty. "What do you want from me anyway?"

"I don't want anything. I'm just checking to make sure everything's okay. It's my job."

"Yeah well, your job isn't to come nosin' in my barn. I'm a private contractor. Just like a landlord, you don't come into my house."

Dusty smiled. "You don't pay any rent, Hannity. You don't own this barn. You don't own these stalls."

"You're all a bunch of socialists."

Dusty had heard that before. "Because we take from the rich and give to the poor?"

"No, that's not what I mean and you know it!"

"I'm just here to find out how the horse is doing. That's all." Dusty walked on down the shedrow and stopped in front of the stall of the horse in question. It was done up all fours and had both its knees wrapped in spider bandages. Dusty took out a notepad and made a notation.

"What are doing? What'd you write down?"

Dusty just looked at him.

"I don't want you in my barn anymore!" Hannity said.

"Really? That's a shame. I'll see you tomorrow," Dusty replied.

Next stop was Rupert's Tack Shop. Rupert looked up from the counter. "Hey, Dusty."

"How's things going?"

"All right I guess. How about you?"

"Everything's okay. I'm just making my rounds."

"Well, if you run into that no-good son of mine, tell him I don't want anything to do with him anymore. Tell him to come get his stuff out of the house."

"I think I'll leave that up to you," Dusty said. "Did you get any more of those molasses treats in?"

"Some came in today. How many you want?"

"Two bags," Dusty said, and paid the man.

The first race was just about to go off. He walked up to the Ginny stand; a bag of treats tucked into both shirt pockets and watched the horses load. The race was six furlongs, coming out the chute.

"And they're off!" He could hear Bud Gipson calling the race from both the grandstand and from the speaker in the Ginny stand. Stereo. Most horsemen when they quit training missed it. Not Dusty. He liked the fact that he was still at the racetrack every day and at the farm every night, but didn't miss the business of dealing with the horse owners. He thought of the little filly at home, Bonnie Bee. He had no idea what he was going to do with her. But in the meantime, he was going to enjoy just having her around.

"Coming down the stretch…."

"Ah, Dusty," said Amadou. "How you do?"

Dusty smiled. "I'm doing good, Amadou. How about you?"

"All well," the man said.

"Taking over the lead...."

"The chestnut on the inside," Amadou said, pointing. "He win, you see."

They both watched intently. From this vantage point the horses were running toward them, hard to tell. "And down on the rail...."

"Ah!" Amadou let out a belly laugh. "I told you, eh?"

Dusty nodded. "Yep, he win."

The horses galloped out in front of them, the jocks talking and yelling to one another, the winning jock singing a song.

"This is a great life, Amadou," Dusty said. "A great life."

"Yep! Don't I know it!"

~ * ~

Dawn led Batgirl out to Tom and Red and stepped aside out of the way. "Bring her back safe," she said.

Tom nodded. He had the mare's halter and bridle draped around the saddle horn to the outside and Batgirl checked up nice and close. She liked Red, he liked her. He had a calming effect on her. Tom patted the mare on the neck. Dawn watched until they made the turn up by the track, then grabbed the muck basket and went to clean the mare's stall. The timing of these two races was almost perfect. It didn't always happen this way. Ben said he'd walk over to the barn after the race. That way Dawn could help Tom give the mare a bath, hopefully in the spit barn, and then either Tom or Dawn could come put B-Bo in ice.

Dawn bed Batgirl's stall nice and deep. Ben was one of the few trainers on the track that still used straw. "You can't teach an old dog new tricks," he insisted. Dawn fluffed it all around and then patted it down, filled the

~ 159 ~

mare's haynet, rinsed out her water bucket and filled it, then topped off all the other horses' water buckets, but B-Bo's. He stood in the back of his stall, knowing. He looked like a mountain of strength, all shiny and slick.

Dawn glanced at her watch, post time. She walked down to the end of the barn, hoping for a good breeze so she could hear the race being called. They'd talked about piping the announcer into the barn area, but all the old trainers, Ben included, voted it down.

"It'll rattle the horses," Mim had insisted. Practically everyone agreed.

"And they're off!"

Dawn heard that loud and clear but that's all she heard. The wind changed directions and she couldn't make out another word. Every once in a while, if there were no horses or vehicles in the way, one could look down the road to the track and see the horses pulling up after a race. She saw one, looked like a bay, then another, and then Batgirl. She recognized their green and white jockey colors.

"Third?" she said. It didn't have to be. It could be that the other two horses just galloped out stronger. She waited for them to come back. Batgirl was one of the first to canter back. A nice canter is good, a trot or a walk, not so good.

Dawn walked back down the shedrow, hung up the hose, and spent the next few minutes raking the footing under the walking machine. With rake in hand, she walked back out to the road, shielded her eyes from the sun, and waited. The spit barn was six barns up. When the horses from the race started down through the barn area, she held her breath. The first horse turned into the spit barn, second one, into the spit barn, and then here came Tom with Batgirl. "Shoot."

"Got beat a neck for all of it," Tom said, when they got closer. "Damn. She run her heart out too."

Dawn took Batgirl from him. He dismounted Red and loosened his girth, ground tied him and Dawn led the mare into the shedrow. Tom took off her bridle, Dawn put her halter on. They gave the mare a drink and then walked her over to the wash rack. Ben came down the shedrow and stood watching them.

His cellphone rang. It was Randy. "How'd she run?"

"She run third, just got beat. She run her race. She run good."

"I'll try and get back for B-Bo's. I'm two counties away."

As soon as the mare was bathed and scraped off, they led her back to the barn, gave her another drink of water and put a cooler on her. Dawn walked her a few laps around the shedrow as Tom and Ben put B-Bo in the ice tub. Another couple of laps around the shedrow, another drink of water, and Tom took the mare from Dawn and hung her on the walking machine.

"It's a shame to run that hard and come up short," Tom said.

Ben nodded and pulled up a folding chair in front of B-Bo's stall and got comfortable. "I might as well enjoy this while I can."

"Oh, Jesus," Tom sputtered, shaking his head.

Ben looked at him over his glasses. "Are you laughing or crying? I can't tell."

"Somewhere in between," Tom said, and they all three laughed.

~ * ~

Wendy paced back and forth in front of the window overlooking the racetrack deeply involved in a three-way phone conversation with George and Glenda. "Well, we have to do something," Wendy said. "Can you see if they'll work a little later today?"

"They won't work after sundown," George said. "Rotty, quit!"

"What's he doing?" Wendy asked.

"Chewing on Dawber's ear. Quit!"

Wendy laughed. Of all the dogs, Rotty was basically hers, a big Standard Poodle with too much energy and a big heart. "I don't know what we're going to do, but I have a feeling we're only going to have until Monday. We've locked the doors before which is why I think this guy wants to come on a race day."

"I'll go talk to the Bishop," Glenda said.

"The Bishop?" Wendy asked.

"He seems to be the foreman on the job. I'll call you back."

"Wait," George said. "Did you make lunch yet? Senior just said Liz made Sloppy Joes."

"Ooh," Wendy said. "A Sloppy Joe sounds so good, especially Liz's." All three of them hung up.

Wendy looked down at the horses in the post parade for the third race. She wished she had a camera handy, and time. There was a pretty gray horse looking at the Forget Me Nots and the contrast of color and the horse's expression was breathtaking. She allowed herself a brief moment to savor the view and then headed out to the Secretary's office. Joe was sitting behind the counter reading the racing form.

"Where's Linda?" Wendy asked.

"I don't know," he said. "It's not my turn to watch her."

"Oh? Then whose turn is it?" she asked, zinging him right back.

Joe blushed, reprimanded. "Actually I think she's in talking to the Stewards for whatever the reason."

Wendy thanked him and walked down the hall. She rarely crossed the threshold of the Stewards office. She tapped on the open door. Linda turned and smiled.

"Excuse me," she said. "Linda, when you get a minute can I see you? I need your help."

"Sure, I'll be right there."

Wendy resumed pacing in front of her office window. "Here's the story. I'm going to need to be off tomorrow and we also have two horses in from Meg's Meadows in tomorrow."

"Love that name," Linda said. "I love just saying it. Meg's Meadows."

"Close the door," Wendy said. "Not all the way." She waited. "As I said, I'm going to need to be off tomorrow."

"Is Matthew okay? Did he take a turn for the…?"

"No, I guess he's okay. I haven't talked to him since I got here today. His appointment went okay, but it sounds like his eyesight challenges might be more than, well, I guess not more than what they said initially just a reinforcement of the fact. It might take a while and then it might not be a complete recovery. Only time will tell." She paused, her voice cracking, and just then her cellphone rang. She looked at caller ID. "It's Glenda, hold on."

"No go on getting the Amish crew to work later or tomorrow. The Bishop said they can be back at seven Monday morning instead of eight and will bring some extra help."

"I think that's going to be too late. Ask the Bishop if he could leave a list of things to do and in what order? I'll hold on."

"Are you going to try and hire someone else to do it?"

"No, I'm thinking maybe we'll do it, you and me and George. Most of the big stuff's done already."

"I'll help," Linda said. "I'm good with a hammer."

"Yes, but I need you here. That's what I was about to ask you. Can you cover here tomorrow in the event that guy from Family Services does show up?"

Linda appeared reluctant.

"It's either that or pony for Tom."

"No," Linda said flat out. "I'm not going back down that road again. No way."

"All right then, so you'll cover for me?"

"Wendy?" Glenda said, back on the line. "The Bishop said okay, he'll make a list. I called Senior too. He said no problem. Wait. What? George says Senior said to tell you we'll start on it tonight."

"Good, good," Wendy said. "I'll see you later." She hung up and looked at Linda. "It's Joe's day off tomorrow, no entries, but he's been coming in anyway. I'm going to make sure he stays home tomorrow and it's best if I'm not here. Richard won't be back for another week or so. You'll be on your own totally."

"So what is it that I'm supposed to be doing?" Linda asked.

"Well, you'll handle the scratches, and then watch the Secretary's office for anyone you don't know."

"I don't know a lot of them. There's a lot of new people here."

Wendy nodded and sighed.

"What's this guy want anyway?"

Wendy glanced at the door and lowered her voice. "I think someone's trying to close us down. I have no idea who or why, but why else all this concern about the old-timers? Why all those articles in the *Morning Banter*?"

"Do you think there's a connection?"

"I don't know, could be. Or maybe it's just a coincidence. So will you do it?"

"Sure. If I screw up, you can always send me back to Erie."

Wendy smiled. "I wish you'd stay."

Linda shrugged and looked away. "Maybe someday."

Wendy hugged her and the two walked back out to the Secretary's office. "Joe, I want to make sure you take tomorrow off," Wendy said.

"Oh?" Joe looked at her suspiciously. "Why?"

"Well, it's your day off for one and you've been really helpful coming in on Sundays, but it's not necessary. Linda's going to be here. I'll be here. Take your day off."

Joe looked from one to the other; Linda standing there looking nonchalant. "I think I'll come in anyway, if you don't mind."

"Well, I do mind, Joe. I think you need the day off. Got it?"

He stepped back.

"Besides, Linda's probably going back to Erie on Monday and it might be a long time before you'll have a chance at another one."

Joe's expression changed entirely. "All right."

"Good. Now if you'll excuse me, I'm going to go track my husband down." As she walked along through the path between the racetrack and parking lot, she couldn't help but think of Matthew. Gone was the day when she could put a band-aid on a cut or scrape and make all the boo-boos go away. Gone were the days when she could jump up in the middle of the night at the first sound of him or Gordon being sick, coughing, running to the bathroom to throw up. "Mom!!"

When she looked up and saw Pastor Mitchell walking toward her and their eyes met she shook her head and instantly burst into tears. "Now, now," he said, putting his arms around her. "Tom tells me your son is going to be fine. It's just going to take a little time and lots of prayer."

"I know, I know," Wendy said, stepping back and wiping her eyes. "Thank you. I know I have to stop crying sooner or later, but...."

Pastor Mitchell looked at her.

"I've never been this emotional in my life. Even when my first husband died, I just did what I had to do, and...."

"Well, if you don't mind me asking, Wendy, how old are you?"

"How old am I? Forty-nine. Why?"

"Just wondering. You're just about my wife's age and things affect her a little differently now."

Menopause. He's suggesting I'm going through menopause. No, I'm not, Wendy thought, I'm too young.

"I'll keep you all in my thoughts and prayers," Pastor Mitchell said. "Now if you'll excuse me, I'm on my way over to watch a few races with the old-timers."

Wendy smiled. Tom was the one that had started calling them the old-timers. It was the night he rescued them in the horse van from the nursing home just before it closed. "Old-timers" was how just about everyone referred to them now, and with affection. "I'll see you later," Wendy said. "Thank you."

As she started down the shedrow, Dawn, Tom, and Ben all turned. "Oh good," she said, "You're all together." Ben and Dawn were sitting on chairs outside B-Bo's stall. Tom was standing at their side.

"Have you been crying?" Tom asked. "What's the matter?"

"Nothing. It's nothing. Well, actually nothing new. I just ran into Pastor Mitchell. I don't know," she said, tears springing to her eyes again. "Oh my God, what *is* wrong with me?"

Ben looked at her. Dawn looked at her. Tom looked at her. B-Bo looked at her.

"Okay, I'm fine now. I'm fine." She wiped her eyes. "Listen, here's the plan. We need to get the old-timers out of here by Monday."

"By Monday?" Ben said. "They're not going to be done with T-Bone's Place by then. We were looking at Wednesday maybe at the earliest."

"I know. It sure is a shame the hotel closed down." Years ago, the hotel across the street was where former owner and management of Nottingham Downs used to put up their high-rolling clients and visiting stake-horse owners. They had two suites which would probably work out perfect right about now, at least for a few days. But that was then and this was now, and even if it was still open, the racetrack budget wouldn't allow it, and then there was the issue of wheelchair access, high seats on the toilets, heavy duty bars on the walls in the halls.

"Wendy?" Dawn touched her arm.

"Oh, sorry, I was just thinking. Anyway, I think we need to proceed as if it's a done deal and just do it. Shoot for Monday around noon. I'll get everything in play as far as transporting them, moving their things, the beds."

"Back to the house," Ben said. "How do you plan to…?"

"I just talked to Glenda and George. They checked with the Bishop on the Amish crew."

"The Bishop?" Dawn nudged B-Bo to keep him from chewing on her shirt sleeve.

"Yes, the older Amish-man. He's their Bishop."

"Wow," Tom said. "I've never known a Bishop before."

"He's going to leave a list of things to be done and in what order. What we don't get done tonight and tomorrow, they'll come early Monday to finish."

"We?" Tom said.

"Senior and George and me and Glenda and Liz. We're going to start on it this evening. I'm going to call Gordon home. He can help too."

Ben recalled when Wendy renovated the attic area next to her and Tom's bedroom at the farmhouse. Aside from hanging the drywall, she'd done most of the work herself, turned it into a right nice cozy, what did she call it, "A room of her own, a room with a view."

Wendy looked at B-Bo. "What do you think, big guy? Think we can do it?"

The horse cocked his head, liking the sound of her voice, perhaps recalling it from the farm. "See," Wendy said. "He thinks we can do it."

Ben tipped his hat back and scratched his forehead. "I have to tell you, whether we get it done or not, the closer it gets to this actually happening, the more nervous I get. This is a huge responsibility. These people are old. Hell, I'm old."

"Oh, geez, not this again," Tom said.

Dusty walked down the shedrow and was brought up to date. Wendy headed back to the office, feeling good about the plan, feeling positive, hopeful.

A young man walked toward her from the grandstand. She didn't recognize him until he came closer.

"Afternoon, Mrs. Girard," he said.

"Good afternoon, Junior."

"I suppose you heard."

"No." She had no idea what he was talking about.

"Lucy's pregnant."

"Oh." Wendy surmised congratulations weren't in order judging from the sad expression on his face. "Is she all right?"

"I guess so. I'll see you later." He walked on with his hands in his pockets, shoulders slumped.

Chapter Fifteen

B-Bo sauntered into the paddock as if he was on an afternoon outing in the park. Because he was so quiet, Tom stayed out on the track on Red with the rest of the pony boys and girls. Dawn held B-Bo while Ben saddled him and then walked him around the paddock. Ben often joked if he could do it over again he would name the horse Big Mack Truck.

When the tote board flashed new odds, Ben squinted. He couldn't make them out this far away. Juan Garcia, B-Bo's regular jockey appeared at his side. "He look good, like always." Next time around, Dawn led the horse past them into the stall.

"You've only got one horse to beat," Ben was saying. Everyone involved knew who he was referring to, Switch and Slide, the big black colt of Sheefer's coming out of the five hole. The two horses were like Alydar and Affirmed, trading wins for years now. Every once in a while they both threw a bad race, but for the most part, the rest of the field were vying for third or fourth.

"Riders up!"

Dawn joined Ben a few minutes later at the fence. She looked over by the track kitchen just before post time and was pleasantly surprised to see Randy's truck pull up next to the Ginny stand.

B-Bo was 7-2. Switch and Slide was 2-1. The race was a mile and $1/16^{th}$.

"The horses are in the gate."

Dawn glanced up at the office window. Wendy had her binoculars poised for the start of the race.

"And they're off! Taking the early lead is Switch and Slide."

The horses passed in front of the grandstand for the first time in a tight pack, hooves thundering.

"It's Switch and Slide in the lead by half a length. Then it's Paper Money, Native Beau Born and on the rail moving up to third is Fortunate Factor. Two lengths back it's Happy To See You and Next Time Around."

"What did they run the first quarter in?" Ben asked.

Dawn looked. "23.4." She did a double take at how hard Ben was squinting to try to see. "The half in 46.3."

Ben nodded. "Good, good."

"On the outside it's Fortunate Factor and a length back it's Native Beau Born."

"What's he doing?" Ben asked.

"He's…." Dawn stretched to see over the tote board. "He's coming. He's making a move."

"Into the far turn it is Switch and Slide, Paper Money and making a move, Native Beau Born."

"Come on, B-Bo!" Dawn said. "Come on, B-Bo!" Then, "Oh no!"

"What?" Ben said, grabbing her arm.

"He got cut off! Damn! Wait, he's coming back!"

"Challenging the leader it's Native Beau Born. Switch and Slide and Native Beau Born battling for the lead. Switch and Slide, Native Beau Born, neck to neck, head to head, nose to nose. Switch and Slide and Native Beau Born. It's Switch and Slide at the wire!! Ladies and gentlemen hold onto your tickets. There is a photo finish."

"Did he get up?" Ben asked.

"I don't think so," Dawn said. At the moment she was more concerned with how little Ben could see. No wonder he'd been so worried.

"How's he pulling up?"

"Good. He's good. Tom's got him."

Switch and Slide was posted as the winner. B-Bo placed second. Paper Money finished third. Happy To See

You ran fourth. Dawn walked around the winner's circle to the track, took hold of B-Bo as Juan dismounted, and followed Tom as he led B-Bo over to the spit barn. Ben waited for Juan to weigh in and walked with him toward the jocks' room.

"He don't get stopped Ben, he win easy! He have his A-game today!"

Ben thanked him, patted him on the back, and walked on. He hoped the horse came back all right. Randy was hoping the same thing. He got out of his truck studying all four of B-Bo's legs as Tom and Red led him off the racetrack. "Shit," he said, under his breath. B-Bo had a big cut on the inside of his left hind leg, dripping blood pretty heavily.

He looked at Dawn. She'd be seeing it soon enough. He waited until the rest of the horses passed in front of him and then drove the back way to the Miller barn. Ben was just coming down the shedrow. Randy got out of the truck, gathered some supplies, and was ready when he got paged to the spit barn. "Dr. Iredell, please report to the test barn. Dr. Iredell, please report to the test barn."

Ben climbed into the passenger seat with a cooler-blanket for the horse. Randy handed him the supplies. "He's got a pretty good gash on the inside of his left hind."

Ben rode along in silence, got out, arms held tight around the blanket and supplies, and followed Randy into the spit barn.

"Aw, Jesus," Randy said.

"Does he need stitches?" Ben asked.

Tom held B-Bo with Dawn standing at his side.

"Maybe not. We'll see."

Randy signed a treatment form and they all followed Tom and B-Bo to the wash area. "Just cold water," Randy said out of habit. He dabbed at the wound. B-Bo kicked out at him and he dabbed again.

Ben leaned down to look and then stepped back. "Did I see bone?"

"Yeah," Randy said.

Ben walked over to a bench and sat down. No sense getting in the way, he said to himself. The track veterinarian came out and drew blood from B-Bo. Randy covered the gash to isolate it and taped it at the top and bottom to keep it from getting any wetter. The horse was given a drink and a quick bath. Tom scraped B-Bo off. Dawn retrieved the blanket from Ben and they all went inside the spit barn. The horse was given another drink of water and Dawn started walking him around the shedrow. As soon as Dawn put the horse in a stall so he could pee, he produced a urine sample. Though it wasn't needed, since the track vet had already gotten a blood sample, the attendant tagged it anyway.

Ben signed the test form and Dawn walked the horse back to their barn. Tom and Red walked alongside. Randy and Ben followed in the truck. "Do you want me to keep walking him?" Dawn asked.

Randy listened to B-Bo's breathing, gave him an injection, and stepped back. "A couple more times." Tom untacked Red and put him away. While Dawn was walking B-Bo down the backside of the barn Tom fed the other horses. Ben finished B-Bo's stall, bed it down, hung his haynet and filled his water bucket. Randy gathered his head-mount LED light and more supplies from his truck. No one said the obvious. An injury this severe could be the end of a horse's racing career.

B-Bo didn't seem to care much about the gash on his leg. Once he was put in his stall, he buckled his knees, took a couple of good rolls in the straw, stood up, circled, went back down and rolled again, stood and shook off, and then walked over to his haynet and started eating.

Randy went to work on the horse's leg. "I'm glad you were here," Dawn said, down on her knees next to him in the straw.

"So what do you think? Is it going to need stitches?"

"I don't think so, Ben. It's almost right on the shin. I'm going to butterfly it." He adjusted the light, applied adhesive staples, sprayed the area with an antibiotic ointment and motioned for Dawn to hand him a non-sticky pad and then the cotton wrap and ace bandage. Dawn did B-Bo's other three legs up. It was standard procedure to do a horse up all fours after a race.

Randy gathered up everything.

"Should we take him home?" Ben asked.

"No, I don't think so. Let's not even go there yet. This is B-Bo, remember. He's got the temperament of a horse that helps to heal himself."

Ben nodded. B-Bo had had his share of mishaps, but mostly on the farm, and they always healed quickly. "I'll see you guys at dinner," Randy said. Dawn walked with him to the truck, and there, gave him a brief update on the evening plan for T-Bone's Place.

"Ah, bet Dad's raring to go."

Dawn smiled and just looked at him.

"What?" he said.

"Helping you just now reminded me of when we first met."

Randy put his arms around her and pulled her close. "I'll see you at home. If I'm late, go ahead and eat dinner without me. I'll be home eventually."

~ * ~

Liz had made fried chicken, oven fries, and coleslaw for everyone and had it all set up at Ben's farmhouse. As a treat for being so exceptionally well-behaved, the children were allowed to sit together at their own table with no adults.

Glenda had run off copies of the list of projects to be completed at T-Bone's Place and they all sat hashing over who was going to do what and which tasks should be tackled first. It was a loud affair, arms in the air, passing food, talking strategy. Judging from the list, there was a lot of painting that needed done. Linda, Glenda, Dawn, Wendy, and Liz opted to do the painting.

"Do we want to each take a room or work all together as a unit?" Wendy asked. "By the way, Matthew, you're staying home."

"Excuse me?"

"You heard me. Ben, would you mind staying here with Matthew?"

"I don't need anybody to stay with me?"

"Oh yeah? Well, I do," his mother insisted.

"I say we each take a room," Linda said, trying to change the subject and avoid a confrontation. "Let's see a show of hands."

All the women raised their hands, Carol included, even though she'd be on child duty and wouldn't actually be there physically to help. "I just like having my say." When the dogs all started barking, Tom leaned back in his chair to look out the window. "It's our resident veterinarian."

After he fussed over the dogs, Randy came in and washed up at the sink. "I just stopped and checked on B-Bo. He's doing good." He tapped each child on the head in passing and sat down next to Dawn. "Ooh, fried chicken."

"All right, so we'll each pick a room to paint," Glenda said, studying the list. "Dawn, since you're the tallest, I think you should take the living room. It's got the highest ceiling. If we get done with the other rooms first, we'll come help you finish. You might want to start at the top. George, we need ladders or buckets to stand on."

"Pass the coleslaw, please," Senior said.

"Do we have more fries?" Dusty asked.

"Yep, there's a whole other tray." Liz retrieved it from the oven where she'd been keeping it warm and refilled the platter.

"Ketchup! Ketchup! Ketchup!" D.R. said.

Randy looked at him. "Do you want more Ketchup or are you just singing its praises?"

The children laughed. "Daddy. You're so silly. I want more Ketchup?"

"Please?"

"Please."

"Pease. Pease," Maeve and Maria echoed.

Tom passed the boy the bottle of Ketchup. "Here you go, little man."

D.R. poured Ketchup on his fries and then poured some on Maeve's and Maria's. Not too much and not too little, to everyone's amazement.

"Say thank you," Dawn said.

"Tank you," the girls sang.

"So, Son." Senior said. "Are you home for the night?"

"Well, I should be." Randy snuck a dramatic peek at his phone. "Yep, so far so good."

"Oh, I almost forgot," Wendy said. "You just reminded me. There's a recent grad coming to see you Monday morning. He's just out of vet school."

"A recent grad," Randy said. "No."

"No wait, listen," Wendy said. "He's thirty-seven years old. He was a Standardbred trainer for years and decided to become a vet."

Randy looked at her. "Seriously? Cool. Where's he from?"

"Arizona I think. Or was it Arkansas? Anyway, he's driving."

"Is he good-looking and single?" Linda asked.

They all chuckled. "I don't know," Wendy said. "I suppose I should have asked."

"I would think so," Linda said. "Who cares if he might not know the difference between a Thoroughbred and a Standardbred? A lot of people don't. If he's single, let's not even think of holding that against him. Okay?"

Everyone laughed.

"Eat up," Senior said. "We have lots of work to do. Time's a wasting!"

~ * ~

The Amish crew had all the boards cut to size for the front and back wheelchair ramps and railings. According to the notations, it basically would be just a matter of screwing all the boards and rails together and installing them. Simple, the women thought. However, the exact process of how to go about it was cause for a lengthy debate amongst the men.

"Do we put them both all together and just attach them or build it as we go along?"

The women had the painting underway. "You gotta see this," Glenda said. The five of them looked out the window and laughed. There the men all stood as if suspended in time, tool belts strapped on, sharpened pencils behind their ears, and at a complete standstill. They hadn't even begun yet.

Once the men determined their course of action, the handicap ramps went up quickly, front and back. They had to have just the right pitch; each board had to be level. Too steep an incline could prove dangerous; wheelchairs rolling too fast on the way down, too much of a struggle on the way up. Then, they installed a new railing on the back porch, extra bracing for added support in the event one of the old-timers leaned heavily on it for balance. They installed outdoor slip guards on the side steps. They measured and cut railings for the hallways, stained them and set them aside to dry. They cut all the ceiling molding and floor trim boards, stained those and set them aside to dry as well.

Ben and Matthew took a walk over to check on the progress. "The blind leading the blind," Ben said. The dogs followed them there and back. There were horses grazing all around in the pastures, the night sky clear, the stars bright, a crescent moon. No traffic, no street lights, and the further they walked, the sounds of distant hammering, buzz-sawing, and home-building for the old-timers.

Just after eleven, Senior announced it was time to call it a night. "We want to get an early start tomorrow." They'd have a smaller crew for most of the day. Tom, Dawn, Dusty, and Randy wouldn't be home until the evening. Gordon would be home around noon. "We have a lot more to do if we're going to even get close to making headway."

Chapter Sixteen

Tom arrived at the barn at the track first and looked in on B-Bo then started down the shedrow toward the tack room. "What?" He glanced ahead. There was a note taped to the door with Vetwrap.

DO NOT DISTURB!!!

He glanced at the latch, lock missing, and opened the door. "What the hell?"

Junior and Lucy were curled up together, asleep on the cot, covered in horse blankets. "Hey," Junior said, waking and sitting up.

"Do not disturb?" Tom asked.

"Well, I didn't want you just opening the door and scaring yourself to death."

"How'd you get in here?"

"I know where the key is," Junior said, yawning. "We didn't have anywhere else to go."

Tom was just about to lit into the boy in his customary manner, but Lucy stirred and woke up and looked so pathetic. Tom shook his head. This was her future? Junior?

"Here." Tom took a ten dollar bill out of his wallet. "Go get something at the kitchen to eat."

Lucy had just sat up, and at the mention of food covered her mouth. Junior reached for a bucket quick.

"Oh, geez," Tom said.

When Dawn arrived a few minutes later Tom shared the story with her. "Where are they now?" she asked.

"I don't know. I guess up at the kitchen. Junior was still standing outside the ladies room a few minutes ago. He's gone now."

"It was cold last night."

Tom just looked at her.

"What are they going to do?" Dawn asked, pouring herself a cup of coffee.

"I don't know. It's not my problem."

"Did you ever hear the story of the Convenient Christian?"

"Don't go there, Dawn. You're as bad as Ben. You two don't play fair at all."

She looked at the training chart. "Will he be back to gallop Whinny?"

"I guess so. Why wouldn't he be?'

Ben walked in behind them, heard the story, and shook his head. Though usually light by now, it was still dark out, rain in the forecast. They heard the sound of distant thunder and swung into action. They only had one horse to track today, the rest to walk. Wee Born was in the third race and Bo-T the ninth race feature. He was favored to win.

"I'll get Bo-T out now," Tom said, hoping to get him handwalked before the storm bore down on them. The colt was difficult enough to handwalk the morning of a race, let alone with fireworks lighting up in the sky. "We'll save B-Bo and Batgirl for last."

Randy arrived at the barn a few minutes later and checked for abnormal swelling in B-Bo's leg. There was a little edema above and below the bandage. "I'll be back this afternoon to change the dressing."

Dawn cleaned one stall after another as fast as she could. The wind was picking up, the dark cloud of rain just over the horizon. "Where's Junior?" Tom asked, muscling Bo-T around the corner of the shedrow the final lap.

"He's here. I just saw him," Ben called from down the shedrow. Dawn was cleaning stalls and he was bedding them.

"Have him tack up Whinny," Tom said.

"I got it," Junior said, following right behind him with Whinny's bridle and exercise saddle. "Red's all ready."

"What?"

"I said Red's ready!" Here came the rain, pelting the metal roof, sending horses bucking and kicking and bouncing around in their stalls and charging their stall webbings.

"You all right, old man?" Tom called out to Ben.

"I'm fine!" Thankfully he was bedding B-Bo's stall right then. Nothing rattled B-Bo.

"Dawn?"

"I'm fine!" she yelled, ducking out of Alley's stall just in time. "I'm fine!" The mare bucked and squealed.

Tom put Bo-T in his stall and shut the bottom Dutch door just in case the horse took to charging the webbing. It would prove no match against Bo-T's strength and determination. He walked down to the tack room, dodging other grooms, trainers, and hotwalkers trying to lead their sky-high horses, and put on his rain gear. "Let's go!" he said to Dawn and Junior as he mounted Red. Dawn gave the young man a leg-up and led Whinny out to where Tom and Red stood waiting.

"Old man, stay here, all right?" Tom yelled.

Ben waved, not about to argue for once. If it started lightning, they'd close the track anyway. There wasn't any yet, but the skies were getting darker and darker. He couldn't see as it was, let alone in a raging downpour.

~ * ~

Linda's major task of filling in at the Secretary's office that morning was heading off trainers wanting to scratch their horses because of the rain. "I wish you wouldn't. I understand, however…." The rain was supposed to let up by noon. Nottingham Downs' track surface was "state of the art" when it came to weather conditions and good drainage. She repeated that fact many times. "Don't tell me. I know that track better than anyone." A flash flood in the morning and it could be a hard fast track by race time. Fortunately, by eight o'clock and the end of scratch time, only five horses had dropped out of today's card.

All in all, she survived the process relatively unscathed. "Guess my old kick-ass reputation comes in handy for something," she told Wendy on the phone. "I just took the list upstairs to the printer. How are things going there?"

"Good. We're getting a lot done. Senior had to run to the hardware store. Liz says we may never see him again."

Linda stepped off the elevator leading to the Secretary's office and noticed a man she'd never seen before hovering around the bulletin board. She approached him. "Excuse me, do I know you?" There was something about this man that signaled alert to her. Plain suit, white shirt, black tie.

"No, I don't believe we've met. Are you Linda Dillon?"

"Yeah, that's me all right. What can I do for you?"

He hesitated, somewhat intimidated by the woman's demeanor. She had really mean eyes. "I'm looking for Wendy Girard. I was told you might know where I can find her."

"Oh yeah? Well that's not going to happen. She's not here today. I'm the best you're going to do. Do you have a pass?"

"A pass?"

"Yes. A pass that says you belong here."

"No," he said, "But...." He hesitated again, watching as she instantly whipped out her cellphone.

"Who are you calling?"

"911. We have a big stake race here today. Security is tight and you breached it."

"I'm no threat. I'm just here to see Wendy Girard and investigate a complaint about residency. I'm with Family Services."

"Oh, you're with the State," Linda said.

"Yes." He took out his wallet and produced his identification.

Linda took it from him, looked at the photo, looked at him and then looked at the photo again. "Not a very good likeness," she said. "Come with me." She walked him down the hall to the Steward's office, knowing no one was there yet, glanced inside and sighed. "They might have been able to help you. Too bad. I guess this isn't your lucky day."

"Well, if you could just show me upstairs."

"Seriously? Do you think I fell out of a fucking cherry tree? Do you think I want to lose my job? Come on, let's go. I know someone else who might be able to help you." She walked him down a ramp to the indoor paddock and over to the horsemen's entrance, ending at the guard shack.

"Do you recall seeing this man?" she asked the guard.

"Yes. He told me he had an appointment with Mrs. Girard. He said he was from the state and showed me his ID."

"This ID?"

"Yes."

"I see," Linda said. "Well he didn't have an appointment because Mrs. Girard is not here today. She's never here on a Sunday so that's bullshit." She turned to the man. "Serious bullshit. What kind of scam you running?"

"None. I told you, Mrs. Girard was expecting me."

"Okay," Linda said. "I'll give her this little identification card here and if it's not bogus, she'll get in touch with you. Have a nice day."

"But…" the man protested.

"Yes? Is there something else?"

"Uh, I need my ID back."

"Oh yeah?" Linda said. "Well, call the cops. Let's see, so far there's misuse of state ID, unlawful entry, trespassing. Keep it up and I'll add harassment. Go ahead. I'll wait."

~ * ~

Wee Born was not iced before a race and was best left totally ignored until it was time to lead her over to the paddock. As was routine, they waited until almost the last minute to groom her, do her legs up in Vetwrap and put her shadow roll and bridle on. She raced in a plain snaffle bit and tongue tie. Also routine in Wee Born's case, when Red was tacked Tom had to lead him around the back of the barn and out to the road that way, so Wee Born didn't see him pass by her stall. Otherwise she'd commence to pitching a fit and be washed out before they got her to the paddock. As long as they could keep her fooled and then moving, she remained relatively sane.

"The race is over. Let's do it," Tom said, mounting Red.

Dusty was going to meet them in the paddock to hold Wee Born for Ben to saddle. Dawn remained back at the barn. Whenever a horse or horses were in, someone had to be at the barn at all times prior to their races. It was a firm Ben Miller rule. Bo-T was in the ninth race. Dawn went about cleaning and bedding Wee Born's stall, filled her haynet, rinsed out and filled her water bucket, rolled her bandages.

When Randy stopped by on his way to a farm call, Dawn had just hit submit on the article she'd been working on that morning. "What's this one about?" he asked.

"Well, basically about *not* fixing races."

Randy nodded and just stood there for a moment.

"What's the matter?" Dawn asked.

"I just got a call from Cindy."

Dawn looked at him.

"She lost the baby."

"Oh no. Do your mom and dad know?"

"Yes. I just talked to them."

"Oh, Randy, I'm so sorry."

"I know. I'll see you later." He kissed her good-bye. "By the way, Veronica called. Seems Hillary was there this morning and coming back this afternoon. They think she's sweet. Can you believe that?"

Dawn smiled sadly. Wee Born's race seemed miles and miles away, another time, another place. She recalled the morning she miscarried. It was the pregnancy between D.R. and Maeve. She remembered going into the bathroom and calling out, "Randy, come quick. Something's happening!"

Off the distance she heard bits and pieces of the race being called, the sound of a muck bin being dropped back in place, heard the sound of a radio, a Sunday song, "If I could have a beer with Jesus…." The questions I would have for him. She thought of Hannah, her dear friend who'd wanted a child so desperately but that had been barren. She thought of blood flowing when it shouldn't have. She thought about Matthew, she thought about Ben, both fearing the loss of their eyesight. She thought about Mim.

"I don't have long," the old woman had told her. "I'm going to make every day count." Dawn wiped her eyes and walked out to wait for Tom and Wee Born.

~ * ~

Senior and George crossed another task off the list and headed upstairs. They'd saved the second floor for last. It had one bathroom and three small dormer-style bedrooms, one of which would be Vicky's. They'd consider it an accomplishment if they could at least get that one done. The Amish had gutted all the walls and ceilings and had put in new insulation, but the drywall needed to be hung, mudded, sanded, and painted. The two men stood debating the timeframe.

"There's no way."

"The paint we're using is non-toxic and fast drying. It shouldn't bother the old-timers and we can close the downstairs door."

Wendy and Glenda walked upstairs to offer their opinions. "Can't you just panel over the insulation?" Glenda asked.

"That's a good idea," Wendy said. "Why does it have to be drywalled anyway? You have all these wood posts to hammer the paneling into. Who would care? What's the difference?"

"The paneling would eventually bow in," Senior said. "It's for backing, sound, additional insulation."

"Does it still have to be mudded?" Glenda asked.

The two men looked at one another. "Well, the ceiling would. The walls? Not necessarily. Plus Wainscoting is pretty expensive. You'll want to keep that in mind."

"Does it come already painted?"

"Primed."

"Good enough. How much do you need? I'll go get it."

The two men stood staring at the walls for a moment and then took out their rulers and started measuring. "Well, if we just do this room…."

"No, let's do all three," Wendy said. "We can do this. What we don't get done the Amish can finish in the morning. Who's got the biggest truck?"

"You're going to have to make two trips," George said. Senior agreed.

"All right, we'll both go," Glenda said. "The quicker we get back the better. Finish measuring and call me. I'll grab a notepad."

"Wow, look at us go. I say we take this act on the road," George said, and they all laughed.

There was no denying there was a sadness hovering over them with the news of the loss of Cindy's baby. But Cindy had assured her dad she was fine, and Senior took comfort in that.

"I guess it just wasn't meant to be," Cindy had said. "Not this time at least."

"You okay?" George asked when Glenda and Wendy had gone and it was just the two men.

"Yeah, but you know what. I'm going to go check on Liz. I'll be right back."

George nodded. "Take your time. If we were allowed a little caffeine around here, I think we could probably work all night."

Senior smiled. "I do admit to sleeping better without it." He walked down the stairs and called back up. "Gordon's here. What do you want him to do?"

The young man stood at the ready, cellphone pressed to his ear.

"Have him start hauling up the drywall."

It was stacked on the front porch.

"Have him bring up the mud too."

~ * ~

Liz stood at her kitchen sink staring out at the weanlings grazing in the pasture. Being a farmer all her life, she was used to the sadness that could surround births. They'd had their fair share. There were times they lost the babes and times they lost the mothers.

She thought about the day she gave birth to Cindy. There were complications, emergency procedures, lifelong repercussions. There would be no more children for her and Senior "We had to do a complete hysterectomy," she heard the doctor say while still feeling the effects of anesthesia. "You'll be fine and your baby is fine."

She turned when Senior walked in the door and looked at him, her husband of thirty-eight years. If anyone knew what she was thinking, it was him. He walked over and put his arms around her. She'd said she was fine when he'd left and went back to T-Bone's after lunch, but….

"It's okay," he said. "It's okay."

"We should have stayed longer," she said, tears falling on his shoulder. "She could have rested more."

"Liz, come on. These things happen. I'm sure she was taking care of herself fine." He rubbed her back. "Come on. We're going to need you to paint."

"I'm a mess," she said. "I'll just stay here and make dinner."

"No." He leaned back and looked into her eyes. "We're going to order pizza. Glenda's already taken care of it. You already fixed us lunch. That's enough. Come on. I'll wait for you."

Liz wiped her eyes. "No, go ahead. I'll walk up. I want to check in on Matthew."

"He was just here for lunch a couple of hours ago, Liz. I'm sure he's fine."

"I know. I know. But did you see how sad he looked when he dropped his fork and couldn't see it at first."

"He's going to have blind spots, Liz. The doctor told him that. Come on, let's go."

"I have dishes to finish up."

"Liz…."

"Fine." She took off her apron. "Fine."

~ * ~

George measured each room, did the math, and phoned Glenda to give her the Wainscoting order. "Get an extra sheet just in case. What time do they close?"

She asked. "Five."

"Oh, geez," George said. "Get two extra then and an extra box of white finish nails. We can always take 'em back if we don't need them."

Wendy and Glenda stood waiting for the dock worker to load their trucks. "It sure is a shame about Cindy," Wendy said.

"I know." Glenda nodded. "I lost two babies in my early twenties. At the time I thought, well I'm not married, so. My boyfriend at the time could care less." She shrugged with a sad far-off look in her eyes. "I think about them every now and then. You know, wondering what they'd be like. Who would they look like? In my family we all look like my mother's side. This nose, big hips."

Wendy smiled. "I like your nose. I'd take it over mine any day. If a person's shorter than me, they can see right up into my nostrils."

Glenda chuckled. "Good thing we're all taller than you then."

"And you don't have big hips."

"Oh, and this from a woman who when we first met used to count every calorie, gram, morsel, and crumb."

Wendy laughed. "God, I was such a bore."

"All set," the dock worker said.

Instinctively, both Wendy and Glenda counted the panels and checked to make sure all the other items were loaded before they left. Glenda's phone rang and then Wendy's. It was Linda Dillon at the track, a three-way call.

"Wee Born ran fifth. Looks like she couldn't get a hold of the track."

"Is she okay?" Glenda asked.

"Looked like it. She pulled up good, cantered back."

"Any more from that Social Services guy?"

"Nope."

"Good." Wendy brought her up-to-date on the progress at T-Bone's.

"Ben went up and talked to the old-timers. They're excited. I'm going to leave early Tuesday."

"Thank you," Wendy said, echoed by Glenda. "Thank you. Though I do wish you'd stay."

"I know, and I appreciate that. I'm just not ready yet, though I have to admit kicking that guy outta here was fun. If I could do that every day...."

All three women laughed and then hung up. Wendy and Glenda had arrived at T-Bone's Place. Both backed into the drive up to the front porch. Gordon was waiting for them. "I'll unload. You both need to go up and mud."

Glenda and Wendy looked at them.

"George says it's easy," he teased. "He said even a woman could do it."

Glenda and Wendy pushed him off the porch, all three laughing.

"Matthew's inside. Don't yell at him."

Wendy let her head drop. "What's he doing?"

"Hooking up the television wiring."

Surely that would have to be a strain on his eyes, his mother thought, but refrained from saying a word to Matthew in passing and walked right on upstairs. Liz had already started on the mudding and smiled. "It's like icing a cake, the smoother the better. And just wait, we get to swirl it too."

~ * ~

Randy pulled his truck up next to the Miller barn, sat talking on the phone for a minute and got out and gathered the necessary supplies to change the bandage on B-Bo's injured leg. Ben was sitting on his favorite ratty old lawn chair outside the barn, dozing in the sunlight. He opened an eye and looked at Randy, nodded, and went back to dozing. He'd been quietly cutting carrots into a bucket to add to the horse's feed tonight. Several of the barn cats roaming the backside had paid a visit, rubbed up against his leg to get their backs scratched. The one purred so loud, so happy. He could hear quiet conversations all around; the barn across from them, the barn next to them. He could hear the soft music of several radios, the horses munching hay.

In the gentle breeze he could smell fresh coffee, Absorbine, straw, cooked oats. In every barn, horsemen were doing chores, watering their horses, picking stalls. A horse was being handwalked two barns down. "Can you hear who win?" a voice asked, far, far away. "Nope, can't hear a thing."

Dawn finished doing up Wee Born and brushed her. She'd heard Randy's truck pull in and park, figured he was in with B-Bo and walked down to check. When she saw Ben sitting outside, head on his chest and snoring, she smiled.

"Hey," Randy said, glancing up at her.

"How's it look?"

"Oh…." He tilted his head one way and then the other to get a closer look. "I've seen worse."

"But you've seen better?"

He shrugged, but softened that with a smile.

"Should I take a look?"

"Not today," he said. "Where's Tom?"

"I don't know. I think he might be at the ReHome barn with Dusty." Dawn stroked B-Bo's face, straightened his forelock, and gave him a kiss on the nose. She glanced at Ben. "Do you think he's going to be all right? His eyes I mean."

"He'll be fine," Randy said. "They do so many of those procedures, they could do it blindfolded. No pun intended," he added.

"But sometimes there are complications. They told him that."

"Yes, and most times there aren't. Not to mention the odds of his losing his eyesight if he doesn't have the surgery."

Dawn glanced at Ben again. Did he just open his eyes? Had he heard them? Was he worrying? No, he looked so happy, so content at this moment. He appeared to be asleep, but was almost smiling. Maybe he's dreaming, she thought.

By the time Randy finished bandaging B-Bo's leg, Tom had returned and Ben was awake. "The track's getting slower," Tom said. "They just ran six furlongs in thirteen and change. They were practically crawling." The rain had continued all morning and only stopped just before the first race. The track drained well, but mud is mud.

Bo-T used to be a closer, but with his being a four-year old now and all testosterone, he didn't take kindly to being rated anymore. Johnny was going to have his hands full. Bo-T was in going a flat mile. Usually he liked to lay right on the lead.

Tom tacked Red while Dawn did up Bo-T's legs in Vetwrap, applied run-down patches, bridled him, and rinsed his mouth. Tom ground-tied Red just outside Bo-T's stall. Red and this colt's history was a good one. Red bit Bo-T on the neck in retaliation of Bo-T biting him one morning while ponying and Bo-T paid heed. Apparently the bite was fair warning; Red had gotten him good and he deserved it. Tom tied Bo-T's tongue; a task Dawn refused to even attempt with Bo-T anymore since he'd gotten so nippy. Done, Tom smeared Vicks VapoRub inside the colt's nose.

Since this was their last horse in today, Dawn would be going over to watch the race. Ben had already started for the paddock. As she walked down the shedrow leading Bo-T out to Tom and Red, she was surprised to see Randy still there. He was sitting in his truck, making notations on various horses' file charts.

~ 191 ~

He looked up, put the files aside, and got out. Dawn handed Bo-T to Tom and looked at her husband. "What are you doing?"

"I'm going to walk over and watch the race," Randy said.

"What?"

Randy chuckled. "I'm going to walk over with you and watch the race."

"Seriously?"

"Come on, you act like I'd never done this before," he said, walking along with her behind the horses.

Tom turned in the saddle. "What's going on? What's the matter?"

"Nothing," Randy said. "I'm going to come watch the race."

"What?"

Randy laughed.

"It's been years, Randy," Dawn said.

Tom pointed at him. "You better not jinx us."

"No, no jinx," Randy said. "I was there the day he was born. Remember?"

Dawn looked at him and smiled, slipped her hand in his.

"I think I need to do more of this," Randy said. "I think I'm forgetting what I'm here for."

Bo-T was the Beau Born - All Together offspring that looked the most like Beau Born. Big, broad, bright shiny new-copper-penny red, he was sensible except when he was sniffing the air for mares; hence the Vicks up his nose. Tom kept him checked up tight when they stepped onto the racetrack behind and in front of two other horses. Tom looked. It was a mare up front. He kept talking to Bo-T, patting him on the forehead, the neck.

Randy got a couple of strange looks from some of the trainers walking back to the barn behind their horses in the previous race. "Who let you out of the cage?" Davidson asked.

Randy laughed.

When they arrived at the paddock, Dawn took Bo-T from Tom but only for a split second, as Tom dismounted quickly - practically in one fell swoop, ground-tied Red, and took Bo-T's reins back. In that split second, Bo-T got a whiff of something in the air and Randy was tempted to step in to offer Dawn a hand, but refrained. Bo-T pranced into the paddock, snorting.

Ben shook his head. This was the oldest he'd ever raced a colt before. He thought about that as he watched Bo-T showing off and pushing up against Tom.

Dawn took her place next to Ben. "He's wound up, that's for sure," she said.

Ben nodded, a lifetime of racing flashing before his eyes, a lifetime of the ups and downs and the highs and the lows. A thought crossed his mind that this might be Bo-T's last race. Or, the last race he would see. He sighed. Oh, Meg, he thought, can you hear me?

Tom led Bo-T into the stall past them, turned him around to be saddled and jiggled the bit in Bo-T's mouth to try to keep him preoccupied. The colt kicked the back wall, and then kicked it again. Saddle in place, girth tightened, the valet put the overgirth over the saddle and Bo-T lunged forward.

"Hey! Hey!" Tom said. "Hey!" He turned Bo-T around, led him back in, the overgirth was cinched, and Tom picked a gap in the parade of horses to walk him around the paddock. Johnny came out of the jockey's room and watched as Bo-T danced past him, nostrils flared and wide-eyed, looking all around.

"Hey, Big Man," Johnny said.

Bo-T pricked his ears. Johnny was the only jockey Bo-T knew. He recognized his voice, recognized him.

"Be good now, be good now," Tom kept saying. They were about to pass the mare being saddled. "Be good!" He turned Bo-T's head to the inside. "Be good."

Ben talked strategy with Johnny. "The track's slow. I don't want you fighting him, but if he goes to the front you might end up with no horse under you at the end."

Johnny nodded.

"Riders up."

Tom kept the colt moving. Dawn gave Johnny a leg-up and took the reins from Tom so he could go out and mount Red. The colt bucked a little and kicked. "Save it for the race, Big Man," Johnny said. The bugle sounded.

Dawn let out a sigh of relief once she handed the horse over to Tom and walked up the ramp to find Randy. He was at the outside hotdog stand. "Damn, these are good," he said. "You want one?"

"No." She shook her head. Her stomach was doing flip-flops. "I'll be back in a minute. I'm going to the ladies room." She checked in with Linda on the way back.

"Everything okay?"

"Yep. I'll see you at the farm."

Randy was standing alongside Ben when Dawn returned. Dusty got there just before the horses were being loaded in the starting gate. He looked worried.

"What's the matter?" Dawn asked.

He shook his head. "I'll tell you later."

They all watched as Bo-T was loaded into the gate. The race being a flat mile the starting gate was right at the wire in front of them. A mare was loaded next to Bo-T. He looked at her, eyes searching. Johnny tapped his neck with the soft whip. "Eh, eh, eh…" he could be heard saying. "Eh, eh, eh."

The last horse was loaded, the latch sprung, the bell rang. "And they're off! …. Taking the early lead is Missy

Banks. Second is Go For The Money. Third is Beau Together. Fourth is Rapid Randy and a length back is…."

The horses pounding the racetrack sounded like thunder.

"The quarter in 23 and 1/5th," Dawn said, for Ben's benefit.

"Where is he now?"

"Still laying fourth," Randy said. "He's tucked in behind Missy Banks."

"Oh dear," Ben said.

"Starting down the backstretch," Bud Gipson announced, "it is Go For the Money and Missy Banks. A length back it's Beau Together and coming up on the outside, Gypsy Voodoo."

"Half in 47," Dawn said.

Ben shook his head. "Too fast for him. He's too close to the pace. What's he doing now?"

"Trying to run up that mare's butt," Randy said, shaking his head.

"Into the clubhouse turn it's Missy Banks and Go For The Money. Beau Together is trying to make a move on the inside. He's got room but not advancing!"

"Three quarters in 13 and 3/5ths," Dawn said.

Ben sighed.

"And now swinging wide, it's Beau Together! Beau Together taking over the lead, Beau Together out by one. Beau Together out in the middle of the racetrack. It's Beau Together."

The crowd started yelling the trademark chants. "Go Bo-T! Come on, Bo-T! Come on, Bo-T."

"Can you see him, Ben?" Dawn said. "Can you see him?"

He nodded. "I see him! I see him! Come on, Bo-T! Come on!"

"It's Beau Together by two lengths, three. It's Bo-T, Bo-T, Bo-T in complete commandddd!!!" Bo-T crossed the wire three and a half lengths in front of Missy Banks.

"Ladies and gentlemen, hold onto your tickets until the race is official."

"Is he pulling up okay?" Ben asked.

"Yes," Randy said. "Tom's got him. Good thing. That's mare's right next to him." He sighed. "I think we're going to have to address this, Ben."

"I know."

Dawn gave Randy a hug and walked down the ramp to the track. Ben and Dusty headed for the winner's circle. Tom dismounted Red and turned the big colt around twice before leading him into the winner's circle. Johnny saluted the Stewards with the traditional wave of the whip.

The photographer snapped the photo and Johnny popped out of his stirrups and landed on his feet and removed his saddle. Ben and Dusty waited until he weighed in and walked with him to the jocks' room. "He's never done that before," Johnny said. "He would have been perfectly happy to stay behind that mare the whole trip. It's like he didn't want to hurt her feelings or something. I'll be good, I'll be good."

The three of them laughed.

"I almost couldn't get him off the rail. Once I got him away, he took to running."

Ben patted Johnny on the back. "Thank you. That was one hell of a ride, Son."

"Thank you!" Johnny tipped his whip and jogged into the jocks' room. He had a mount in the tenth.

Ben glanced at Dusty as they walked down through the parking lot the back way to the barn. "So what's going on?"

Dusty shrugged. "Junior's old man pulled a gun on him."

"Is he all right?"

"Yeah, it wasn't loaded, but still...."

"Here at the track?"

Dusty nodded. "There has to be consequences. We can't let this go unanswered."

"Where's the gun now?"

"I have it."

"Good," Ben said. "Give it to me."

Chapter Seventeen

By the time Dawn brought a very tired Bo-T back from the spit barn, Tom had his stall done, the rest of the horses fed, and was raking the limestone underneath the walking machine. He glanced at her. "Ben and Dusty went back over to the grandstand. Randy went on a farm call."

Dawn wished Dusty hadn't told Tom about Rupert pulling a gun on Junior. Tom didn't much like Junior, but disliked his father even more. The two had almost come to blows several times over the years. Plus, it wasn't sitting well with Tom that Ben had told him to "stay out of this." And that he meant it.

"This has nothing to do with you," Ben insisted. "We hired Dusty to do a job, now let's let him do it."

"Why? This has nothing to do with horses and liaison. This is about a poor excuse of a man who should have been kicked off this racetrack years ago."

"Enough," Ben said. "I know how you feel. You've made that clear. We have enough going on in our lives right now. This has nothing to do with you, Tom, and already you're taking it personally."

Dawn stood in front of Bo-T's stall, watching as the big colt laid down and rolled in his stall. For a second, she wondered if he was planning to ever get back up. He just laid there and moaned. Tom walked up next to her. "He's body sore. You can't run a race the way he ran it and come back without feeling the effects."

"He's going to be all right though, right?" Dawn asked.

"Yeah, he'll be fine."

The big colt groaned again, mashing and grinding himself into the straw bedding, then stood up and shook off. "They wouldn't think of gelding him, would they?" Dawn asked.

"No." He shook his head. "Run for the hills, Bo-T, just in case."

Dawn smiled. "Did you talk to Wendy? I guess they made a lot of progress on T-Bone's Place."

"Yeah, she called me. She wants me to pick up the sign? The guy's going to wait for me. She had it rush-ordered special. Are you gonna be all right if I leave?"

"I'll try hard without you."

Tom nodded, smiling. "Good thing I taught you everything you know."

"Yes, I just wish you'd teach me how to not worry about Ben."

"That I can't do," Tom said. "I'm just as guilty."

~ * ~

Ben was oblivious to their concerns at the moment. He had more important things on his mind and hadn't given thought to his pending eye surgery for hours now. He and Dusty sat across the table from Mim, wanting her advice, her wisdom, her no-muss no-fuss frankness.

"I never liked that man," she said. "The odd part is some people do. It's like he's Dr. Jekyll and Hyde. What's he got against the boy? So Lucy's pregnant, big deal. Life goes on. That *is* life."

"I don't know," Dusty said. "I don't understand it either."

The old-timers had just finished dinner and most were resting. They all planned to watch the Secretariat movie tonight. "We've seen it a dozen times and never get tired of it," Mim said. "Chef Diamond Lou made us hull-less popcorn drizzled with sugar-free Bavarian chocolate. I'm going to miss that guy. Lordy, Lordy."

They laughed and then grew serious again. "So what do you think we should do?" Ben asked.

"Well, like it or not, he's like family. Proceed accordingly. Let us not forget Billy Martin. And remember, when I die, no wearing black."

Ben smiled. He'd already assured her of that so many times. Vicky walked with them to the elevator. "So tomorrow's the day, huh?"

"Yep. We're probably looking at around noon if all goes well," Ben said.

"I meant your eye surgery."

"Oh!" Ben laughed. "I can't believe I forgot about that."

Dawn was gone by the time Ben and Dusty returned to the barn. Ben looked in at all the horses: all eating hay, all looking content.

Dusty walked on. "I'll see you at the farm." He checked on the horses in the ReHome barn. They too were eating hay and content and he was just about to leave when Junior and Lucy pulled in off the highway. As many times as he'd seen Junior in that souped-up pickup truck of his, a rather imposing-looking vehicle sitting up high, it occurred to him that Junior suddenly looked lost.

The young man rolled down his window. "Do you have any idea where we could stay the night?"

Dusty looked at him.

"I can sleep in the truck. I'm thinking about Lucy. She's not feeling so good."

Dusty smiled. "You okay, Lucy?"

"Not really." She tried to respond happily, but felt just plain awful.

"We only need it for one night. I get paid from Brickman tomorrow and we can get a room."

"All right, follow me." Dusty drove over to the grandstand. "Come on," he said, steadying Lucy as they walked to the elevator. Vicky looked up when the doors opened.

"Well, what do we have here?"

"A couple needing shelter for the night. What about that couch in the hall?"

Vicky nodded.

"And maybe some ginger ale, something to eat."

"I ate. Don't worry about me," Junior said.

"No you didn't," Lucy said. "You haven't eaten since breakfast."

Vicky ushered them in. "Go ahead, Dusty. I got this covered."

"All right. If you need anything, call me." Dusty watched the three of them walk away, Vicky gripping Lucy's shoulders to guide and comfort her, and Junior trailing behind them carrying Lucy's sweater and tiny purse.

"How far along are you?" Vicky asked.

"A little over nine weeks," Lucy said.

"Any bleeding?"

"No, just puking."

"Oh, that's good. You're gonna be fine. Come on, you're gonna be just fine."

~ * ~

No time for a celebration at The Rib tonight. Everyone sat down for a late pizza and salad supper at Ben's, a packed house with practically everyone talking at once. It was a good day at the races. It was a good day of progress on T-Bone's Place.

"The Amish should have no problem finishing up tomorrow by noon."

"Transportation is all lined up."

"Pass the salad."

"The movers will be at the track around eleven to load up the beds and furniture. The old-timers will have lunch in the clubhouse. Chef Diamond Lou is going to make them their favorite meal, turkey and dressing and mashed potatoes and gravy."

"I hope he doesn't make them all cry. I've never known a man so emotional before."

"He cries tears of happiness too."

"Remember that day Mom hurt his feelings and he quit," Matthew said.

"Don't remind me," Gordon shook his head. "God, that was embarrassing."

"We look and there he comes, crying a river."

"Wait a minute," Wendy said. They were all laughing. "I didn't mean to hurt his feelings. I was just pointing out that the salad dressing was sour."

"And you didn't think that would devastate him?"

"Rather that than everyone get food poisoning."

"Is there any more pepperoni pizza?"

"Bread sticks?"

"More juice, Mommy."

"Me too."

Tom passed the juice down. Linda poured.

"So the plan tomorrow is?" Tom asked.

"Well," Dawn said. "I'm going with Ben for his surgery."

Ben sighed.

"Dusty, you're going to help Tom, right?"

"Right."

"We only have the one to track," Ben said. He'd marked the horses' training chart for the whole week, all except for Bo-T. "Uh...." He cleared his throat. "I think...."

Everyone looked at him, even D.R., Maeve, and Maria.

"I think I've decided to retire Bo-T."

"Oh?" Dawn said. "We're not...?"

"No, we're not selling him. That's the one thing I can thank my age for; I won't have to make those decisions. We're going to lease him to Breezeway Farm for stud. We keep racing him he's going to hurt someone, not to mention himself. He's proved he's a great racehorse. Let's see if he can prove he's a great sire. He deserves the chance."

Everyone let that news settle over them for a moment, the children all looking from one adult to the other, sensing something important happening.

"Are we all in agreement?" Ben asked. "Let's see a show of hands."

Everyone raised their hands, the children included. They loved this game.

"All right," Ben said. "It's done. He'll stay here until breeding season. The sooner you bring him home from the track, the better," he said to Tom.

Tom nodded. Talk then went to the situation with Junior and Lucy, and ultimately Rupert. "Do you have a plan?" Randy asked. They were all careful not to mention the word "gun" for the children's sake.

"Yes," Ben said. "Well, part of one. I dropped it off at Matt's office on the way home. I want to see whose name it's registered in. I don't want to get the uh, authorities involved," he said, not wanting to say police. "We'll go from there. The fact that it wasn't loaded...."

~ 202 ~

Dawn reached for another piece of pizza and stilled the room with her next comment. "Maybe you should just let Uncle Matt take care of this."

Ben looked at her, Dusty looked at her, Wendy looked at her, Tom looked at her, Glenda looked at her, George looked at her, Randy looked at her, Liz looked at her, Randy Sr. looked at her, Linda looked at her, Carol looked at her, Gordon and Matthew looked at her, Maria, Maeve and D.R.

"What?" she said, glancing at all of them.

"You're not suggesting…?" Tom said.

"I'm not suggesting anything. Just let Uncle Matt take care of it."

"So that uh…?" Tom wanted clarification, as did all the other adults judging from their expressions. "So that uh… Rupert never points a finger again?"

"Not that one," Dawn said.

Everyone hesitated a moment. When Ben went back to eating, they all went back to eating. Dessert was Cassada cake. It was always Cassada cake with pizza. When the dishes were done and everything was cleaned up, the evening came to an end. Ben stood out on the porch and watched them all leave, the children holding hands, their tiny voices echoing in the night, their laughter. He waved to Glenda and George as they pulled out of the drive, and smiled at Dusty. He was headed out to the pasture where the little filly Bonnie Bee was grazing with Poncho and Biscuit. No doubt, he had a pocketful of molasses treats for them.

He glanced in the direction of T-Bone's Place, dark but for the porch light. "Oh, Meg…" he said. "There's so much going on. I wish you were here."

"I am, Mr. Miller," he heard her say. "I'll always be here. Now go get some rest. You have a big day tomorrow. I'll be waiting for you back here at home."

Tom got out of the shower and dried off, wrapped the towel around his waist and walked down the hall to check on Wendy. They had the upstairs to themselves, bathroom, bedroom, and the adjoining attic turned into a cozy, sprawling den. Wendy was sitting at her desk.

"I'm going to bed."

She nodded and smiled. "I'll be right in."

"All right, but if you wait too long I'm going to be sound asleep."

Wendy laughed. "Come here and look at this." It was an article written about the number of Thoroughbred racetracks that had closed over the past five years. Tom scanned the page and yawned. Ben had said no to "slots" and Dawn and Tom had agreed. Ben said he'd close the doors first. He and Richard had gone round and round about it.

"We'll simulcast, we'll run promotions, do giveaways, the tours, the videos, the articles, all of that and more, whatever you guys come up with, but no slots. We're not a gambling casino; we're a racetrack."

"You know what I think?" Wendy said.

"No, I don't," he said. "Come to bed and tell me. Tell me anything you want." He took her by the hand. "Tell me stories. There once was a man who lived on a farm, and…."

Wendy laughed, following him. "Okay, but if I lose my train of thought."

"I'm counting on it," Tom said, turning out the light.

Chapter Eighteen

Ben and Dawn walked down the corridor at the hospital, checked in at the surgical desk, and sat down in the waiting room. Dawn laid her laptop down on the empty chair next to her and reached for one of the cataract-surgery pamphlets on the table.

"Let's see, it says right here that the procedure is brief and painless and that most patients are back to normal activities the next day."

"What?" Ben said. This was the first he'd heard of that.

Dawn read him bits and pieces of the description of the surgical procedure. "In preparation for your surgery, a sterile drape will be placed around the eye. Did you put your drops in your eyes this morning?"

"Yes," he said.

"Okay, good." She read further. "To begin your surgery, the surgeon will make a very small incision about an eighth of an inch or less at the outermost edge of the cornea." She cringed. "I'll skip ahead."

Ben nodded.

"Let's see, rarely needs stitches, self-sealing, a clear artificial lens, it's folded and then unfolded, set in the correct position. Humph. That's interesting."

"Terribly," Ben said, glancing at her.

She chuckled. "Okay, here, this is good. During your surgery you will be aware of the surgeon, the staff, and the operating room surroundings, but you will not be able to see images of the surgery being performed. Your surgery will take less than 15 minutes per eye...."

"Per eye?"

"You're only having the one done today. Remember?"

"I remember. I just hope they remember."

"Mr. Miller."

Ben stood, looked at Dawn as if he was seeing her for the last time and walked through the doorway with the nurse. Dawn continued reading. "If you experience pain during the procedure it is important to tell your surgeon.

The use of eye drop anesthesia is sufficient for most cataract patients. Most experience little if any discomfort."

She folded the pamphlet and leaned her head back against the wall. "All we are saying is give peace a chance…" she sang softly. "Why am I singing that song? Oh, the wall, that's why." She closed her eyes, said a prayer for Ben, and sat staring through her eyelids. She couldn't imagine what Ben must be going through. It was so important for him to be independent. It was so important to Matthew.

When someone sat down in Ben's chair next to her, she opened her eyes and smiled at the tiny little woman. A middle-aged woman, perhaps the daughter, was standing at the counter. The tiny woman looked up at her.

"Good morning," Dawn said.

"Mom, don't bother the lady," the woman standing at the counter said.

"I'm not bothering her."

"She's not," Dawn said.

The daughter rolled her eyes and sighed.

"She thinks I'm senile," the mother whispered. "I'm not; I'm just forgetful."

Dawn smiled. "So am I."

"It's just that I have so many things on my mind. I'm missing bridge you know."

Dawn looked at her.

"I'm supposed to be playing cards right now."

"Well, we can fix that," Dawn said, opening her laptop. "At least until they call for you."

"Oh, I'm not having anything done. She is. I'm just supposed to sit here."

The daughter rolled her eyes again.

Dawn pulled up an online bridge game. "We will be playing against two virtual opponents."

"Huh?"

"Fake players. You and I will be on the same team. How good do we want them to be?"

"Well, let's keep it interesting," the little woman said. "I'm pretty darn good."

Dawn smiled. "All right."

The two of them won the first game, lost the second one, and won the third. When the woman's daughter returned from whatever surgical procedure had taken place, apparently not her eyes, the little woman sighed. "It was so nice to meet you."

"You too," Dawn said.

The woman patted her arm. "I hope the man 'who's like a father to you' does well in his surgery."

"Thank you."

The woman's daughter opened the door for them to leave. "Like a father? she muttered. "He's probably her sugar-daddy. She has pampered written all over her."

"Oh no, dear. She works hard. She works at the racetrack."

"I'll bet," her daughter said. "Come on; let's go. Don't dawdle."

How sad, Dawn thought. You have no idea how lucky you are. Oh how I wish my mom was still alive, my dad too. She checked her e-mails and smiled. There was one from her Aunt Maeve.

Hello, my dear Dawnetta. I hope you are well and those darling children and handsome husband of yours too. I am facing day-to-day challenges of aging. I know now why they say getting old is not for sissies. Climbing a mountain is not quite as easy as it once was. Love, Aunt Maeve

Dawn e-mailed back. Dear, Aunt Maeve. When you get to the top, don't look down. It makes you dizzy. Love, Dawnetta

"Mrs. Iredell?"

"Yes?"

"Mr. Miller would like to see you."

Dawn gathered up her things and followed the woman down the hall. An image of Ben the first time she saw him after he'd had his stroke flashed in her mind. He'd looked so frail, so weak, so....

Ben looked up when she walked in the room and smiled. He had a big patch on his right eye. "It wasn't bad at all. I only have to wait a few more minutes and we can leave."

"Really?"

"Yep," the nurse said. "He did great." She handed Dawn a list of post-operative instructions and left the room

"What's it say?" Ben asked.

"It says to keep the patch on until your appointment tomorrow, only light physical activity, no heavy lifting and no aerobics."

Ben chuckled. "No risk of that."

"You can take acetaminophen for pain. Don't rub your eye. It may feel as if you have something in your eye, that's normal. No driving for twenty-four hours, no alcohol, you can resume your medications."

"What about eating?"

"It doesn't say. We'll check with the nurse on the way out."

~ * ~

In between bouts of nausea, Lucy proved to be a great help to Vicky. She packed the old-timers' clothes in bags. She stripped the beds, stacked the pillows, packed up all their meds, their books, their magazines, their racing forms.

"Keep sipping the ginger-ale," Vicky insisted, whenever the girl looked a little green or felt woozy. "Here, have some more Saltines."

The old-timers were down in the clubhouse enjoying an early lunch. Closed on Mondays when there was no racing, they had the whole dining area to themselves. They sat reminiscing, planning, anticipating. The thought of moving out to Ben's farm was exciting, but it was also frightening. Change came hard for them at their age.

Chef Diamond Lou came out with his serving crew and gave them all a hug. "I will see you. I promise," he said, wiping his eyes. "Now eat! Eat! I make so special for you, always!"

Vicky and Lucy joined them a few minutes later. "Try and eat a little mashed potatoes," Vicky told the girl. "If it stays down, get brave."

"Oh no, so I hear," Chef Diamond Lou said, bringing out a special dish. "For you, little lady." He'd made her fresh lemon-lime gelato. "Eat tiny amount a time. Make tummy feel good."

Lucy nodded and started to cry. "You are all so nice to me."

"Oh my," Mim said.

"Nonsense, nonsense." Diamond Lou hugged Lucy gently. "You so special. Woman with child is God gift."

"Okay, enough" Mim said, that sentiment causing even her to get a little teary-eyed. "Can we just eat now?"

Chef Diamond Lou clapped. "Yes, yes! Eat, eat! Where Pastor Mitchell? He supposed to come!"

Pastor Mitchell walked in behind him. "I'm right here."

"Oh, good, good, good!"

Pastor Mitchell sat down next to Lucy and they all bowed their heads. "Dear heavenly Father, bless this food. Bless these people. Bless this place. Bless this young mother to be and her unborn child. Be with them all as they embark on their new journey. We pray in Jesus' name, Amen."

Chef Diamond Lou sniffled and looked at all of them. "I so happy, so happy for you all." He glanced at the feast he set before them and gasped. "Oh no! Who forget cranberry sauce? I make special, no sugar!" He hurried into the kitchen, returned in a flash and doled out a scoop for each person, waited for them to taste it, and left happy.

~ * ~

As soon as Tom and Dusty finished up at the barn, they drove over to the grandstand, parked in the basement level used for deliveries and waited for the moving van to arrive. The transport vehicles for the old-timers were expected later. Since Jeannie and Clint were in wheelchairs, they had to have separate vans because of liability. The others were going to be driven in a limo bus. The hope was for their beds and furniture to be in place before they arrived at T-Bone's Place, so they would feel right at home, which is why they were all in the clubhouse and not on their floor. It might be hard on them to see their belongings being packed up and hauled out.

Tom motioned to the guard shack by the horsemen's entrance at a shiny black BMW with tinted windows. "God, I'd love to be there," he said. It was Dawn's Uncle Matt. The two of them watched the vehicle wind its way through the horsemen's lot and park outside Rupert's Tack Shop. The driver got out and opened the door. Tom smiled when Uncle Matt emerged. The man was always dressed in black.

When the tack store door opened, Rupert looked up from the counter. Uncle Matt made no pretense of shopping. "We're here to see a man named Rupert," Uncle Matt's assistant said, locking the door behind him. "Would you happen to be Mr. Rupert?"

Rupert nodded warily. "Is there some reason you locked my door?"

"Yes, we don't want disturbed," the assistant said. "We'll only take a moment of your time."

Uncle Matt put on a pair of black Corinthian leather gloves. "I mean you no harm," he said. "But it's been brought to my attention that there was a little incident here yesterday involving a gun."

Rupert looked from one to the other.

"This is private property, this establishment, this racetrack, it's all...how can I say this, it's all under my jurisdiction."

Rupert's Adam's apple moved up and down in his throat.

"Guns make me nervous," Uncle Matt said. "Right, Angelo?"

His assistant nodded. "Yes, they make you nervous, Boss."

"So you see, when I had this gun in question run for registration it made me even a little more nervous and I don't like that."

"No, he doesn't like that," Angelo said.

Uncle Matt hesitated. "What kind of man pulls a stolen gun on his son?"

"I didn't steal that gun. I bought it years ago at a gun show. For burglars."

"I see," Uncle Matt said. "Lucky for you, the gun ends up in my hands."

"It wasn't loaded."

"I don't like a bluff," Uncle Matt said. "I don't like a bully. Your son is well thought of. I don't want to see any harm come to him. You, I don't know and I don't care."

"He doesn't care," Angelo said.

"So let me make myself clear. Nothing happens to your son. Nothing."

"Capiche?" Angelo said, unlocking the door.

"One more thing," Uncle Matt said. "I don't like the smell of this place. Clean it up."

Angelo stepped back and followed him out, opened the car door, closed it and got in behind the wheel. Uncle Matt looked at him in the mirror. "Capiche?"

Angelo laughed. "Hey, I thought it was a nice touch."

Tom and Dusty watched as the black BMW snaked its way back out of the horsemen's lot to the road. And here came the moving van.

Chapter Nineteen

Loading up all the beds and furniture and the old-timers belongings took very little time. Fortunately they were able to use the industrial-size commercial elevator. Between the two movers and Dusty and Tom, it was all done in less than an hour. Tom tipped the men each twenty dollars and he and Dusty went back up to the third floor to make sure nothing was left behind. They swept the rooms, the bathrooms, hallways, and took the bagged garbage down to the basement dumpster. Tom looked out across the parking lot.

"I can't stand it," he said. "I've got to go feel Rupert out."

"Now wait a minute," Dusty said. "Ben told you to stay out of this. Remember?"

Tom just looked at him.

"All right, I'll come with you," Dusty said. "I'm warning you though, if you say one word about that gun, I'm going to drag you out of there by your ear!"

"Ooh." Tom pretended to be afraid, the two of them laughing.

Tom opened Rupert's Tack Shop door and Dusty walked in first. It had been quite a while since Uncle Matt paid his visit, but Rupert still looked visibly shaken. "What can I do for you two?" he said, scrubbing the floor.

"I need a, uh, box of Vetwrap," Tom said. "Green."

Rupert motioned. "You know where it's at. What about you?" he asked Dusty.

"Oh." Dusty hesitated. "Another couple bags of those molasses treats if you still have some."

Rupert propped his mop against the wall and walked around behind the counter to get them. Dusty paid the man. Tom's Vetwrap was put on Ben's account. The two walked to the door and another customer entered.

"Hey, Jack," Dusty said.

"Hey, Dusty. Hey, Tom."

Dusty nudged Tom out the doorway. Randy's truck was parked by the first barn past the kitchen. They tossed their wares onto the front seat and walked back to the grandstand. When the two of them entered the Secretary's office, they saw Linda talking to a man that neither had seen before. At first they thought it might have been the agent from Family Services but when she looked up and waved them over, they figured not. She seemed rather happy to be making this fellow's acquaintance.

"This is Dr. Simmons."

"Mark," the man said, shaking their hands.

"He's the new vet here to see Randy. This is Tom. He kinda sorta owns the place."

"Not really," Tom said.

"And this is Dusty. He is the Nottingham Downs Liaison Official. He makes sure that everyone on the backside behaves and he watches out for every horse here on the racetrack."

Mark Simmons smiled, impressed. He was a short, stocky man, already graying at age thirty-seven, with big blue eyes.

"He's divorced," Linda added. "Loves children, has two, and they're in high school."

Tom laughed. "Did you read that on his forehead or something? How long you been here?"

"Not long." They all laughed. "I tried having Dr. Iredell paged from the guard entrance, but he never showed. I waited quite a while and then decided to come over here."

Wendy had left a visitor's pass for him at the gate.

"Come on," Dusty said. "I'll take you to go see Randy."

When the two men walked away, Tom teased Linda. "You're drooling."

"Yeah, but not so much. He's got a girlfriend. She's why he's divorced. I don't want any part of that." She walked back around behind the entries counter. "Have you seen Joe?"

"No, why? He's not here?"

"Nope."

No sooner said than he came rushing through the doorway pushing people aside. "Excuse me. Excuse me."

Tom stared at the man. "What's the matter with you?" He looked like the walking dead.

Joe shook his head. "I think my wife's trying to poison me. I've never slept fourteen hours straight in my life."

"I'll be upstairs," Tom said.

Dusty walked with Mark Simmons down between the racetrack and horsemen's lot to the backside. "Where are you parked?"

"By the front gate," Mark said.

Randy's truck was still sitting outside barn two. Dusty glanced up and down the shedrow. "He's around back," one of the grooms said. The two men walked around to the other side of the barn.

"Randy?"

"Down here, Dusty. Good, you can give me a hand."

"I can do better than that," Dusty said, finding the right stall.

Randy looked up. He was attempting to bandage a horse that had torn its tendon and trying to go down in the stall, probably from shock. Mark stepped past Dusty and braced the leg. "Mark Simmons," he said.

"Oh, shit." Randy said. He'd forgotten the man was coming this morning. "Here." He paused to make sure the man had a good hold of the horse's leg. "I'll be right back."

Mark braced the mare with his stocky body. "There now, there now," he said.

Randy returned. "This might backfire so be ready." He administered a small dose of a stimulant, IV, and stood watching the mare's eyes. She blinked a couple of times and started looking a little more alert. "All right, let's do this," Randy said. "Dusty."

Dusty took the shank from the trainer, nudged him out of the way, and Randy and Mark Simmons worked on the tendon. When it was all said and done, Randy stood up and the two men shook bloody hands.

"Nice to meet you."

"You too."

"Thanks for the help."

"My pleasure."

~ * ~

Mim walked to the ladies room on the clubhouse floor and after using the facility, washed her hands, leaning on her cane, and looked in the mirror. Hers was a weathered face and she rather liked it that way. It showed where'd she'd been; the hard roads she'd traveled. Her eyes were almost silver now, but still bright. She thought about her dear friend Janie Pritchard who'd passed away last year. As she stared into the depths of her own eyes, she could almost see Janie, standing close to her shoulder, smiling.

"Mim, are you okay?" Vicky asked from the door.

"Yes, fine, fine. Stop fussing over me."

Vicky smiled. "Tom's here. He wants to talk to everybody."

"Oh my," Mim said, drying her hands. She steadied herself with her cane, made her way back out and took a seat next to Lucy. The poor girl was experiencing another bout of nausea. Mim touched her gently on the back. "Think poopy diapers."

Lucy chuckled and took another sip of ginger ale.

"Mim…." Vicky shook her head.

"What?" Mim said. "She laughed."

Tom sat down and took off his cowboy hat. "First of all, I want you all to know Ben's cataract surgery went well. Dawn said he just wolfed down two hamburgers."

"That's good news," Clint said. "An appetite is always good news." Clint had had most of his stomach removed and didn't start feeling alive again until he found he could still enjoy eating.

"He's back at the farm. Dawn says he's supposed to take a nap, but we all know Ben."

They all smiled.

"So, here's the update. Everything upstairs, and I mean everything, is on its way to the farm."

Several of the old-timers gasped; a whoosh of collective breathing in and out.

"I think you're going to like the place. We need just a little more time to get it all set up, so you're going to have to stay here just a little while longer, and then we're going to all head on over. Okay?"

"What about my wheelchair? Clint asked.

~ 216 ~

"You're all set. Both of you are," Tom said, looking from him to Jeannie. The rest of you will ride together in a limo."

"A limo?" Miguel said. "Sheeet! Uptown!"

Everyone laughed.

Steven glanced around at his friends, his family for all practical purposes since he had no family anymore. "We feel bad, all this expense and…."

"Come on," Tom said. "You're all pitching in and you know that. Everyone is helping out and doing what they can and that's all anyone can ever ask for. Right?"

"Right," they all said, nodding.

"So, I'll be back in a little while when it's time and we'll all go together."

With that, Lucy promptly got up and ran to the bathroom.

"What about Lucy?" Mim asked. "What's going to happen to her?"

Tom hesitated. "Junior's getting them a room today. She'll be fine."

~ * ~

Senior and George walked from room to room observing the Amish at work. Everything was just about completed. "You all did well," the Bishop said. "You do good work."

"Thank you," George said. "It took a whole lot of hands and we made some mistakes along the way, but we did it." He looked at the list. All the tasks were checked off but for hanging the signs Wendy had ordered.

"Let's do it."

The two men dug the holes for the Meg's Meadows sign announcing Ben's Farm, lined up and leveled the posts, and then filled the holes around them with a quick-drying concrete. "Wish we didn't have to wait for the concrete to dry to hang the sign."

"Brace it." The Bishop had walked down to join them and stood puffing on his pipe. "Just brace it on this side and it'll be fine. Get the wood, I'll show you."

"Alrighty then," Senior said. They cut the braces the size the Bishop specified and stood back while the man eyeballed the sign to level it. George and Senior were a little uneasy about that, but neither one wanted to question the discretion of a Bishop. When the sign was in place, the three men stood back, the Amish Bishop nodding. Then they went back to T-Bone's Place to hang the other sign.

"I suggest you hang it to the right so when people open the door they can still see it," the Bishop said, still puffing on his pipe. "In my community we revere the elderly. This is good what you are all doing."

Senior and George smiled, both feeling as if they had just been blessed. Wendy came outside with Matthew behind her. "I just got a call from the mover. They're about five minutes away."

The men hurried and hung the sign. "All hands on deck," the Bishop said.

They all laughed.

"It's showtime!"

"Matthew, don't you dare lift a thing," Wendy said. "I mean it. Gordon, what are you still doing here? Shouldn't you be at school?"

"Are you kidding me?" Gordon said. "Mom, I wouldn't miss this for the world. Cool sign. I like the one for Meg's Meadows too."

Wendy glanced past them. Dawn was walking down between the barns. Wendy waved. Dawn motioned she'd be right there. There'd be dishes to put away, clothes closets to organize, bathrooms to organize, beds to make. Wendy felt a flutter of anxiety, a rush of blood gushing to her face. "Oh Jesus," she said to herself. "It's true, my first hot flash."

"Here they come," Matthew said.

Gordon took out his cellphone and snapped a photo of the moving van as it backed into the drive. The Amish crew gathered all their tools and put them out by the garage. The two moving-men got out, slid the back door open and for a second, everyone just stood looking inside. Vicky and Lucy had labeled everything; beds, mattresses, tables, and clothing bags with each person's name.

Wendy consulted her chart. Jeannie and Mim had the first bedroom. Steven and Bill the one in the back. Jack and Clint were in the first one on the other side of the hall, Miguel and Frank behind them.

"Here." Matthew took the notepad from his mom and wrote the old-timers' names in pairs in big letters on four pieces of paper. "Do you have tape?"

"Yep." She pulled a roll of masking tape out of her utility belt. Matthew posted the names on the bedroom doors and the unloading began.

~ * ~

Linda put the phone down and stared out the window at the racetrack for inspiration. She didn't have long to think, to devise a plan. When she heard a knock on the open door, she turned. There stood Joe with the Social Services man from yesterday.

She shook her head. "Weren't you supposed to make an appointment? Mrs. Girard isn't in today."

"I don't need an appointment. I have a court order," the man said. "And I want my ID back."

Linda glanced at Wendy's desk where it lay. "I've got this, Joe," she said. "Go ahead."

"You sure?"

"Yes. Thank you." She reached for the court order and handed the man his ID. "What do you want?" she asked.

He examined his ID and put it into his wallet. "Well, as you can see, I'm here to investigate a complaint about unsafe housing in a non-residential building."

"There's no one here," Linda said.

"Fine, that's all you have to show me. And don't think you're going to pull any more games on me either."

"I wouldn't think of it." She motioned for him to walk out the door and followed him. She took her cellphone from her pocket as they boarded the elevator. The man looked at her with sudden rage in his eyes.

"Don't you be...."

"What? Doing my job? Do you think you're the only thing I have going on today? Think again, oh annoying one."

The man glanced away, giving her just enough time to finish the text. "Besides, do you seriously think I can make all these people listed here on this piece of paper disappear with a phone call? Oh yeah, watch me go! Hey, get rid of all the old people," she said into the phone. "Hurry! You have about five seconds. Poof!"

The man shifted his weight.

"Did you say third floor?"

"Yes." He looked away. "We'll inspect the second floor on the way down."

"Good thinking, 'cause they might go there to hide."

The man shook his head. "You're very entertaining, you know that?"

"I try."

When they got to the third floor, the two of them stepped off the elevator to nothing but emptiness. The man walked down the hall, looked into all the rooms, looked into the bathrooms, looked into the closets. Nothing, not even a tumbling tumble-weed dust bunny!

The man walked back toward the elevator. "Second floor."

Linda followed him. The man was starting to sweat. She glanced at the court order again. "Who is this?" She pointed to a name written in the complaint.

"It's of no importance to you," the man said. "Do you want to push the button?"

"Sure," Linda said, taking out her cellphone again and texting the name she'd seen on the court order to Dawn.

"What are you doing?" he asked.

"Confirming a lunch date. It's of no importance to you," she said, throwing his comment right back at him. "Ah, home sweet home." They stepped out onto the clubhouse floor. "There's no one here at all on dark days. You're wasting your time and mine."

"We'll see," he said, and walked down the hall to the dining room. Empty. All the tables were set up, silverware, napkins, glasses, ready for tomorrow. No signs of anyone. He looked all around, checked the restrooms and opened the door leading to the general seating side of the grandstand. Nothing. Not a soul.

"What part of *dark days* don't you understand?" When he motioned to the large swinging doors to the kitchen, Linda shook her head. "You're kidding me?"

He pointed to the court order.

"All right," she said.

The man pushed open one of the doors and met with Chef Diamond Lou. "What you do here?"

"I'm just here to look around," the man said. "I'm just here to look around."

"Not my kitchen!! Campylobacter! Campylobacter! Campylobacter! Shoes! Shoes!" he screeched. "Germs! E-Coli! Health department!! Out! Out! No breathing! Out!!"

The man backed up. Chef Diamond Lou towered over him.

"Out!!! Out!!!"

The man was silent on the way down in the elevator to the first floor.

"Did you want to look anywhere else?" Linda asked.

He glared at her. "I'll be back. You mark my words, I'll be back."

"Oh yeah. Well, maybe I'll be here and maybe I won't. Maybe this is all just a figment of your imagination. Next time, why don't you bring a fire-breathing dragon along with you too."

~ * ~

Ben woke from his nap and looked out the kitchen window. He couldn't remember the last time he took a nap, a legitimate nap that is. He could easily doze throughout the day at any given time. But to actually lie down on the bed, pillow under his head, and cover up with a blanket? No. He looked out the window. The moving truck was parked outside T-Bone's Place. He put on his hat and a pair of sunglasses and decided to take a walk over. When he got to the end of his driveway, he saw the Meg's Meadows farm sign for the first time. He stood next to it and traced the letters of beloved wife's name.

Meg's Meadows
Home of the Legendary Beau Born

"I'm here," he could hear Meg say. "I love it too. Thank you." He tried not to blink and wiped the tears from his eyes as he walked out onto the road. The sight of the sign on the front of T-Bone's Place choked him up again. He took out his handkerchief and blew his nose.

T-Bone's Place
Retirement Home for Old Racetrackers

Ben got the Grand Tour. He even walked upstairs. "This is nice. This is so very nice. It feels like home. I think they're going to like it here. When are they due?"

"They're loading up now," Wendy said, closing her cellphone and slipping it into her pocket. "Tom says they'll be here in about half an hour."

Jeannie was first to board. The ambulance driver pushed her up the ramp and backed her into place, secured her wheelchair, fastened her seatbelt and pulled ahead to wait for the rest. They wanted to go all together. Clint's "sweet ride" as he called it, had a lift platform. He was wheeled onto it, his chair braced in place, and up he went. The attendant wheeled him in then, snapped his wheelchair in place and secured his seat belt. They moved forward and the limo bus pulled up to the loading ramp.

One by one, the old-timers were helped inside and made comfortable, seatbelts buckled, and all facing forward. Miguel lowered his window. "Pardone me. Do you have Grey Poupon?"

They all laughed. When everyone was loaded, Vicky looked at Lucy and then at Tom and Dusty. Tom sighed. "Go on, get in. Junior can pick you up at the farm. Do you need a bucket?"

"No, I have…." Lucy clutched a sick tray in her hand. "I'm fine. Can I ride up front? I think that would be better."

"Sure," the driver said.

Dusty walked outside the building, looked one way and then the other, and waved for the convoy to pull out. "All clear, let's go." He and Tom followed them in their trucks. It was a short ride to Ben's farm. There was very little traffic this time of day. In a little over twenty minutes, the two transport ambulances and the limo bus were pulling into the driveway at T-Bone's Place.

The Amish crew had been picked up and were gone, but everyone else was still there. The ambulance attendants opened the ramps, Clint was lowered down. Jeannie was wheeled down the tiny ramp. The other old-timers all stepped out of the limo bus. Walkers, canes, together as one family, they made their way up the ramp to the front door. They gathered on the porch in front of the sign for a family photo and crossed the threshold, one by one. "Welcome home," Ben said. "Welcome home."

~ * ~

Randy and Mark Simmons took a late lunch break at the track kitchen and sat talking about the history of Nottingham Downs, its dedication to the life of the Thoroughbred, its mission, the highs and the lows. "I remember when you guys made national news for bringing in the soft whip," Mark said. "Damn, that was big!"

"Yeah, there were some ups and downs with that, that's for sure. The worst part was the derby the following year when some of the top contenders didn't want to come in for the race. We really didn't have a problem this year though. I'll be right back. You want more coffee?" Randy asked, pointing to Mark's cup.

"No, thank you. I'm done."

Randy came back, sat down, and sipped his piping hot coffee, then yawned. "So here's the deal," he said. "Everyone in my family is telling me I work too many hours. I have eight farm calls yet to do today. My younger sister is a vet. She just went back for additional equine. She's always been small animal." Randy stifled another yawn. "She was supposed to move here this year with her husband. He was going to transfer within his company. He's a corporate up and comer, nice guy. Damn," Randy said, yawning yet again. "Anyway, she's had some health issues, and now's not the time to, you know, move ahead. So tell me what *you're* thinking."

"Well." Mark looked around the track kitchen, a few trainers and grooms dotted here and there. "I like the racetrack. I always have. I grew up at the trotters."

"So, I've heard." Randy took another sip of coffee.

"I don't know what happened to me, but somewhere along the way, I started paying more attention to the horses' physiology. I wanted to know why certain things happened. And I didn't want anybody else telling me. I wanted to know for myself." Mark shrugged. "The rest is history. I went to school, got my license, and here I am hoping for a chance to get my feet wet."

Randy looked at him. "How did you pay for your schooling?"

"I owe a fortune in student loans."

Randy nodded. "I just paid mine off last year." His cellphone rang. It was Dawn. "Excuse me," he said. "Hello."

"Oh, Randy," Dawn said. "You should have seen the old-timers. They are so happy. I just left there and they're all sitting around in the living room in their favorite chairs, talking. Some were dozing. They love their rooms. They love the kitchen and the porches. They love being able to see the horses grazing in the pastures. They love it! They absolutely love it."

"It all worked out okay, huh?"

"Yes, it was amazing. I'm so proud of Ben for doing this. I'm so proud of everyone." She paused. "So how did it go with interviewing the vet?"

"Good, good. We just had lunch at the track kitchen. I'm heading out on farm calls now. I'm not sure if he's going along or not. I've been working him to death."

"I'm in," Mark said.

"Okay," Randy said. "Where's dinner tonight?"

"At your mom and dad's. Oh and I have to tell you, when Miguel was introduced to your dad he called him Señor and now everyone is calling him Señor, even Liz. He loves it."

Randy laughed. "I'll see you at dinner. I'll try and be on time."

"Wait! One more thing. The man from Family Services showed up again today. He didn't see anything, but Linda noticed something odd on the court order and called me and then I called Uncle Matt."

"What is it?"

"Are you ready for this?"

"Yesss...." he said, playing along.

"RJR Enterprises."

Randy sat back. "Why does that sound so familiar?"

"Uncle Matt says it's the money behind a bunch of big Las Vegas casinos."

"Oh shit."

Dawn sighed. Her sentiments exactly.

~ * ~

Linda stood at the exit of the Secretary's office and took one last look around. It would be so tempting to stay. After all, Nottingham Downs had been her life for so many years. But then again, she thought, those years weren't always so great. She recalled a time when she had walked into this same office so high she didn't even know her own name let alone why she'd come over here.

What was it? How did it begin? Partying all night? It was the thing to do back then. Being so tired and hung over in the morning she welcomed "pep" in the form of a pill. How many horses did I gallop this morning? Twelve? Seriously? And ponied seven too?

"You're pregnant," the doctor at the Free Clinic said.

"How?"

"How...?" The doctor turned his back on her.

~ 226 ~

"I mean, I don't even eat right. How's a baby supposed to…?"

"Well, I suggest you start eating right. You're about four months. Didn't you realize you weren't having periods anymore?"

"No." Days, weeks, months, meant nothing to her. She pressed her hand to her stomach. "If it hadn't been for feeling like there was something moving around inside of me all of a sudden."

The doctor looked at her. "Well, hopefully that's an indication of a healthy baby. Unless there is cause for suspecting otherwise, you are not eligible for an ultrasound unless you can pay for it yourself."

Linda closed the Secretary's office door and secured the lock. Joe had disappeared hours ago. She was the last one to leave, the last one left in the entire grandstand. She glanced up at the third floor windows. Dark. She smiled, thinking about her encounter with the Social Services guy. "Well, at least I accomplished something today."

She looked out at the racetrack, raked and pristine with perfectly furrowed rows. She breathed in the scent of earth, grass, Forget Me Nots.

"Some day I'll feel worthy of coming back. Don't leave me," she said to the pale moon in the distance as she walked on. "I need to be able to find my way home."

When her cellphone rang, she glanced at the number and smiled. "Hello."

"Mommy?"

"Yes."

"Señor says to tell we are wading for you to eat. He said to tell you even Wandy is here."

Linda chuckled at the fact that Randy was home - for one. And two, the way Maria said Señor. How natural it sounded rolling off her little tongue. Her father was Mexican. A man Linda could hardly remember anymore but for his coal black hair and intense eyes. He'd said he loved her. Or did she imagine that?

"I'll be home in a few minutes."

"She be home in a few minutes!" Maria shouted.

Linda laughed.

"Bye, Mommy!"

"Bye." Linda hung up the phone and walked down through the parking lot. It was practically empty, a long walk. The sight of her car sitting there all by itself near the stable gate brought tears to her eyes. "God, I am so lonely. How did this happen to me?"

It wasn't like her to feel sorry for herself. She didn't have a bad-ass reputation for nothing. She'd developed a hard crust early on and maintained it, except for when she was at Ben's farm where she could be herself. "What would I do without that old man?"she said, wiping her eyes. "Without all of them?"

The stable guard stepped outside his guard shack. "You okay, Linda?"

"Yeah," she said, wiping her eyes again. "I'm fine. If you ever tell anyone you saw me crying, I'll beat you to a pulp. You hear me?"

The guard smiled. "I didn't see anything."

~ * ~

The children had talked Ben into wearing D.R's pirate patch over his bandaged eye and he looked rather imposing sitting at the head of the table. Even so, Mark Simmons, the newcomer, found himself thoroughly delighted with this homey scene.

"You eat like this every night?" he asked. "All together?"

"Well, we switch houses, but basically, yes. Sometimes we eat alone, but not often." Everyone was present, even Gordon, who decided not to return to the frat house tonight and leave early in the morning instead.

Linda planned to leave in the morning too, but a little later.

Mark glanced around at everyone. "So right here, sitting at this table, is basically Nottingham Downs. Right?"

"Yep!" Tom said.

"So, what do you all do? I mean uh…what do you do?"

Everyone laughed. "We wondered the same thing back when we were thinking about getting into this," Dawn said.

"And even after that," Ben added. "I have no idea what I do. I go over and I sit at the desk a couple times a day. I look at Wendy. She looks at me. I wave and leave."

Everyone laughed again. "That's pretty much the way it is," Wendy said. "And I wave back."

Mark smiled. "Who runs what?"

Tom nodded in Wendy's direction. "Wendy is the Assistant General Manager. She and Richard run the office."

"Richard's been on medical leave," Wendy said. "He's due back any time now. He does most of the PR and marketing. I do a little of the marketing, and actually have had to do a lot more lately, but basically I oversee the daily operation of the racetrack."

Mark looked at Tom. "And you…?"

"I pony horses. That's all I do."

Everyone chuckled. "Tom has his hand in everything," Randy said. "Don't let him fool you."

"And, Dusty, you're liaison. You do…?"

"I actually *do* do everything," Dusty said, and they all laughed again. Everyone was in a good mood, a celebratory mood. The old-timers were home. They'd dodged the bullet with Family Services. Ben's surgery had gone well.

Mark looked at George.

"Me and Glenda run the farm," George said.

Glenda nodded. "I let him think he's boss."

Mark looked at Carol.

"I am the nanny to these little ones. Children," she said, "Show Mr. Simmons your happy face."

All three children tilted their heads to the side and cupped their hands to their chins.

More laughter!

Liz looked at Mark. "I'm Randy's mother and official doting Grandma."

Senior smiled. "I am Señor Iredell. I do whatever I can."

All eyes fell on Linda. "I am, let's see. I am Maria's mother. She has given me purpose, as has everyone else here at the table." She hesitated, not more tears, she thought. No. Tough it up. "I'm a clocker up at Erie, which is why Maria and I are going back there tomorrow. And…." Here came the tears. She waved her hand in front of her face. "And, I'm thinking next year that we'd like to come home for good."

Everyone clapped, the children included, and Linda wiped her eyes. "Move on," she said. "Gordon, you're next."

"All right," Gordon said, "But don't expect any tears and touching speeches from me. Holy crap!"

Linda smacked him and they all laughed again.

"I'm Gordon. I'm Wendy's youngest son. I'm studying marketing. This is my brother, Matthew. Tom's my dad. Ben's my Gramps."

Tom and Ben both sat back, everyone silent for a moment.

"Oh, Jesus," Gordon said. "Mom, now why are *you* crying?"

"No reason." She dabbed at her eyes with her napkin.

"Matthew," Ben said. "I believe it's your turn."

Matthew put his fork down. "Well, I'm Matthew, Wendy's oldest. I'm studying economics and computer science. I almost died last week and I'm still a little blind at the moment, just like Ben. And um, this is my home. This is my family. We're all family."

More tears. Even Mark got a little teary-eyed.

"What the hell?" Tom said, sniffling. "Somebody pass me the rolls. Enough of this already!" Everyone laughed.

"What can I say," Ben said, looking at the newcomer. "It's been quite a week."

"I see that," Mark said.

There was a knock on the door, and Junior entered. They all looked at him.

"Would you care to join us?" Liz asked.

"No. Thank you. I'm just wanting to thank you all for taking care of Lucy."

"Did you get a room?" Tom asked.

"No. Brickman didn't pay me. He says he'll pay me tomorrow."

"He's always stiffing somebody," Linda said.

"So where are you going to stay?" Wendy asked.

The boy waved and started out the door.

Tom threw his napkin down on the table and followed Junior out onto the porch, about to lit into him, but there was something about the defeated look in the boy's eyes that caused him to pause. "You need to grow up."

"I'm trying, Tom."

Wendy got up to intervene. Linda touched her arm. "I think I need to handle this. I can relate." She walked out onto the porch and closed the door behind her. "Tom, what the fuck is wrong with you? He is trying! Can't you see that?"

Tom stood looking at her.

"Vicky says Lucy can stay over there tonight," Junior said. "I'm going to sleep in the truck. If it's all right with you, I'll park over there by the main barn."

Tom shifted his weight and sighed.

Junior looked at Linda. "I hear you're leaving tomorrow. Have a good trip."

"Thank you."

Junior walked down the steps.

"Did you eat?" Tom asked him.

"Yeah, yeah I ate." Junior waved over his shoulder and then stopped and looked back. "Don't take this out on Lucy, Tom. Okay? None of this is her fault."

Tom stood looking at the young man.

"What am I supposed to do?" Junior said, hands out to his sides. "I'm nothing. I've got nothing. I've got this fucking truck," he said, kicking the bumper. "What the hell is wrong with me?"

Tom swallowed hard.

"You've said it yourself, Tom, how many times. I'm a loser. I'm a piece of shit. What kind of father is that little baby going to have? I have five dollars in my pocket. Five fucking dollars."

"And whose fault's that?" Tom said.

"Mine!" Junior said. "You think I don't know that?"

"Tom," Linda said. "Do you know why I'm leaving tomorrow?"

He looked at her.

"Because there are people who won't let me forget who I used to be." She shook her head. "Don't do this to Junior. He's just a kid."

Junior climbed into his truck, slammed the door shut and pulled over to the barn and turned off his lights.

"Leave him alone," Linda said. "Just leave him alone."

When she went back inside, Tom hesitated and followed. He walked to the kitchen sink and stared out into the night. T-Bone's Place was all lit up. He reached in the cupboard for a plate and in the drawer for some silverware.

"He's lying" he said. "He didn't eat. I know that boy." He walked to the table, started putting food on the plate, and passed it around. Everyone added something, even Mark. Liz got up to get a can of soda for the boy. Wendy grabbed a pillow and a blanket.

"Here." She tucked the pillow under his arm, blanket over his shoulder, and soda in his shirt pocket. "He won't want to come in, not tonight."

Tom nodded. "He's such a pain in the ass."

Wendy smiled. "Yes, I know."

Ben looked down the table at Mark Simmons, who sat taking this all in. "Welcome to the family," Ben said. "There's never a dull moment."

Chapter Twenty-One

Tom arrived at the track first, as usual, checked the horses' feed tubs, fed them their morning oats, made coffee, and sat down to look at the Overnight. Dawn arrived a few minutes later, poured a cup of coffee for both of them and handed him his.

"How was Ben this morning?"

"Cranky. He said the bandage on his eye bothered him all night. He can't wait to get it off."

"He's going to have to sleep with one on at night for at least a month I believe."

"Seriously?" Tom looked at her. "Does he know that?"

"I don't think so. I didn't get that far in the pamphlet yesterday before they took him back."

"Well, that'll make his day. What time's his appointment?"

"Eleven?"

"You taking him?"

"Yes."

"Well, then you'd better get your ass in gear."

Dawn laughed.

Tom finished reading the Overnight and looked at her. "It seems odd without the old man here. He'd better never die on us."

Dawn nodded and sipped her coffee. "So what do you think about this RJR Enterprises thing?"

"I don't know. That's some scary shit."

"It sure would explain a lot of things."

"That's for sure."

Dusty came in and poured himself a cup of coffee.

"What if the new vet is a spy?" Tom asked.

"How can that be? We called him," Dawn said.

"Oh yeah, that's right. I actually kinda like the guy, so that's a good thing."

"Well, someone's leaking information. I'd like to know how Family Services got involved in the first place. None of the old-timers had family that objected, not initially, no estates. That was the point of getting involved. They had nowhere else to go? Who would raise these questions?"

Tom and Dusty nodded.

"Not only that, how did Family Services find out about Mim? She hadn't been upstairs but for about a week and half now. "

Junior came walking down the shedrow.

"Shhh…" Tom said.

Dawn shook her head. "Yeah, right. Like it's Junior. I wish you'd get off his case."

"I have. I am. Watch me."

"Good morning, Junior," Tom said.

The boy looked at him. "What now?"

"Nothing. I'm just saying good morning. Help yourself to some coffee."

Junior turned around and walked out. Dawn chased after him and coaxed him back. "We only have one to track. Do you want to tack up now?"

"Well, look at you," Tom said to Dawn. "The old man ain't here one day and you're running things."

Dawn laughed. "Weren't you the one just telling me to get my butt in gear?"

"Oh? So now you're listening?"

Dusty laughed, took his coffee, and left. He only had three horses in the ReHome barn but he liked getting them out early. Randy was meeting him there at seven to look at one of the horse's knees.

~ * ~

Lucy walked down the stairs and when Vicky turned from cooking something on the stove, she smiled. "Can I help?"

Vicky had looked in on the girl earlier, sound asleep on the makeshift bed of piled-up pillows and blankets. "I don't know. How are you feeling?"

"Pretty good so far," Lucy said.

"All right. You finish the bacon and I'll start the eggs."

Mim was making the toast. "Morning," she said.

"Good morning."

The rest of the old-timers were all sitting in the living room, reading the paper, watching the news, reading the racing form. "Can you believe?" Miguel said. "They deliver right to front door, five o'clock. That Wendy, she think everything."

T-Bone's place had a huge dining room. The new table sat twelve. Lucy pushed Jeannie's wheelchair up to the table on the one end and met Clint on his way in and pushed him around to the other side. It's where they both ate dinner last night and seemed most comfortable. The others were still trying to decide where they would like to sit. She and Vicky brought the food in from the kitchen. By then they were all seated. Steven said grace.

"Thank you for our home. Thank you for this food. Amen."

Mim scowled. "You're certainly not Pastor Mitchell, but you'll do."

Everyone chuckled.

Lucy ate two pieces of toast and an egg and drank some ginger ale. The rest were all good eaters. Vicky was happy to notice that when she first signed on. She hadn't been looking forward to coaxing finicky appetites. She glanced around the table. For the most part, they were all healthy for their ages. Mim was the one she worried about most.

"This Sunday starts the football pre-season games," Steven said. "Would we be allowed a beer? I haven't had a beer in years."

Vicky smiled. "I'll check for contraindications with your medicine."

"Check mine too," Jeannie said. "I could go for an ice-cold Bud Light."

They all laughed. "Oh, I can see I'm going to have my hands full," Vicky said. "Lucy, you might have to stick around and help me keep them all in line."

"Okay. I like beer and football," Lucy said.

They laughed again.

Bill looked around the table. "There must be something in the water here. We're all just too happy."

"You all deserve to be happy," Vicky said. "If it's the water, let's all drink lots of it, and maybe an occasional ice-cold Bud Light too."

~ * ~

Ben decided to walk over and check in on the old-timers. Dawn wasn't due for an hour or so to come take him to his doctor's appointment. He wasn't used to having time on his hands and was restless. "I'll be glad when I get this patch off," he muttered, walking along. It was odd seeing out of only one eye. "I would have figured I needed to have two eyes to have depth perception." He didn't. He held his arm out in front of him.

"Hello to you too, Ben!" he heard Mim call out. He'd recognize her gravelly voice anywhere. He looked ahead and saw her sitting on the back porch overlooking the pastures.

"Ah, it's a shame about her, Meg," he said, walking along. She had been Meg's best friend. "Them damned cigarettes finally got her." They were all three the same age.

Mim stood with the support of her cane and walked to the porch railing. "Gorgeous morning, isn't it?"

"Yes, yes. Gorgeous," he said, "At least half of it anyway."

Mim laughed. "Come sit with me. I want to talk to you." Ben climbed the ramp and sat down on one of the chairs. Mim sat down next to him and motioned with her cane. "I want to know who all these horses are."

Ben looked out over the pastures. "Well, let me see," he said. "We'll start with the ones closest, I can see those. Those are the yearlings." There were four of them. "The gray one is out of All Together by Beau Born. The bay is out of...." He had to stop and think. "She's out of the Native Dancer mare. I never can remember her name. The two chestnuts belong to Breezeway. They're both by Beau, the Native Dancer filly too."

"They're nice, Ben. And nice how you're letting them grow up the way God intended and not cooped up in a stall most of the time."

"We keep them out as much as we can. A big storm or something we'll bring 'em in, but aside from that, we

~ 237 ~

leave them out. They'll be turning the two broodmares out soon. They come in at night. Oh, and then there's the old broodmare, Sissy. She's barren now and keeps an eye on the babies."

"Who are the three in this pasture here over the hill?"

"Oh, that's Linda's old ponies Biscuit and uh...Poncho, yes, Poncho. They belong to Dawn now and she and Wendy ride them all over. The kids have ridden them too. The little black horse is Bonnie Bee. Dusty just brought her home."

"He's such a softie. I can't believe he hasn't brought more of them home."

Ben nodded. "I keep on them all about that."

"Yeah, and you're tough too." Mim smiled.

Ben sat back. "Well, at least I try."

Mim motioned. "What about the weanlings?"

"Well, there's just the three of them." Ben had to admit he couldn't see that far. They were in the pasture just this side of the half-mile training track. "There's a chestnut filly out of that Native Dancer mare and a chestnut filly out of All Together. The dark one is out of a Seattle Slew mare, a granddaughter. That filly's going to be a nice horse. We just have the two, two-year-olds this year. The Seattle Slew mare slipped that year." He looked around, could make out the main barn. "They're usually kept in the biggest pasture just past the stallion barn."

"I see them," Mim said. "They're nice looking."

Ben nodded. "That All Together - Beau Born combination has proved to be a good one. The other colt's going to be nice too. He's got a bit of an attitude, but that's all right. That doesn't bother me."

"Me neither," Mim said. "Some of the nicest horses I've had would chase me out of the stall just for the hell of it."

They both laughed.

"Beau was like that on the track, except with Dawn. And All Together, geez, that filly was nuts come race day. I thought she was going to kill Dawn a couple of times. Now granted she wasn't mean, she just got wound up."

Mim looked at him. "You think the world of that girl, don't you?"

He nodded. "Meg would have loved her too. She's the daughter we never had."

They both sat looking out at the horses for a moment. "Let's see. Did I leave out anybody?"

"Well, I'd know that one anywhere," Mim said, motioning again with her cane. A large chestnut was being turned out into a pasture with a bay. Beau bellowed his long and loud stud-horse whinny. "And it is Beau Born in complete command...." Mim sang.

"Yep, we knew from the day he was born. You know that feeling you get, Mim?"

She nodded. "It's a shame Meg didn't get to see him run." Beau was bucking and playing and jogging down the fence line, calling to the mares.

Ben smiled. "She watches him."

Mim patted his hand. "And I'll watch them too. That's why I want to get to know them. I'll want to watch over all of them."

~ * ~

Randy and Mark parked outside the barn at Shifting Gears. There were two other cars there. One Randy didn't recognize. "There's a high school senior that has been shadowing here. I think that's probably her car. She can be rather rude."

Mark looked at him.

"Why am I telling you this? Because she's also some kind of animal communicator. She can sense what the horses are feeling and even thinking." He shared the story about Hillary knowing the Foregone gelding's bloodline.

~ 239 ~

"You're kidding."

"Nope," Randy said, getting out of the truck. "The main reason we're stopping is I want you to meet Veronica and Karen."

The women were not expecting Randy and were pleasantly surprised to see him. "Hello! Who's this?" Karen asked.

When introduced, Veronica shook Mark's hand. "Randy, you're not quitting on us are you?"

"No. I just want you to get to know each other in the event Mark decides to stay and I decide whether or not I want him to stay. So far, so good."

They all laughed.

"So who's here?" Randy asked.

"Hillary. Come see what's she's done."

Randy could only imagine. At least they sounded happy about it, even Veronica, the habitual worrier that constantly fretted over the "what if's" of any given situation.

"Look!"

The young girl had bed the horse's stall with dirt.

Randy stared. Mark stared. It must have taken her days. Hillary glanced at them. She had on soft mittens and was massaging the horse's neck and side. "He likes this," she said.

"I see that," Randy said. The horse had put on some weight and appeared steadier on his feet. He even looked bright-eyed. "What's with the dirt?"

"It's natural," Karen said. "He has better footing on it. Hillary said he was afraid to move before."

"I see," Randy said, repeating himself for lack of anything better to say.

"He's eating. He's drinking," Veronica said. "Who'd have ever guessed?"

Hillary looked at them. "He actually would have preferred being outside. But since that can't be until he starts doing better, I brought the outdoors to him."

"It's not just the footing; it's the earth," Karen said, obviously repeating something Hillary had said.

Veronica nodded. "It's true."

"I wish I could bring him the sun," Hillary said.

Randy just stood there, imagining holes over the stall in the barn roof tomorrow. "Okay. Well, since everything's good here, I think we're going to head on out now. Keep up the uh…the good work."

Hillary glanced over her shoulder, still massaging the horse. "He's glad he's not getting a shot today."

Randy looked at her and then looked at the horse. The horse let out a sigh.

"Tell Dawn I said hi," Hillary said.

Randy nodded. "Sure thing." Mark followed him out. The two exchanged glances in the truck. "Don't ask me," Randy said.

"Me neither."

They rode in silence. "You know," Mark said, after a while. "Dirt actually has healing properties, so maybe…."

Randy put on his blinker and pulled into the driveway of his Veterinary Office. "The flatness of the stall makes sense, a little I guess, sturdier footing. When you think about how we've taken the horses out of their natural environment, particularly racehorses and show horses, maybe horses that are healing need that natural environment."

Mark agreed. "I guess it might go back to why do horses eat dirt?"

"He's probably eating some."

"Well," Mark paused. "Dirt *is* a living, dynamic ecosystem of organic matter; a veritable universe of microbes, bacteria, fungi, other tiny organisms, minerals, water, and plant roots."

Randy marveled at him. "Is that right off the top of your head? Damn, you're good! What did you do, memorize the textbooks?"

Mark raised his cellphone. "No. Actually I just Googled it."

Randy laughed. "Come on, you get to meet our one and only employee."

Betty, a woman in her mid-fifties looked up from her desk when they walked in. She smiled. "So you must be Mark."

"Morning."

She handed Randy several messages. He sorted through them and took out his phone. "This one first." Betty reached for them and sorted them back to the way she had them initially.

"I hate talking to this man," Randy said. "He doesn't want me to come out. He just wants to talk my ear off." He handed the message to Mark. "Here, you call him."

Mark read the message. "Horse acting strange for days now, eating good, peeing and pooping good." He looked at Betty. "Huh?"

"That's what the man said."

"Okay," Mark sat down in the waiting room. "Hold all my calls," he said.

Betty and Randy laughed.

While Randy made several trips back and forth to his truck loading up supplies, Mark talked to the man. Randy went to the men's room, came back out, and Mark was still talking to the man. Randy motioned to his watch.

"So," Mark said. "What time would you like me to stop by today?" When he paused to listen, Randy and Betty exchanged knowing glances.

"Okay," Mark said. "Four o'clock it is." He looked at Betty. She shrugged and then nodded. "Let me write down your address. Oh, we have it? All right, I'll see you then."

"Sold!" Randy said. "He's all yours!"

Mark gave Betty his cellphone number in case she needed to get ahold of him and he and Randy headed back to the racetrack. "So basically," Mark said. "You don't do any small animal and no clinic exams whatsoever."

Randy nodded. "I couldn't keep up. We did everything at first, but basically Doc Jake's practice was all large animal. I sold that building when it became obvious I was never there and we set up where we're at. Betty does all the billing and orders supplies, makes appointments. She's part-time."

"So it's all just mainly Thoroughbreds?"

"No, I do other breeds, but Thoroughbreds are the bulk of it."

Mark was quiet for a while. "So, uh, when do you want me to start?"

Randy looked at him. "I don't know. How about yesterday?"

"Works for me." The two men shook hands. "Thank you."

Chapter Twenty-Two

Ben sat with Dawn in the doctor's office and waited and waited and waited. "Five more minutes, I'm taking this patch off myself and we're leaving," Ben said. "What's the point of making appointments?" He opened the door and looked up and down the hall. "Excuse me. Is anybody home?"

Dawn smiled. She had to admit she was getting a little tired of waiting herself. At least she could read a magazine. "Maybe they had an emergency," she suggested, flipping pages.

"Maybe they forgot we're here," Ben said.

"I'll go check," Dawn said.

There was no one at the desk. She stood listening, couldn't hear anyone anywhere. Finally a nurse came out from a closed door, sipping a cola. "Can I help you?"

"Yes. I'm with Mr. Miller. We've been waiting to see the doctor."

"Oh my!" the woman said. "The doctor has gone."

"Well, then get him back," Dawn said.

"Um...." The woman turned around, half circle, then full circle. "I'm so sorry. This has never happened before."

Dawn sighed. "Where *is* the doctor?"

"Probably in his office or at lunch I would think."

"Okay," Dawn said. "Surely you have an emergency number for him. I suggest you contact him and we'll either go to his office or he can just come back here."

The woman looked up the doctor's office number, dialed the phone, and got the answering machine. "I'm sorry. They're closed until one."

"Give me the address," Dawn said.

The woman wrote it down, talking fast. "I'm sure they're going to have appointments, so I'm sorry, but it might be a wait."

"No, I don't think so," Dawn said, just as calm as could be. "I'm going to count on you to make sure we're the first one the doctor sees. I'm sure you understand the situation. Thank you." She walked down the hall, gave Ben a quick version of the story, and off they went.

"This is just how old people get treated," Ben said. "Nobody pays attention to us."

"What? What were you saying? Is there someone talking to me?"

"Very funny," he said.

"I don't think this has anything to do with age, Ben."

"Fine. But when you look at how the old-timers were being treated."

"Not anymore," she said.

Ben nodded. "That doctor better be there."

He was. He was expecting them and was entirely apologetic. "I have no idea how that happened. I am so sorry."

"Yes, but you knew I had an appointment this morning," Ben said. "You yourself told me to make it. Didn't you notice I wasn't there? I just had my surgery yesterday. Shouldn't that have concerned you?"

The doctor removed the bandage on Ben's eye. "I did so many procedures yesterday, Mr. Miller, I can't even tell you how many."

"See," Ben said to Dawn. "I'll bet they were all old people too."

"Well, actually," the doctor said, examining Ben's eye. "They probably were. It is the nature of the beast, cataracts. Everything looks good. You're going to have to keep up with the drops in your eyes and you'll need to wear a patch at night until I see you again." He glanced at Dawn. "Is the other eye scheduled?"

Dawn looked at Ben, deciding Ben should be the one to answer that. He had a point. Old people do get treated differently. "In a month," Ben said. "That's if I decide to keep it."

~ * ~

Dusty paid a visit to the Brickman barn, hoping to catch him there and talk to him about paying his bills. It was not uncommon for a trainer to fall short on cash now and then, some more often than others, but this particular trainer had been doing this for far too long. The majority of exercise riders and pony boys and girls got paid cash for their work and lived week to week if not day by day. They needed to be paid on time.

The man was cleaning tack. "Afternoon," Dusty said.

Brickman looked up. "It's a nice day, that's for sure."

Dusty sat down on a bench across from him and stretched out his legs.

"How's Ben doing? I hear he had surgery on his eyes. Is he okay?"

Dusty nodded. "Cataract. One now, one later. It went well. Knowing him, he'll be back here tomorrow."

"He's a tough old man," Brickman said.

Dusty paused. "How's things going?"

"All right. I got one in tomorrow. He's got a good shot."

"Good, good. Buster Bay in the seventh?"

The man nodded, surprised Dusty knew.

"There's not much I don't know," Dusty said, reading his expression. "Not when it comes to this racetrack." He looked around. "We've come a long way, haven't we? It wasn't that many years ago, we were falling apart. I thought we were all doomed."

The barns were in good repair now, painted every year. They had good lighting. The roads and wash racks were kept clean and with rubber mats for safe footing. There were ice machines at every other barn, muck bins out of the way and dumped daily, awards and recognition for the best-kept barns. It was a backside to be proud of.

"Ben's done well by us," Brickman said.

"I know. And we all have to do our part too."

"Meaning...?"

"I don't know. Keeping up our share of the bargain. We had to weed out quite a few at the beginning. They weren't paying their bills. They were stiffing their exercise boys and ponies. Some we helped out; some we showed the door."

Brickman glanced at him and continued cleaning his tack.

"Let me ask you something," Dusty said. "What do you think about Hannity taking Jackson's horse?"

The man hesitated. "Claiming's claiming. You win some, you lose some."

Dusty nodded. "I lost my fair share." He stood and glanced around. "You've got, what, five head now?"

Brickman nodded.

"I'm glad you're doing well and taking care of business."

"Thank you," the man said.

"Well, I think I'm going to rattle Hannity's cage a little. That's just not sitting well with me. He had the right to take that horse according to the rules of racing. But I think there's an ever deeper set of rules with some things. No, it's just not sitting good with me." He nodded and walked down the shedrow. "Good luck tomorrow."

Dusty walked through six more barns to get to Hannity's. The man wasn't there but his groom was, new to the track this year. Dusty stopped in front of Jackson's horse's stall. He wasn't done up today but looked like he'd just had his knees painted. "How's he doing?"

The man shrugged. "No speak Engless."

"That's all right," Dusty said. "I speak rather good Spanish." He started to ask the question again, but the man held up his hand.

"He sore."

"Thank you." Dusty patted the horse on the neck. "Tell Hannity I was by."

The groom nodded.

Dusty walked on to the next barn, and the one after that, and then walked up to the HBPA office. So much had been going on lately, he'd all but forgotten about the Annual Banquet this Saturday. Irene, the head volunteer opened the office religiously Monday through Friday from 2:00 – 5:00 in the afternoon.

"How's everything?"

"Well, I'd wish we had more signed up by now."

"How many do you have?"

"Oh." She reached for a chart. "Fifty-three."

"Ouch," Dusty said.

"Twenty bucks is cheap, but twenty bucks a head is still twenty bucks a head."

Dusty chuckled. "Maybe it's the price on their head part that's keeping them away."

Irene laughed. "Well, we're still going to have it either way, a bunch or a little."

"Maybe we need a theme."

"We tried that. It didn't work. Remember?"

Dusty paused. "Oh, yeah. Mardi Gras. That was a bust." He scratched his head and stared off. "How about a 'Come as You Are'?"

"Are you kidding me?" Irene said. "Do you have any idea how people might show up?"

"Well, if it helps sales...."

"No," Irene said, and then, "Let me think about it."

"I can spread the word for you. Just give me the nod."

Irene hesitated. "All right. What do we have to lose?"

"Good. I might as well get started now." He glanced back from the door. "You're not planning on wearing that, are you?"

She threw a pen at him and laughed. "I like this mumu! It's comfortable. Get outta here!"

"Thank you." Dusty picked up the pen and put it in his pocket. From there he walked over to the Secretary's office, picked up registration papers for the two horses shipping out of the Rehab and ReHome barn today and stopped to talk to Wendy for a few minutes.

"Have you heard from Linda?"

"Yes, they arrived safe and sound."

"What about Ben?"

"Oh, you won't believe. They're just leaving the doctor's now. He's fine, but now he's saying he's not having the other eye done. He says he's going to stage a protest on the front steps of the hospital in support of old people everywhere. He says he's tired of just being a number and he's not going to stand for it anymore."

Dusty smiled.

"Where are they going?" Wendy asked, motioning to the registration papers.

"Well, this one," Dusty said, "is going to be a hunter-jumper prospect. And actually the new owner is going to donate money to the program."

"That's good."

"The other one is going to be a pasture buddy for one of Randy's warmblood customers. Randy says he's going to have the 'Life of Riley.'"

"What do you think of the other vet? That Mark guy?"

"He seems nice. He sure got indoctrinated yesterday between Randy running him ragged and then dinner last night at the farm. Where's Joe?"

"He left right after entries. Between you and me, I am not missing him. He's been like a cat on a hot tin roof lately."

~ * ~

Ben and Dawn stopped for lunch at a fast food place. "Let's just eat in the car," Ben said, still fuming. "Do you know what I need?"

"Yes, you need to calm down," Dawn said. "Eat."

"Oh geez, I'm being told when to eat now."

Dawn smiled.

"Seriously," Ben said. "I need a pair of sneakers."

"Sneakers? You mean tennis shoes?"

"Yes. I need a pair of tennis shoes."

Dawn looked at him. At least he was eating and thinking of something else. "Have you ever owned a pair of sneakers?"

"When I was a kid, yes."

"Okay." Dawn slurped her chocolate shake. "Let's see. There's a sports store just down the road." As soon as they finished eating, off they went.

The young woman salesperson was quite amused by Ben. "Seriously, you've never owned a pair of tennis shoes?"

"No. I never played tennis either."

Dawn laughed, fighting the urge to move this along.

"What size shoe do you wear?"

"Ten and a half, wide."

The woman came back with several pairs. "These are all-purpose. These are for jogging. These are for running. These are for walking."

Ben motioned to the walking ones, white, with bright red, blue, and purple stripes. "Do they come in brown? Those look like something a Martian would wear."

"A Martian?"

Ben tried the shoes on and laced them up. He walked down the aisle, looked in the mirror, and walked back. "Black maybe?"

"No. Those are in case you walk at night. You'll glow."

Ben stared at his feet. "Really?"

"Really."

"How much are they?"

"$89 plus tax."

"What? They'd better glow then. Eighty-nine dollars? For sneakers?"

The young woman hesitated. "Do you still want them?"

"I guess." He looked at Dawn. "If they don't glow, I'm bringing them back."

"Just make sure you save your receipt," the young woman started to say.

"He's kidding," Dawn said.

Ben looked at her. "No, I'm not."

"You'll be wearing them home?"

"Yes." Ben put his old shoes in the box, tucked it under his arm, and rocked back and forth on his new walking sneakers. "Where do I pay?"

~ * ~

Tom was at the barn picking out stalls when Randy came by with Mark to change the bandage on B-Bo's injured leg. He leaned over their shoulders to take a look. "Holy shit, Batman!"

"Actually it's a little better today," Randy said.

"I'm glad I didn't look at it yesterday then."

While the two veterinarians dressed the wound, Tom finished picking stalls and then topped off all the water buckets. He had the feed already mixed. As soon as Randy finished up, he'd give the horses their dinner. Bo-T bucked and squealed in his stall, not one to wait.

"When's he going home?" Randy asked, ducking out of Bo-T's way as he walked past his stall. "Watch out," he said. Mark ducked.

"Tomorrow."

"I might send B-Bo home too, maybe for a week or ten days. We can turn him out in the paddock and keep him moving that way. Where's dinner tonight?"

"Your house. Promptly at seven."

"We'll be there. We're on a roll."

"Dr. Iredell to barn eleven," the stable guard announced. "Dr. Iredell to barn eleven."

"I'll see you at the farm," Randy said, and got into his truck.

"Which house is his?" Mark asked Tom.

"The big colonial in the back. Where's your truck?"

Mark motioned that it was parked up by the stable gate. "How far are we from Brigadoon Road?"

Tom looked at him and smiled. "Buffert's place?"

"Yes."

"Oh, aren't you gonna have fun. It's not far, about twenty-five minutes."

Mark pulled into Brigadoon Farm ten minutes early and parked by the main entrance of the rather grandiose two-story, ten-stall barn, white with hunter-green trim and shutters. It looked more like a house, a mansion. Mark stood admiring it for a moment and walked inside. The aisle way between the stalls was brick-paved laid in a herringbone pattern. The lighting was a row of chandeliers, and judging from their bright glow, LED bulbs.

A man dressed in English riding attire walked down the aisle to greet him. "Hello, you must be Dr. Simmons.

Mark shook the man's gloved hand. "Nice to meet you, Mr. Buffert."

"Please, just call me Buffert. Everyone does."

"All right," Mark said. The name "Buffert" didn't seem to fit the man. He looked more like a Rockefeller or a Kennedy, chiseled profile and all. "Well, where is the horse in question?"

"Follow me."

As Mark walked along, he couldn't help but notice the empty stalls; all bed two feet deep in wood shavings, the stall walls lined in thick rubber sheeting. "The horse in question" was in the last stall and not exactly what Mark had expected, given the phone conversation with the man and the appearance of this barn. It was a big non-descriptlooking bay gelding standing about 16 hands, rubbed shiny clean, short mane, squared-off tail, no forelock, and feet that looked as if they were at least six inches in height. His feet gave him the appearance of being on his tip-toes.

"See," Buffert said, standing with his arms crossed and supporting his chin. "He just looks funny."

"Has he ever had trouble with his feet?" Mark asked.

Buffert stared and was still suffering shock from that question when Mark added another. "Has he always been shod that way?"

"Precisely what do you mean? Besides, what would his feet have to do with him just looking funny?"

Mark studied the horse and without realizing it, had taken on the exact same posture of Buffert. Arms crossed and supporting his chin. "And you say he's sound?"

"Oh yes!"

"And eating good and uh 'peeing and pooping'?" He remembered the note.

"Yes. That's what's so puzzling."

Mark nodded. "Can you get him out of the stall and let me see him walk."

"Sure." Buffert took the horse's halter and lead-shank off a brass hook hung outside the stall and slid the horse's door open. The gelding stepped forward obediently and lowered his head. Buffert gave the horse a stiff pat on the neck. Mark couldn't determine if that was affection or a command. Buffert walked the horse out into the aisle way. Mark listened to the sound of the horse's hooves clunking on the herringbone brick. Each sounded the same. He watched the way the horse put each foot down. Watched the way his shoulder lifted and relaxed, lifted and relaxed. He studied his stifles, his hocks.

"Can we go outside and jog him?" When Buffert looked hesitant, Mark glanced over his shoulder, confused. "Are there other horses out back?"

"Well, no. He's the only horse here, but...it's....uh, can I just jog him in here?"

"No," Mark said. He pictured Randy hiding somewhere, laughing, and saying I warned you. "I need to see him outside, uh, on the uh, the earth."

"Oh, okay," Buffert said. "Watch out."

Mark stepped back and followed them. The horse stopped just outside the barn and gazed out at the lush green pastures. Mark stood marveling as well. They looked as if they'd just been mowed. It was a beautiful sight, all fenced in white. Out of the corner of his eye, he noticed the horse starting to quiver.

"I'd better take him back in," Buffert said. "He's not used to being out this time of day. Maybe you can come back in the morning."

"Why don't you just turn him out?" Mark suggested.

Surprisingly, Buffert handed him the horse's lead-shank. "I'll get the gate."

Mark followed, leading the horse, who by now resembled a 747 jet revving up for takeoff. "Easy now," Mark said. "Easy now."

"Oh dear, "Buffert said. "This is why I don't put him out this time of day." He unlatched the gate, pushed it open hard and hurried over to grab it from the outside and keep it from closing on the horse.

Mark instinctively grabbed hold of the horse's ear. "Easy now, easy, easy...." He released the horse's lead shank, let go of the horse's ear and for a split second the horse just stood there. Then like an explosion, he turned and took off running. And he ran, and he ran, and he ran.

"How long has it been since he was turned out?" Somewhere around this point, Mark forgot he was a vet and reverted to being just a horseman. Every time the horse came charging up to the gate he just stood enjoying the show.

"I try to get him out a couple of times a week."

"Why not every day? Work?"

"Oh no, I'm retired."

The man didn't appear to be fifty years old. Mark looked at him and then stepped back when the horse made another charge toward the fence and turned at the last minute. It was then Mark noticed something odd about the horse. "Something funny."

"How often do you ride him?"

"Oh, I don't. Not anymore."

Yet, the man was dressed to ride. Mark stood tugging at his ear, thinking, and when the horse came up to the fence the next time, he clapped his hands. The horse took off running again. "He hasn't bucked once. He hasn't rolled either."

"Oh, he never bucks. He's not allowed."

"Never?"

"Never."

"What about rolling?"

"Nope. He's a real clean horse. He was trained well."

"Okay…." Mark pictured Tom hiding somewhere nearby now and laughing. "And he's the only horse here?'

"Yes. I don't want any other horses. I'll just fall in love with them and when Trojan goes…."

"Trojan?"

Trojan ran up to the fence and took off again. The horse hadn't grazed yet either. He hadn't even sniffed the grass. "Well," Mark said. "I think we need to change that." Again, as a horseman and not necessarily a veterinarian, Mark climbed the fence and stood on the inside, lead-shank in hand.

"What are you going to do?" Buffert said.

The horse trotted right up to Mark, all obedient like, and stood blowing. "Good boy, good boy," Mark said. He stroked the horse gently on the neck, snapped the lead shank on him and led him to a real lush spot and proceeded to drop him down gently – horse whisperer style.

Buffert gasped. "Wh...! What!"

"He's all right," Mark said, when the horse just lay there. "He's all right. He's just in uncharted territory."

"Get up," Buffert gasped.

"Seriously," Mark said, pointing a finger at the man. "Shhhh...." He released the lead shank from the horse's halter and when the horse continued to just lay there, took the horse's halter off. "It's okay," he said. "It's okay."

When the horse laid his head down and started moving it back and forth against the grass, Mark stepped away. The horse moved its legs back and forth, eyes closed, and looked like it was sleepwalking, walking and walking. Then it rolled onto its back, up and over, and then back up and over again.

Mark got to the fence just in time. When the horse rose, he shook, bucked, and bucked and bucked and bucked. Mark climbed the fence and sat on the top rail, watching and smiling. The horse reared, pawed the air, circled, and then went down and rolled again.

"It's a miracle," Mark said, jokingly.

"I know," Buffert uttered breathlessly.

Another roll, another fine show of bucking and rearing, and the horse finally put his head down and started nosing the grass and ultimately took to grazing.

"He's been out all along on the pasture, right?" Mark asked.

Buffert nodded.

The horse was a little sweaty, but not overly. "He'll be okay," Mark said.

"What was wrong with him?"

Mark's chosen profession came to the forefront as he looked at the man. "Uh…" He hesitated. "I think he might have had a little kink in his back. You'll want to make sure you get him out every day from now on. If you don't see him rolling and bucking, call me. What's your e-mail address?"

Buffert rattled it off. Mark recorded it on his cellphone. "I'm going to send you some pictures of the correct angle of a horse's foot. Your blacksmith has him standing up way too straight and way too long. That might have started this whole thing. Have him angle them gradually."

"But his feet look so pretty."

"Pretty is as pretty does," Mark said, imitating Forrest Gump's voice. "What would you rather have, pretty feet or happy feet?" He pulled up a website on his phone and showed Buffert a photo of a healthy-shaped horse's hoof. "When we get him right, we'll pull the shoes all together. For what you're doing with him and the barn setup, he should be barefoot. You also might want to get him a goat or a companion horse. You're wasting a lot of really nice grass by mowing all the time."

Buffert looked at him. "I'll think about it. Uh, what do I owe you?"

"I have no idea," Mark said. "Betty'll send you a bill."

Chapter Twenty-Three

When Ben and Dawn approached T-Bone's Place, most of the new residents were sitting out on the front porch, so Ben had Dawn drop him off. "I'll walk the rest of the way," he said, closing the door and waving.

His new shoes were a hit. "Whoo whoo!" Miguel said, whistling. "You uptown now, Mr. B!"

Ben laughed. "No, but this way I figure if I start walking in my sleep you'll all see me coming. They glow!"

"No kidding?" Clint said, peering at them with curiosity.

"Nope. I'm going to test them out tonight." Ben sat down on one of the empty chairs and looked around. "Oh geez, here come the dogs. Nobody move."

They all laughed. They'd been visited by the pack several times already today. The five yellow Labrador Retrievers and one Black Standard Poodle bounded up the steps and milled all around them.

"What's this one's name?" Mim asked, of the tail-wagging wiggle-worm at her side.

"Let's see." Ben paused. "That one there's easy, that's Gimpy. He's got a slight limp. All these Labs are from the same litter. Randy saved them and brought them all home one day. We had baby bottles and puppy shit everywhere."

The old-timers laughed.

"Rotty's the poodle. He's pretty much Wendy's. He took a liking to her. We all did."

Everyone agreed.

"That's Sloopy and that one's Dawber. He's the biggest. That's Piccolo and the smallest one there is Runt." Once the dogs all got petted and fussed over, they took off. "Don't feed them snacks or you'll never get rid of them," Ben advised.

Steven nodded, then looked around and sighed. "Is this Iowa, Ben?" he asked, a variation of a line in one of his favorite movies, "*Field of Dreams*."

It happened to be one of Ben's favorite movies too. "No, Steven, this is heaven," he replied in kind.

Lucy and Vicky walked outside after doing lunch dishes and changing the beds. Lucy smiled a shy smile. "Thank you, Ben."

He nodded. "Well, I'd best get going. These shoes are made for walking."

"Oh my," Vicky said, pretending she needed to shade her eyes. "How did your appointment go?"

"Good," Ben said, flipping his sunglasses up to show her. "A patch at night for a while and I'm good to go."

"When's the next one going to be done?"

"Never," Ben said.

"Ben," Vicky scolded. "You know you can't put it off."

"I know." He gripped the railing as he started down the ramp. "I know."

"Hold up a second. I'll walk along with you." Ben waited for her. "I could use the exercise." When they were well out of hearing distance, she told him, "They're all so happy. I can't thank you enough for what you've done for them, and for me, and for Lucy."

"What's the plan with her?" Ben asked.

"That's basically what I wanted to talk to you about. Is there any way we could just let her stay here with us for a while, just until she gets through all the morning sickness? She's no trouble. In fact, she's actually a lot of help."

"Well, let me run it by the "Board," Ben said, smiling.

"She's a hard worker, tell them. She wants to earn her keep."

"I'll let them know."

"They also want to know if they're allowed an occasional beer or glass of wine?"

"Gosh, I don't know. Why not? I'll ask them about that too."

"Thank you." Vicky headed back toward T-Bone's Place. "Oh, I almost forgot. Mim got a phone call from someone at Family Services today. She told them she was senile and to bugger off."

Ben chuckled. "Tell her it comes in handy to be crazy sometimes. Tell her thank you." Mim was the sharpest of all of them, Ben included. She could remember every detail from her whole life and most everyone else's too.

Ben got a standing ovation when he walked into Dawn and Randy's house. "Enough, enough," he said. "You'd think these were magic slippers or something."

"Well, they are," Tom said. "Look at you walking all over the damn place."

Ben waved them off and glanced back at T-Bone's Place. "Wonder how far a walk that actually is?" It was one thing to walk the distance from his farmhouse, but all the way back here to Dawn and Randy's was at least twice as far, and further yet if dinner should happen to be at Liz and Senior's.

"I'd say about three quarters of a mile at least," Randy said.

Mark took out his cellphone, asked for the addresses and punched in the numbers. "Point seven two miles."

"I wonder what the track record is?" George asked.

They all laughed.

"Now don't be trying to time yourself, old man," Tom said. "The world ain't ready for the sight of you running up and down the road in jogging shorts!"

Ben laughed. They all did and sat down at the dinner table. Matthew motioned to Mark to hand him his cellphone. "Sweet," he said. It was the latest version of a Stylus Smartphone. When Tom promptly took it from him and handed it back to Mark, Mathew laughed.

This evening's dinner was an abundant roast pork, mashed potatoes and gravy, with hot rolls affair. No salad.

Never any salad when this menu was served. Everyone dove right into the main course. Liz had made a chocolate-chocolate cake for dessert with peanut butter ice cream.

The children had already eaten and were watching a dinosaur cartoon in the living room. "Wait! Look!" D.R. said, "He's going to eat the whole tree."

"I know!" Maeve said. "Stop telling me!"

The adults laughed.

"So how'd it go at Buffert's today?" Tom asked Mark.

Randy smiled. He'd already heard the story. "It went okay," Mark said. "After I got the horse to roll in the healing powers of the earth, it was clear sailing."

Tom laughed. He'd heard the Hillary-earth-story, but listened to both accounts again as Randy and Mark told everyone else.

"Well, you know," Senior said. "Being a pig farmer, I can attest to the joy a pig experiences wallowing in the mud. They squeal with delight!"

"We raised pigs once, my ex-wife and I," Mark said.

"Oh?" Senior looked at him. "What kind?"

"Whiteshires."

"You're kidding?" Senior reached over and shook his hand. "Hot damn! Raised them all my life."

"Yes," Liz said. "Four-thousand three-hundred and twenty-two of them."

"Raised them right too," Senior said, and let it go at that. Dawn never liked to hear about the butchering part, even with it being done at home and humanely. "I had a pet sow once. She hated Liz."

"She did," Liz said. "She used to chase me all over the place squealing, Liz Liz! Liz Liz!"

The children echoed her from the living room in little piggy voices. "Liz Liz! Liz Liz!"

Randy passed the mashed potatoes to George. "If I recall, Mom, when her time came, you called me home and you held her and cried."

"I didn't say I didn't like her. I said she didn't like me."

"Point taken," Randy said. "And then dad and I had to bury her."

"She was old," Senior said, pragmatically. "Nine, ten. She wouldn't have been good for food anyway."

Liz looked at him.

"Getting back to the dirt," Dawn said. "I think there's something to that. People go for mud facials, mud body treatments."

"Well, in Malaysia..." Mark said.

"Give me that damned phone! I'm on to you now," Randy said.

Everyone laughed.

Randy proceeded to read some of the article highlights out loud. "Detoxification, found in antacids, kaolin, essentially clay, isolated from the earth mass, slippery, stays in your mouth…."

"Well, if that doesn't sound lovely." Dawn took the phone from him and passed it back to Mark. Matthew intercepted it and the way he studied it, moving it all around to bypass his blind spots, caught his mother's attention.

Matthew passed it on to Mark. "How much did it cost?"

"About four hundred. I got it on a payment plan." Mark glanced around the table, around the room. Randy and Dawn's house was larger than he'd expected. Driving up to it this evening, he'd have to admit it was rather imposing. It looked like the Big House of a country estate. Thankfully, inside, though large, the house had a warm feel to it, a down-home feel. Even so, he couldn't help but wonder where all the money came from.

Glenda passed the rolls. "When I visited the old-timers today, they asked about you Señor."

Senior smiled. "I like that. Beats all the confusion all the time."

"Let's see a show of hands," Randy said. "Señor?"

"Señor!"

When the bowl came back around, Glenda buttered a roll for herself.

"Speaking of the old-timers," Ben said.

It was not Mark's imagination that everyone sat up a little straighter. They knew by Ben's tone that the conversation was about to turn serious. "It's about Lucy. They'd like her to stay there for a while if that's all right with everyone."

Tom sat back. If it were just Lucy….

"That would be three people sharing a bathroom upstairs," Dawn said.

"What do you mean, three?" Tom asked.

Dawn ignored that.

"Is there a way to install another bathroom up there?" Dawn asked.

Mark looked at her, knowing now who was most accustomed to having money and fine things.

"If they take care of Lucy then Junior's off the hook," Tom said.

Wendy shook her head. "I don't agree."

"It's not a matter of you and me agreeing. It's Junior we're talking about."

"Either way," Ben said. "I told Vicky I'd let her know."

"They'll need bedroom furniture," Wendy said.

"And linens," Liz added. "Towels."

Tom sighed. It was obvious he was alone in his thinking. They all knew the boy. They saw his strengths and his faults. They knew his work ethic, which aside from being notoriously late, was fairly hard to beat. Tom thought of the boy as a good hand with horses. They all saw the boy as family. He lowered his eyes. Admittedly, deep down, he too saw the boy as family.

"They'll need a crib."

"So this is long term?" Tom asked.

Dawn looked at him. "I think they need to know they have a home. They might decide they want to move on someday, but until they get on their feet…."

When Tom nodded, everyone looked at him, including Mark. He knew very little about this particular situation but was starting to put two and two together.

"Mim has some furniture in storage at the racetrack," Dusty said. "I'll talk to her. Maybe we can just bring it here."

"All right," Tom said. "We'll have room in the van when we bring Bo-T and B-Bo home tomorrow." Without anyone asking for a vote, there was a unanimous show of hands.

"Done," Ben said. He thought about the day Mim received her diagnosis. Her "death sentence" as she'd called it. He recalled the spirit in which she had taken care of business. She dispersed her horses, making sure they went to trainers who had good track records. She listed her condo with a realtor she instructed not to quibble over price. She bought a hospital bed and had it delivered upstairs at the racetrack. Then without even looking back, she dusted off her hands and walked stoically down her shedrow with the help of her cane, and climbed onto her golf cart for a final ride to the grandstand.

"What do you think about the plumbing, Señor?" George asked.

"Well, there's plumbing already up there. I don't know about a second toilet. I guess we could put one in back-to-back somehow."

"Oh, and they want to know if they're allowed to have a beer now and then?"

"Why not?" Randy replied.

"Well, I think they think they need permission from someone."

"Certainly not something I want to comment on," Tom said. "I think it's up to them."

They all just sat there a moment. It was an odd question, given that the old-timers were all adults who had spent their entire adult lives making their own decisions, and yet....

"Or Vicky," Liz said. "She knows their health situations better than any of us. And their medications. Aren't Miguel and Mim diabetics?"

Ben nodded. "I think so. All right, I'll tell Vicky it's up to her discretion." He sat back out of the way when Glenda started stacking plates and reached for his. Over dessert, Dawn brought up the subject of the RJR Enterprises situation at the racetrack. It was the first Mark had heard of it.

"Wait a minute," Randy said. "Get a sharp knife. Mark needs to drip a little blood and be sworn into the covenant of secrecy first."

"What?" Mark said.

"Look it up," Randy teased.

Dusty explained. "What is said in these discussions at the table or in the barns, anywhere here, when it's just all of us, it stays between all of us."

"Got it," Mark said. "Though all of you are actually the only people I know."

"Come on, Mark. You know Buffert," Tom said. "Hut, hut. Tow the line! Hut!"

They all laughed.

"Seriously," Ben said. "this has to stay between us." Everyone looked at him. "We suspect someone might be trying to put us out of business and we've come too far to fail now. You name it and we've done it to try and get the crowds back. Wendy and Richard have done a fine job. Dawn writes the articles to counter the attacks, and now we have this…." He waved his hand. "I don't want to talk about it. It just aggravates me."

"What's going on now?" Carol asked.

"Well, it's seems like a big casino conglomerate from Las Vegas is trying to undermine us," Dawn said.

"How?"

"By finding us at fault in something, anything," Dusty replied.

"I suspect they're behind the *Morning Banter* articles," Dawn said.

"I think they're the cause of all of the Family Services inquiries," Wendy said. "I stopped by on the way home and asked Mim about her daughter. She said there's no way that her daughter would ever file an inquiry."

"Into what?" Mark asked.

Well, see, that's the thing," Tom said. "We can't figure that out, because our main concern has been to just keep buying time. But now that the old-timers have moved here…."

"Uncle Matt says we still have to lay low though. He says if we could somehow just walk away from this Family Services issue now, he'll see what he can do to get it all buried in the archives."

"Uncle Matt?" Mark said.

"Matt Fioritto," Randy said. "Dawn's uncle."

Tom grinned. "Google that one."

"No, don't," Randy said. "Not unless you want to be paid a visit tonight. Where are you sleeping?"

Mark smiled. "Is that because his name is like the Mafia Don fella?"

"Like?" Tom said. "How about one and the same?"

"Is that who I'm named after?" Matthew asked.

Everyone laughed.

"More cake?"

Wendy fanned herself with her napkin. "I'm wondering about a lot of things that have happened over the last couple of years. Is it hot in here?"

No one answered.

"Remember when you put the zero tolerance on drugs into effect?"

"You mean when a third of the trainers left?" Tom said.

"Yes, that precise day. Actually they trickled out over a couple of weeks," Wendy explained to Mark. "But the writing was on the wall."

"I wanted to stand at the gate and wave," Ben said, "But Dawn wouldn't let me. She insisted the headline the next day would say, 'This confirms it. Ben Miller has lost his mind. There it goes. Hitch a ride.'"

Everyone laughed.

"The most puzzling for me," Dawn said, "is that all these articles most certainly have to be initiated by the same person. There's no other explanation."

"So let me get this straight," Mark said. "You introduce the soft whip, you do away with drug violations, essentially, and you've increased the crowds. What would this person or persons' complaint be? What is their problem?"

"The fact that we don't make any money," Dusty said. "We just get by. We have a monopoly on the area. We have the facility, the reputation, the integrity. We don't want the slots, but the slots are out there to be had. What else can they do but try and bring us down?"

Mark nodded.

"They feel there is money to be made by adding slots, a lot of money," Dusty said. "We've ridden out the storm of failing crowds. We got them back. There's a big interest in our ReHab and ReHome program. We hardly ever have to stable many ReHab horses very long now; that's how supportive the community has become. They know we care. If we start running it like a strictly-for-profit business and only a business...."

Ben sighed. "Did you know that you're not allowed to stay in business if you don't turn a profit? Seriously," he said. "It's not enough to employ people, pay them a good wage, offer benefits, and share in the cost. It's not admirable to even pay all your bills, not unless you have a profit margin. I don't understand that kind of thinking. At the end of the day here at the farm, if we've all eaten, the horses have all eaten, we all have roofs over our heads and we don't owe anybody, why isn't that good enough for a business? Why isn't that at the end of the day considered a job well done? Somebody tell me that. Somebody explain that to me once and for all."

~ * ~

When they all parted for the night, Ben's glow-in-the-dark walking shoes lit the way. "They really do work," he said. "I'll be damned."

When Liz and Señor were almost to their house, Señor called out, "We can still see you!"

Ben laughed. George and Glenda and Tom did night check in the barns and Wendy and Matthew turned up the walkway to Ben's house. "I'll be back in a few minutes," he said. "I'm going to walk over and let Vicky know what we decided."

Matthew and Wendy stood on the porch and watched Ben's feet glowing in the night, each foot lighting up a little more than the other whenever it was put to the ground. "He coming!" they heard Miguel say. "Come see! He coming!!"

"We can still see you!" Señor called out.

Dawn and Randy watched from their porch steps, each holding a child! "We see you, Grandpa!!!"

Ben waved, called back, and kept walking.

"Here he comes! Look!" Steven said. "Would you look at that!"

George and Glenda passed him in their truck. "We see you!" they both said.

By the time Ben got to T-Bone's Place, he was so winded from laughing and calling back to everyone, he had to sit down and catch his breath.

"Would you like a glass of water?" Vicky asked.

"Don't mind if I do."

When she went to get it, Ben looked around the living room. Mim had been reading a book. "A racetrack novel," she said, holding it up. "It's not bad." Steven and Clint were playing cards. Jeannie was knitting a scarf to donate to Headstart. Jack was doing a crossword puzzle. Frank and Miguel were watching TV. Bill was reading the racing form. The scene was like an old racetrackers' Hallmark card.

"Tomorrow we're going to hang win pictures," Vicky said, coming back with the glass of water.

"Thank you." Ben took a drink and looked at her. "Everything's okay."

"Good," she said. "I'll let Lucy know."

"Where is she?" Ben asked.

"She and Junior went to town to get us some milk. We ran out."

"That's because Steven drank it all," Jeannie said, knitting away.

"Yeah, well that's because Vicky's pot-roast was so good."

Jeannie smiled.

Her knitting reminded Ben of Meg and how she used to sit in the living room in the evenings and knit for hours. He loved listening to the sound of the needles tapping together, and how she'd say, "Oh dear, I dropped a stitch."

"Well," he said. "I'll see you all tomorrow."

Vicky walked out onto the porch with him. "What about Junior" she asked. "You know, he really is a nice kid."

"I know," Ben said. "We're going to look into getting some furniture. We'll work out the bathroom up there too. Señor is on it."

"Thank you." She smiled at the way he'd said Señor and looked back in at the old-timers, all in their glory. "Having some young people here will be good for them. I know it'll be good for me. I also think having a young man around will make the old-timers feel safe. Me too," she added.

Ben walked down the ramp and waved. Junior and Lucy had just pulled off the road into the driveway. "Wait a minute, Ben. Let me take the groceries in and I'll give you a ride home."

"No, that's okay," Ben said. "You stay here. I need the exercise."

"You sure?"

"Yep."

Vicky gave Junior the news.

"Thanks, Ben," Junior called to him. "Hey, cool shoes!"

Ben chuckled and walked on. He didn't realize how much harder it was going to see now that it had gotten a little darker with his one eye still blurry and the other one with the cataract. When he was about midway between T-Bone's Place and the main drive to the farm, he slowed

~ 270 ~

his pace. There was a car coming down the road. It blinded him for a moment. Then he saw something in the road up ahead. A person, a person walking toward him. The person came into focus. It was Matthew.

"The blind leading the blind," Matthew said when he drew close.

Ben smiled.

Up ahead, Tom stood waiting for them. "You two are going to be the death of me," he said, chewing on a toothpick and falling into rank next to them. Junior waved to them. "Him too," Tom said.

Chapter Twenty-Three

There was no talking Ben into staying home another day. He arrived at the racetrack right after Tom and Dawn, looked in on B-Bo, ducked out of Bo-T's way, and checked all the other horses. "You'd swear you'd been gone a month to watch you," Tom said.

Ben nudged him. "Get out of my chair."

Tom laughed. He'd heard Ben coming and sat down in the old man's chair on purpose. "I marked the training chart for you."

Ben looked at him. "You'd better be kidding."

"I am," Tom said, pouring a cup of coffee.

Dawn walked in behind them. "Where you been?" Tom asked.

She sighed in disgust and showed them the headline on the Sports page of the *Morning Banter*: "Feeble Attempt to Appease Fans at Nottingham Downs."

"Feeble attempt?" Dawn said.

"Who is this son of a bitch?" Tom asked.

"I don't know." Dawn shook her head.

Dusty walked in all red in the face, sporting a copy of his own. "I think if I read it one more time my head's gonna explode."

Then here came Junior. "The motherfuckers - did you read this? They're messing with my livelihood. I got a baby on the way!"

Tom looked at him and somehow managed to not say a word.

"Who is this guy?" Junior asked.

"Actually," Dawn said. "I could be wrong, but it seems to me it's a woman writing this. I think that's why it's gotten so personal. The author uses only an initial for a first name, which traditionally indicates male, but...."

"Well, I say you go kick her ass," Junior said.

Tom laughed and then cleared his throat and looked away.

"Well, let's put this all aside and get to training," Ben said. "One thing's for sure: we all know where we stand and this person's accusations are bullshit."

"I say we sic Mim on them," Dusty said.

Dawn looked at him a second. He was right. Mim would go right to the source. "That's a good idea. Thank you." She grabbed a lead-shank and headed out of the tack room.

"Where you going?" Tom asked.

"To walk Bo-T. And he'd better not mess with me. Not today."

The four men all nodded, agreeing. Dawn didn't get angry often, but when she did....

"What time are you taking him home?" Ben asked.

"Who?" Junior asked.

"Bo-T," Ben said.

"Right around ten, right after the track closes."

"Why's he going home?" Junior asked. "What's the matter with him? Is he all right?"

"He's fine. He's done. Ben's retiring him to stud," Tom said, wondering why he was even having this conversation with the boy.

"What? What about the Burgundy Blue Stake. He's a shoe-in!"

Ben looked at him. He hadn't forgotten about the Burgundy Blue, but admittedly with his eye surgery and everything going on with Matthew and the old-timers, it had obviously been pushed far into the back of his mind. And apparently everyone else's.

"He's just gotten so…." Ben shrugged.

"The old man's made up his mind," Tom said. "He's going home. He's done. He's leasing him to Breezeway. He keeps messing around he's going to hurt himself. All he can think of is mares."

"So?' Junior said.

"You saw how he ran," Tom said. "Johnny could hardly get his nose out of that mare's ass."

"Yeah, but there's no mares in the Burgundy Blue."

Ben stared. Tom stared. Dusty stared.

"Even so, that's weeks away," Ben said. "We can't train him sharp for that long and expect him to fire. That, and every time you lead him to the track, you chance him trying to mount every mare and filly in sight."

"This isn't right," Junior said, grabbing Alley's tack. "This is what makes fans mad. Look what happens every time they retire one of the fucking Derby winners or the Preakness winners or the Belmont winners. Fans get pissed off everywhere. They want to see great horses run. It ain't all about their stud careers or breeding the next runner." He walked out of the tack room and down the shedrow shaking his head.

Tom looked at Ben and Dusty. "Fucking Derby winners?"

"Tedious, isn't it," Ben said.

Tom laughed. "I never sounded like that."

"Oh really?"

Thus the day's training began. Alley galloped. Whinny galloped. Wee Born walked. Batgirl walked. Morning Dew galloped. Bo-T and B-Bo were hand-walked. Ben nursed his doubts all morning, waffled back and forth, but when it came time to load B-Bo and Bo-T, he decided to go ahead and send them both home. "I need time to think," he said to Tom and Dusty. "Go. We can always bring him back." Dusty climbed into the passenger seat, filled the necessary paperwork out at the stable gate, and he and Tom drove the van over to the grandstand to load Mim's things out of storage.

The blacksmith showed up a little after ten and Dawn led Batgirl out first. It wasn't often they had more than one or two horses due to be reset on any given day. This morning there were four of them to be done.

Brownie had been Ben's blacksmith for years. At the end of the meet each year Brownie talked about retiring and moving to Florida for good, but always returned. Every time Dawn saw him, his back seemed to be bent a little more, his walk a little slower. But his wit and the stories he could tell were as good as ever, if not better.

"Stop," she said, laughing on numerous occasions today. "That possibly could never have happened."

"I kid you not," Brownie said. "Butt crack and all!"

Randy stopped by with Mark.

By then, they'd worked their way down to Morning Dew. Dawn introduced Brownie to Mark and the blacksmith tried standing up straight to shake the man's hand and ended up just nodding. "Nice to meet ya!"

"Another Brownie?" Mark said. The man who ran the kitchen was Brownie too.

"Ain't no relation," Brownie joked.

Dawn swished flies off Morning Dew with a towel.

Randy looked inside both empty stalls, checking. "What time did they go home?" When he arrived earlier, he'd signed all the necessary paperwork on his end as the attending veterinarian.

Dawn yawned. "Just before eleven."

"Are you okay?"

"Yes," she said. "It's just that article…."

"I read it," Brownie said, from under the horse. "What the hell's wrong with those people?"

"I don't know." Dawn sighed. "Wish I could get them to come here for just a day."

"Why don't you try?" Randy kissed her and walked to his truck with Mark right along with him. "It can't hurt."

Dawn nodded. "I'm going to go by there on the way home. Enough's enough."

~ * ~

As much as Ben liked having the old-timers home on the farm, he had to admit he was going to miss going up to the third floor of the grandstand to see them every morning. He walked past Joe and several trainers playing poker and into the downstairs general office. Wendy looked up from her desk.

"I think Richard's coming in this afternoon. I actually think he's working this morning. I've gotten several texts from him."

Ben sat down in his "owner's chair." It never ceased to amaze him how the day-to-day operation of the racetrack *operated* without him. He was happy that's the way it was, but still found it amazing. "Have you talked to him?"

"Yes."

"About the RJR thing?"

Wendy nodded.

"What's he think?"

"Well, I actually think that's what he's working on now, judging from his texts. He had me take a photo of the court order and e-mail it to him. He said he was clear across town."

"This is all so complicated." Ben sighed. "All of it. This, the newspaper articles…."

"I know," Wendy said.

"Did you talk to Matthew this morning?"

"No. Why?'

"I'll let him tell you."

"Ben, come on."

"Well," Ben hesitated. "He says he wants to quit school. He says in the grand scheme of things, it's all a waste of time."

"When did he tell you this?"

"This morning before I left."

Wendy stared. "I think he's just depressed."

"Well, he's got good reason," Ben said, blinking instinctively as he thought about Matt's failed eyesight. "I'm just telling you this because I think when he gets around to telling you himself, you might want to just listen."

Wendy nodded. When there was a tap on the open door they both turned and smiled. Richard was back.

~ * ~

Dawn parked outside the *Morning Banter* and marveled. It was huge. On second glance, she noticed that the majority of the building appeared to be empty. She got out of her car. The main doors to the building were locked tight. Reading the handwritten sign, *Morning Banter* – Second Door Around Back, she drove to the rear of the building.

There were two desks in the small *Morning Banter* office, both occupied by middle-aged women dressed casually and looking quite busy. "May I help you?" the one asked, noticing a copy of the newspaper in Dawn's hand.

"Yes, I'd like to speak to F.D. Crenshaw."

"Who shall I say is here?"

"My name is Dawn Iredell. I write for the *Herald* and also work at Nottingham Downs."

The other woman looked up. "F.D. Crenshaw is a syndicated writer."

"From where does she write?" Dawn asked.

Both women stared at her. "Uh, she…" the one stammered. "She is from New York I believe, or maybe Chicago."

"Well, that's pretty far," Dawn said. "Not to mention the proximity of one to the other. Would you mind looking it up? I'll wait." Dawn walked over to one of the chairs in the waiting room and sat down.

"Um," the one woman said.

Dawn looked at her. "Surely there is a trail that would lead to her."

"Well, yes, but…."

"Seriously," Dawn said. "Take your time. I don't mind waiting." She wished Mark was here. He could use his Smartphone and Google this F.D. Crenshaw. She wished she had her laptop. While the two Banter employees talked among themselves, she called her Uncle Matt's office. "Jamie, could you look up an F.D. Crenshaw for me? She's a syndicated columnist out of either New York or Chicago." The two women looked at her. "Yes, I know, that's what I said. Throw in Cleveland just for the heck of it."

The two women busied themselves while Dawn waited. "You're kidding," they heard her say. "Well, that's odd." And then, "All right, keep me posted." She stood up and walked over to the two women. Both were staring into a computer screen and appearing as if they were still trying to find the reporter's location. "Let me guess," Dawn said. "No such person."

"Well, syndicates are sometimes…."

Dawn held up her hand. "I don't need a lesson in syndication. Thank you for your time."

"I'm sorry," the one woman said as Dawn started out the door. "We just work here."

"Thank you," Dawn said. "I understand."

What she didn't understand and what nagged her all the way home was why? Why would anyone, any person, any syndicate, imaginary or real, want to target Nottingham Downs?

Meg's Meadows was a welcome site. Carol had just put the children down for a nap. Dawn peeked in on them and walked down to the main barn to check on Bo-T and B-Bo. Both had settled in and were eating hay. George and Glenda were just finishing up chores.

"What's the matter?" Glenda asked.

"Is it that obvious?" Dawn said.

George nodded. "You want some coffee? I just made a fresh pot."

"Yes, thank you." The three of them sat down on the bench outside the barn and watched the horses grazing in the pastures.

"So what's going on?" George asked.

Dawn recounted the story about the *Morning Banter* and the three of them just sat there, nodding and wondering. "I just don't get it," she said, thinking out loud. "I just don't get it."

~ * ~

Ben rocked in his office chair staring out at the racetrack and mulling over everything Richard had to say. It wasn't sitting well. He didn't want a dispute with the man his first day back on the job after gallbladder surgery and the infection that followed, but…. "I think you're off base, Richard. I don't think this has anything to do with slots."

"Ben." Richard shook his head. "This is me, remember. I know how you feel. You and I almost parted ways over this. But I'm telling you, there can't be any other reason for RJR Enterprises to be sniffing around."

Wendy's cellphone rang. It was Dawn, wanting to let her know about her dead-end encounter at the *Morning Banter*. "You're kidding," Wendy said.

"No. Uncle Matt's people are trying to come up with something, but so far, nothing. I'll keep you posted." Wendy hung up and shared the news with Ben and Richard.

"Now let's not go and immediately think these two situations are related," Ben said.

Richard sat back. "Even if they're not, Ben, and I'm thinking they are, you're going to have to start turning a sizable profit soon or it's going to be Uncle Sam knocking on your door."

Ben sighed. "I'm going to the barn."

Wendy watched him walk out and looked at Richard. "Did you have to be so hard on him?"

"He wouldn't want it any other way and you know that."

True, Wendy thought. Still….

"Come on," Richard said. "You know I love that old man just as much as you do, but I have to tell him how it is and he's going to have to face this."

Wendy sat looking at him. "Do you really think there's a connection?"

"I think we're going to find out. What's that fella's name again, the one from Family Services? I think I'm going to pay him a visit."

"Dan Gotbert." Wendy located the man's card and handed it to him. "Should I call ahead and warn him?"

"No. Turnabout is fair play." Richard smiled. "God, it's good to be back."

It was good having him back. "Call me," Wendy said. Richard nodded, waving over his shoulder.

~ * ~

George and Señor spent quite some time assessing the upstairs bathroom situation at T-Bone's Place. They decided that with a little luck it shouldn't be all that difficult to install another toilet, sink and tub. It would obviously cut the size of the third bedroom, but, "It just might work." Off they went to the plumbing warehouse.

Meanwhile, Tom and Dusty hauled Mim's furniture upstairs. There was a double bed, a dresser, two-night stands and a rocking chair. "Perfect," Lucy said, hands on her skinny hips and her little baby bump starting to show. "I love it! Thank you!!" She yelled downstairs. "Thank you, Mim!"

"Jesus," Mim mumbled. "You're welcome." She lowered her voice again. "For such a little thing, she sure does have a big set of lungs."

"God help us when the baby comes," Jeannie said.

Lucy glanced around the bedroom. "Do you think you could maybe move the dresser over there and the rocker here? I want to be able to hear if Vicky or one of the old-timers needs me. We can put a crib there then."

Tom looked at her. There's that mention of crib again, as in staying here that long.

"Good. Now that's perfect," Lucy said.

"You said that before," Dusty teased. "You sure?"

"For the time being." Lucy smiled. "Yes."

When George and Señor returned, Lucy had the bed made, had some of her things placed on the dresser, and was sitting rocking in the rocking chair. "I love it," she said. "I don't ever want to leave."

Vicky called up the stairs. "Lucy!"

"Yes?"

"Do you want to come down and give me a hand?"

"Yes, I do!" Lucy said. George and Señor laughed at the enthusiastic way she'd said it. "Coming!"

"Hey, slow down," George said. "Use the railing. That's what it's there for?"

Señor thumped the wall between the bedroom and the bathroom. "I hope we know what we're doing."

George laughed. "Ain't no mountain we can't climb. Let's do it!"

Mim cringed each time she heard the pound a hammer or the long drawn-out screech of a crowbar. "I think I'm going to go for a walk," she said.

"You sure?" Vicky asked.

Mim nodded. "Not far. Just down to see the horses." She stood with the support of her cane and walked out onto the back porch, rested for a moment, and then made her way down the ramp. She drew in a breath, as deep a breath as she could, and glanced around. "Oh my," she said, "Well, would you look at that. Hello there."

~ * ~

Richard stood facing Dan Gotbert in the dingy lobby of the Family Services building. He shook the man's hand. "I wonder if we could go to your office and talk a moment."

"I don't have an office," Gotbert said. "I have a cubicle. What can I do for you?"

"My name is Richard Spears. I'm the General Manager of Nottingham Downs."

Gotbert just stared for a second, then lowered his arm and tucked his hands into his pockets.

"Are you sure there isn't any place we could talk in private?" Richard asked.

"No, this is it. Do you have a case number?"

"No. As a matter of fact I don't," Richard said, with a sardonic smile. "Maybe there's someone else that can help me."

The man hesitated. "That won't be necessary. Your case has been closed. As of this morning, apparently it never existed."

"Well, that saves me filing a restraining order against you, since that was going to be my next stop."

The man just looked at him, a myriad of barely controlled emotions coloring his face.

"RJR Enterprises," Richard stated simply. "I guess I'll just head there instead. You wouldn't happen to know if they have a local office here in the area, would you?"

Again, the man just looked at him.

"I guess not." Richard turned and left.

The man followed him halfway out the door, careful not to cross the threshold with the security camera pointed right at him. There was something he obviously wanted to say.

Richard looked back. "Yes?"

The man shook his head. "Have a nice day at work."

"You too," Richard said, and got in his car. "What the hell's that supposed to mean?" He phoned Wendy down the road to let her know he'd be awhile.

"Any luck?"

"No." He told her what the man said. "I guess it was more how he said it that makes me wonder. Is he telling me it would be a waste of time?"

"I don't know. I have my own drama going on at the moment," Wendy said.

"Why? What happened?"

"Apparently someone shut off the main water line to the grandstand."

"What? Did you get it back on?"

"Yes. But why was it turned off?"

"All right. I've had enough," Richard said. "I think I'll go back in for some more surgery now."

Wendy chuckled. "It does rather coincide with your return I might say. If I check your car and there's a big monkey wrench in the backseat you're in big trouble, Mister."

Richard laughed. "I'll see you later. If the power goes out, don't call me I'll call you."

~ * ~

Matthew walked outside and just stood on the porch for a while, then decided to go for a walk up the road. Mim saw him coming. "Young man! Young man!"

Matthew waved. The woman was over near the garage next to T-Bone's Place.

"Can you come give me a hand please?"

"Sure," Matthew said.

Mim stood supporting herself with her cane and gazing down at her old golf cart.

"Wow. Now this has been around a while," Matthew said.

"So have I," Mim said. "What's your point?"

Matthew laughed. "What are you trying to do?"

"Well, if we could push it into the garage, I can charge it. It was running good the day I parked it. It must have lost its charge."

"Don't tell my mom," Matthew said, steering it with one hand and pushing it with another.

"Wait a minute! Wait a minute! Are you Matthew? Oh yes it is you. Stop!"

"I'm fine," Matthew said.

Mim hooked him with her cane. "Stop!"

Matthew laughed. "Honest. I'm fine. I'm not using my eyes. Watch, see, I'll look at you the whole time."

Mim shook her head. "No, wait. All right. Here, let me help." The old woman started pushing the back of the golf cart with her butt.

Matthew could hardly steer for laughing.

"Are we almost there? There's a plug just inside on the left. I looked."

Matthew was still laughing. "Okay, we're close. Just another little push. Okay, okay, we got it."

"Wonderful," Mim said, dusting off her backside. "We'll need a rag too to wipe off the seats." She looked around the garage as Matthew hooked up the battery charger. "Here's one. Oh dear, what a dreadful smell. What the hell *is* that?"

Matthew took a whiff. "Skunk!"

"No!" Mim said. She took another whiff. "Really?"

"Really," Matthew said. "Stay here." He turned the hose on and rinsed her hands, careful not to interfere with the way she balanced herself with her cane under her arm. "Use the back of my shirt to dry."

Mim wiped her hands dry and stood tall with the help of her cane. "Well, thank you, Matthew. We should be all set now. I'll find a rag inside. Thank you."

"You're welcome," Matthew said, and looked around.

"What do you see?" Mim said, studying his sudden sad expression.

"Not much," Matthew said. "It comes and goes."

Mim gripped his shoulder hard. "Go talk to the horses."

Matthew smiled. "What good will that do?"

"It'll make you feel good," Mim said. "And it'll make me feel good too."

Matthew smiled when she persisted and walked down to the pastures.

"Those three there will be the safest." Mim pointed to Biscuit, Poncho, and Dusty's little filly, Bonnie Bee.

Matthew squeezed between the fence rails and looked back at her.

"Go on, go on," she said, waving. "Go on. Talk to them."

"Hey, horses," Matthew said, laughing at himself.

"See," Mim said. "You're feeling better already."

Matthew smiled and patted Biscuit on the shoulder, stroked his neck. He rubbed Poncho's face and combed his fingers through the filly's mane.

"They like you!" Mim said. "Sit down. Let them graze around you."

Matthew looked at her warily.

"It's all right. Dusty does it all the time. Sit!"

Matthew buckled his knees and sat down Indian style and watched the three horses grazing. The little filly nudged him and he moved slightly to the left. Apparently he was sitting on some really good grass judging from her actions.

"This is fun," Matthew said, touching the horse's face and looking at Mim.

"I told you!"

"Thank you!"

Mim waved and nodded, then turned and walked to the house. She stopped to rest, to try and catch her breath, then walked up the ramp and inside the back door, where she stopped again and looked back. Matthew had lain down in the grass and the three horses were grazing all around him. The young man was grinning from ear to ear.

~ * ~

Dusty spread word throughout the backside about the HBPA banquet "Come as You Are" theme and checked back in with Irene. "I've gotten a few more," she said. "Keep up the good work."

"Have you seen Junior?"

Irene shook her head. "Why?"

"I don't know. His truck's here. It's been here all day; I haven't seen him though." The seventh race was about to go off so Dusty walked downstairs and out to the Ginny stand to watch.

"And they're off!"

Dusty smiled. The grandstand was packed; a good turnout today.

"It's Buster Bay taking the early lead…."

When Dusty's cellphone rang, he answered it and plugged his other ear. "Hello."

It was Wendy. "Have you seen Tom?"

"Not for a couple of hours. Why? What's up?"

"Nothing, I just…." Wendy hesitated. "If you see him, tell him I'm going to be a little late. I'm going to stop and look at a car for the boys."

"You're kidding."

"No. Why? I need to get mine back. I can't keep borrowing Glenda's. Never mind, here he is."

Tom walked into her office and straight to the window to watch the end of the race.

"And it's Buster Bay, Buster Bay, Buster Bay, wire to wire!"

"That's good. Brickman can pay him now."

"Who?"

"Junior. Brickman's been stringing him along."

Dusty made a point of walking outside the Ginny stand just as Brickman led Buster Bay off the track on the way to the spit barn. "He run good!" Dusty said.

Brickman nodded. "Yep, he win easy."

Tom smiled, even from a distance he knew. "That Dusty's always on the ball."

"I just talked to him. I wanted him to tell you I'm going to be a little late getting home. I'm going to stop and look at a car for the boys."

Tom looked at her. "What?"

"I want my car back. Glenda's being really nice letting me use hers, but…."

"You're not going to let them pick out their own car."

"Not unless they plan to pay for it."

"Wendy!" Tom laughed. "Honey!"

"Don't 'Honey' me. This car's just like the other one they had."

"Isn't that kind of freaky?"

Wendy stared. She hadn't thought of that. All she knew was that the make and model had been affordable, economical on gas. "Do you think I'm being…?"

"A mom? Yes. I gotta go," he said. "I'm meeting with Pastor Mitchell and Junior in about five minutes."

"What for?"

"I don't know. I'll let you know." He winked at her and stopped short of leaving. "What's that look for?"

"You don't think I should pick out a car for the boys?"

"No," he said. "I don't. Now come on, cheer up. I gotta go."

Wendy sat biting her bottom lip.

"Aw, Jesus," Tom said. "You gotta stop this shit." He went over and put his arms around her. "It's no big deal. I'll take them and go find a car."

"Oh, and that's different somehow?"

"Than their mommy? Yes."

"Go on. Get out of here," Wendy said. "Go on."

Tom tipped his cowboy hat and left.

~ * ~

Ben was careful to wear sunglasses driving home and was pleased he could see fairly well. He waved to the old-timers in passing. Some were sitting out on the porch. He figured he'd grab a quick snack, don his walking shoes, and go visit with them for a while before dinner.

Matthew looked up from watching TV when he walked in. "Tell me that's not what you've been doing all day," Ben said, washing his hands at the kitchen sink. "That can't be good for your eyes."

"Actually I was outside quite a bit today. I was out communing with nature and the horses. Mim told me to...."

"Well, I'll be damned." Ben looked out the window and laughed. "What the hell?"

Here came Mim down the driveway in her golf cart with Jack in the passenger seat and Miguel sitting square in the middle of the back seat holding on to the roll bars on each side.

"Yeah, we charged it," Matthew said. "We took a tour of the whole place. We even rode it around the training track."

Ben walked out onto the porch drying his hands and smiling.

"Hey, Mr. B!" Miguel said. "How you do?"

"I'm good, I'm good," Ben said. "Mim. Jack."

"Hey, Ben," Mim said. "Imagine my surprise when I walked outside and found it by the garage. Oh how I've missed this dear old thing."

Ben laughed.

"We're on our way up to the stallion barn. Jack and Miguel haven't seen Beau Born in years. Hop on."

Ben climbed into the back seat when Miguel moved over and off they went. "How fast does this go, Mim?" Ben asked.

"Oh, I don't know. Once upon a time it could go pretty fast. I'd say about three miles an hour or so now." When Mim pulled up next to the barn and put on the brake, they all piled out. Mim reached back in for her cane the way she'd done a gazillion times over the years, and the four of them walked into the barn. Ben was just about to warn them of Beau's habit of screaming like a banshee to greet visitors when Beau let out a whinny that could probably be heard for miles.

They all jumped, Ben included, and then they all laughed. "Well, that'll get your heart going," Jack said.

"Oh look at you," Miguel said, to Beau Born. "You so beautiful."

Beau tilted his head, liking the sound of Miguel's voice. "I remember you," Miguel kept saying. "I remember you, you big horse!"

Beau sniffed and snorted and flirted a little, then went back to eating his hay.

"He looks fantastic," Mim said. "I rode down this afternoon and just sat watching him out in the pasture." She smiled and then heaved a little sigh. "All right, boys, Lucy said dinner was in ten minutes."

All four climbed back into the golf cart and Mim dropped Ben off at his house. "You're not going out on the road, are you?" he asked.

"No." Mim imitated the warning she received earlier today from Vicky, "It's not allowed."

"Señor going to make path tomorrow," Miguel said. "We go now outside of pasture."

Ben stepped back and waved.

Matthew walked out onto the porch.

"Where's dinner tonight?" Ben asked.

"Glenda and George's."

"Good. You'll be up for a walk, right?"

"You bet."

Chapter Twenty-Three

Tom sat down in one of the front row seats of the chapel and said a prayer. Pastor Mitchell once told Tom the day he started praying with his actions and not words, he had become a better Christian. Tom still liked praying. He'd just given up all his preaching. He said a prayer for

Wendy for what she was going through. He said a prayer for himself, hoping he got through it too.

Pastor Mitchell and Junior walked in together.

Tom opened his eyes and turned. "So what's up?"

Pastor Mitchell motioned for Junior to grab two chairs and the two of them sat down across from Tom. "Junior wants to marry Lucy."

Tom looked at the boy. "And…?" They seemed to be holding back something.

"And I want you to be my best man," Junior said.

Tom looked at Pastor Mitchell and sat back. So this was why the man had him meet them in the chapel, knowing full well the surroundings would temper his response. "Why me?" Tom asked.

"Because you're like a father to me," Junior said.

Tom shifted his weight. "You have a father, Junior."

"Yeah, but he's not a friend," the boy said. "You are."

Tom stared. Jesus, he thought, why me for sure? "What's involved in this? What do I have to do?"

"You stand with him in friendship and support. It's a lifetime commitment."

"A lifetime?"

Junior chuckled. "You mean like an anchor around his neck?"

"No." Pastor Mitchell smiled. "It's spiritual and it's concrete. Tom, it means you'll be there for him in difficult times and in good times. Not all marriages work."

"That's a nice positive note," Tom said.

The three of them just sat there for a moment, absorbing the situation. The odds of people staying married on the racetrack weren't all that good. It was like Hollywood in that respect. "So are we talking about a big wedding? What?" Tom asked.

"Just a small service here in the chapel. Just a few people," Pastor Mitchell said.

Junior was staring down at his hands in his lap.

"What does Lucy think about all of this," Tom asked.

Junior kept his eyes averted. "She doesn't know yet."

Tom just looked at the boy.

"Junior wanted some spiritual guidance from us first."

Us? Tom sighed. "I don't know what to say, but…."

"Just say yes, Tom," Junior said. "Just say yes."

Tom nodded, wondering how it is that someone can grow up so fast in such a short amount of time. "All right, I'll be your best man. But if you screw up…."

"I know," Junior said, smiling. "You're going to kick my ass. Oops," He ducked. "Am I allowed to say that in here?"

"Yes," Pastor Mitchell said, smiling. "And I was a witness to it."

"You got that," Tom said. "We'll all be watching you now."

The boy nodded. "Thank you. I won't let you down. I'm not going to let anybody down, Lucy, the baby. I want to live a righteous life just like you said, Pastor Mitchell. I want to live a life that will make you all proud."

~ * ~

Up until about a year ago, dinner at Glenda's and George's had always been a buffet-style scattered seating affair. Some ate in the kitchen, some in the small dining room, some in the living room. Then George decided to knock down the wall between the dining room and kitchen, opening it up, and he and Senior made a table that sat fourteen people. Since they had just torn down the wall between the bathroom and the bedroom upstairs at T-Bone's Place today, the process brought back memories of the reconstruction here. It had not gone "without a hitch."

"Señor here had to get ten stitches in his hand the one day," George told Mark.

"Not even a week later, George got a concussion when an overhead board fell and hit him in the head," Señor said. "I'd never seen a person's eyes roll back in their head before."

Everyone laughed.

"Who's that?" Ben asked when he saw headlights pulling into the driveway.

George leaned over to look. "Ah, it's Richard!"

Richard tapped on the door and came inside. There were lots of hellos and how are you's since most hadn't seen him since he'd gotten home from the hospital.

"Sit down, sit down," Ben said. "We just got started."

Richard washed up at the sink and sat down near the end of the table. A platter of rigatoni and Italian sausage was passed to him, salad, garlic bread. He helped himself and passed them on.

"What do you want to drink?" Glenda asked.

"Water's good," he said.

Randy reached for the pitcher and filled his glass. "How are you feeling?"

"Good, everything's good," he said. "Well, not everything."

Ben pointed his fork at him with just a hint of a smile on his face. "How about you let me finish my meal first?"

Randy introduced Richard to Mark and the two shook hands across the table.

"So," Richard said, settling in. "What did I interrupt?"

"Well," Liz said. "We were all fondly reminiscing about the remodeling project in this house last year and all the trips to the emergency room."

Richard chuckled and waved to D.R. and Maeve.

They both giggled.

"So how did it go next door today?" Dawn asked. "Did you get started on the bathroom construction?"

"Started?" George said.

"We finished it," Señor said. "All we have to do tomorrow is paint the walls."

Dawn smiled. "You're kidding?"

"Nope. We're getting this down pat."

"And not one trip to the emergency room," Glenda said. "How do you like that?"

They all laughed.

"How are *you* doing, Matthew?" Richard asked.

"Oh, all right I guess. I had a good day." He moved side to side and then forward and back. "Is that you, Richard?"

"Very funny," his mom said. "His eyesight is going to return completely. It's just going to take time."

"Could you pass the rigatoni," Dusty said.

Carol held the platter for him to help himself.

"Thank you," Dusty said. He glanced at Ben. "I'd like to bring up a subject. I guess it's not too controversial. Not really. Well, maybe." He reached for the grated cheese. "We've talked about this before and I'm not sure what the ramifications would be, but what about if we establish a kind of gentlemen's, well, ladies and gentlemen's code of sorts to…."

"Dusty," Ben said. "What are you talking about?"

"Hannity claiming Jackson's only horse."

"Oh." Ben nodded. Just about everyone nodded.

Mark looked at Randy. "The horse I examined today?"

"Yep," Randy said. "The plot thickens."

"I have a feeling Hannity's going to lead him back over there on the raise with the hopes that Jackson'll claim him back."

"How sore is he?" Tom asked. "Will he finish the race?"

Mark shrugged. "He shouldn't race, not for a couple of weeks at least."

"Jackson loves that horse," Glenda said.

"Eat, D.R.," Randy said.

"I'm full."

"Me too," Maeve said.

"Then I guess you won't want any of Grandma's angel food cake, will you?" Dawn said.

"Yes!" they both chorused.

"All right. Then finish eating."

"Mark's going home tomorrow," Randy said.

"Oh?" Ben looked up.

"I'm going to go get some of my things, close up the condo, try and talk my girlfriend into coming back with me. I found a furnished place close by here I can rent."

"Speaking of girlfriends," Tom said.

"Oh?" Wendy looked at him.

"Lucy," he said. "I'm talking about Lucy. They're going to get married."

"Well, that's good news," Ben said, everyone echoing those sentiments. "When?"

"As soon as possible," Tom said. "Pastor Mitchell's going to marry them in the chapel. I'm going to be the best man."

Wendy smiled. He'd told her this at home and she was so proud of him for saying yes.

"Well, well," Randy said. "That's interesting."

Tom looked at him. "I know what you mean."

They all laughed. Tom and Junior's constant bickering was well-known by everyone.

"He had a good idea, old man," Tom said.

"Oh, and what's that?"

"He thinks you ought to race Bo-T off the farm in the Burgundy Blue."

Ben looked at him.

"He says he's going to be here every day anyway. Why not let him gallop him and keep him fit and decide down the road?"

Ben sat back.

"That last part, I added," Tom said.

Ben nodded, figuring as much. "I'll think about it."

"What's the horse's problem?" Mark asked.

"Too much testosterone and bred too well to cut," Randy said. "He's a Beau Born - All Together colt and track record holder. He's got a breeding career ahead of him."

"Ah," Mark said.

Ben looked at Dusty. "All right, so let's get back to Hannity. What are you thinking? What were you trying to say?"

Dusty sighed. "I'm thinking we can't let that horse start. Not until we're sure he's okay."

"How does that work?" Mark asked. "How do you stop them?"

"I don't know," Dusty said. "It's uncharted territory."

"We," Randy said, "as an attending veterinarian can't flag the horse."

"So, can't you just have the track veterinarian scratch him?"

Dusty looked at him. "Well, doing that in the non-socialist, hands off ownership, we're all private contractors here way, is the bailiwick. What if the track veterinarian doesn't see anything out of the ordinary with the horse? What if he's walking sound in the paddock, in the post parade? What if two steps out of the gate…?"

"Oh, Lord," Richard said. "I'm wishing I had two gallbladders. I could go get the other one removed and you could all call me when this situation is over."

They all nodded. It was said in jest, some even laughed, but it was a serious matter and no one knew that better than them. They took each and every horse's wellbeing seriously.

"How would we be dealing with this right now if the horse wasn't sore?" Tom asked. "That's the question. But at the same time, if Hannity doesn't think Jackson's going to claim the horse back on the raise, no trainer's going to lead the horse back over on the raise. Not if he's sore. They're going to patch him up and wait out the time limit and drop him down."

"That's just not right," Dawn said. "I hate that part of racing."

"Claiming races keep racing honest," Ben said; something he'd told her time and time again. "Without a designated price of that horse's worth…."

"Speaking of a horse's worth," Richard said.

"Aw, Jesus," Ben said. "All right, go ahead." Richard had practiced a great deal of restraint listening to everyone else's concerns. It was obvious whatever he was about to say was utmost on his mind - and big. Ben reached for another piece of bread.

"I have a feeling, backed up by some fairly good circumstantial evidence, that the driving force behind RJR Enterprises wants slots at Nottingham Downs and they're not going to let anything stop them, even if it means shutting us down."

"Now what benefit would that serve them?" Ben asked.

"Well, assuming you wouldn't just sit on the property and have to sell, the sooner they buy it the better. It would become the new and improved Nottingham Downs and

Casino. We've already brought the horse-racing fans back. They'd just target the rest."

Ben sat back. Dawn sat back. Randy sat back. Tom sat back.

"That's just not right," Liz said. "You all have worked so hard to build the integrity of the sport at Nottingham. That's just not right."

Richard nodded. "Right or wrong, slots are what they're in it for. They can put them downtown. They can put them down by the river. They can put them wherever they can get the zoning. But Nottingham Downs is where it'll succeed the most. I guarantee you that's what they're thinking. They want Nottingham and they want it bad. They're going to keep after us until they bring us down, and there'll be no racing with integrity after that, I promise you."

When everyone remained quiet, he continued. "Do you think anyone else will care as much as you all do about the soft whip, the zero tolerance for drugs, or even this trainer whose only horse got claimed? Do you think they're going to care about each and every Thoroughbred that ships in and out of here? I don't think so. It'll all be about the bottom line, the profit margin." He pulled a piece of paper out of his pocket. "This is mind boggling. The CEO of RJR Enterprises made three billion, four million and twenty-five thousand dollars last year. Do you think he cares about anything any of us at this table hold dear?"

Silence permeated the room until Maeve tugged on her mother's arm. "Mommy, can we have dessert now? I ate ev'ything."

"Yes," Ben said, answering for Dawn.

Mark looked at Randy. "This is great. Now you tell me. I was just getting attached to all of you."

Randy laughed. "We've been here before. Though admittedly," he added, looking at Richard, "this might be our toughest fight yet."

When the evening ended and they all parted, Tom, Ben, and Matthew started the walk home. The nights were getting cooler. "I'm still glowing," Ben said, watching his feet move forward. "Guess that says something."

Tom and Matthew laughed. The moon was big and bright. The horses could be seen grazing in the pastures. As they approached T-Bone's Place, they saw Junior sitting in the bed of his pickup truck, drinking a beer.

"What's going on?" Tom asked.

"She said no," Junior said.

"What?"

"I asked Lucy to marry me and she said no."

"Why?" Tom asked. "Did she say why?"

"Well...." Junior took a swig of his beer. "She said she thinks I'll probably make a good father, but that she's not so sure I'd make a good husband."

"That's what she said?" Tom asked.

"Yep. Her exact words."

"Well did you tell her that you've changed? Or that you're going to change?"

"Yes. I told her all of that."

"What did she say then?"

"She said she'd think about it."

"So what are you doing out here?"

"I'm thinking about it too."

"Well, that's good I guess." Tom hesitated, just looking at the boy. "We're going to go on home now. You okay?"

"Yeah, I'm fine."

"Good night."

Chapter Twenty-Four

What Richard had said last night at the dinner table weighed heavy on everyone's mind, and worse when Dawn arrived at the racetrack and was handed a copy of the *Morning Banter* opened to the Sports page. "Nottingham Downs owner Ben Miller sees the Writing on the Wall." Under a photo of a horse van was the caption, "Ben Miller ships his own horses South."

She stormed into the tack room to find Ben already reading the article and Tom leaning over his shoulder. "That's not even our van. How can they do this?" The article had been written by the same supposedly syndicated F.D. Crenshaw. "Who's feeding them this information?"

Dusty walked in behind her, paper in hand, and speechless. He sat down on the cot.

"Well, at least it says I'm a kindly old man," Ben said. "The sons of bitches."

Dawn looked at him and drew a breath and sighed.

"It's lies," Ben said. "That's all it is, just lies."

"Yes, but people believe what they read in the paper," Tom said.

"Good. Dawn will write another article and tell them it's not true."

"And then they'll say that's all lies, and then the next day…." Tom threw up his hands. "How did….? How did…?"

Junior came in behind them with a copy of his own. "Who is this fucking Crenshaw guy?"

Dawn made room for him to sit. "I think we all need to calm down. We all need to just pause for a minute and calm down." She was saying this as much for her own sake as theirs, but it gave them a moment to collect their thoughts.

"You know what's freaky about this," Tom said. "Wondering *where* they're getting their information? Are they sitting somewhere across the street watching us come and go? I mean, come on, aside from us, Randy, and the stable guard...." Tom started across the tack room.

Dusty grabbed his arm. "Wait a minute. Let's think this through. If it was Jason or any stable guard, they'd have the horses' names and precisely where they were headed. In this case, the farm."

Tom looked at him. "All right, so tell me this. Why do we all of a sudden have so many copies of this newspaper? Why is Jason giving them out to everyone?"

"Well, maybe he's not. Maybe he's just giving them to us," Ben said. "Junior, go find out how many he's got. Don't ask him anything. Just say you need an extra one."

They all waited for Junior to go and come back. "He's got a stack this high," the boy said. "He's says they're delivering more of them these days. And yes, he's passing them out to everyone."

"Now that's just suspect," Tom said. "That's not right."

Ben read the article again, as did Dawn. "You know what's odd," she said, "the use of the word ships. Ben Miller *ships* his own horses South. That's distinctly a racetrack term. A van's not a ship. Why would they say ship? Nothing else in the article sounds like they know racetrack life, just that one word."

Johnny walked into the tack room, *Morning Banter* in hand. "You shipped Bo-T to Mountaineer?"

Ben looked at him. "I told you yesterday we were taking him home."

"Yeah, but...."

"What made you say Mountaineer?" Tom asked, suspecting everyone and anything at the moment.

"The West Virginia license plate on the van."

Everyone looked at their own copies. Tom started to say something, but Dawn stopped him. "Bo-T's at home, Johnny. Just like Ben said. B-Bo's home too."

"That's who the second horse was?"

"Yes. All the other horses are still here. We're not going anywhere. B-Bo will be back and actually Bo-T may be back."

"What do you mean?" He looked at Ben. Next to Beau Born and All Together, Bo-T was the finest racehorse Johnny had ever ridden. Bo-T had put his career on the fast track.

Ben looked at Dawn. She wanted him to go on with this, to say something. "We're uh, thinking of running him off the farm in the Burgundy Blue and waiting to retire him after that. The meet'll be almost over. It would work out good."

"I'm going to gallop him," Junior said.

Johnny pressed his hand to his heart. "I'll come out too if you want. Just let me know."

"You'll be the first to know," Ben said. "Now let's just all get to work." He looked at the training chart and realized how much clearer everything looked this morning, how easy it was to read. "We have two to gallop, one to pony, Whinny, half-mile breeze, Morning Dew walks. Let's get started."

~ * ~

Wendy picked the note up off her desk and quickly phoned Tom. "Joe's going to be late. Can you come cover for him? I don't know how to take entries."

Tom had just finished tacking Red. "Here," he said to Junior. "Pony Alley for me. I'm gonna go do entries till

Joe gets in." Off he went, chaps, helmet and all. "I'll be right back, Ben. I've gotta cover entries."

"Joe's late again?"

This wouldn't be the first time Tom had filled in on entries, but it had been a while. "Yep."

It was after eight before Joe arrived, looking frazzled. "What's going on with you," Tom asked, when there was a lull in entries and it was just the two of them.

"It's nothing. I just have some family problems."

"Well, you need to get them taken care of. If you need help, let somebody know."

"Thank you. I will," Joe said.

"All right, I'm going back to the barn. By the way, would you happen to know anything about those articles in the *Banter*?"

Joe looked at him. "Why would I know anything? Why are you asking me?"

"Don't go paranoid on me, Joe. I just asked a question."

"No," Joe said. "I don't know anything."

~ * ~

Richard boarded the plane and found his seat. "Excuse me," he said, to the tiny woman on the aisle seat. "Would you rather the window?"

"No, I'm fine," she said. "Thank you for asking."

Richard stashed his carry-on in the compartment overhead and squeezed in past her. There was a time he used to always fly first class. He smiled at the memory. Ben put a stop to that as soon as he took over ownership of the racetrack.

"What's so funny?" the tiny woman asked.

"Oh nothing," Richard said. "I was just remembering my first day on the job. Well, actually it wasn't *my* first day on the job, it was the new owner's. I was recalling how I used to fly first class up until then."

The tiny woman nodded. "And you prefer this now?"

"Actually, I don't mind. I've gotten used to it. The people are a little friendlier back here."

The woman chuckled. "I wouldn't know. I usually sleep the whole time. There's something about the roar of the engine. I can't keep my eyes open."

Richard smiled. "So do you live in Vegas? Returning home?"

She shook her head. "I'm going to the Casino. Me and my two lady friends." She pointed to the two women across the aisle. Richard leaned forward. Both women waved.

"Good morning," Richard said.

"They talk too much," the little woman at his side whispered. "I can't sit next to them. It drives me crazy. They talk and talk and it's like I'm in a bad dream. They live together. What more can they have to say?"

The stewardess walked by, glancing at everyone's laps checking for fastened seatbelts.

Richard hunkered down, figuring he'd take a nap too, and sensed the old woman looking at him. He opened one eye. "Yes?"

"You remind me of someone?"

"A movie star maybe?" Richard asked.

The woman laughed. "No. But I never forget a face. What line of work are you in?"

Richard closed his eyes again. "I'm a CEO."

"Where? In Vegas?"

"No, here. Nottingham Downs."

"That's where I saw you! Virginia, Nancy, he's from Nottingham Downs. He's the C-E-O."

Both women waved again.

"We go every Wednesday," the woman said.

"Senior day," Richard said, eyes closed again.

"No, Rueben day!"

"Oh…" Richard said. "I can't remember whose idea that was, but it's a hit."

"It was *my* idea. I suggested it at one of the Meet the Team Breakfasts a few years back. That's where I met you. You were a real stuffed shirt then. That's why I couldn't quite place you. I never forget a face." She took in his turtleneck and jeans. "Look at you now!"

Richard smiled. "Thank you. I think."

The little woman nodded. "I told you I never forget a face."

~ * ~

Lucy finished drying and putting away the morning dishes and filled the coffee pot to have it ready for lunch. It took about twenty minutes to perk. The old-timers loved their coffee. She glanced into the living room and smiled at the sight of several of them all comfortably situated in their favorite chairs. They each had their own which was not to be shared. She and Vicky each had their own chair now too, thanks to Mim's extra furniture. All the old-timers felt at home here. So did Lucy, and in such a short amount of time. They hadn't even been here a week.

She felt the baby move and pressed her hand gently against the fluttering motion. She could imagine living here forever and helping to take care of the old-timers. But nothing lasts forever. She thought about Junior, the look on his face when he asked her to marry him, and then the look of hurt in his eyes when she said no. She loved Junior. As much as any eighteen-year-old girl could love any eighteen-year old boy. He was fun. He always made her laugh. He made her pregnant. They had shared a lot.

But he also made her cry. He'd cheated on her several times, said it was nothing when she heard and cried her heart out. "I should have been more careful," she said to herself. "How do I know he won't do it again?"

She walked out onto the back porch and took in a deep breath. Mim was sitting on her golf cart way over by the main pasture. She looked so happy, so resigned to her life drawing to a close. Lucy's baby fluttered again.

She wished she could talk to her mother. But her mother wasn't talking to her. "You have shamed me," her mother had said. "You have shamed us all. People are talking all over the racetrack. Couldn't you at least have had the decency to come tell us first?"

Her father wouldn't even look at her.

"You okay, Sweetie?" Jeannie asked.

Lucy turned, wiping her eyes. She hadn't realized Jeanne was sitting on the back porch. "I'm fine," she said.

Jeannie tapped the seat next to her wheelchair. "Come sit. You've been working all morning." Lucy sat down next to her and sighed. Jeannie patted her on the arm. "So what's the matter?"

"Oh…." Lucy shrugged.

"Let me guess," Jeannie said. "You're going to be a mother."

Lucy laughed and wiped her eyes.

"I think that's why God makes pregnant women nauseated in the beginning. It gives them something to think about besides the wonder of what is happening inside of them."

"Did you have children, Jeannie?"

"Three of them." Jeannie nodded. "Two of them have passed."

"Who's left?"

"My son. He lives far, far away. He's gonna come see me someday, he says."

Lucy gave her a hug.

"And here I was trying to cheer you up," Jeannie said, wiping tears from her eyes.

"Is there anything harder than being a mother?" Lucy asked.

"Possibly," Jeannie replied. "Maybe being a father."

Lucy nodded. "I think I'm going to go for a walk."

Jeanne patted her on the shoulder.

"Tell Vicky I'll be back." Lucy followed the already-worn path in the grass from Mim's golf cart and stopped along the way to talk to the horses in the various pastures. When she got to the main barn she climbed onto the golf cart next to Mim and she and Mim just sat there for a moment.

"It's such a gorgeous day," Mim said.

Lucy gazed off into the horizon. "It looks like rain."

Mim looked at her. "That's what I mean. We need the rain."

Lucy smiled and motioned to a large gray horse in the pasture. "Which horse is that?"

"Oh, well that's All Together. She belongs to Dawn and Ben. In case you haven't noticed, she's in foal too."

"I see that. I wonder if she has any doubts."

"About what?"

"Life. Liberty. The pursuit of happiness."

Mim laughed. "You're going to do just fine. Junior too."

"I wish I had a crystal ball."

"Well, you don't," Mim said. "Besides, then you wouldn't live in the moment and look how much you'd be missing out on."

Lucy nodded.

"Do you want a ride back or do you want to walk?"

"I think I'll walk. Thank you." Lucy walked up past the barns, waved to Glenda and George, waved to the children playing in the back yard, waved to Carol, and walked to what looked like the end of the world and stood staring out at the training track. She loved the smell of the racetrack, the dirt. She always had. She held onto the rail and tried to see into her future, her baby's future. What kind of mother will I be? What kind of father will Junior be?

"Lucy…?"

She turned.

"You okay?" Junior asked. "Jeannie said you went for a walk. Mim said she thought this was where you were headed."

Lucy shrugged, wiping her eyes. "I was thinking about all the babies that got started here. How they probably bucked and played and then galloped. How they learned to break from the starting gate and they didn't think too far ahead. They didn't worry."

Junior walked toward her.

"What are you doing here?" she asked. "Shouldn't you be at the racetrack?"

Junior shrugged. "I was worried about you. I was worried about us."

Lucy smiled and reached for his hands, held them both tight. "I think we're in this together. The baby's going to need you. I'm going to need you. And I want to always be there for you. I want us to be a family."

"Does that mean yes?"

"Yes."

Chapter Twenty-Five

Dusty walked into the Stewards' office and was greeted warmly by all three men. "What can we do for you?"

"Well, I'm wondering if we can have a conversation off the record?"

When the answer was yes, Dusty initiated a discussion about claiming races, the policies, the grievances, complaints, the upside, the pitfalls. They covered everything.

"Why are you asking about all of this, Dusty?"

"Well," he paused. "I'm dealing with some issues on the backside that have brought it all to the forefront for me. I appreciate that claiming has been a practice since as far back as the 1930's and I think it's served its purpose in its day. I guess what I want to know and I'm just speaking for myself here…."

All three Stewards smiled. They knew better.

"What if we try and change it around? This is state jurisdiction, right?"

All three nodded. "What kind of change?" Simpson asked.

"I don't know exactly. We talk about honesty and integrity when it comes to claiming races. That it's to keep racing honest is waved like an honor flag. But I'm just not so sure there's a whole lot of honor to it any more. Or if it hasn't outlived its usefulness."

"How else would we determine the horse's worth?"

"Well, again, I don't know. It's just something I've been thinking about. I don't think it's fair. I don't think it's fair to the trainer or the owner. I don't think it's fair to the horse. I just don't think it's right. Then you have the trainers trying to unload a horse by dropping them down. How many times have we seen that happen? Too many to count. Where's the honesty and integrity there?"

Fitzgerald, the State Steward, leaned forward, perhaps agreeing. "I have no idea about the logistics of trying to change claiming races. As to whether they're fair or not…? I have to say I hadn't given it much thought, but I don't see a change happening. Not in our lifetime."

Dusty nodded. "Thank you all for listening. I'll do a little research and get back to you. How would that be?"

"That would be on the record," Fitzgerald said, smiling.

"Fair enough," Dusty said. As he walked back to the barn area, a thought occurred to him. Years ago he had an owner who refused to run her horses in claiming races when they had won their lifetime conditions and were no longer competitive in allowance or starter allowance races. She'd said she couldn't sleep nights not having a say in those horse's lives. Not being a good "steward" to the horse. Two of her horses could have gone on to be very competitive in upper claiming races, not to mention several of the others as middle claimers.

"I bred them," she'd said. "I raised them from babies. How do you tell one of your babies: if you don't perform at the top, I'm going to put you up for grabs at the bottom and you'll go from trainer to trainer to trainer? How do you turn your back on them? What kind of person does that?"

"There has to be another way," Dusty said to himself. "There just has to be."

Ben looked up from his desk in the tack room when Dusty walked in.

"What are you doing?" Ben asked.

"I'm contemplating life."

Ben laughed.

Dusty sat down on the cot and leaned his head back. "I feel like this claiming race issue is my purpose in life, at least here."

Ben turned and looked at him.

"What do you want to accomplish, Ben? What is your main goal here?"

"Well." Ben scratched his head. "I've said it before. I even wrote it down somewhere. I figured you could all find it when I'm gone and decide if I'd accomplished it." He searched his top drawer, then the side drawers, and sat back. "Oh there it is. He'd taped it to the top of the calendar from last year. He took it down and unfolded the piece of paper. He thought he'd have trouble reading it, since it was so faded, but not so.

"Okay," he said. "This is what I wrote. 'Simply put, though no easy task, I want to change the course of history in Thoroughbred racing in this country.'"

"You've done it, Ben. You have made a difference. You've made a big difference. You *have* changed the course of history," Dusty said. "I want to make a difference too. I know what it's like to lose horses through no fault of my own. There isn't another business that I know of where this happens. It's one thing for someone to outbid you on a price at a sale. It's one thing to buy and sell a horse. But when you're trying to make a living and running your horse where you think it belongs and doing everything right by that horse, it's just not fair to have it claimed out from under you. It's just not fair."

~ * ~

Matthew dug through his closet for his sketch pad and uncovered an old tam he forgot he even had. He put it on, found his art pencils in his top dresser drawer, and walked down to Biscuit, Poncho, and Bonnie Bee's pasture. He fussed over them, petting them, talking to them. He'd brought carrots which he broke into pieces for them. Then he sat down in the grass and started drawing.

It had been a long time since he'd done any sketching. He'd doodle now and then, but that was the extent of it. He marveled at the shape of the three horses' ears. Each pair was so different from another. Then again, he reminded himself, I'm not seeing them in their entirety at a glance. He found if he moved his head up or down or sideways in either direction, he could almost find the missing parts. When he couldn't he left them blank. His eyes tired easily.

"Afternoon, Matthew!" Mim called from her golf cart up on the hill.

"Good afternoon, Mim!"

"Rain's coming! Be careful!"

"I will! You too!"

"I'm heading back now!" she said, and moved along.

Lucy came out to see what all the commotion was about. "Do you need a hand?"

"That would be fabulous!" Mim said.

Lucy helped her park the golf cart well to the back of the garage. Its battery was just about dead and she needed a push. Lucy hooked up the charger and helped Mim up the ramp to the back door. The wind swirled all around them.

"Matthew!" Mim called, looking back.

"Yes?"

"You look like a beatnik."

Matthew laughed and waved. "Bon Jour!"

Mim laughed.

Lucy helped her in the rest of the way. "I feel so sorry for him. It's a shame about his eyes."

"Don't be," Mim said. "He's seeing brand new things every day. Life is not always about what you can read in books. Sometimes you just need to spread your wings and fly."

~ * ~

Vicky lay down on her bed and closed her eyes. She could hear the old-timers talking downstairs. She could hear them laughing. She could hear Lucy laughing. It was music to her ears. How did I get here, she wondered. This small cozy bedroom: my sanctuary from the storm. My *own* bathroom. She relished the sound of the steady rain.

She was never a huge racehorse fan. She'd never been around horses much at all. She was a city girl most of her entire life. Yet here she was, living on a working Thoroughbred horse racing breeding farm, and loving it.

Living on the third floor of Nottingham Downs all those months with the old-timers was nice. It was interesting. It certainly was different. But there were times when it felt a little too clinical; all that tile and slate flooring, the eighteen-foot ceilings, the huge long walk to the bathrooms, the florescent lighting. This was home. A real home in every sense of the word.

She dozed and woke to the sound and smell of popcorn being made and hot chocolate. She glanced at her bedside clock and was amazed. She'd slept for over an hour. This was so unlike her. "That's what you get for being so comfortable," she said to herself, smiling.

"I need a six-letter word for arrow holder," Frank said.

"Quiver," Jack said.

"No. Yes. You're right. That's it."

"Would you two be quiet," Jeannie said. "I can't hear myself think."

"That's 'cause you don't think," Clint said.

"Very funny."

When Vicky walked down the stairs, yawning, Lucy looked up and smiled. "I'm learning how to knit. Jeannie's going to teach me how to crochet too."

"That's lovely, Lucy." She poured herself a cup of hot chocolate, *cocoa* as Mim called it, filled a small bowl with popcorn and sat down in her chair amongst everyone. She glanced around. All accounted for, all content. "When did it stop raining?"

"About ten minute ago," Miguel said. "More rain tonight."

Vicky sipped her hot chocolate, ate some popcorn, and sipped some more hot chocolate. Such a lazy afternoon. "So what did we decide on for dinner tonight?"

"Chili," Steven said.

"My chili," Miguel said.

"Not too spicy," Vicky cautioned. "Remember we had to throw out the last batch."

"I remember," Miguel said. "Such a waste."

Vicky chuckled. "I'll be standing at your side, making sure."

Jeannie watched Lucy's knit stitches. "Are you counting?"

"Yes," Lucy said, concentrating so hard. "Oops."

Vicky smiled. "It just doesn't get much better than this."

"Lucy put a touch of cinnamon in the cocoa," Mim said. "Can you taste it? It's divine."

"I taste it. It's divine indeed."

~ * ~

The dogs would most always hole up in the barn during a rainstorm and as soon as the skies cleared, would go in search of mud puddles. Señor laughed when he saw them coming and quickly ducked back inside. Muddy dog prints everywhere. "Go! Go play!" He figured he'd hose the porch off once they left, otherwise Liz would be out there with her mop and bucket at first sight. She'd always been a good housekeeper, but now she seemed obsessed.

"I want everything to stay brand new," she'd said. "I've had very little brand new in my life."

"What's that supposed to mean? You didn't like our farmhouse?"

"No, that's not it. I loved it. It was my home for close to forty years. I adored that old house. But it was also your mother's house, and…."

Señor frowned at her. "Well, all your fussing so much makes me glad we don't live in a mud hut. You'd probably scrub us a brand new window every day."

They both had laughed.

The dogs bounded down the porch steps sounding like a herd of buffalo, in search of more mud puddles no doubt and Señor hosed down the porch. Liz came outside a short time later and sat down on her rocking chair next to Señor in his. She laughed at the site of all six dogs romping down through the pasture headed for the pond.

"They're bad," she said.

Señor nodded. "But in a good way. What a life they have. What a life we have." He gripped the top of her hand gently. She patted the top of his hand and looked at him.

"What's the matter then?"

"I don't know," he said. "There's nothing to do tomorrow. We finished the painting today in the bathrooms. It's all done up there."

"I know what you mean." Liz sighed. "I know exactly what you mean."

He looked at her. "These are our golden years, Liz. Or at least silver," he said, referring to the color of their hair.

"Yep." Liz laughed and then sobered. "It's like I want to plow a field or go feed an army. I want to make the biggest batch of stew you've ever seen and feed the world. I want to do everything! We have so much here. I want to give something back."

"You've always given something back, Liz. You were the best volunteer City Church ever saw."

"But I want to do more. Wait," she said, on her feet and heading inside. "I want to show you something." She came back with a pamphlet and opened it up. "Pastor Mitchell says…"

"Pastor Mitchell?"

"From the racetrack. He stops by to see the old-timers. I told him what I was thinking about and he says he knows what I mean and that's why he goes on these missions every year. No preaching, no sermons, just offering a helping hand to those in need."

Señor read the mission name out loud. "Seniors Helping Others."

"See. You build," Liz said. "You feed. You help others learn tasks. You commit for two weeks a year. There are places to go all over."

Señor nodded, looking for the locations.

"I want to go to Appalachia. We can drive there."

"Sounds like you've given this a lot of thought."

"I have," Liz said. "Do you want to go with me?"

Señor smiled. "Have I ever said no to you?"

~ * ~

Dinner was at Ben's tonight, the menu; chicken Paprikash, cranberry Jello salad with fruit and nuts, and hard crusty rolls. Dessert was Millionaire's Pie, Glenda's mother's favorite recipe. She'd made two.

While waiting for everyone, Wendy decided to straighten up the living room. She folded Matthew's sheet and blankets, tucked them under his pillows in the corner of the couch. He left them out all day. "Why put them away?" he'd say. "Ben doesn't care."

She picked up Matthew's sketch book lying on the coffee table. Once upon a time he had wanted to be an art major. She'd talked him out of it. She opened the sketch book and sat down slowly, staring at the drawing he'd been working on. The tree-line in the pasture was blurred, fuzzy, an odd stroke of pencil angle, not scribbled, but erratic. The horses were defined, but unfinished, parts missing....

Oh my God, she thought, is this how he sees things?

When she heard someone coming down the hall she quickly closed the sketchbook, laid it down, and walked into the kitchen.

"Hey, Mom," Matthew said, drying his hair with a towel

Wendy looked at him and smiled, fought back tears.

"What's the matter?"

"Nothing," she wiped her eyes. "It's just your hair. It's so pretty."

Matthew shook his head. He most always wore his hair in a ponytail. It wasn't often it was loose, and hung well past his shoulders, thick and black.

Wendy tried to remember how old he was the day he said he didn't want to cut it anymore. Thirteen? Fourteen maybe? Aside from a trim every so often, "Just the bottom, Mom," he hadn't cut it since. He was a handsome boy, slight in build like his father. Muscles were never their strong suit. She wished she hadn't talked him out of pursuing art as a profession. His talent was a gift. What had she been thinking? And now with his eyes the way they were and no certainty for his eyesight in the future....

"Mom, if you cry at dinner, so help me God, don't you dare blame it on my hair."

Wendy laughed and wiped her eyes again.

Ben walked in the door. It wasn't dark enough outside for him to glow yet, but he was glowing indeed. "They're all so happy over there. It just warms my heart."

Tom walked in behind him. One look at Wendy and he turned. "Ben, you have to stop making Wendy cry."

"It wasn't Ben. It was my hair," Matthew said.

"Well, now *that* I can understand," Tom said, putting his arms around Wendy. "It makes me cry sometimes too."

Matthew laughed. Ben laughed.

Glenda and George arrived, then Dawn and Randy and the children. Carol had the evening off and was going with her lady friends to play Bingo. Liz and Señor arrived, Dusty arrived. They all went about the business of setting up dinner.

When they sat down to eat, D.R. could hardly wait to share his news. "I know how to spell Brontosaurus Rex." Sure enough, he spelled it out. Bro…n…to..s..aur…us … Rex."

"Good boy," Randy said. "Who taught you that?"

"I learned all by myself," he said. "I taught myself."

"I know too," Maeve said. "B r t s x."

"Almost," Randy said, ruffling her hair. "Just slightly abbreviated."

"Abbreviated," D.R. said. "Abb…rev, e..ate it."

Everyone laughed at the way he said "it" at the end, D.R. included, though he had no idea what had charmed the grown-ups. He liked being the center of attention. Liz volunteered her news next. "Randy and I…I mean Señor and I are going to do a mission trip to the Appalachians."

"Really?" Tom asked, with everyone looking on.

"Well, we're going to check tomorrow to see when and where we're needed the most. Pastor Mitchell says we should make sure to ask a lot of questions first. He said he went on one of these mission trips once, and what was really needed the most was just funding. The people had all the repairs underway on their own. He said he ended up just getting in their way. I don't want to get in anyone's way. We want to be able to help."

Matthew looked at them. "Maybe I'll go with you."

"That would be great," Señor said.

"Did Mark get off all right?" Ben asked.

Randy nodded. "Which reminds me, Dusty, he mentioned Standardbred claiming races where the horse's worth is dictated by times." His mother looked at him.

"Their claiming price is based on an average of how fast they run," he added, for her benefit. "He says it doesn't keep owners and trainers from claiming them, but as a rule, he thinks it deters some of the games associated with claiming."

"I got called into the Steward's office once at the trotters," George said. "My horse threw a big race with a big payoff. They said fine, if he throws two big races, you have to run him higher next time. They really watch things like that. It's all about consistency. Longshots winning is not as common at the trotters unless there's a pileup. It's pretty hard to *hold* a trotter."

Dusty sat listening, the wheels turning in his mind. "I talked to our Stewards today just to feel 'em out. They agree that the practices of claiming races are outdated, but they don't seem too anxious to take it on."

Ben looked at him. "I'm right behind you, Dusty. You push and I'll shove."

"If it's the last thing I do," Dusty said.

They all nodded, smiling, knowing.

"Where's Richard?" Randy asked. It's not as if Richard came every night, but with so much going on at the moment.

"Vegas," Wendy said. "He left early this morning and I haven't heard from him since." Almost as if by magic, no sooner had she said that her cellphone beeped with a text message. She took it out of her pocket, looked at it, and chuckled. "It's from Richard. It says he's wining and dining."

"What's that mean?" Señor asked.

Wendy smiled. "Knowing him, it means he's on the job."

"Pass the Paprikash, please," Ben said.

Liz looked at Wendy. "Wining and dining who?"

Wendy shrugged. "My guess would be RJR Enterprises."

"Hope he finds out if they're behind those articles," Dawn said.

Tom looked at her. "You're awful quiet tonight. What's the matter with you?"

Dawn shrugged and then shook her head. "I'm just bothered by those articles. They're lies and this is getting personal and we all know how I feel about that. I don't like it. It makes me nervous."

"Why you nervous, Mommy," Maeve asked, tugging on her shirt sleeve.

"Oh, honey, it's nothing. I'm nervous that Uncle Tom is going to eat all the Paprikash and I want some more."

Tom smiled and passed her the platter.

"Me too," Maeve said.

Dawn dished out a serving for both and handed the platter back to Tom. When he winked at her, she smiled. "I know," he said. "I know what you mean."

Randy looked at them both and nodded. Randy would protect Dawn with his life and right behind him would be Tom. He and Dawn weren't blood-related, but they were as close as a brother and sister could ever be.

Ben looked at all of them. "This isn't personal and it's not going to be. And if it does get personal, it's coming to me. Now come on, eat. All of you. You're giving me indigestion with all this talk."

"Indigestion," D.R. said. "I n d i…ges…t..ion."

"Yes! Yes, little man," Tom said, high-fiving him. "Yes!"

As they ate it started to rain again, and it rained and it rained and it rained. With a big bolt of lightning, the power went out, so they lit candles around the living room and one in the main bathroom. Tom looked out the kitchen window at T-Bone's Place. They'd lost power too, but some of the lights were on.

"It's good having Junior there," Tom said.

"What?" Ben looked at him in the flickering light of the candles.

"He's got the generator going."

"Good."

When a car pulled up to the farmhouse, Tom went out with an umbrella to protect Carol from the storm. "The power's out everywhere," she said, taking off her jacket. "Clear up past Monticello."

She sat down with the others in the living room amidst the glowing candles and joined in as they all told "Remember When," stories. Even after both children were sound asleep, cuddled up next to Randy and Dawn, they were still sharing memories.

Chapter Twenty-Six

Dawn was pleasantly surprised to not see an article about Nottingham Downs in the *Morning Banter*. Jason, the stable guard, smiled. "Like my momma used to say, when the devil comes charging, open the door wide and sometimes he might just go right out the back."

Dawn chuckled. "And they can just keep right on going as far as I'm concerned."

"I hear ya."

Tom had coffee made. Ben was sitting at his desk in the tack room. Dusty arrived shortly after Dawn. Then here came Junior.

"Is everything okay at T-Bone's Place?" Ben asked.

"Yep." Junior poured a cup of coffee and stood staring at the training chart. "We have three to gallop, one to walk, one to pony. Are you ponying or am I?" he asked Tom.

Tom just looked at him for a moment. "You're asking that because…?"

Junior sipped his coffee. "Because you're getting old. I'm just lookin' out for ya."

Ben laughed. So did Dawn and Dusty. "What goes around comes around," Ben said, and laughed some more. "God, I needed that!"

Tom looked at them all and shook his head. "All right, screw all of you. I'm heading over to the Secretary's office to see what's going on and Joe had better not be late again. Pony Alley and I'll be right back." He started down the shedrow, pointing at Junior. "And don't you be worrying about me being an old man. On your best day…"

"Yeah, yeah," Junior said. "I hear ya."

Joe was on the job but in his usual-of-late frazzled state. Tom walked past him and into Wendy's office, not wanting him to think he was checking up on him, which would probably only add to whatever frustrations the man was going through.

Tom stood at the window looking out over the racetrack. Dew still covered the infield. He recalled Dawn saying once it was, "Like diamonds on green velvet."

He watched several horses being galloped, watched as one just about dumped its rider, and smiled at how the boy hung in there and righted himself. Feeling a little nostalgic after last night and all the reminiscing, he hoped when the day came to step down off his horse, that he'd know and that'd he'd handle it with the sense that Ben had. He hoped to be able to deal with life the way Mim was facing it. He hoped….

"Shit!" he said. He saw a loose horse coming down the stretch, reins and stirrups flapping. He hurried outside, stood watching from the rail, and smiled when both outriders closed in on the horse and the one nabbed him.

"Who was it?" Tom said.

"Billy."

"Is he okay?"

"Yeah."

Tom strained to look up the head of the stretch. Billy was walking back down the outside rail, mud from head to toe and limping a little. Tom waited to make sure he was all right, gave the boy a leg-up on the horse, and the outrider jogged them off and turned them loose.

Tom walked back to the barn, arriving just in time to pony Batgirl to the track to gallop, Johnny aboard. Dawn watched as he led them down between the barns to the gap and then hurried to get her stall done, clean her water bucket and fill her haynet. Having only five horses at the track was almost like a vacation. It wasn't even seven o'clock yet and there were only three more horses to go.

Randy stopped by. "Did I just see Richard?"

"Yep, he's back. He took the red-eye home."

"What's going on?"

"He wants to meet with all of us after the track closes. He said around ten or so. Can you make it?"

"Where at? Over at the office?"

"Yes, upstairs."

Randy looked at her. "Wow."

"Please try to be there. I have a feeling this is something really big."

Randy nodded. "If it's at all possible, I'll be there."

~ * ~

Joe watched a steady stream of management personnel board the elevator over a ten-minute period of time and stood trying to fend off a threatening panic attack. "What are they doing?" he said to himself. "What's going on? Are they convening to fire me?"

When Randy walked into the Secretary's office headed for the elevator, Joe stared. This was highly unusual seeing Randy here, particularly this time of morning.

"Is everything okay?" Joe asked.

"Fine, fine," Randy said, the doors closing.

Joe gathered all the entries and sat down, watching the door, wondering, worrying, fretting....

Dawn looked up when Randy entered the office and made room for him to sit next to her. Tom was seated over next to Dusty. Wendy sat at her desk, Ben at his.

"Where to begin..." Richard said.

Ben motioned for him to just dive right in.

Richard cleared his throat. "Well, considering how it wasn't difficult at all to meet with the head of RJR Enterprises, I can't say for sure that they're behind everything that's been going on, but I'm pretty sure they are. I'm also pretty sure they're not going to stop until they bring us down totally or we stop them."

"How?" Ben said.

"Well...."

"If this is going to be about us and slots, no," Ben said.

"Ben, it is about slots. It all comes down to slots."

Ben stood up to leave.

"Ben," Richard said. "You'll have one more year, two at best without slots, and that's an optimistic estimate."

Ben turned and looked at him. "This is a Thoroughbred racetrack, Richard. Not a goddamned casino."

Dawn looked from one to the other. "Richard, we've been over this. You know how Ben feels, so unless there is something new...."

"There is," he said. "Ben, please. Sit down. Hear me out."

Ben sighed and sat back down.

"Here's what I proposed. And this was going in as if I had no idea they're trying to bring us down."

"What kind of proposal?" Randy asked.

"I proposed we combine operations."

"No," Ben said, shaking his head. "Nobody's going to tell us what to do. They don't know racing, not from our standpoint. They don't know what we go through, what every horseman goes through."

"And they don't want to," Richard said. "You're right. They could care less. Listen, I met this elderly lady on the plane with her friends. She loves Nottingham Downs, but she also loves the slots. If we had them here, do you think she'd go to Vegas? I don't think so. We'd have Vegas here for her and her friends, for everyone. Ben, this isn't going away. This is here to stay."

Ben shook his head.

"What good are you going to do for racing, Ben, when the doors close? Slots will bring in more money, bigger crowds, higher purses, better horses." He corrected himself. "A higher value of horse."

Ben looked around the room at Tom, Dawn, Randy, Dusty, Wendy. They were all looking to him.

"Here's what I propose," Richard said. "We don't have to have anything to do with them. We can let them run their operation and we run ours. We're doing fine. With money from them and higher purses, we'll start turning a profit. It's a win-win situation. We don't have to change anything. We are running Nottingham Downs the way we want to, the way that makes us all proud."

"And how do you 'propose' we do this?" Ben asked.

"We lease them the third floor," Richard said. "It's as simple as that."

Everyone looked from him to Ben and back.

"It's empty."

Everyone just stared.

"We turn it from a liability into an asset."

"How would that work?" Ben asked.

"They come in and redo the entire floor themselves. They access it from inside the grandstand. They cover all the costs. We lease them the floor and they not only pay us for the space; we get a percentage of the revenue."

Ben sat for a moment, thinking. "What's the catch?" he said.

"Well, there is one," Richard conceded. "From that point on and for however long we are associated with RJR Enterprises, we'd be known as Nottingham Downs and Casino."

"It would be on the program that way?" Dawn asked.

Richard nodded. "I tried, Dawn. That's the deal."

Ben stared down at the floor and sighed. "I'm going to have to think about this. When do you have to let them know?"

"As soon as possible."

Ben nodded. "All right." He looked around at his friends, his family, his loved ones. "Give me a couple of hours." He walked to the door.

Tom stood up. "Are you going to the barn?"

"No," Ben said. "I'm going home." He waved over his shoulder, boarded the elevator, and was gone, leaving them all behind.

Chapter Twenty-Seven

Ben drove past Glenda and George's, past T-Bone's Place, and into his driveway. He looked back and was glad no one had been on the porch at T-Bone's, as he was so preoccupied, he didn't even look that way or wave. He parked and got out, walked into the main barn, and was happy no one was there. He didn't want to talk. He didn't want to debate the issue. He didn't want to listen. He just wanted to be left alone. He sat down on the bench outside the tack room and leaned his head back.

"Ah, Meg," he said. "What am I going to do?"

"You're going to do the right thing," he could hear her say. "You always do."

"Yes, but what's right for me, might not be right for everyone else. What would this place be like if Dawn and Randy weren't here anymore? Or Tom and Wendy and the boys? Glenda and George? Randy's parents? There's plans to build a large animal vet hospital here someday. What would be the point if there's no place to race close by?"

He sat in the quiet of the barn, so many memories, so many horses over the years. He thought about the good times and the bad, the endings and new beginnings. He thought about the day Dawn came home.

"Maybe I should let them make the decision. Maybe I should just back away."

"Could you live with that?" Meg asked.

"I don't know." He turned when he heard a noise and smiled at Mim, standing just inside the barn aisle way supporting herself with her cane. "Hey, Mim."

"Ben." She hesitated walking any further. "I'm just out for a ride if you want to join me." When she turned and slowly made her way back to her golf cart, Ben stood up and walked outside.

"Where we going?" he asked, climbing aboard.

"Oh, everywhere," Mim said.

Ben enjoyed the ride. They didn't talk. They just rode all around the property, down between the pastures, up over the hills. She'd even forged a trail on the tree line separating his farm from the rest of the world. She motioned to Matthew sitting in the pasture with Poncho, Biscuit, and Bonnie Bee. Ben smiled.

They rode up to the training track and drove slowly around the outside rail. "This is a nice track, Ben."

He nodded.

"Junior says you'll be running Bo-T off the farm in the Burgundy Blue."

Ben nodded again. "That's what I hear."

Mim smiled. "We're looking forward to that. We'll all be up here watching."

"Save room for me," Ben said.

Mim looked at him. "What do you mean?"

"Oh. Slots."

Mim sighed, the two of them looking out at the training track. "It's a sign of the times," she said. "There's not much you can do."

"I can say no."

"What will that accomplish?" she asked.

"Nothing." He told her about Richard's proposal and sat dreading her response. He knew she'd agree with him and that would make his decision even harder.

"So, basically they would run the slots and everything else will go on as usual at Nottingham Downs but for sharing the space and a name?"

Ben nodded.

"That's it?"

"Yes."

"And you trust Richard Spears?"

"Yes."

"Then what's the problem?"

"Well...when you put it that way, I don't know."

Mim laughed and so did Ben.

"Oh, it's not about us anymore, Ben," Mim said. "Not really. It's about the next generation. It's about the babies; the hopes for them and the dreams. They've got to have a place to go. You want to send them all away? You don't want to do that, do you?"

Ben shook his head.

"Well then." She pressed her foot to the pedal. "It's time for my nap." She dropped him off at his house and with a wave, took the new path back to T-Bone's Place. Ben climbed the steps and sat down on the porch glider. The dogs had apparently been waiting for Mim's return and all milled around her. She must have treats for them, he decided, because each dog approached her and then ran off. Lucy came outside to help her get off the cart and then helped her climb the ramp.

Ben smiled. He was seeing pretty good, and in more ways than one. He took out his cellphone and speed-dialed Dawn.

"Tell Richard go ahead," he said.

"Are you sure?"

"Positive. Tell everyone to keep it to themselves until it's a done deal. We'll make an announcement at the banquet."

~ * ~

Ben rarely spent leisurely time at the farm during racing season. Since the horse racing business operated seven days a week, most full-time trainers and grooms were at the track all day, each and every day. Some went home for a few hours on dark days or when they didn't have a horse in that day. But for the most part, the option of Ben having the afternoon to lounge around and do anything he so desired was a treat.

He searched the kitchen cupboard for a can of potted meat, checked the date, and made himself a sandwich. It didn't taste as good as he remembered. He ate about half of it, and then made a pot of coffee and sat down on the porch to wait while it perked.

"Hey, Ben," George said, tooling by on the tractor.

Ben waved. "What's for dinner tonight?"

"Beef stew. Liz's making it. We're eating there."

What a life I have, Ben thought. And so many years, I was alone. "Not good to live alone," he said to himself. "It makes you too set in your ways." He felt as if the weight of the world had been lifted from his shoulders. He still didn't like the idea of slots at Nottingham Downs, but once he'd made the decision, he resigned himself to it.

He closed his eyes and breathed in the farm air. Horses. He'd had a lifetime of horses and he would never tire of them. "Ever." Well, so what do I do now?

He'd already toured the farm with Mim. Everything was in good order. He wished he had a horse to ride. Maybe Poncho or Biscuit? "Nah, no sense falling on my head." How long had it been since he'd ridden? He laughed, recalling, it was right about the time Tom started ponying for him on a regular basis.

He propped his feet on the old wicker couch table, hunkered down, and leaned his head back on the chair. Maybe I'll take a nap. He opened his eyes when he heard Matthew come up the steps. Matthew gave him the peace sign and Ben went back to snoozing.

Matthew closed the screen door quietly and laid his sketchbook and pencils on the table, searched the fridge for a snack, and smelled the opened can of potted meat. "Ew." He made a face. Out the kitchen window he saw Ben stir. He made a peanut butter and jelly sandwich, poured a glass of milk, and went out to join him.

"Hey," he said.

Ben nodded. "What are you eating?"

"PB&J. You want half?"

"Yeah." Ben reached for the half sandwich. "You feel like bringing me a glass of milk?"

"Sure." Matthew handed him his and went and got another one and came back out.

The two sat eating and drinking their milk. "Like *Romper Room*," Ben said.

Matthew looked at him.

"Never mind. It was before your time." Ben smiled.

They watched the horses in the pastures grazing. Watched the birds perched on the fence, preening. Watched a plane overhead. Ben had no idea how much of anything Matthew was seeing, but he seemed to be enjoying the view as well.

"I've been thinking," Matthew said.

"Oh? About what?"

"The Appalachian Trail. I'm thinking when I go down with Liz and Señor that I'm going to hike the trail back."

"By yourself?"

"Well, yes, unless you want to come along."

Ben laughed. "We wouldn't get very far."

"I think you'd be surprised," Matthew said.

They both sat quietly for a moment.

"Yes, by myself," Matthew said.

"Your mother is going to have a fit. You might want to go see the doctor first and get clearance. That way…."

Matthew nodded. "Good idea."

Another moment of quiet passed.

"What if he says no?"

"Then you'll have to rethink your plan."

Matthew smiled. "What about if I just say I went?"

"What? You don't think she'll check?"

"I'm twenty-two years old, Ben. She can't, not really."

"Then off you'd go with a lie."

"Oh geez," Matthew said. "Why'd you have to go and say that?"

"Because it's true."

"Fine, I'll go see him."

Ben nodded. "Don't be lying to the doctor either."

~ * ~

Tom followed Dusty's truck out of the parking lot and headed home. Not a mile down the road, he noticed Joe

Feigler following along behind them. He didn't think much of it at first, but the closer he got to home, the more it started to bother him. He phoned Dusty.

"What the fuck?" he said. "Joe's following us. Did you invite him to dinner or something?"

"No." Dusty glanced out his sidemirror. "I'll be damned."

"Let's separate and see what he does."

Tom put his blinker on and turned right. Dusty put his blinker on and turned left. Joe drove straight ahead. "I guess the guy has me paranoid now," Tom said, laughing.

They hung up, doubled back around and there sat Joe in a parking lot ahead. Dusty phoned Tom. "Don't look. Just keep driving."

"I see him. What the hell is wrong with him?"

Dusty and Tom drove on by, both looking in the opposite direction and Joe pulled out and started following them again. "All right, that did it." Tom hit the brakes.

Joe screeched to a stop and just missed slamming into the back of the truck. "Oh my God!"

Tom got out and stormed back to Joe's car. "Are you following me? What are you following me for?"

"I'm not following you!"

"Don't give me that shit!"

Dusty backed up and parked in front of Tom's truck, got out and walked back. "What's going on? Joe, what are you doing?"

Cars and trucks slowed and drove around them. Then a cop car pulled in behind them, lights flashing. The officer got out of his car. "Everything all right?"

"Yes," Tom said. "There's no damage. He hit me, but it's nothing."

The officer took a look. "Yep, don't see any damage. Ya'll need to just get off the road now. We're about to get into rush hour."

"Thank you," Tom said. He and Dusty walked back to their trucks. Tom glared in his sidemirror at Joe. Joe looked away and then back, the two just staring at one another for a second. Tom motioned for Joe and Dusty to follow him. When they approached a fast-food restaurant, Tom put on his blinker and all three pulled in and parked to the back.

"Get out of your car," Tom said. "I'm not talking to you sitting in there like some kind of idiot scared to death." He yanked Joe's door open. "Get out!"

Dusty glanced around the parking lot and tapped Tom on the arm. There were several people leaving the restaurant watching them. Tom stepped back.

"It's your turn to treat," Tom said, nudging Joe toward the restaurant entrance. "Come on, let's go."

The three walked into the restaurant and stood in line. "Three cokes," Tom said.

"One diet," Joe said.

Tom rolled his eyes, paid for the cokes, and the three of them went over to a table and sat down. "Now don't be pissing me off," Tom said, in a real low voice. "No bullshit. Why are you following us?"

"I'm being watched."

"What?"

Joe nodded, wide-eyed. "I'm being watched. At first I thought it was my wife. She's been acting really strange lately."

"Stranger than you?" Tom asked.

Dusty kicked him under the table.

"Okay, so if it's not your wife, who is it?"

"I don't know. I thought it might have been you."

"Me? Why the hell would I want to follow you? I can't wait to get away from you every day. You're turning into a loony tune."

"I am not," Joe said, apparently trying to convince himself by saying it with conviction. "It was after the day that guy started talking to me."

"What guy?"

"I don't know. That guy."

Dusty and Tom exchanged glances.

Joe slurped his diet coke, eyes darting left and right. "He said he was there to apply for the racing secretary's position. He was in the parking lot."

"Where?"

"At the track. Where else?" Joe said.

Tom shrugged. "But we're not looking for a secretary. Although we may be if you keep this shit up."

Joe licked his lips, darting his eyes back and forth again. When he went to take another drink of his Coke, Tom took it away. "I think you've had enough caffeine for the day."

"I can't sleep."

"That makes sense."

"I pace all night."

Dusty and Tom looked at one another.

"And then when I do fall asleep, it's time to get up."

Tom sat thinking. He loved a good story. "Why would you think your wife's following you?"

"Because she's going through the menopause."

Tom stared.

"It's not her though."

"Good," Tom said.

Joe reached across the table for his Coke.

"One sip and that's it," Tom said, handing it to him.

Dusty chuckled. Joe even cracked a jittery smile.

"The guy wouldn't have made a good secretary. He didn't know anything about horses."

Tom and Dusty looked at one another long and hard, both thinking of Dawn's comment about the Banter article.

"What?" Joe said. "What?"

"Nothing," Tom said. "Don't be talking to him anymore."

"Yes, but if he's following me…?"

"I'll tell you what," Tom said. "How about if we draw up a contract saying your job is secure, at least until the end of the meet and you get your act together."

"But?"

"I know. Ben doesn't like contracts, but we'll talk to him."

Dusty nodded.

"All right?"

"All right," Joe said. "Thank you."

"And don't talk to strangers."

~ * ~

Everyone assembled for dinner expected Ben to be in a bad mood, considering the day's decision on slots, but were pleasantly surprised when he and Matthew walked up to the Señor and Liz's together. Ben was wearing his walking shoes and appeared to be on top of the world.

"It's over. It's done, I don't want to talk about it," he said. "Let's eat."

"We're waiting for Pastor Mitchell," Liz said. "He's joining us this evening."

No sooner said than Pastor Mitchell knocked on the door.

"Come in, come in," Señor said. "Come on in."

Pastor Mitchell shook all the men's hands and gave all the women a hug. He'd eaten dinner with them before, but it had been a while. They all sat down. Also customary when he dined with them, was his saying grace. Everyone bowed their heads and closed their eyes.

"Lord," he said. "Bless this food and these lovely caring people. Guide us in our daily lives so that we may do your service. Guide us in the decisions we make in our everyday lives and here tonight."

Ben opened an eye and looked at the man, then looked at Tom, who coincidently had opened one of his eyes and was looking at him. Tom shrugged.

"Thank you for the home provided for the old-timers. Thank you for this lovely farm."

"Amen," Maeve said.

"Amen" Everyone laughed. "I was just about done anyway, little one," Pastor Mitchell said, smiling.

Everyone passed their bowls down and Señor ladled out the beef stew. "Smells good, Liz." Platters of French bread and butter and jam were passed around.

"That was a fairly loaded prayer if you don't mind my saying so, Pastor Mitchell," Ben said. "Do you have something on your mind?"

"As a matter of fact, I do. It's about Junior and Lucy's wedding nuptials."

"Their nuptials?"

"The wedding ceremony. As you all know, Tom is going to be the best man. Lucy's best friend Judy is going to be her maid of honor."

"Okay," Ben said, dipping his bread in the stew.

"We need someone to walk Lucy down the aisle."

"What aisle?" Ben said. "I thought they were getting married in the chapel at the track. That's not much of an aisle."

"Well, see that's what we wanted to talk to you about."

"We?" Ben glanced at Tom and Dusty.

"We discussed it this afternoon and…."

"You three?" Ben asked, motioning.

"Yes," Pastor Mitchell said.

Dusty and Tom kept their eyes on their food.

"See, this is a big commitment for these young people, especially with a child on the way."

Ben had visions of the horse-drawn carriage these three men had cooked up for Billy Martin's funeral a few years back. What had started out as a simple memorial for the man's passing turned into a media event on the evening news.

Dawn and Randy sat eating quietly. They were also remembering that day; the procession down through the barn area, the bagpipes playing....

"We thought maybe a little more elaborate ceremony...."

George and Glenda were recalling watching the news the night of Billy Martin's funeral, how they all sat around the television. It was the first time they'd met Wendy, a first date for her and Tom. Wendy was remembering that night too. They were all at Ben's. She was overdressed. Everyone was in tears over a man no one really even liked.

"We're thinking perhaps...."

Dusty stepped in. "I don't know if you know it or not, Ben, but the tickets for the banquet aren't exactly selling like hotcakes this year, even with the Come-as-You-Are theme. Times are hard."

Ben reached for his coffee cup and took a drink.

"So," Dusty said. "We got to talking and thought maybe, well, just maybe Junior and Lucy could get married at the banquet. We checked with the hall. They can arrange for an aisle down the center of the room between the tables. We can have the ceremony. They say their vows and we eat. We already have a band, food. We'll just need to get a wedding cake."

"I can make one," Liz said. "I can make two!"

"The Lord works in mysterious way," Pastor Mitchell said, buttering his bread. "It's as if this was all meant to be."

"All except for...." Tom cleared his throat. This was where he was supposed to step in. "Lucy would like you to walk her down the aisle, Ben."

"Me? Why me?"

"Well, maybe because of your new tennis shoes."

Everyone laughed, Ben included.

"When we talked to her about it...."

"You already talked to Lucy about this?" Ben said. This was getting better by the minute.

"Well, yes. She was the one that suggested you could walk her down the aisle."

Ben sat nodding. Maybe if he hadn't have had that meeting today about slots. Maybe if he wasn't in such a good mood. "I'll tell you what," he said. "I'll walk her down the aisle, but only after you, Pastor Mitchell, go and talk to her father."

"I have talked to him."

"About this?"

"Well, no, but about Lucy and Junior in general."

"Good. Let me know how it turns out and we'll go from there. If he says no, I'll step in. But something tells me you're going to be able to convince him that it's not only the right thing to do, but something he'll be proud of for years to come."

Dawn smiled, as did Glenda, Wendy, Liz and Carol.

"There's just one other thing," Dusty said. Ben glanced at Tom and Pastor Mitchell. Both obviously knew what Dusty was about to say. "We thought maybe, since this is going to be a wedding too, that we might cover the cost out of the Emergency Fund. That way everyone who wants to come, can, and won't have to worry about buying a ticket."

"We thought if they want to donate anything, it can go to Junior and Lucy. They don't have any insurance for the baby," Tom said.

"It'll just be a wedding box," Pastor Mitchell said. "They're not a charity. This is their wedding."

"Well, it sounds good to me," Ben said. "Go for it."

Señor ladled more beef stew for Dusty. Randy passed his bowl down too.

"How will you be letting people know?" Wendy asked. "The banquet is only two days away."

"I'll let everyone on the backside know, and in case I miss someone, maybe we can have Joe tell everyone that comes into the Secretary's office. Maybe even put up a flier."

"Who?" Liz asked.

"Joe Feigler, the racing secretary."

Pastor Mitchell looked around the table. "I don't know what's happened to that man lately, but he sure has gotten strange."

Tom shared part of the story of Joe following him and Dusty home.

"Well, we have been excluding him quite a bit," Wendy said.

"That's because he can't keep anything to himself," Tom said. "Hell, I'm surprised he didn't blab all over the place about the old-timers being upstairs."

Everyone looked at one another, the possibility of that descending over them. "Well, they're here now," Tom said. "That's all behind us."

Dusty sighed. "We can only hope."

Chapter Twenty-Eight

Jason stepped out of the guard shack and handed Dawn a copy of the *Morning Banter* folded open to the Sports page. Dawn read the headline: "Nottingham Downs the Future of Thoroughbred Racing."

"Do I want to read this?" she asked.

"Oh yeah," Jason said. "It's positive for once."

Dawn walked to the barn with her eyes glued to the page. Respectful treatment of the horses, conscientious employee relations, family-run operation, upstanding community involvement…. She walked into the tack room to find Ben, Tom, Dusty, and Junior, all glued to their own copies.

"I'm speechless," Tom said. "To what do we owe this turnaround?"

"Well," Dawn said. Junior wasn't privy to the slots information or Richard's visit to Vegas twice in two days. "I'd say we should not look a gift horse in the mouth."

Ben smiled. "Good answer."

"Entries are open," they heard over the loudspeaker.

"This is strange," Tom said. "Are we all in one another's dreams?"

"If so, Joe's here too," Dusty said.

They all laughed.

Junior poured a cup of coffee and stood looking at the training chart. "Why are you ponying Alley two days in a row?"

Ben turned slowly and just looked at him.

"I'm just wondering," Junior said sheepishly in response.

"Well, don't," Ben said.

Dusty and Tom laughed.

"Because…?" Junior said.

"Are you second-guessing my training or you really don't know?"

"I don't. She's fit. She win her last time. Why aren't you galloping her?"

"Because by my way of training, taking into account this particular horse as with all the horses I train, each one being different…."

Tom wrote something on a piece of paper and handed it to Dawn.

"Because she *is* fit, she doesn't need to be trained hard. You save the wear and tear and it gives her a mental freshness. Consider this your first lesson in Training 101. You don't make any money in the morning."

Dawn read Tom's explanation on the piece of paper. "She's fit - doesn't need trained hard - keep her loose – keep her frisky."

"Okay," Junior said, when Tom passed him the note. "You ponying her or am I?"

Tom smiled. "I'll do it. I need the exercise."

Morning training began. Dusty only had one horse in the ReHab and ReHome barn, so he got an early start on informing the backside about the HBPA banquet also being Junior's and Lucy's wedding celebration. He walked up and down each shedrow, and ended up in Hannity's barn as Jackson's horse Sunrise Sam was being hand-walked. The horse looked more body sore to him than anything else. He made a point of watching the horse walk all the way down the shedrow, knowing Hannity was watching him, and waited until the horse was led back around before approaching Hannity.

"Morning!" Dusty said, and to the groom, "Buenos Dias."

"Buenos Dias." The groom smiled.

Dusty shared the news about the banquet with Hannity, and then repeated himself in Spanish to the groom.

"Gracias," the groom said.

Dusty walked on to the next barn, glancing back several times at the horse, and met up with Randy at the Greentree barn. "When's Mark supposed to come back?"

"Tomorrow I think," Randy said. "Why?"

"Nothing. Just Hannity."

Randy looked at his clipboard. "I'll be heading over there soon. Apparently he's off his feed."

"Oh wonderful," Dusty said. When he reached the last barn, he doubled back to make sure to catch anyone who might have been at the track or at one of the wash racks the first time around, and came upon a groom getting after a horse for something and shanking him pretty hard.

"What's the crime?" Dusty asked.

"Ah, this common motherfucker."

Dusty grabbed the shank from him. "Enough. All right?"

The horse stood wide-eyed and trembling.

"Enough!" Dusty repeated.

The man looked at him.

"Oh. You gonna pick a fight with me now? How about I write you up?"

"No. No," the man said, walking away to try and calm down. "No."

Dusty talked to the horse, petted him on the neck, calming him, and walked him down the shedrow. His groom was waiting for him when they came back around.

"I'm sorry," the man said.

Dusty nodded. "You heard about the banquet, right?"

"Yes."

"All right," Dusty said. "We'll see you there. Make sure you go register with Irene. We need to know how many's coming." He continued on to the kitchen, making sure everyone there got the wedding news.

Several people were reading the *Morning Banter*.

"About time they get it right," Brickman said.

Dusty smiled, agreeing. "Hope to see you at the banquet."

Randy's truck was parked outside Hannity's barn as he walked back through the barn area. He was tempted to go down and observe the exam, but figured that might be crossing a line of sorts and walked on. He held a horse for Atwood at the wash rack, talked to the horse, and when done, handed the horse back and walked on.

Ben was coming from the opposite direction. "Last one," Ben said. Tom and Red were leading Whinny to the track, Junior aboard. "Did you tell everybody?"

"I think so."

"Wendy posted something." Ben dodged a horse and jockey side-stepping in front of him.

"Hey, Ben," the jock said.

Ben nodded and looked at Dusty. "Garcia's looking for you."

"What for? He say?"

"No." Ben walked on.

Dusty backtracked to Garcia's barn. The man was cleaning a stall. "What's going on?" Dusty asked. "You wanted to talk to me?"

Garcia nodded, hesitated and sighed, leaning on his pitchfork. "Any way I go borrow to pay my feed bill?"

"How much do you owe?" Dusty asked.

"Two month. $210. I pay back soon."

"All right." Dusty said. Garcia had borrowed money before and though he didn't necessarily pay it back soon, he did always eventually clear his debt. "I'll be back through in a little while. I'll bring it then."

"Thank you, Dusty."

"You'll be at the banquet, right?"

Garcia nodded. "My Missus too."

"Let Irene know."

"I will."

By post time of the first race, Irene had close to two-hundred people registered for the banquet-wedding. Richard had returned from his second trip to Vegas, contract in hand, and would be flying back later today to personally deliver the signed copy. He met up with Ben at the barn and sat down with him in the tack room.

Ben looked at the contract, looked at the four signatures from RJR Enterprises. "You say Matt looked it over?"

"Yes. He says it's a good deal."

"Oh, I don't doubt that."

Richard nodded. "Thank you."

"I sign here?"

"Yes."

Ben signed his name and sat back as Richard signed his name as a witness. "When will this all take place?"

"Soon. They'll get their PR department on it right away."

"I'd like you to make the announcement tomorrow night at the banquet. You'll be back in time, right?"

"Yes."

"The horsemen need to hear this from us," Ben said. "Don't let them broadcast this until then."

"I won't. Trust me."

Ben nodded. "Did you see the paper?"

"Yes. It pretty much confirms what we suspected, doesn't it?"

"I'd say. It's the same syndicate name. I'll tell you, life sure was easier when I was just a trainer."

"Yeah, but Ben, look at what you have done for racing. Look at what you've done for the horses."

"Well, I didn't do it myself. I had lots of help."

"Thank you," Richard said. "For everything." He smiled. "Who knew boots and jeans could be so comfortable."

~ * ~

Liz got word of the "head count" by way of Irene at the racetrack and took off to the store for cake mix. She'd made wedding cakes before but not for this many people. She waved to the old-timers as she passed T-Bone's Place. Some were on the front porch. Some were sitting under the big oak tree by the driveway. The leaves will be starting to turn soon, she thought. She looked forward to that. Autumn was her favorite time of year. She wondered what the plans were for Labor Day. A picnic? It would be nice if we could all picnic together.

She decided she'd make a big sheet cake. Sixteen cakes, double-decker, frosted all as one, all white. She bought sixteen aluminum foil pans, sixteen boxes of cake mix, six boxes of powdered sugar, vanilla, and eggs. She stood at the checkout counter, staring into her cart, wanting to make sure she hadn't forgotten anything. She already had a decorator set.

"Shortening!" She had some at home. "I'd better get another can." She found the aisle, got two just in case, and pushed her cart back to the checkout counter.

"Ah, a wedding cake I bet?" the cashier said, running the items over the scanner.

"Yes. The wedding is tomorrow night."

"Oh my. You're going to be exhausted."

"Actually I'm looking forward to it."

Señor came out to help her when she pulled into the driveway. "I made the platform," he said, grabbing all the grocery bags with two hands. "You'll have to let me know what you want it covered with."

"I'm thinking a white tablecloth." She followed him inside. "We can tape the underneath. A big piece of white cardboard would be nice too."

"I wonder where I could get that?" He put the bags on the counter.

"The craft store maybe," Liz said. "If you can't find any, get white poster board."

"I'll be right back," Señor said. He waved to Mim, Steven, and Miguel, out for a ride on Mim's golf cart. "Liz's starting on the cake."

They all waved back, looking forward to tomorrow. Liz had four cakes ready to go in the oven when Señor returned. "These go to Ben's. Matthew has the oven preheated. Set the timer for twenty-eight minutes."

She mixed four more before he came back. "These go to Glenda and George's. She's waiting for you." The next batch went to Randy and Dawn's. Carol had their oven ready.

"These stay here," she said, when he returned. "Go check the cakes at Ben's."

"They're not ready yet."

"Go!" she said. "Every oven's different. Here, take these toothpicks. Check the centers. No wait, stay here, I'll go."

"I know how to check a cake," Señor insisted. "Stay here, for Christ sake." Off he went.

"Frosting, frosting," Liz said to herself. "Should I make it now, or should I wait? I'll make it now." She whipped up five batches of regular, made another stiffer batch for the flowers and edging, and put them all in the refrigerator. She looked out the window. "Where is he?"

Chapter Twenty-Nine

Pastor Mitchell walked down Guciano's shedrow. With fifteen horses between the two of them, both of Lucy's parents were most always at the track all day. The tack room door was open, the feed-room door open. "Tony?" he called out. "Loretta?" No answer. He decided they couldn't be far, not with the barn open, so he sat down on the bench to wait. It faced the ReHab and ReHome barn. He waved to Dusty.

"Have you seen them?"

"Not for a while."

A few minutes later, Lucy's parents came walking down the road between the barns, each carrying a bag of fast food and a soda. "Don't start with me," Tony said.

"I don't recall finishing with you," Pastor Mitchell replied.

Loretta walked past him and sat down on a chair outside their tack room. Tony walked into the tack room to sit down.

"Do you want me to lay this on you now or come back after you eat?" Pastor Mitchell said.

No reply from either.

"I suppose you heard Lucy and Junior are getting married tomorrow."

Silence.

"I see you were signed up earlier for the dinner and now you're not."

Loretta looked at him. "It was just the banquet before. We always go."

"And now because it's also a wedding, your daughter's wedding…?"

"An ass-backwards wedding," Tony said, from inside the tack room.

"Well, it's not in the customary order. I'll give you that, considering the child on the way."

"You're wasting your time, Pastor. We're not going," Tony said.

"All right. Ben said he'd walk her down the aisle if you won't." Pastor Mitchell hesitated. "But it's a girl's dream to have her father walk her down the aisle on her wedding day."

"Yeah? Well it's a father's dream too. But not this one, not this way."

"Because?"

"Because she's pregnant."

"And that somehow changes the fact that she's your daughter and that she looks up to you as her father. And you, Loretta, she looks up to you as her mother. How does she stop being a daughter because she's with child?"

"With child?" Tony said, on his feet now and standing in the tack room doorway. "Don't try and make it sound like she's right out of the Bible."

"What would you rather I say about this grandchild of yours that she's carrying? Shall I call that child names instead? Shall I damn that child to a life of hell?"

Silence....

"Should I turn my back on Lucy too? Should I call her names? Shall I curse her? You're both turning your back on her. Maybe I should too. Why should I care?"

More silence except for the sound of Loretta crying.

"Maybe nobody should be supporting them," Pastor Mitchell said. "Maybe nobody should be standing up for them."

"No," Loretta said. "That's not right."

"Loretta?" Tony cautioned.

"I'll walk her down the aisle, Pastor, and I'll be proud. You tell her that."

"Loretta?"

~ 347 ~

"No, Tony. No one's going to tell me I can't stand up for my daughter. And no one better ever tell me I can't hold my grandchild. No one."

Tony threw his food in the trash and walked past her down the shedrow. "Don't expect me to be there."

"Fine. But I'll be there," Loretta told Pastor Mitchell. "Tell her I'll be there. And if the Lord willing, her father will be there too."

Tony turned and looked at her.

"Then we'll both walk her down the aisle."

~ * ~

Dusty walked up the ReHab and ReHome shedrow to the feed room, mixed feed for his one and only horse, and was startled when he heard someone behind him. It was the young girl, Hillary. "Oh! Hello," he said, hand pressed to his heart. "I didn't see you coming."

"Sorry."

"What can I do for you?" he asked, walking down to grain the horse.

Hillary followed him. "I'm not sure."

"Everything okay at Shifting Gears?"

She nodded, looking in at the horse.

"I have very little to do here," Dusty said, in case she came to help. "It's just this one horse at the moment."

"He seems happy," Hillary said, puzzled by that fact.

Dusty glanced at her. "I think I have a direct home for him."

Hillary nodded, but then shook her head.

"What?" Dusty said.

She shook her head again. "It's not him."

"What's not him?"

She pressed hard against the bridge of her nose and shook her head yet again. "Did you call me?"

"No."

"Not by phone, you know…." She pointed to her head. "Did you…? Never mind. It wasn't you. I gotta get out of here."

"Wait!" Dusty said.

She turned.

"Do you want to take a walk with me?"

She lowered her eyes. "Knees, knees," she said, appearing to be in sudden pain. "My shoulder."

"Come on," Dusty said.

"Okay, just give me a second." She dusted herself off everywhere, including her head. "It's the only way I'll get through the barn area," she said. "Otherwise…."

"That's got to be hell," Dusty said.

"It is." Hillary nodded. "But if I can help."

The two walked down through the barns to Hannity's shedrow. The man was standing outside the tack room talking to a middle-aged couple; perhaps two of his owners. Dusty smiled. "Good afternoon!"

The couple returned the greeting.

"Just out making my rounds," Dusty said. He introduced himself. "My name is Dusty Burns. I'm the Nottingham Downs Liaison Official. I'm here to make sure everyone in the neighborhood is happy."

The man and woman chuckled. Even Hannity chuckled.

"Nice day," Dusty said, glancing around the barn area. "Will we be seeing you all at the HBPA banquet tomorrow?"

"Definitely," the woman said. "We're new to horse racing this year. We're looking forward to it."

Dusty nodded. "It's a great sport." He glanced out of the corner of his eye at Hillary. She'd been petting the horses and was now standing in front of Jackson's horse.

"Is he for sale?" she asked.

"No," Hannity said.

"Oh?" She looked into the horse's eyes, ran her hand down his nose, pressed her cheek against his muzzle.

"He may bite you, you know," Hannity said.

"No, he won't," Hillary said. "Of course I came," she told the horse, patting him on the neck. "I understand. I'll see you again."

Hannity fidgeted and probably would have said something objectionable, had it not been for his owners standing there.

"Well, we'd better get going. See you all tomorrow," Dusty said. He and Hillary walked over to the next barn, up that shedrow then down the other side, and then back toward the ReHab barn. "You okay?" he asked.

"Fine," she said, strolling along.

"What about the horse?"

"He's getting better physically." Hillary looked at him. "He's worried about you."

"Me?"

"Yes. You and someone named Sir."

"Sir?"

"That's what he said. He said he misses him. And that he is causing you both distress."

"Distress? Horses actually say that word."

"If they've heard it before."

Dusty nodded. "I guess that makes sense."

"He says he doesn't understand why Sir doesn't come to see him anymore. He doesn't feel at home. That's why I wondered if he was for sale."

Dusty walked her to the gate.

"So what are you going to do?" she asked.

"About what?"

"Duh!" she looked at him. "The horse, Sunrise Sam."

"You know his name?"

"He knows his name. Why wouldn't I know his name? He is why you called me here, right?"

Dusty stood staring down the road between the barns. "I guess so. I've been really worried about him and his situation. I have been rather 'distressed' as he put it." He laughed. "I can't believe this conversation."

"Dusty, you hear the horses. Maybe in a different way than I do, but you hear. You hear them loud and clear." Hillary walked to her car and waved. "You need to find Sir, whoever that is. And you need to find him now."

Dusty watched her drive away and walked to the Secretary's office. He hadn't seen Jackson for days. He looked up his owner information in the files and sat down and phoned the man.

"Hello."

"Jackson?"

"Yes. Who's this?"

"It's Dusty from the track. I have a really odd question for you. Does the name Sir mean anything to you?"

Jackson hesitated. "It's a nickname my father called me, after Stonewall Jackson. He called me Sir."

Dusty nodded to himself.

"Why are you asking?"

"Oh, that's a long story. Are you coming to the banquet tomorrow?"

"I don't know. I think if I run into Hannity, I'd probably shoot him."

"Then don't bring a gun," Dusty said. He told him about the wedding. "It would mean a lot to Junior and Lucy if you come."

"I'll think about it. What time?"

"Seven. It's Come as You Are. No dressing up."

"No chance of that," Jackson said, laughing.

Dusty paused, a momentary silence between then. "You okay?" Dusty asked.

"I don't know, Dusty," Jackson said. "It's like my will to live is gone. That horse was my life. Me and him were partners."

"I know. He's doing okay, by the way. I just thought you'd like to know. I'll see you tomorrow."

"Good-bye. Thank you."

Dusty hung up and looked around the room. Joe Feigler was watching him. Dusty walked over and sat behind the counter next to him and crossed his arms and sighed.

"What's going on?" Joe asked, happy Dusty wasn't avoiding him.

"Nothing, I was just talking to Jackson. I haven't seen him in a while."

"He came in and cleared his account out."

"He did?"

Joe nodded. "Yep. Down to the penny."

~ * ~

Putting all sixteen rectangular cakes together to become one big cake became a challenging family affair. Some of the cakes decided to stick with apparently no intention of coming out intact. Carol and Liz recalled the old round cake pans that had a metal bar on the bottom that slid all the way around to loosen the cake. "We could use a version of that now."

They carefully loosened each one, with only a few pieces in each cake falling apart. "Get out the glue," Liz said.

Glenda laughed.

Señor had made a fine platform. Dawn covered it in a white linen tablecloth, folded it neatly on the back, and taped it securely. The white cardboard Señor found after going to five different stores was cut to size. It was just a matter now of picking the cakes up, turning them over, and not having them fall apart anymore than they already had. "What we need is an industrial-sized spatula," Liz said.

Carol nodded.

"We have one of those pizza oven thingies." Glenda said. "You know, the thing you put the pizza in and out of the oven on."

"That might work."

"I'll be right back." Off Glenda went. George came back with her.

"All right, let's get'er done," George said. He and Señor held up clean hands, ready to flip the first cake over. Liz sprinkled powder sugar on the pizza board.

"Stand back," Señor said.

They all laughed. George held the pizza board tight to the cake while Señor gently but quickly flipped the cake and put it in place. Then they slowly, with the women holding their breath, nudged the cake while pulling the board out from under it.

"Perfect." They repeated the process with seven more of the cakes, creating a big sheet cake. Liz, Carol, and Wendy applied the icing. "Professionals peel off the crumbs."

"What a waste," Carol said.

"That's what I say," Liz said.

When they got the first layer all covered in frosting, George and Señor repeated the process with the top layer. "Oops." One fell apart.

"No problem," Liz said, motioning for them to keep going. "We'll fix it with icing. It'll be the bonus piece." They pieced the cake back together and when all eight top layer cakes were in place, the real icing process began. They used flat metal spatulas.

"Can we help?" Señor asked. "I have plenty of drywall spatulas in the garage."

"Get out of here!" Liz said, laughing. "Go! This is serious business." The women worked for well over half an hour getting all the frosting on, even, and smooth. "Now comes the fun part."

Glenda had the steadiest hands for the roping around the base of the cake.

"Oh, how pretty."

Carol was really good at making leaves. She practiced with a few on a saucer, transferred them over, and got brave and started making one for every inch around the bottom of the cake. Meanwhile, Liz started making the roses.

"Where did you learn to do that?" Glenda asked.

"Actually I taught myself. Some of my earlier attempts were very interesting looking." She pointed at Señor. "Don't say a word."

He laughed. "I'd seen piles of chicken shit that looked better."

"Go on! I said get outta here." Liz gave him a shove, everyone laughing.

"What's for dinner? Does anybody know?"

"Pizza and salad at Dawn and Randy's," Glenda said. "If it's still warm enough we're going to eat out on the deck."

"Cassada cake too?"

"Yep."

The three women worked on the cake for the next forty-five minutes, then stood back to admire it. "It's beautiful, Liz."

"Thanks to you two," she said. "Wow!"

"It's a good thing we don't have to refrigerate it," Carol said of the size. "We *don't* have to refrigerate it, do we?"

"No," Liz said. "But I am wondering how we're going to get it there. It's not like we can put it in the back of a pickup truck."

"One of us needs to have an SUV for occasions like this," Liz said.

Glenda agreed. "What were we thinking? Oh look," she said. "There's a little frosting leftover. We wouldn't want to waste it, would we?" They scraped the bowl clean with their fingers.

~ * ~

Everyone gathered on Randy and Dawn's back deck for dinner under the starlit night. Tiny white Christmas lights twinkled throughout the landscaping. Soft music played from speakers hidden under the rhododendrons.

Everyone had a story to tell. Dusty went first and they all marveled at his account of Hillary's "perception" and collectively worried about Jackson. "You don't think he's suicidal, do you?" Liz asked.

"I don't know," Dusty said.

Both he and Ben and Tom had known Jackson for years, but admittedly didn't know much about him outside of the racetrack. "I think he'll be at the banquet though. He likes Junior."

"Speaking of Junior, I videoed him galloping Bo-T this afternoon," Dawn said. "I sent a still shot along with an article to the *Banter*."

"How'd he go?" Randy asked.

"Good!" George said. "He had a crowd."

Ben smiled. "Well, if for no other reason…."

"He got a little rank with Junior coming back by the two-year-olds," George said.

"Pretty little fillies," Tom said. "Junior get him okay?"

"Yeah. Oh yeah."

"He's a good hand," Señor said, repeating the comment George made during Bo-T's shenanigans. "I was surprised how everyone got real quiet."

"They know," Ben said. "We could write a book about every one of them and their experience with horses. Jack was one hell of a jock. So was Frank. Frank getting hurt so young was sad."

"And look at him now," Glenda said. "He sure is a happy guy."

"Speaking of happy guys," Matthew said. "Señor took me to see my doctor today."

"Oh?" Wendy said. "Why? What's wrong?"

"Nothing. I was just getting an okay on the Appalachian trip."

"Does he say it's okay?"

"Yes," Matthew said. "I'm going to hike the trail back."

Wendy looked hard at him. "Are you sure?"

"He says it's up to me. Right, Señor?"

Señor nodded. "He didn't exactly recommend it, but he said he understood why Matthew would want to do it."

"Why?" Wendy asked.

"Well," Matthew said, taking a big bite of pizza. "My eyes are about the same, no better, no worse. I told him I'd always wanted to hike the whole trail, and he agreed maybe now's the time to do it."

Wendy let those comments settle in and looked at Señor.

He nodded. "That's pretty much what he said."

"I'll be fine, Mom."

Wendy hesitated, thinking. "Maybe we can replace your phone and get one with a GPS like Mark's. I don't want you getting lost."

"It's a trail, Mom, a well-worn path. Besides, I don't want a cellphone."

Tom looked at him. "Seriously?"

"Seriously. There's check points. I'll keep in touch."

"How long does it take?" Liz asked. "A couple of weeks?"

"Well, to do the entire trail, about five to seven months."

"What?" Tom said.

"I've already done better than half."

"What if it snows before you finish?" Dawn asked.

"I have gear. I have my backpack. There's lodging along the way and I have my savings?"

"It costs money?" Glenda asked.

"Yes, I'll need to eat. I don't think I could get used to eating just seeds and roots," Matthew teased. "Not with the way we eat here."

Everyone laughed and ultimately Wendy sighed. When he'd hiked the trail the first time it was with two friends. Now alone? And with his eyes the way they were? She bit at her bottom lip.

Matthew looked at her. "Mom…?"

She swallowed hard.

"Seriously, Mom" he said. "I have to do this."

She nodded and for some reason thought of the phrase, "She wears busy-busy like a badge, and it's so sad." How busy she kept herself all those years….

"So you just walk?" Randy asked, reaching for another piece of pizza.

"Well, I'm going to sketch too. I forgot how much I enjoy it. It might take me a little longer that way, but…." He paused. "I'm really looking forward to it."

~ * ~

Junior took Lucy to the mall to buy a dress. She tried on at least ten and finally found one she liked and that she could wear for a while as the baby grew. It was pink with an empire waist and had tiny white daisies on the sleeves and on the hem.

"Do you need shoes?" Junior asked.

"Yes."

They headed for the shoe department where Lucy found an inexpensive pair of white slip-ons. "They're so soft," she said, and cringed at the price tag. $19.99

Junior took them from her and headed for the check out. "You have to have shoes."

"I have so many at home."

"Yeah, and I have a dress pair of boots at home. Lot of good they're doing me there. I'll clean these up." Next, they went to the jewelry department and bought two thin gold wedding bands.

The old-timers were waiting for them when they got home, all sitting in the living room and having all signed a card. "For the happy couple," Vicky said, handing it to Lucy.

Junior stood at her side as she opened it and looked around the room at each one of them. "We don't want your money," he said.

"Why not?" Mim asked. "It's a wedding present. Shut up!"

Everyone laughed.

Lucy wiped her eyes. "I don't know what to say?"

"We figure you can buy a baby bed with that."

Lucy nodded, tears falling onto the money in the card.

"Thank you," Junior said.

Lucy nodded again, turning and pressing her face against his shoulder.

"Thank you."

"Sit," Miguel said. "We got old, new, borrowed, blue." He waited for them to both sit and handed them a wrapped box.

Lucy took her time untying the ribbon, a cause for chuckling. "Too late now," Jeanne said.

"For every ribbon you break, means a baby," Lucy explained to Junior.

"Take your time," he said. "No twins."

Everyone laughed.

Inside the box was a delicate handkerchief, edged in lace and faded in color, but so pretty. "That's your something old," Mim said. "And believe me, it's old."

Lucy smiled. "Thank you, Mim. It's beautiful."

Underneath the handkerchief was a tiny rose pin.

"That's your something new," Jeanne said.

"Thank you."

Something borrowed came from Jack. It was his Medal of Honor.

Lucy smiled. "Thank you. I hope I don't lose it."

"Hey, then I'll just have to go earn another one."

Everyone laughed.

Something blue followed; a pale blue ribbon for her hair. "Marry in blue, lover be true," Vicky said.

"It's so soft. Thank you." Lucy looked around at each and every one of them. "I am so blessed. Not too long ago, I thought…." Her voice cracked. "Thank you," she said.

Frank handed Junior a tiny box that held a silver coin. "To put inside Lucy's shoe before the wedding so you will always have good luck and prosperity."

"Thank you." Junior said, his arm around Lucy and holding her tight. "I think we're all set now. What could possibly go wrong?"

Chapter Thirty

Jason stepped out of the guard shack and handed Dawn a copy of the *Morning Banter*. "Nice photo. He's looking good."

"Thank you." Dawn read the headline. "Beau All Together Training Like a Champion." The caption below the photo read, "Burgundy Blue Here He Comes."

She walked into the tack room. Ben, Tom, Dusty, and Junior had all read the article and were having coffee. "Nice," Tom said.

"Thank you."

"Very nice," Dusty said.

"Hope it doesn't jinx us," Ben said.

"Those aren't my titles," Dawn said. She knew how superstitious Ben could be.

"Wow, do I look good!" Junior said, imitating the stronghold he had on Bo-T. "Yeah, Baby! Look at them muscles in my arms!"

They laughed. What an ego.

"Let's see about looking good this morning." Ben studied the training chart. "If there's no objection, I see we have four to gallop and one to walk."

Junior smiled, still admiring the photo of him galloping Bo-T.

"Randy said B-Bo's leg's looking good. Why don't you get on him at home too," Ben said.

"Are you trying to work me to death? It's my wedding day for Christ sake."

"You're not getting married till seven," Ben said. "You've got plenty of time."

"The Secretary's office is open," Joe Feigler announced over the p.a.

Tom looked at the others. "Is he going to do that every morning?"

"Don't forget tonight's the HBPA banquet. Seven o'clock sharp for Lucy and Junior's wedding. Don't get shut out," Joe added.

Tom laughed. "Don't get shut out? Who does he think he is, Bud Gipson?"

Thus the morning began. Batgirl was scheduled to walk today so Dawn started with her first. She took off the mare's standing bandages, wrapped her legs in fleece wraps, and hung her on the walking machine then went to work on her stall. Tom tacked Red, Junior tacked Whinny. Ben walked up to the racetrack. Dusty got paged to barn twelve.

Gulliver, a relatively new trainer to Nottingham Downs stood outside one of his horse's stalls. "Good morning, Dusty," he said.

"Morning." Dusty looked in at the horse. "What's going on?"

"He came back a little owie after the race yesterday. Doc was just here. He'll be right back. Nothing's broken, but he pulled that ligament pretty good."

The horse was standing on three legs. Dusty was glad Hillary wasn't around. The horse was obviously in a great deal of pain. "Did Randy give him anything?"

Gulliver nodded.

"What's the prognosis?"

"He said with complete rest he might be okay a year or so from now. No more racing though. He said even if it healed, it probably wouldn't hold up."

Randy pulled up in his truck, got out, and walked towards them, talking on his cellphone. He motioned he'd only be a minute and finished his conversation.

"I tried the owner," Gulliver said. "He's not up yet. He was at Mountaineer last night."

Randy nodded. "I'd rather he stay here, at least for a couple of days. It's a long walk to the ReHab barn. I don't want him going up a ramp yet either, no trailering him. I'll tape it good tomorrow and hit him with some stiffer pain killers."

"What'll I do with him today?"

"Well," Randy said. "After you talk to your owner, let Dusty know. He'll take care of him here until we move him."

"We have a waiver form for you to sign," Dusty said.

The man sighed.

"Don't worry. We'll take good care of him."

"I know. I've heard. I just hate this part of racing."

"We all do," Randy said. "That's why we're in this together."

"I'll be back in a little while," Dusty said. "Once you sign the waiver, he's no longer your responsibility. Your owner will need to go in and sign the papers over. He'll go down as a Do Not Race. He'll get rehabbed and we'll find him a good home, however long it takes."

"Thank you," Gulliver said. "I appreciate this. This is the way it should be done."

"We think so too," Dusty said. "I'll be back in a little while."

~ * ~

Pastor Mitchell walked into Rupert's Tack Shop and greeted the man in his usual way. "Good Morning! God's blessings upon you!"

Rupert glanced up from the counter. "Morning, Pastor."

Two horsemen were in the store shopping.

"It's a glorious day," Pastor Mitchell said.

Rupert looked at him. "Is it ever not a glorious day with you, Pastor?"

"At times. Sad times. But even then, there is glory in God."

Rupert nodded. "What can I do for you?"

"I'm just wanting to touch base with you about this evening."

"Dusty's already been here."

"That was about the banquet. I'm here about the wedding."

Rupert glanced at his two customers, still shopping. "I don't plan on attending neither," he said, in a low voice.

"That's a shame," Pastor Mitchell said. He bowed his head and closed his eyes.

"What are you doing? Don't you be praying for me."

"Actually, I was praying for your unborn grandchild."

Rupert stepped back and looked around the room, a hesitation in the way he moved. "I don't have time for this now. As you can see, I'm busy."

"Ah, more of God's blessings. I will leave you to your work. You close at six, right?" Pastor Mitchell pointed to the hours on the door. "That's just enough time to lock up and come as you are. Your business is an integral part of Nottingham Downs. How lucky you are, how lucky we are, to have you on our grounds. "

Rupert just looked at him.

"I will leave you with these parting words. Everyone here would like to see you attend this event. Come hungry for fellowship and fun and good food. Horsemen stick together. It's the only way we can support one another and prosper unto the Lord."

Rupert stared at the door in the man's wake, perhaps reading too much into what the man just said. Was it related to the visit he received the other day from that Mafia guy and his thug?

About half an hour later Ben opened the door and walked in. "Rupert," he said.

"Ben."

It was just the two of them. "It would mean a lot to your son if you'd attend his wedding."

"Did he say that?"

"He's your son, Rupert. Do you walk around saying how you feel?"

Rupert just looked at him.

"I am a man of few words," Ben said. "I think you know that. So hear me out. I never had a son and I wish I had. Don't let foolish pride get in the way of doing the right thing. That's all I have to say."

When the door opened about forty-five minutes later, Rupert looked up with resignation in his eyes. "Enough already, all right? I'll be there."

"Good," Tom said. "If you're not, you'd better not be where I can find you." He started out the door. "Don't come with an attitude either."

~ * ~

Dusty came back to Gulliver's barn and had the man sign the release form. "I'll be taking complete care of him from here on in. You say you get ahold of your owner?"

"Yes. He's in total agreement. I don't think he's ever actually seen the horse but for the winner's circle, but he says he wants to do the right thing by him. He's run hard and did well for the man."

Dusty nodded and looked in at the horse. "When this hay is done, don't give him any more. I'll be back with a haynet full before dinner. Don't grain him."

"What about watering him? Carrots?"

"That's fine."

"It's just that, you know, him being here, and I'm so used to taking care of him."

"I know what you mean. He'll be fine." Dusty patted the man on the back. "He'll be fine."

From there, Dusty walked to Hannity's barn. It was still training hours, the barn bustling with activity. As he stopped to look in at Sunshine Sam, Hannity walked out of the tack room.

"How's everything?"Dusty asked.

"Good."

Dusty nodded, glancing back in at the horse and noticing grain still in his feed tub. He turned and looked at a horse on the walking machine, a large chestnut. "That would be Forever Colin? He's running tomorrow, right?"

"Yes. Why? Why are you asking?"

Dusty patted this man on the back too. "I'm just making an observation. I hope he runs big for you. Throwing that bad race last time out, he'll have good odds." A final look in at Sunrise Sam and he walked on down the shedrow.

Ben was coming back from the track. Dusty caught up to him. Tom, on Red, was leading Alley back to the barn, Jenny Grimm still on board. "How'd she go?"

"She galloped strong."

"When are you running her back?"

"There's a race for her on Friday."

Dusty nodded and headed in the opposite direction. Irene was attending to last-minute details for the banquet and was becoming a bit unraveled. "I think I have everything. We haven't had this many people in years. I hope they have enough bathrooms."

Dusty laughed. "It's a banquet hall. Why wouldn't they?"

"I don't know. I just don't want anything to go wrong."

"What could possibly go wrong?" Dusty said.

Bill Squire, the HBPA chairman walked in behind them. "Are we all set?"

"I think so," Irene said, wringing her hands.

"Are you all set," Dusty asked.

Bill nodded and pulled a copy of the agenda out of this pocket. "I'll give a brief financial report, thank the horsemen for their support, then introduce you, then Ben, then Richard. That's the lineup order Wendy gave me."

"All right, I'll see you two this evening." He stopped at the door. "Irene, please don't wear that mumu. The other one either."

Irene laughed. "Go!

~ * ~

Tom met Gordon and Matthew at the car dealership, where the three of them walked up and down the dozens and dozens of rows of cars, all colors, all sizes.

A salesman came out, handed all three of them his business card, and shook their hands. "What can I get you in today?"

"The car's for the boys," Tom said, looking into the interior of a four-door sedan with a sun roof. "I've always wanted a sun roof."

"Will there be a trade-in?"

"No," Tom said. "Not unless you want it in pieces."

"I see," the man said, smiling. "Large car? Small car?"

"Small," Gordon said.

"Medium," Matthew said.

"Color?"

"Red."

"Blue."

"Financing?"

"Family financing," Tom said.

The man looked at him.

"Debit card."

"Wonderful, wonderful," the man said.

Tom followed around behind the "boys" for better than a half hour, took two phone calls, and sat down on the curb outside the sales office to take a third. Matthew and

Gordon had settled on a make and model by this time and were debating accessories and options.

"Stick."

"Automatic."

Tom hung up his cellphone, stretched out his legs, and crossed his arms. The salesman walked past him a few minutes later. "They're still debating color."

"Tell them to flip a coin," Tom said. "What the hell? I could have been to the moon and back."

The salesman laughed. "You sure you don't want to trade in that fine truck?"

"No, I've only had it three years. I'm just getting it broke in. Excuse me," he said, and took another call. Matthew and Gordon walked up a few minutes later, having finally chosen forest green. "It's your mom." Tom said.

Matthew and Gordon both held up their hands. Tom laughed. When the salesman came back outside, Tom leaned slightly to get his wallet out of his back pocket, phone pressed between his shoulder and his ear. He took out his debit card and handed it to the man. "Put the car in their names," he said.

"We can only do one," the man said.

"Then flip a coin," Tom said, his answer to apparently everything today.

Gordon and Matthew walked inside with the man. Gordon stuck his head out a few minutes later. "Do we want the extended warranty?"

Tom nodded, still talking on the phone, this time to Pastor Mitchell.

When the deal was all said and done, the boys came out with the salesman, carrying keys and license plates. The man handed Tom his debit card. Tom nodded and put it in his wallet; still lying on his lap. He stood and walked with the salesman and the boys to the car they'd picked out, looked at it and nodded. "Nice."

All set, the salesman shook Matthew and Gordon's hands. "Your dad's a busy man."

"He's planning a wedding."

"Oh? Which one of you are getting married?"

"Neither of us," Matthew said. "It's for Junior."

Tom hung up the phone, shook the man's hand, and walked away.

"He owns a racetrack," Gordon said.

"Really? Which one?"

"Nottingham Downs." They both smiled proudly, watching as Tom reached into his shirt pocket for a toothpick and popped it between his teeth as he climbed into his truck.

"I like playing the ponies," the man said. "I just wish they had slots. My wife loves playing blackjack."

~ * ~

Señor spent hours building a box for transporting the cake. His first thought was to make it so he could set the cake down inside and top it with a lid. "No." It would have to be tight enough to not slip around inside and that wouldn't allow enough hand space for putting the cake in and lifting it out. He decided to take one of the sides off, called George for help with lifting the platform, and the two of them slid the cake in slowly.

"Careful," Liz said.

"Don't make me nervous," Señor said.

"Well, you're making me nervous."

"Shhh…." The two men finished sliding the cake inside, felt the platform butt up against the back, and tacked on the side and top panel.

"Do you want to take it now?" George asked.

"Yes," Señor said, "before I have a heart attack."

Liz opened the screen door and stood back.

"Damn!" Señor said.

"What?" Liz asked.

The same thing just occurred to George right at the same time. They set the cake back on the table. Señor took out his ruler and measured the box; way too wide for the doorway. "Well, we could probably tilt it and make it."

"No," Liz said. "It'll slide and be ruined. Go out the garage."

"We still have to go out a door to get to the garage, Liz!" Senior wiped his brow. "Let me think." He glanced around the house. "The window. Let's take it out the window."

"Oh my God," Liz said.

Señor opened the window and raised the screen. "Plenty of room. George, you go out and around and Liz and I will hand it to you."

"We're going to drop it," Liz said. "I just know it. We'll be serving their wedding cake by the spoonful."

"We're not going to drop it, Liz, could you just…." Señor motioned for her to pick it up. "Come on, it's not that heavy."

Outside, George positioned himself to receive it by straddling two Burning Bushes. Señor and Liz lifted the cake box and carried it slowly to the window. When they placed it on the windowsill, Señor instructed Liz to hold the side while he went out to help George get it down off the sill and to the truck. That part went fairly easy, except for George's pant leg getting hung up on a shrub branch. He came so close to falling. "I'm okay, I'm okay," he said, balancing his box on his shoulder while he wiggled his leg free. They placed the cake box in the back of Señor's pickup and closed the tailgate.

"What's to stop it from slipping and sliding around?" Liz asked.

"It's not going anywhere," Señor said. "Besides, the base is a tight fit in the box."

"But? But?"

"Fine." Señor climbed into the truck bed, sat with his back to the cab, and braced the cake box with his feet. George walked around and got in behind the wheel.

"If we're not back in an hour," Señor said. "Call 911."

Liz clutched her hands to her chest, watching as George backed the truck up and turned it around, driving slowly down the driveway and out onto the road. She watched until she could no longer see the truck.

With wide doors at the banquet hall accustomed to large deliveries, unloading the cake and getting it inside went without a hitch. George and Señor took the top and one side off the box, then slid the cake out gently and placed it on the serving table. Both men stepped back and heaved huge sighs of relief. "I think I just lost ten years off my life," Señor said. He phoned Liz to let her know all was well. Then he and George helped themselves to an ice cold beer from one of the kitchen coolers.

~ * ~

Junior honked when passing T-Bone's Place to let the old-timers know he was on his way to the barn to gallop Bo-T. Mim and her golf cart brought up one load and went back for another. Vicky pushed Jeannie up in her wheelchair. Lucy pushed Clint up in his. Señor and George had plans to build a small set of bleachers with back rails. In the meantime, they'd hauled up lawn chairs. Mim sat in the driver's seat of the golf cart, her cane at her side. Vicky sat next to her.

"What a day!" Mim said.

"A perfect day for a wedding."

Mim nodded. "I'm glad I'm still here to see it, to see this."

Junior was riding Bo-T up the path to the training track. The colt was a little better behaved today but still full of himself, jigging and snorting. Matthew was on the path behind him, staying way back and carrying his sketch book.

"Don't forget to get my biceps," Junior said.

Matthew laughed. "I'll try. That's if I can see them. Can you go slow when you go by in front of me?"

Mim heard that and chuckled, then coughed. Vicky placed a hand on her shoulder. "You okay, Mim?"

The old woman nodded. "I'm fine. I just wish I had an idea of when. I'd like a warning somehow."

"I know," Vicky said, giving her a hug.

"And no theatrics I hope. I would hate that."

Junior jogged Bo-T onto the training track and clicked to him.

"What a grand-looking horse," Mim said.

Bo-T snorted and bucked.

"Don't be dumping me in front of my bride now," Junior said.

"I've seen you get dumped before," Lucy said.

"Yeah, but it ain't that often." Bo-T broke into a trot and then a nice fluid canter. "Start drawing, Matthew!" Junior said, glancing back over his shoulder and flexing his arm muscles.

Everyone laughed.

"This is just too much fun," Mim said.

"My heart feel so good," Miguel said.

Clint smiled. "He looks like Secretariat!"

They all watched as Junior galloped down the backstretch of the training track, into the turn, and past them again. Junior smiled at his bride. "Am I looking good?"

She laughed. "Yes! You're looking real good!"

Bo-T had his head down, neck bowed and pulling hard against the bit, and with each stride, did that Thoroughbred grunt thing with his nose and throat.

"I love that sound," Jack said. "It's like a racecar revving up." He imitated it. "Baroom, baroom."

They all nodded in agreement.

Junior pulled Bo-T up on the backstretch and turned him around and trotted through the turn and then walked down the track in front of them. The colt was breathing hard, but not overly. It was a good workout. "I'll be back in a few minutes," he said, walking Bo-T off the track and onto the path.

"Back?" Bill said, all wondering the same thing.

"I'm going to gallop B-Bo."

They all smiled, settling in for the wait. One racetrack story led to another and then another. Lucy pressed her hand against her tummy. The baby was moving. She read in a book yesterday that babies in the womb are said to sense what is going on around them judging from their mother's reactions and emotions. She smiled. "My baby's happy. Here comes Daddy," she said.

B-Bo looked a lot like Bo-T, having the same sire, but was slightly taller and not as wide. Being a gelding, he had a little more refined Thoroughbred racehorse look to him, and a lazy yet commanding way of going.

Mim watched the horse closely as Junior walked him onto the training track. "Why don't you just walk him for a bit. That back leg's still a little stiff."

"Yes, Mom, I mean Mim," Junior said, grinning. There wasn't anyone there including him that would even think of disagreeing with Mim about anything - let alone horses. If Ben were here, he probably would have agreed with her too. Both practiced the same old-school way of training.

Matthew turned the page in his sketch book and started a new drawing. The angle of the sun being behind them now made it somewhat easier for him to see the horse. He moved over by Mim and sat down on the grass and looked between the bottom rail and the ground; at times the way he was seeing but a thin line between the two barriers.

Mim glanced at his sketch and smiled. "Do you have any idea how lucky you are?"

Matthew nodded. "Yes, I do," he said, drawing feverishly. "I'm learning that more and more every day."

"Right there," she said, pointing to the horse's chest. "Capture his heart. The rest you can fill in later."

Chapter Thirty-One

Transportation to the wedding banquet for the old-timers also turned into a family affair. Wendy had lined up a double-wheelchair transport vehicle for Jeannie and Clint. Two more rode with Glenda and George in Glenda's car. Two went with Tom and Wendy in Wendy's car. Two went with Vicky in her car. Bill rode with Dawn and Randy and the children. Dusty and Ben went together in Dusty's truck. Junior and Lucy came in his pickup truck. Gordon and Matthew came in their new car.

The plan was to arrive early so the old-timers could get themselves situated. They'd been given the option of mixing in with the other horsemen, but chose to sit together at their own table. "They're more comfortable that way," Vicky said. "I will be too." Carol opted to join them.

The banquet personnel had arranged the round tables to seat eight and nine people, depending on whether or not the table was on the aisle, so that worked out well. Dawn, Randy, the children and Liz, Señor and Glenda and George sat at the table next to the old-timers. Wendy and Tom, Ben, Dusty, Matthew, Gordon, and Richard and his wife Heather were to be seated at the table on their other side. Pastor Mitchell and his wife were going to sit with Junior and Lucy after the wedding ceremony along with Lucy's best friend Judy, her boyfriend Max, and Joe Feigler and his wife June. The HBPA officers' table was across the aisle.

Junior and Lucy, who had been standing just inside the door, ended up serving as the greeting committee. The mood was loud and festive. Pastor Mitchell stood outside the door, waving people in, shaking hands with the men and giving gentle welcome hugs to the women.

He glanced ahead and saw Lucy's mother Loretta. "Oh, please..." he muttered to himself as she walked toward him. Right behind her was Lucy's father Tony. He hadn't told Lucy that her mother planned to be here. Hadn't told her for fear Tony would forbid it and Lucy would be even more disappointed. He hadn't told her there was a possibility her father might show, and if he did, if he'd want to be involved with walking her down the aisle. He wanted to spare her that also, in case....

Loretta must have been reading his mind or the expression on his face, because as soon as they drew close she said, "We're here to walk our daughter down the aisle." Pastor Mitchell looked from her to Tony. The man nodded.

"All right, let's go get ready," Pastor Mitchell said.

Lucy looked up from greeting Jenny Grimm and saw her mother and father standing next to Pastor Mitchell. She instinctively reached for Junior's hand and gripped it tightly. Junior followed the direction of her eyes and had Pastor Mitchell not been smiling....

"You look beautiful, Lucy," her mother said.

Lucy bit at her trembling bottom lip.

Tony shook Junior's hand. "Shouldn't you be up front somewhere waiting for us to give her away to you?"

Junior nodded, taking his hand and placing it on Lucy's. "I'll be waiting for you. Okay?"

Lucy nodded with big tears running down her face.

Junior glanced back from the doors leading into the banquet room.

"I'm sorry, Daddy," Lucy said.

"Me too," he said, hugging her. "I'm so sorry."

Loretta wiped her eyes again and again.

Tom walked up next to them, assessed the situation in a glance and relaxed. He shook Tony's hand and kissed Loretta on the cheek. Judy, the maid of honor and her boyfriend Max continued greeting the guests who streamed steadily inside and into the banquet room to take their seats.

Pastor Mitchell ushered them into the corner. "Okay, in just a few minutes, Tom and I will go up front with Junior. The band will start playing the bridal march and you three will walk down the aisle." He positioned them, Tony on Lucy's right, Loretta on Lucy's left.

"Do you have the rings?"

Tom patted his shirt pocket and nodded.

"Okay. I think we're all set."

Wendy hurried through the door, looked around and rushed over with Lucy's bouquet. "Can you believe it wasn't ready?" She handed Judy hers, the same but for the ribbon.

Lucy smiled. "It's beautiful. Thank you." The old-timers had given Wendy a blue ribbon that matched the one in Lucy's hair to be put into the floral arrangement of daisies; Lucy's favorite flower.

"Is Richard here?"

Tom nodded. "Yes."

Wendy gave Lucy a kiss on the cheek and Tom walked with her inside to take his place next to Junior.

"Are we ready now?" Pastor Mitchell asked, of the bride and her parents.

"Yes," Lucy said, smiling. Just then, in the back door walked Rupert.

Pastor Mitchell turned. "Oh dear God," he said softly.

Rupert looked at all four of them, nodded, offered something that had the semblance of a smile and walked into the banquet room.

"Okay." Pastor Mitchell took a deep breath. "Let's get this underway. Remember, when you hear the music…."

Tony nodded.

Pastor Mitchell walked down the aisle to where Junior and Tom stood waiting. "Your father's here," he said to Junior.

Junior glanced around the room, he and his father's eyes met, and the band struck up the introit to the wedding march. One of the banquet employees opened the doors. Judy walked down the aisle, a hesitation in her step to match the music. At the head of the aisle she turned and smiled at her best friend.

As the bridal march began, Lucy stood perfectly still between her mother and father. When Pastor Mitchell nodded, the three of them started down the aisle. Lucy had tears in her eyes. So did Junior. He watched her every step of the way and smiled when she stood facing him.

"Dearly beloved," Pastor Mitchell said. "We are gathered here today to join this man and this woman in holy matrimony." He looked at Lucy and Junior. He looked at Lucy's mother and father. He looked around the room. "The Lord is smiling upon you all," he declared and paused. "Who gives this woman today in marriage?"

"We do," Tony Guciano said, "Her proud mother and father."

They both gave Lucy a tearful hug and turned. Pastor Mitchell's wife motioned for them to sit next to her at the first table. Logistics could be remedied after the ceremony.

Pastor Mitchell smiled. "Love is the reason we are here. In marriage we not only say, "I love you today. We say I promise to love you all of our days."

Tom looked at Wendy. Randy put his arm around Dawn. Ben thought of Meg the day they took their vows. Just about everyone in the room entertained a promise, past, present, or future, a sweet memory. Some bittersweet; some sad.

"You are among family. A bigger family than most, but make no mistake, we are all family." A succession of amen's could be heard throughout the room. "Lucy and Junior, in the days ahead of you, there will be good times and there will be stormy times, times of conflict and times of joy. As you go through life together, I want you to remember this advice. Never go to bed in anger. Learn to compromise. Know that it is better to bend than to break. Believe the best of one another instead of the worst. Confide in each other. Ask for help. And Junior, ask for directions."

Junior laughed along with everyone.

"Remember true friendship is the basis for any lasting relationship. Give one another the same respect and kindness you bestow on your friends. Be courteous. Be loving." Pastor Mitchell paused. "Now if you will face one another and join hands."

Lucy looked up at Junior with tears sliding down her cheeks, trying desperately to swallow and gain composure. Junior smiled at her in support and when that didn't work, he did something that probably had never been done in the history of weddings, let alone one Pastor Mitchell presided over, Junior pulled her close and gave her a hug. "It's all right," he whispered. "It's all right."

Tom looked on with tears in his eyes, seeing Junior growing up in a flash.

"It's all right."

Lucy nodded, sniffled, and picked her head up.

Pastor Mitchell smiled. The moment called for brevity if the ceremony was going to continue, as there were a lot of tears in the room. "If I might quote a scripture from the Bible that seems rather fitting at this moment," he said.

Everyone either chuckled or laughed as Pastor Mitchell turned the pages in his Bible, one, two, three, four…. "Ah yes. Luke 19:41. 'And when he came into view of the city, as he approached it he broke into loud weeping, exclaiming: Oh that at this time you knew, yes, even you, on what your peace depends.'"

He looked at the bride and groom. "Douglas Rupert Junior, do you take Lucy to be your wedded wife? Do you promise to love her, comfort her, honor and keep her, for better, for worse, for richer, for poorer, in sickness and health, forsaking all others and to be faithful only to her, so long as you both shall live?"

"I do."

"Lucy, do you take Junior to be your wedded husband? Do you promise to love him, comfort him, honor and keep him, for better, for worse, for richer, for poorer, in sickness and in health, forsaking all others and to be faithful only to him, so long as you both shall live?"

"I do."

"May I have the rings please?"

Tom took them out of his pocket and handed them to the minister.

"This ring, an unbroken, never-ending circle, is a symbol of committed unending love. Junior, as you place this ring on Lucy's finger, repeat these words after me. "With this ring, I thee wed. "

"With this ring, I thee wed."

"As this ring has no end, neither will my love for you."

"As this ring has no end, neither will my love for you." Junior's voice cracked.

"Lucy," Pastor Mitchell said. "Repeat after me. With this ring, I thee wed."

"With this ring, I thee wed."

"As this ring has no end, neither will my love for you."

Lucy looked up at Junior with abundant love in her eyes. "As this ring has no end, neither will my love for you."

Pastor Mitchell smiled. "There is an Apache blessing I would like to share with you both today, and the little one. 'Now you shall feel no rain, for each of you will be shelter for one another. Now you will feel no cold, for each of you will be warmth for one another. Now there will be no loneliness, for each of you will be companion to one another.'"

Pastor Mitchell put his book down and paused, looking at the bride and groom. "Junior and Lucy, I have known you both since you were little children. I have watched you grow into adulthood. Today, in front of family and friends, you have committed yourself to each other in marriage by the exchanging of vows and by the giving of rings. With the authority invested in me, I now pronounce you husband and wife. What God has joined together let no man put asunder. You may now seal your vows with a kiss."

Junior leaned down and gave Lucy a sweet tender kiss and Pastor Mitchell had them turn and face the guests. "Ladies and gentlemen, I present to you Mr. and Mrs. Douglas Rupert Jr."

All of the guests that could, stood, and clapped accompanying whistles and hoots of celebration.

"And now, from what I understand," Pastor Mitchell said, "Tom would like to say something."

Tom looked at him. His expression priceless, as a speech was not in the script. Everyone laughed; even Junior and Lucy.

"Well," Tom said. "Since we all know I've never been at a loss for words before, let me think." Everyone laughed again. "Junior, Lucy…I wish you happiness. I wish you good health. "

Gordon and Matthew looked on proudly from a table in the middle of the room.

"My wish is that you walk in the path of the Lord. And I want you to know that I will be there for you both, whenever you need me."

"Amen," Pastor Mitchell said. "Lucy and Junior will be milling around after we have our dinner, which I understand is ready to be served. And the cutting of the wedding cake will follow."

Irene stood up and faced the guests. "Let's eat!"

~ * ~

The menu for the banquet was down-home roast beef, mashed potatoes and gravy, corn, peas, and carrots, fried chicken, broccoli casserole, and a tossed salad - and lots of everything. A terrene of extra gravy was placed on each table along with rolls and butter. There was coffee, soft drinks, milk, beer and wine to drink.

The band played an assortment of songs during dinner, heightening the festivities, and then the noise lessened and a wave of silence followed Bill Squire as he stepped up to the microphone at the front of the room. Time for some HBPA business.

"I want to thank you all for coming. This is a great turnout! Junior, Lucy, congratulations and thank you for doing your part to get everyone here tonight."

Everyone clapped. Junior bowed. Lucy smiled.

"I have just a few budgetary items to go over." Bill put on his glasses and read from a report. "Expenditures this year, $3,045. I'm rounding this off," he said. "Income, donations, $3,982. I already did the math," he said, chuckling. "We have...."

"$937," Big John Myers said from one of the tables halfway back.

Everyone laughed. Myers was notorious for instant numbers tabulation in his head.

"So, I'm happy to report we are in the black for the second year in a row."

Everyone clapped.

"Irene, would you like to say something?"

"Yes." She stood up and walked to the microphone. "I want to thank you all for coming. I want to thank Junior and Lucy too. God Bless you both. I want to thank Ben Miller."

Everyone clapped again. Irene waved to everyone and sat back down.

"Now I think Dusty, you have a report on the finances of the ReHab and ReHoming Thoroughbred Project."

Dusty nodded and stepped forward. He too, had a list of figures. "We're happy to report that as of today and for this past year, we have found homes for twenty-two Thoroughbreds and they all are doing well."

More applause.

"Total donation figure of $5,734.37. Total expenses...." He paused. "I'm leaving the change in to put you to the test, Big John."

John Myers laughed. "Bring it on."

"Expenses. $4,932.66."

"Balance....?"

"Eight hundred and twenty-one dollars and seventy-one cents," Big John said, reaching into his pocket.

Dusty looked at him, a hush falling over the room. "No, actually that's $801.71."

Big John held up a twenty dollar bill. "Not with this donation added."

Everyone laughed and clapped, passed the twenty dollar bill up front, and clapped again when Dusty held it up. "Thank you!" Dusty sat down and Bill Squire stepped back up to the microphone.

"Now we're going to hear from Nottingham Downs General Manager Richard Spears."

Everyone clapped as Richard stepped up. "I have a lot of news to share with you this evening," he said, looking around the room. Some of the faces he knew; many were relative strangers to him. "Good news. Nottingham Downs is alive and well!"

Everyone clapped.

"And things are about to get even better." When Richard paused, looking around the room, Wendy smiled. He was playing the crowd, doing what he did best. "I have wonderful news to share with you. As we all know, our illustrious owner Ben Miller can be a little stubborn."

"Hey, hey, watch it now." Ben shook his head, pointing at him as everyone laughed.

"He can be a little set in his ways," Richard added.

Ben laughed along at that.

Richard paused. "But you're not going to find a more thoughtful, more knowledgeable racetrack owner anywhere."

Everyone clapped boisterously.

Richard waited for the applause to quiet down. "We're all aware, every one of us, how tough this business can be. How competitive it can be. How at times, how utterly impossible it can be."

You could have heard a pin drop.

"I want you all to know we are not oblivious to the competition. I want you all to know how much we appreciate each and every one of you. We want to thank you for backing us in our efforts to clean up racing. We are setting an example for every other racetrack in this country. We have a lot here that they don't have. Number one, we have a professional horseman at the helm."

More applause for Ben. "Jesus," he said to Tom in a low voice. "I'm dying to hear what's next, and I already know what he's going to say."

"So getting to the news, and I don't mean the *Morning Banter*."

Everyone laughed. Lots of them booed.

"Is this. The only thing that a lot of other racetracks have that we don't have is slots."

Once again, you could have heard a pin drop.

"But that's about to change."

It took about two seconds for the implication of that to settle in, everyone looking at one another, looking at Ben, and then looking up front at Richard again.

"Nottingham Downs has entered into an agreement with RJR Enterprises to bring slots to Nottingham Downs!"

Cheers and applause and whoops and hollers rocked the room, many of the horsemen on the feet!

Richard waited for the cheers to run themselves out and for everyone to sit back down. "We're excited too. This is positive for the future of Nottingham Downs in many ways. Increased revenue means higher purses. It'll mean more in terms of profit for everyone. It'll mean more in the HBPA coffers. It'll give us the revenue we need to finalize hospitalization for backside employees.

It'll mean more outreach for the community." Richard held his hand up. "What it won't mean, is a change in the way we do business here at Nottingham Downs." Ben nodded when he looked at him. "We won't allow horses to be put at risk for the extra dollars. The racing industry has learned a hard lesson there. We won't make those same mistakes. Just as our Nottingham Downs creed states, 'Where no Thoroughbred is ever Forgotten,' we won't forget you. You have stuck by us. You have stepped up to the plate. We won't let you down." He paused. "Ben," he said.

Ben rose and walked to the microphone to thunderous applause. He looked around the room. "Well," he said, clearing his throat. "As one of the oldest people in this room, I can say I've known many of you all of your lives."

The people laughed.

"I want to talk about several things tonight. Most important on my mind is integrity. We've tried to do what's right. Like Mim said, it's about change. And hopefully change for the good. We're going to do our best to stand by you horsemen here tonight and we're going to continue to do what's right for the horse. Make no mistake about that. I can see in some of your faces some of the same concerns I had. What about the little guy? What about the trainer with one or two horses? Three or four? Is there room for him or her when the line starts forming and Joe Feigler has a stack of stall applications from every stable far and wide looking to bring in a string of horses?"

Joe smiled.

"Yes," Ben said. "That won't change. It's part of the agreement." He hesitated, glancing at Dawn and Tom, the successors to complete ownership someday. They both nodded and smiled. "Equally important to me in reference to the fear of big trainer little trainer, small stable big stable, I want to address the issue of claiming a trainer's only horse."

Silence permeated the room.

"Dusty and I have been deeply troubled by this issue." Ben held up his hand. "Now, I know, maybe some of you might be thinking we're just getting a little sentimental in our old age, but quoting Mim again, with age for some of us, yes, she said some, comes wisdom."

Mim smiled.

"We have it in the works to introduce a bylaw that will prevent a horseman from having his one and only horse claimed. We think everyone here at Nottingham Downs has a right to make a living, whether it's the owners, the trainers, the grooms, the riders, hot walkers, everyone. Claiming has been a Thoroughbred racing practice for almost a hundred years. We've all claimed horses. We've all lost horses. Here, at Nottingham Downs, we think it's time for change. Just because something's old, doesn't make it right. We're going to work on it. We're going to make it right."

"Ben," a man said, from the back of the room.

Ben looked toward the sound of the voice, as did everyone else.

"I want to thank you," Jackson said, standing and walking up front. "I want to thank you and Dusty for sticking up for us small owners." He looked around the room and let his eyes fall on a man at a table midway through the room. He took a wad of money out of his pocket and held it up. "I want my horse back, Hannity. This here is what you paid for him plus a week's care. I want him back."

All eyes went from him and the wad of money to Hannity. The man was seated with his wife and six of his owners.

"I want him back," Jackson repeated. "Not only did you take my only horse, you took away my livelihood, my reason for getting up in the morning. I want him back. I want my life back."

Hannity stared straight ahead, feeling the weight of a room full of eyes weighing on his shoulders, not to mention his wife's glare. "Uh, what about the vet bill," he said, trying to save face.

Randy held up his hand. "I'll waive it," he said.

Everyone looked at Randy, then back at Hannity. When the man finally nodded, Jackson walked to his table, gave the man the money and shook his hand. "I'll be coming to get him in the morning. I mean you no disrespect and harbor no hard feelings. I just want my horse back."

~ * ~

As soon as Jackson returned to his seat, the mood changed back to a festive one. The band started playing and it was time to party. Junior and Lucy visited each table, chatting with each person. Some offered name suggestions if the baby was a girl, a boy. People came up to see the old-timers, visit and reminisce. Children were everywhere. They took to running around, squealing, and dancing.

Rupert shook his son's hand and darted his eyes at a man standing at the back door all evening, arms crossed. He could very well be a banquet employee, but he couldn't help thinking that the guy looked like a bodyguard.

"Congratulations," Rupert said to Lucy.

"Thank you."

"It's time to cut the cake," Irene announced. Perfect timing, Junior thought.

Cutting the wedding cake turned into a photo shoot. The cake-makers first stood at the newlyweds' sides.

Lucy's mother and father stood at their side. Lucy and Junior smiled for everyone snapping their cameras.

"I hate to cut it. It's so pretty," Lucy said.

George and Señor motioned for her to move the process along. Both had plates and waiting. Junior and Lucy fed one another a piece of cake, no mess, and Liz and Glenda took over cutting the rest. The bride danced with her father. Junior danced with Lucy's mother. His mother lived several states away. The old-timers sang along when the band played, "My Old Kentucky Home."

Juan Garcia stepped up to the band mike and sang a stellar rendition of "The Run for the Roses." The floor was swarmed with Texas-style line-dancers when "Boot Scootin' Boogie" began. Gordon and Matthew had hooked up with several young women at the table next to theirs. The girls pulled them out onto the floor, thinking they were going to teach them the dance and were surprised they both knew how. They were all laughing, everyone having a great time.

"Too loud," Ben said, at one point.

"What?" Mim said.

They both laughed. The chicken dance had just about everyone dancing, on the floor, in their seats, around the perimeters of the tables. When the song "YMCA" was played, there was even louder singing and flailing of arms. The children all giggled and laughed, mixing up their letters and falling down deliberately.

The Electric Slide song came next, clearing the floor, those that knew how from those that didn't. Some in between bravely gave it a go. More singing at the mike, more dancing, more cake, more trips to the bar.

When the banquet hall closed at midnight, they had to shoo people out. "Here." Tom tucked the wedding donation box under Junior's arm and handed him a key.

"You're booked next door for the night. Leave your truck here."

Junior nodded. "Which way?"

Tom laughed. "Wait a minute. Maybe you ought to leave that with me." He had no idea how much money there was inside the box and Junior obviously was just a little drunk.

Randy had gone for Dawn's car and she was standing inside the door with the children. "I'll follow them," a distinguished-looking muscular gentleman said.

Tom looked at him.

"Thank you, Vito," Dawn said. "Junior, Vito's going to follow you to the hotel to make sure you and Lucy get there all right. Okay?"

Junior turned and had to look way up to see the man eye to eye. "Thank you, Vito. That's so nice of you. Do I know you?"

Vito laughed. "I'm family."

"Should we go now?" Lucy asked, supporting Junior.

"Just a moment," Vito said. He waited until Dawn and the children were in the car with Randy.

"Who else came with us?" Randy asked.

"Me," Miguel said.

"No, you didn't, I did," Bill said.

"It doesn't matter," Tom said. "Just get in."

When Dawn and Randy were loaded up and pulled out, Vito escorted Junior and Lucy to the hotel next door, rode up the elevator with them, and as they closed their door, bid them goodnight.

Chapter Thirty-Two

Jason stepped out of the guard shack and greeted Dawn cheerfully. "Morning! Great banquet! Here's your paper."

Dawn smiled. "Thank you." Noticing it wasn't opened to the Sports section she was just about to tuck it under her arm when she saw the headline: "Nottingham Downs Says Yes to Slots." The subtitle: "Ain't no Mountain High, Ain't no Valley Low."

When she walked into the tack room, Ben, Tom, and Dusty looked up at her. "All right," she said. "So I didn't get enough sleep, but what's this supposed to mean?"

"I don't know," Tom yawned. "Is it directed at Mountaineer?"

"That's a possibility," Dusty said.

Ben leaned back. "The article's not bad. At least it makes the distinction between the two operations."

Dawn poured a cup of coffee and turned when Jackson walked into the tack room. "A thought occurred to me in the middle of the night last night," the man said. "I don't have a stall."

The four of them laughed.

"This late in the year, your old stall and tack room are still available," Dusty said. "I'll let Joe know."

"Thank you." Jackson hesitated at the door. "I want you all to know how much I appreciate what you did for me."

Ben nodded. "We're going to fix the claiming system. Next year will be a brand new year all around. Claiming is never going to go way. We're just going to try and make it right."

No sooner had Jackson left than Junior made his way in. "Whoa." He sat down ever so slowly with his head spinning. "Did anyone get the license plate number of the bus that hit me?"

They all laughed. "Lucy drop you off?" Tom asked. It would be hard to imagine Junior driving in this condition.

"No, she's still in that big bed…with all the pillows. There were so many pillows."

They all laughed again.

"I walked here. I pointed myself toward the smell of horse shit and here I am."

Dawn handed him a cup of coffee, all of them laughing again.

"Well, it's not every day you get married," Tom said.

Junior nodded, and then held his head still. "I ain't never getting married again." He looked at Ben. "Tell me there's no one to gallop."

Ben glanced at the training chart. "Three."

Junior stared - first at Ben, then at the wall, the floor, and then into his coffee cup.

"Go get something to eat," Tom suggested.

"You're kidding," Junior said.

"Nope, it'll help you 'man up.' Get some bacon and eggs and eat some grits."

Junior rose to his feet, coffee cup still in hand. To watch him as he hesitated at the door, one would think he was contemplating climbing a mountain. "I'll be back," he said. "I hope." He returned about a half hour later, laid down on a stack of hay in the hay room for about an hour, and woke ready to go. Batgirl was first to be galloped, then Whinny. Wee Born walked. Morning Dew was galloped. Jenny Grimm worked Alley Beau a half mile. Tom and Red ponied her up and back.

From the moment Wendy arrived at her office, she got little done for fielding questions on the phone from numerous newspaper sports reporters, radio sports talk-show hosts, sports television figures, and racing fans in general, wanting to air their pros and cons about slots. By noon, she decided to make a recording, programmed in the option for more information by pressing five, listed the information to date, and stepped away.

As she walked out into the Secretary's office and glanced ahead she smiled. Gloria and Charlie had just come inside. She gave them both a hug. "Does Ben know you're here?" Whenever Charlie and Gloria paid a visit up from Florida where they'd retired, it was a surprise because Gloria insisted surprises kept people young.

"No," Charlie said. "We were just at the barn and no one was there."

Wendy glanced at her watch. "Did you try the kitchen?"

"Yep."

"What's this I hear about slots?" Charlie asked. The man had been a stable guard at Nottingham Downs for over forty years and was Ben's best friend. He'd heard it all and had seen in all when it came to the backside. "I never thought Ben would go for it."

"Well, like he says, 'He went kicking and screaming.'"

The elevator door opened and out stepped Ben. "Well I'll be. Look who's here!" He shook Charlie's hand and gave Gloria a hug; the woman who saved his life years ago. An image of that day flashed in his mind, as always whenever he first saw her again. He smiled. She still smelled like lilacs.

"How long are you staying?"

"Oh, just a few days," Charlie said. "Gloria's grand-niece is getting ordained."

"Have you been out to the farm?"

"Not yet. We thought we'd stop by here first."

They always stayed at Ben's or Dawn's when they were in town.

"So what else is new?" Gloria asked.

"Well, we named the farm," Ben said. "We're calling it Meg's Meadows. How about we go upstairs and get some lunch and talk?"

"Sounds good," Charlie said.

Gloria agreed. "Though I'm not that hungry. I don't eat that much anymore."

Ben winked at Wendy. Whenever food was mentioned around Gloria she always said that, even though she was a good doer, as the horse saying goes. "Do you want to join us?"

"No," Wendy said. "Thanks, but I haven't gotten anything done today except answer the phone. I'll stop up in a while if I get a minute. Otherwise, I'll see you all for dinner? We're at Señor and Liz's tonight."

"Señor?"

"Miguel called him that and it stuck. It beats trying to differentiate Randy from Randy Senior all the time. Junior got married, you know. He and Lucy are expecting."

"So we heard. Wished we could have made it in for the wedding and the banquet, but we both had doctor check-ups," Gloria said. "The story of our lives."

~ * ~

Dusty paid a visit to Jackson's barn to check up on him and Sunrise Sam. Both were settled back in and happy as can be. "He saw me coming and cried like a baby," Jackson said. "He just kept whinnying and nickering."

The horse was standing at the front of his stall pulling hay out of his haynet and chewing contentedly. Dusty patted him on the neck. "You're happy to be back home, Sam, aren't you? That a good boy." From there Dusty walked over to check on the horse in Gulliver's barn. The plan was to move him tomorrow. Dusty checked his water. It looked like it had just been topped off. He turned the haynet, checking to see how much the horse had eaten since this morning. He picked his stall. There were several piles, always a good sign.

From there he walked to the Stewards office and tapped on the door. Two of the three Stewards had attended the banquet last night so they were expecting this visit. Dusty sat down across from them and hesitated.

"Well, as you know, we've been giving this a lot of thought."

"Slots or claiming races?" Fitzgerald asked.

"Both. But slots is a done deal. We're going to put our full attention on the practices of claiming races. We want to try to get a revised policy into effect for the next meet."

"I don't know, Dusty. We've already gotten calls this morning. I'm not at liberty to say from whom. But the word's out and it's not being warmly embraced, to say the least."

"Well, we're not foolish enough to think it's going to be easy," Dusty said. "There's been talk for years in this business about change. If the change has to start here, so be it. We're not talking about trying to do away with claiming all together. We just want to make it fair. How does anybody with integrity keep looking the other way? How do our industry leaders keep looking the other way?"

The three men just looked at him, not agreeing, not disagreeing.

"All the talk lately is about the betting public and their opinion of Thoroughbred racing, how we treat our horses, what happens to them when they no longer race. I don't think the average fan knows much about the process of claiming. I don't know that they care, so essentially this is an internal issue. This is a practice that is flawed and is being allowed to continue year after year. And the biggest flaw is trainers dropping a horse down hoping to get it claimed. Meanwhile, the bettor is betting on this horse because the horse has class and they think he has a shot at winning, when we all know as horsemen that the majority of horses dropping down are dropping down for a reason. They're sore. They're tired. They're done."

When Dusty stood up and walked to the door, the Stewards sat back. "Thank you for your time, gentlemen."

All three Stewards stared at the door. All three smiled.

~ * ~

Wendy set up Dawn's video of Bo-T galloping at the farm, complete with narrative and music, then programmed it to run throughout the day on the monitors in the grandstand in between live racing and simulcast. The racing fans had come to expect the various videos and seemed to really enjoy them. She spent time updating the Nottingham Downs website, another of her regular tasks. It felt good to be back on the job, so to speak. Now that Matthew was doing well....

"Is he?" she wondered, and there went her good mood. "What if...?"

Dusty stopped by to check in with her. "What's the matter?" he asked.

"Nothing." She wiped her eyes. "It's just me. I keep running hot and cold, literally."

Dusty smiled. "I just talked to the Stewards about the claiming races. I think the more people we get to thinking about this the better off we'll be."

"What did they say?"

"Actually, they didn't say much of anything, but I got the feeling they might be onboard."

"Did you see Charlie and Gloria? They just came into town."

"Really?" He smiled. "Did they go to the farm?"

"No. They're up in the clubhouse."

"Well, I'll go up and say hi. You sure you're okay?"

"I'm fine. It's just whenever I think about Matthew...." Here came the tears again.

"Listen." Dusty hesitated. "For what it's worth, if I was Matthew I'd be doing the same thing."

"Thank you, Dusty." Wendy wiped her nose with a tissue. "I think the more I hear that too, the better off I'll be. It's hard to let them grow up."

"It's even harder for them though if you don't."

Wendy looked at him. "How did you get to be so wise?"

"It comes with age." Dusty waved. "I'll see you at the farm."

~ * ~

Junior dropped Lucy off at T-Bone's Place and drove on to Meg's Meadows. Since he'd galloped horses all morning in his wedding clothes, jeans, boots, and a white shirt, he figured there was no sense changing now. Besides, he was only galloping B-Bo today. By the time he tacked up and walked him up the hill, the crowd had assembled at the training track, his bride included. Matthew followed along behind him toting his sketch pad and pencils.

B-Bo walked calmly at a slow pace, hardly favoring that injured leg at all. Mim turned in her seat on the golf cart to watch him approach. "What did Ben say to do today?"

"Warm him up long at a trot and let him canter easy."

Mim nodded, agreeing.

It was a gorgeous day with just a hint of distant autumn in the air. The Cleveland Browns pre-season game was being broadcast at four that evening. Carol and Lucy were going to make home-made pizza for the event, but with no pepperoni, since it gave just about every one of the old-timers indigestion. Junior started singing a song. "I'm gonna be a wheel someday, I'm gonna be somebody."

Matthew chuckled. "I think you need to keep your mouth closed or you're not going to like this drawing."

When they all laughed, Mim started coughing and blamed it on the stirred up dust. She'd brought a bottle of water with her and took a drink. Three women started up the hill behind them. Vicky turned, as did the old-timers. Mim recognized the two. "Well, hello!"

"Hello, Mim," Veronica said.

"Hello!" Karen echoed.

The girl walking with them just shrugged.

"This is Hillary."

"Ah, Hillary," Mim said. "I've heard about you."

When the girl just looked at her, Mim laughed. "Ah, if you could read people the way you read horses, you would know, little girl, that we are kindred spirits."

Hillary smiled. "I just don't like being fooled."

Mim nodded. "I can relate to that also," she said, and went about introducing everyone. "That's Lucy. She's gonna have a baby."

Lucy waved and touched her tummy.

"That's Jeanne, that's Miguel, that's Steven. This is Vicky, our patron saint. That's Bill, that fella over there is Jack, that's Frank, that's Matthew, and I'm Mim. Bitch Number One; stand in line."

Hillary laughed.

"Everyone," Mim said. "This is Veronica and Karen of the Shifting Gears Thoroughbred Rescue Farm."

They all said their hellos and turned and watched as Junior and B-Bo passed in front of them in a nice, fluid canter. Hillary studied the horse, the way it moved, the look in his eye.

"And that is Junior," Mim said, "Lucy's husband."

Hillary nodded, her attention totally on the horse.

"He had a hind-leg injury," Mim said. "That's why he's here."

"I know. I see," Hillary said.

Mim glanced at Veronica and rolled her eyes, not offended in the least by the girl's curt response. She apparently *did* see.

"So what you do?" Miguel asked of the girl.

"Uh…." She hesitated. "I…"

"She's been helping us out," Veronica said. "She's very good with the horses. They love her."

Junior pulled B-Bo up on the backstretch of the training track, turned him around, and walked him back. Hillary looked at Matthew. "Why are you staring at me like that?"

"Uh...I don't see well. I'm trying to decide if you're pretty or not."

Hillary just looked at him. "Is that some kind of joke?"

"No," he said, showing her his sketch of the horse.

Hillary looked from his sketch to him and then back. She looked at Mim.

"I told him to capture the horse's heart."

Hillary glanced at the sketch again and then watched the horse as Junior led him off the racetrack. She nodded.

"Hey," Junior said.

Another nod. Her eyes on the horse. She chuckled. "Oh if every horse could be this happy."

The entourage turned and started down the hill. Four on the golf cart, Lucy and Vicky pushing Clint's and Jeannie's wheelchairs, Miguel walking along with Veronica and Karen, and Matthew and Hillary bringing up the rear.

"This is a nice farm," Hillary commented as they walked along. "So were you born blind?"

"No, and I'm not exactly blind. I just have blind areas of seeing."

"Is everything blurry?" Hillary asked.

"No, what I see, I see very clear. You have a mole high on your cheekbone. But a lot of the rest is missing."

They were all at the barn by now. "Where is Dusty's horse, Bonnie Bee?" Veronica asked.

Mim motioned to the far pasture. "The little black filly. Is that who you came to see?"

"Yes."

"I'll take you," Matthew said. "I'm headed there next anyway." He opened the sketch book and showed Hillary his sketch of the filly, Biscuit, and Poncho.

"We're going to go visit with Mim then," Veronica said, walking alongside the golf cart and following the old-timers.

Hillary motioned to the pasture where Beau Born and Hurry Sandy were grazing. "Wow!" she said. "Wow!"

"I know. I can't get close enough to draw him though."

"He's magnificent," she said. Beau looked up at her. "And he knows it."

Matthew nodded.

"He's the sire of the horse you just saw gallop."

"I know," Hillary said.

"Do you want to see Bo-T?"

"Sure." The two walked down past the stallion barn, past the foaling barn, and into the main barn. Junior was hosing down B-Bo in the wash rack. Hillary looked at him. "He's thinking about dinner."

"Always," Junior said.

Matthew stopped in front of Bo-T's stall and nudged Hillary back when he feared she was standing too close. Bo-T charged the stall gate and bucked and kicked, bit the air and put on a show.

Hillary looked at the horse's eyes and shook her head.

"What?"

"Nothing." Hillary chuckled. "It's all x-rated. Apparently that's all he can think about."

"You got that right," Junior said, finishing up at the wash rack. He led B-Bo past them to cool him out. When Bo-T lunged at him, B-Bo never even blinked.

"Brothers," Hillary said.

"I can relate to that," Matthew said, walking out of the barn with her.

They stopped to look at the horses in each pasture, the mares, the weanlings, the yearlings, the two-year-olds. "This is a peaceful place," Hillary said.

"All except for when Beau starts screaming. You should hear him in breeding season."

"I can imagine."

They walked down past Ben's farm house to the golf-cart path and climbed between the fence rails into Poncho, Biscuit, and Bonnie Bee's pasture. The three horses looked up at them from the distance and then went back to grazing. They were used to Matthew coming every day and Hillary posed no threat.

"Where do you usually do your drawing?"

"Well, I sit right with them mostly."

"That's cool." The horses looked up again when they approached and then all three walked over for their carrots. Matthew handed her the one for Bonnie Bee. She broke it into pieces and fed it to her, then stroked her face gently.

"What did Dusty want you to come see her for?"

"Shhh…." Hillary said.

"Sorry." Matthew looked around for a lush spot in the grass and sat down. Hillary sat down next to him, not close, not far. She wanted to see him draw. The filly gravitated toward her.

"She'll eat the grass right out from under you," Matthew said softly.

Hillary smiled and moved slightly closer to him. "He said he just wants to make sure she's happy here."

"Is she?"

"Yes. Very."

"What about the other two?"

Hillary studied the Palomino, Poncho. "He's happy…now."

"He hasn't always been?"

She shook her head and chuckled. Bonnie Bee was nibbling around behind her back and tickling her.

"What about Biscuit?"

She looked at the bay gelding, just looked at him a moment. "He has some concerns." She paused. "He's older than people think he is," she said softly. "He worries, no…not worries, he's concerned that his age might bother people."

"Why?"

Hillary looked at him. "Well." She didn't want to say, not in front of Biscuit.

"This is their home."

Hillary was still looking at the horse. "He's heard that before."

Matthew studied her profile, the angle of her neck.

"He says no one tells him that anymore. He said when he first came, they told him all the time. Now they don't."

"Well, I think that's because they think he should know. They love him. Everyone does."

"He needs to hear that," Hillary said. "They need to reassure him every now and then. Everyone needs to hear that now and then."

Matthew nodded. "So, uh, aside from this," he said, implying her "talking" to horses, "What do you do?"

"I'm still in high school. I would have graduated last year, but I skipped too many classes. What about you?"

"Well," Matthew said, drawing and looking up at the horses, "up until my car accident last month, I was a classic over-achieving grad student. A geek."

She looked at him. "You got the geek thing down pat."

Matthew laughed.

"Go ahead, draw. Don't mind me. This is the most relaxed situation I've been in, in a long time." She watched him sketch Bonnie Bee's eye and pointed. "Her lashes are longer than that."

"Easy for you to say," Matthew said, smiling.

Hillary chuckled and laid back on the grass and looked up at the sky. "Did you ever think about how insignificant we are?"

"No, can't say that I have," Matthew said.

"I mean, in the grand scheme of things, as individuals we're nothing. We're just part of this big huge universe."

Matthew glanced at her. "We could be everything. Maybe inside each one of us is everything."

She spread her hands in the grass and felt the earth. "Wake me in ten minutes," she said. "If I sleep during the day any longer than that, I turn into a real bitch."

~ * ~

Dinner at Señor and Liz's turned into an even bigger party than usual. Gloria and Charlie were there, Mark had returned with his girlfriend Susie. Gordon came home for the night. Richard and his wife Heather came by. There were people eating and talking and laughing all over the house. Gloria had brought treats for the horses and the dogs and all six of the dogs were sprawled out on the front porch. The menu this evening was pork chops, roasted potatoes, a zucchini casserole, homemade applesauce, rolls and butter.

"We stopped for a visit at T-Bone's Place," Charlie said. "It was so nice to see everyone. The place looks great!"

They all nodded, eating, drinking, and sharing stories.

"Mim looks frail."

"I know," Ben said. He and Charlie and Dusty had known Mim for over fifty years.

"What's the prognosis?" Gloria asked.

Ben looked at her, again the memory of her saving his life that day flashing in his mind. "She's on borrowed time."

"When you borrow something, you should always return the item," D.R. said.

Everyone laughed. "Out of the mouths of babes," Ben said. "Thank you, D.R. That's a good reminder for us all."

D.R. smiled proudly.

"So, Matthew," Gloria said. "I hear you're going to hike the Appalachian Trail."

He nodded. "Did we get a date yet?" he asked, looking at Liz.

"Not yet. I hope soon though. I don't know how much help I'd be in cold weather." Liz shared news about the volunteer project.

"I did Habitat once," Charlie said. He looked at Mark's girlfriend Susie. "So what do you do?"

"At the moment, nothing. I'll start looking for a job in the morning." She looked around the room. "Do you all know each other from the racetrack?"

"Yes," George said, and that paved the way for more stories from everyone.

"Once upon a time, I was one of Ben's owners," Gloria said. "I had a wonderful horse named Tom Cajun. Oh, how I loved that horse."

"When I had the stroke at the racetrack," Ben said, "It was Gloria's quick action that saved my life."

"Ben introduced me to Gloria," Charlie said, giving Gloria a hug. "And we got married."

"I'm the Assistant General Manager," Wendy said. "I met Tom through Ben when they bought the racetrack."

"I'm the General Manager," Richard said. "This is my wife, Heather."

"I work with Hospice," Heather said. "Nottingham Downs saved our marriage."

Wendy looked at her, the two of them smiling. "Nottingham Downs saved my life."

Tom looked up from eating. "I pony horses."

Everyone laughed, as usual whenever he said that.

"Junior says you're about done ponying," Charlie said.

Tom shook his head. "I'm gonna smack that boy."

Everyone laughed.

Matthew and Gordon raised their hands. "We're Wendy and Tom's."

Susie had already met Randy and Dawn, along with Carol and the children earlier in the evening at their house.

"I'm George. I'm the farm manager. This is my wife, Glenda. I've known Ben and Tom and Dusty forever. We've been here at the farm for years now."

Glenda smiled. "We were both trainers. We went from the trotters to Thoroughbreds."

"I am the conscience of the racetrack and I live here at "Meg's Meadows," Dusty said, emphasizing the new farm name. "And as of today, I own a pretty little filly named Bonnie Bee."

Matthew smiled, sharing the story. "Hillary says she's happy here."

"Hillary?" Gloria asked. "Who's Hillary?"

"Oh, long story," Dawn said. "A young activist, animal communicator. She has a gift for sensing what horses think and feel."

"Which reminds me," Matthew said. "She says Biscuit will need constant reassurance of 'love.'"

"Don't we all," Heather said. When everyone nodded, Maeve looked around the room and nodded too. Not to be outdone, D.R. then nodded, and with great conviction. Randy ruffled his carrot-top hair and tickled Maeve's nose.

Dawn looked at Matthew. "Did she say he was unhappy?"

"No, just that he'd need reassurance that we all love him, that in the back of his mind he has doubts. She says he's older than we think and he worries that that's going to matter somehow?"

"Oh, how sad," Dawn said. She looked at Randy. "How old is he?"

"I don't know." He turned to Mark. "Do you have your Smartphone with you?"

Mark laughed. "No, but I'm pretty good at judging."

"Good." Randy looked at George. "When did we have him floated last?"

"About six months ago. His teeth were fine. I never thought to ask about his age."

"Don't look at me," Señor said. "I've got good teeth."

Everyone laughed. "I'm Randy's father, Dawn's father-in-law. Liz and I also have a daughter Cindy, who will be moving here next year and hopefully go into practice with Randy and Mark."

All eyes fell on Liz. "I'm Randy's mother and grandmother to these two darling children. I'm looking forward to when Cindy and her husband Marvin move here. I love living here at Meg's Meadows."

Carol smiled. "I'm the nanny. I came into this family by way of Dawn and Randy, and everyone here is my family now. I love them all, even those dogs out there."

Everyone turned and laughed. All six dogs were sitting at attention outside the screen door.

"I don't know who ever started feeding them table scraps," Ben said.

Everyone laughed again. "You!"

Ben shook his head. "I'd also like to know how they know we're done eating."

"Because it's time for dessert," George said.

They all helped clear dishes and sat back down with banana cream pie and coffee.

"You eat this way every night?" Susie asked.

"Not every night," Dawn said. "Just most nights."

"This is the Meg's Meadows commune," Dusty said.

Wendy laughed. "When I first came on the scene I was so obsessed with not eating, I feared I was going to get kicked out of the fold. Up until that point, I don't think I even enjoyed food. I was always so afraid of being overweight."

"I don't eat much," Gloria said, fork in hand.

"How do you figure out who cooks what?" Susie asked.

"Well, we usually just take turns. Someone does the main dish most often, and then we all bring sides. Cost-wise, we probably save money eating all together," Liz said. "We can buy bulk this way. Which reminds me, I talked to Vicky today about doing their shopping for them. When I go do ours, I'll just stop and get their list."

Susie smiled. "Is theirs a separate operation?"

"Well," Wendy said. "The idea is for them to be self-supporting. That's how they wanted it set up. They take great pride in that. We do too."

"See what I told you," Mark said. "You're going to love it here. These are your kind of people."

Chapter Thirty-Three

Nottingham Downs didn't make the *Morning Banter* headline, but did make the Sports page. "Beau All Together Favored to Win the Burgundy Blue Stake."

"Ah, Jesus, they're starting already," Ben said, sitting in the tack room. "It's a jinx. The race is six days away. I hate this. It's just like with the Derby. I knew better than to second-guess myself."

Tom stared at the training chart. "Two to gallop, three to walk. Let's get going." They were all superstitious. If something bad happened to Bo-T, chances are his stallion career would be gone as well. Plus there was no way to just change their minds at this point without a lot of scrutiny. It had been rather nice the past few days not getting negative press.

Dusty walked down to Gulliver's barn, fed the horse, stood talking with Gulliver for a moment, and then headed off to the ReHab barn to set up the stall for the horse.

"The Secretary's office is officially open for entries," Joe Feigler announced over the loudspeaker. "Come on over."

After Dusty squared everything at the ReHab barn, he started making his rounds through the barn area. He heard quite a few comments and suggestions about the claiming race issue. As was his usual routine, he would hold a horse for a trainer, give an exercise rider a leg-up, just sit and talk a minute or two with a trainer, feel things out, look things over. He once had a trainer accuse him of having eagle eyes, but added, "In a good way." Dusty didn't miss much.

He and Ben met up at the kitchen after the track closed for training and had a cup of coffee. There was plenty of coffee back at the barn, but their being here was also a way of listening to the other trainers, owners, and grooms about current issues. It was also a time they enjoyed, one-on-one as two old-timers themselves. Brownie, the owner of the kitchen, sat down with them, another old-timer. These three weren't ones to dwell on the past. They were more interested in the way they could help things be today.

Several trainers pulled up chairs to join them. They talked about horses. They talked about food. They talked about the weather. When Dusty glanced at his watch; time to meet Randy and move the horse out of Gulliver's barn, the party broke up and they all went back to work.

Randy blocked the horse's leg, so it wouldn't feel any pain and wrapped it tight. Gulliver went along with Dusty and the horse to the ReHab barn. The horse walked as if he hadn't a care in the world. Gulliver had one hand resting gently on the horse's withers. The necessary paperwork had all been finalized and Dusty had already put the word out that the horse needed long-term rehab and a home. He led the horse into his new stall, bed deep in straw and turned him around and took his halter off. Randy redid the bandage, not as tightly this time, and the three men stood looking in at the horse.

"Wish I had a magic wand," Randy said.

"I don't know, Randy. I think you come pretty close," Dusty said.

"Thank you," Randy said, patting both men on the back. "You two make me proud." He left them and checked in at the Miller barn. They were still doing horses up, still had one on the walking machine.

Ben picked his keys up off his desk and walked out into the shedrow. "I think I'm going to go on home and watch Bo-T and B-Bo gallop. If I don't come back, don't worry about me."

"You all right, old man?" Tom asked.

"Yes." Ben nodded. "I'm fine."

Dawn, Randy, and Tom exchanged concerned glances.

"You sure?" Dawn asked.

"Yes, I'm sure," Ben said, making an effort to smile reassuringly. "I'll see you all at the farm."

Tom looked at Dawn and Randy after he left. "Was that weird?"

They both nodded.

"I wonder if all of this is just too much for him anymore," Tom said.

"Well, we can always tell him that and piss him off good. That'll get his fire back!" Randy said.

Dawn and Tom laughed.

Ben stopped to talk to Jason at the guard shack on his way out. "How long have you been here?" he asked, seemingly out of the blue.

"Full-time? Well, since Charlie left. I was part-time until then. Why?"

"I don't know. I'm guess I'm wondering what you think about the way things are going?"

"Well, I think things are headed in the right direction if you want to stay open."

Ben looked at him.

Jason shrugged. "You asked."

"Yes, I did," Ben said, nodding. "Thank you."

On the way home, Ben stopped at the grocery store for some liverwurst. He had a taste for a liverwurst and onion sandwich and couldn't remember the last time he'd had one. He honked and waved to the old-timers when he passed T-Bone's place and checked in with George in the main barn, who appeared surprised to see him.

"You okay?"

"Yessss," Ben said, shaking his head. "What is it with everyone asking me if I'm okay? I'm okay."

"Good," George said. "Then get out of my way. I have things to do."

Ben laughed. "How are the boys today?"

"Well, Bo-T chased me out of the stall and B-Bo's taken two naps already today. And talk about snore…."

Ben chuckled. Randy had scoped B-Bo several times over the years just to make sure everything was okay in the breathing department. The horse obviously just liked to snore. He liked to nap a lot too, flat out on his side.

"I'll see you later," Ben said, turning. "There's obviously nothing for me to do here either."

"Wait, Ben. There is," George said.

Ben stopped and looked back. "What's that?"

"Keeping us together. You're the reason we're all here."

Ben smiled. "Wait a minute. Did Dawn call you?"

"Yes, and Randy and Tom and Wendy too."

Ben smiled. "Ah, see. I do have some usefulness. I'm keeping everyone on their toes with worry."

George laughed. "Junior will be here about two-thirty." He looked in at B-Bo, buckling his knees and going down for another nap.

"I'll see you then." Ben walked up to the house to make his sandwich. Much like the potted meat sandwich last week, liverwurst didn't taste quite as good as he remembered. He ate it all anyway, put on his walking shoes, and headed outside and down the driveway. The maple leaves were just starting to turn. He patted the top of the Meg's Meadows farm sign and decided to turn right instead of left and walked alongside the road taking in the sights.

He couldn't remember the last time he'd been down this way. It had probably been years. Everything in his life apparently seemed to come and go from the other direction. A young neighbor woman, dressed to ride, had just checked her mailbox and waited for him.

"Hello," she said.

"Hi, I'm Ben Miller from…"

"From Meg's Meadows. Yes, I know. I love your new sign. It's so nice to finally meet you." She shook Ben's hand. "We've been neighbors a long time."

"Oh?"

"My husband and I have lived here about five years now."

"Well, I'll be," Ben said. "Nice place." The house was big and modern, nice big barn, indoor arena. "Well, I'd best be on my way."

"Bye, Mr. Miller."

"Ben," he said. "My wife's name was Meg."

The woman waved and watched him for a moment. "I like your shoes!"

Ben laughed. "Me too. Have a good day!" He walked for quite a while, maybe a mile, maybe two, and decided to turn back at the crossroad. He switched over to the other side, saw all sorts of new scenery; a little cottage way back in the woods, a ranch house with a huge wind turbine out back, a cow and a rooster. He glanced ahead and saw Junior's truck turn into the driveway. Perfect timing.

~ * ~

Mark and Randy met up at the Brubaker barn and after treating a horse there, went up to the track kitchen for a late lunch. They sat down in front of one of the monitors and watched the running of the third race, then sorted out the rest of the day's calls and had a second cup of coffee. Jackson came and got a burger and hot tea and sat down a few tables away.

"Hey," he said, nodding to Randy

Randy nodded back."Everything okay?"

"Yep, everything's great."

Randy lowered his voice and brought Mark up to date on Jackson's horse.

"And he's sound?" Mark looked at the man.

"Apparently," Randy said.

"He's fine. Why wouldn't he be?" Jackson asked, having heard every word.

Mark shrugged. He wasn't going to say, because I examined him twice last week and he looked like he wanted to die, even though that's what he was thinking.

Jackson took a big bite of his burger. "I'll probably enter him tomorrow. He's kicking the barn down."

Randy and Mark both raised their eyebrows.

"That's how I know," he said, sipping his hot tea. "If there's anything I know, I know my horse."

Both Mark and Randy nodded. What was there to say? They looked at the monitor as it played a video of Bo-T galloping at the farm. "I saw it yesterday," Jackson said. "He looks great! Wish they'd stop talking about him in the paper. It's bad luck. Remember that Turn To colt some years back. Papers talked about him way too much. They put the jinx on him."

Randy sighed. He'd had to put the horse down that day.

"If I had my say, I'd forbid the newspapers from talking about him. Yep, that's what I'd do. 'Course then you'd have people saying that wasn't right and they'd write about that and then talk some more."

Dusty came in the door and walked over to Randy and Mark's table. He nodded to Jackson. "Hey, how is everything?"

"Good, good." Jackson held up his tea cup. "Couldn't be better."

"I'm glad to hear it. All's well that ends well, eh?"

Jackson nodded, downed the rest of his tea, and left.

"Have you seen Ben? I can't find him anywhere?"

"He went home. He says he went to watch Bo-T and B-Bo gallop and wouldn't be back."

"Well, that's odd. Is he okay?"

"That's what Tom and Dawn and I were wondering."

"Why? What's wrong with him?" Mark asked.

Dusty and Randy just sat there.

"Is he sick?"

"No," Randy said. "He just had cataract surgery, but aside from that and needing the other one done now, he's fine."

Mark looked from one to the other.

"He had a stroke a few years back," Dusty said.

"But you wouldn't know it unless we told you," Randy said. "He recovered remarkably well for his age."

"So you worry about him because…?"

Randy looked at him and then smacked him on the arm, laughing. "Get outta here! Who asked you? Don't you have anything to do?"

Mark laughed. "I'll see you later."

Dusty and Randy looked at one another after he left.

"I think we owe Ben an apology."

"I think you're right," Dusty said. "It's one thing to worry about him and quite another to hover over him all the time. Which reminds me, I keep thinking about what Hillary said to Matthew about Biscuit. I think we need to realize that horses, whether they can communicate or not, have feelings. I mean, think about it. People fear when they get old what's going to happen to them, who's going to care for them, or if being old will be their downfall?"

Randy nodded. "I've known horses that I swear no sooner have they eaten, they start fretting over their next meal. Seriously. They watch the corner for more hay. They check their feed tubs. They live in the now as far as reacting, but I think there is so much more that goes on in their heads. They worry and they wonder. And it's not just fright and flight. It's honest to God feelings." Randy chuckled. "Oh listen to me."

"No, I agree," Dusty said. "I'm a believer."

~ * ~

Ben walked up the hill with Matthew behind Bo-T and Junior to the training track. Liz waved from their porch.

"We're at your place tonight, Ben."

"What are we having?"

"Dawn's slumgullian."

"Wonderful!" he said. It was everyone's favorite.

"What's for dessert?" Matthew asked.

"Dirt cake."

"Oh baby," Matthew said.

Ben laughed. "Watch, watch," he said, nudging Matthew back. "He's thinking about pitching a fit."

"How can you tell?" He knew about a horse pinning its ears when it was unhappy or mad, but pitching a fit?

"Just watch him. Look at his eyes."

They were wide open, the sclera about the pupils showing all around and white. Just then, Bo-T hopped sky-high in the air and bucked and kicked and squealed. "If we make it to the race Saturday it's going to be a miracle," Ben said. "Get after him!"

Junior chuckled and urged the colt into a trot onto the training track in front of the assembled crowd. Ben sat on the newly constructed lower rung of the bleachers next to Steven and Frank. Vicky and Lucy were on the top rung. Mim had Miguel, Bill, and Jack on the golf cart with her. Clint and Jeanne were in their wheelchairs on the other side.

They all said their hellos and sat back to watch the show. Bo-T fought the bit, yanking and flinging his head back and forth.

"Give him an inch and he'll take a mile," Jack said.

Junior smiled. "Don't you worry. I got him."

Bo-T propped just then and tried taking off down the track. Junior turned him back around and trotted on up well up into the turn.

"He look like his daddy," Miguel said.

"Oh, don't say that," Lucy said.

"The horse," Miguel said, laughing. "Beau Born."

"Oh good. Sorry. I thought you meant Rupert."

They all chuckled.

Junior turned Bo-T around, allowed him to trot a little and then let him break into a canter. Still fighting the bit, trying to pull it out of Junior's hands, Bo-T bowed his neck and settled into a nice stride when Junior clicked to him. Ben smiled.

Matthew was sketching as fast as he could. "Wish I could freeze-frame him."

"Not with a beating heart," Mim said.

Matthew smiled, still sketching feverishly. Everyone watched Junior gallop the horse down the backstretch and into the turn. Bo-T had picked up speed, but still had his neck bowed and was under wraps. Junior had a strong hold on him.

Ben glanced at Mim. She was smiling, moving slightly with each of Bo-T's strides. "I feel like Penny Chenery," she said. "Go Big Red."

Everyone laughed.

Miguel stood up and waved his arm high in the air. "You about to see something you ain't never seen before!"

Everyone laughed again.

"I think we've watched that movie one too many times," Vicky said.

"Never," Steven said.

They all watched Junior and Bo-T come back around; Bo-T was still galloping strong, all business now and floating along.

"He's got an amazing stride," Mim said. "Just like Beau Born."

Ben nodded. "I would have loved to have seen them race against each other."

"Who do you think would win?" Steven asked.

Ben paused. "Well, time-wise Bo-T with the track record would probably make it a horse race. But their personalities are so different. Beau Born was tenacious. He just flat loved winning. Bo-T; all he can think about is the girls."

Junior pulled Bo-T up deep into the backstretch, almost into the turn, turned him around, loosened his rein and let him walk back.

"Sure was nice seeing Charlie," Mim said.

Everyone agreed. They'd all known one another forever. Charlie had greeted them every morning for decades during racing season.

"Always a happy man," Steven said.

"I wasn't so sure how that marriage was going to work," Jeanne said, "Charlie being a bachelor all is life. But he seems happy. We're all going to have dinner tomorrow together."

"Really," Ben said. "Where?"

"I don't know," Vicky said. "George and Señor said it's a surprise."

Lucy looked over Matthew's shoulder. "You're very good," she said.

"Thank you." He glanced up at her and smiled.

"He looks alive," Lucy added. "Mim, his heart is beating."

"Let me see?"

Matthew passed the sketch book to her by way of Ben. Mim smiled, handing it back, and thumped her hand against her chest. "When you capture his right eye and left ear, it'll be a masterpiece."

Matthew blushed. "Thank you."

They all watched Junior walk Bo-T down the rail past them. He turned the horse to the inside in front of the open gate, bowed to the infield, and everyone laughed. "You're such a ham," Lucy said.

Junior just grinned. Bo-T was nice and calm and just stood for a moment.

"I got it," Matthew said. "I got it."

Ben looked over his shoulder and nodded.

Junior turned Bo-T toward the fence.

"Hold up a second," Ben said, climbing down and going over and holding Bo-T's rein. "Finish the ear."

Matthew sketched with a frenzy, looking up the horse, back at the sketch, erasing, sketching again.

"Does he want to run?" Steven asked.

When Ben looked at him, Steven motioned. "You're supposed to look him in the eye and he's going to tell you if he wants to run."

Ben chuckled and played along. He'd seen the Secretariat movie his share of times too. He stood in front of the colt and looked into his eyes, looked long and hard. Then he smiled. "All right then," he said. "Let's show them what you're made of."

Everyone laughed. Even Bo-T seemed to enjoy the little performance. He nodded his head up and down, rubbed up against Ben, and then Ben stepped out of the way and sat back down.

"George is going to hose him off," Junior said. "He should have B-Bo tacked. I'll be right back."

"All right. We're not going anywhere." Ben heaved a sigh and looked around. "It's such a gorgeous day. It just doesn't get much better than this."

Everyone nodded, even the two from the younger generation.

"I've spent a lot of my life on this farm. It's nice to be able to just sit here and do nothing but enjoy it for a change."

"It's called retirement," Vicky said.

Ben looked at her. She'd come out of retirement to take on the care of the old-timers. It was a tremendous day-to-day responsibility, yet she really didn't think of it as a job, she'd told him. She was just "living."

Sitting there, Ben decided he was going to do a little living too. Afternoons like this and no horses racing that day, why not come home? Richard and Wendy were at the helm. Tom and Dawn and Junior could take care of things at the barn. Junior was helping out more and more. Dusty was there. Why not?

"You're smiling, Ben," Mim said.

"I know." He pointed to the other side of the training track. "I walked way over there today. Do you hear a rooster in the morning?"

Miguel looked at Frank. "I tell you I hear rooster! You say I crazy!"

Everyone laughed.

"Yep," Ben said. "There's a rooster back there and a cow too."

Jeanne placed her hand to her forehead shading her eyes to try and see.

"It crowed at me in broad daylight strutting all around. He made Bo-T look tame."

They all laughed, especially when Ben imitated the rooster bobbing its head and scratching. Then here came Junior up the hill on B-Bo. Glenda was walking along behind. "I haven't seen him gallop since he was a two-year old," she said.

B-Bo walked onto the training track and stood tall and lazy. He just gazed around the track a moment, then looked at everyone and yawned a great big yawn, showing all his teeth and rolling his eyes.

Ben studied his hind leg. It was done up in Vetwrap and only slightly swollen. Glenda sat down next to Lucy. "How are you feeling?"

"Good," Lucy said. "I'm not nauseated anymore, but I'm awfully sleepy all the time."

"That's because your body is working twenty-four hours a day seven days a week wide awake or sound asleep. You need lots of sleep."

Lucy smiled. "I'm getting it. Vicky is always making me go take a nap."

Junior walked B-Bo down to the turn and let him stand and look around some more. Ben watched him walk then trot when he started toward them and nodded to Junior to let him canter. Mim was nodding as well.

"He's like a semi. It takes him a while to get going and then…."

B-Bo gave a little buck and they were all surprised including Junior. "You showing off, Big Man? You showing off?" B-Bo tossed his head and took to cantering along and went around three times like it was nothing.

The entourage followed him back down the hill singing, *"Oh happy day, oh happy day…when Jesus washed, oh when he washed, when Jesus washed…he washed my sins away! Oh happy day…"*

George looked out of the barn, laughed, and sang along in a deep baritone voice, *"He taught me how to watch…fight and pray, fight and pray. And he'll rejoice in things we say, every day. Oh happy day….Oh happy day…."*

They were all still singing as they went their separate ways, arms waving and their voices fading in the distance. It was a happy day indeed. Ben decided he might as well take a nap before dinner and stretched out on the porch couch.

"Matthew!" he said. "Can you bring me a pillow?"

"You want a blanky too!"

"Now that you mentioned it, it is cooling off a little."

Matthew brought him a pillow and an afghan. "You're really taking this retirement business seriously, aren't you?"

Ben laughed, fluffed the pillow and covered up.

~ * ~

Slumgullion was one of Dawn's two signature dishes she'd perfected over the years and always a big hit. Made with browned ground beef, tomato sauce with onion, garlic, and macaroni noodles, topped with grated Parmesan cheese, not only did the adults in the family love it; the children loved it too. It went really good with a tossed salad, Roquefort dressing, and Italian bread.

Three huge serving bowls were placed on the table, close to everyone. Mark and Susie sat across from the children and were thoroughly entertained with their cute little antics. Maeve made a kind of Slumgullion sandwich which was quite a mess and sat eating one bite after another. D.R. took a big drink of milk after shoveling in each mouthful and had a pretty impressive white mustache going.

"Pass the butter, please," Dusty said.

Mark handed the butter dish to him and got the bowl of salad in return. He helped himself and passed it along. Gloria and Charlie were at her grand-niece's ordination ceremony. Richard had gone to a benefit dinner of one of their vendors.

"How does that work?" Mark asked. "The tellers? The food vendors? The janitors? The parking attendants."

"They're all union," Tom said. "We have very little to do with them from our standpoint. That's basically Richard's department. They're all under contract."

Wendy nodded. "Occasionally I have to be the go-between, but for the most part, everything on that end is union. They manage themselves."

"I hope it stays that way," Ben said.

"Why wouldn't it?" Tom asked.

"I don't know. I'm just saying. Never mind. It's been too nice of a day." He shared his 'went for a walk, met the neighbor lady, saw a cow and a rooster' story, and the children's eyes got big.

"A real rooster? A cock-a-doodle-do rooster?" D.R. asked.

Ben nodded. "And a moooo cow too."

Maeve giggled.

Dawn, Tom, and Randy refrained from asking him if he was sure he should be walking that far from home, though that's exactly what all three were thinking. "How nice," Dawn said instead.

Matthew picked up on their vibes and changed the subject. "I drew Bo-T's beating heart today. You can't actually see it, but Mim says it's there, and I think so too. Something happened and...." He held up both hands. "All of a sudden, it was there."

Wendy looked at him and paused. "I owe you a thousand apologies."

"Well, if it's all right with you," Matthew said, fearing she was about to have another crying jag from the way she was looking at him, "can we just eat."

Wendy smiled. "I love you, Son."

Matthew just looked at her, tried making a joke of her comment, tried lightening the mood. "I love you too, Mommy Dearest."

"I love Mommy," Maeve said, Slumgullion all over her face. Everyone laughed.

"I should have let you go to art school." Wendy was determined to get this off her chest, determined not to cry. "I should have. I'm sorry. I advised you wrong."

The table fell quiet.

"Actually, Mom, I don't think I would ever have been able to draw a beating heart in art school. I would never have even wanted to. It would never have crossed my mind. I'm where I should be, this moment: right now." He looked around the table. "And if someone would pass me some more Slumgullian, I'd be even happier."

Everyone chuckled.

"Well now that I've gotten that off my chest," Wendy said, smiling. "I'll have some more too, please."

Susie looked around the table. "This is the most amazing family. I am in awe."

Tom laughed. "You ain't seen nothing yet. Wait till we have a fight. We get down and dirty!"

Everyone laughed. "No, we don't," Dawn said. "Just Tom."

Tom threw a piece of bread at her and laughed. "Don't you start with me!"

Randy caught the bread mid-air and buttered it. "Thank you!"

Ben looked at Liz. "What's this I hear about a surprise dinner with the old-timers?"

Liz smiled. "It's a surprise, Ben. Don't you like surprises?"

"Noooo." Just about everyone answered for him and laughed.

Ben looked at all of them. "That was the old Ben. The new Ben likes surprises. Don't tell me. I don't want to know. I'll be surprised too."

Señor looked at him. "We've got a lot of work to do in the morning to pull it off, so stay away. Otherwise it'll ruin the surprise."

Ben nodded. "I'll see what I can do."

There was a knock on the door and everyone turned. A man as tall as a tree stood in the doorway. "I heard Nottingham Down is getting slots and I had to come see for myself."

"Cracker Jack!" Ben said. "Come on in! Sit down! Mark, Susie, this is Cracker Jack Henderson."

Cracker Jack shook Mark's hand and smiled at Susie. "Nice to meet you, Darlin'!" He sat down as if he had just been there yesterday and not away for over a year. "Ooh, Slumgullion! This is worth eight hundred miles for sure!"

Susie stared at Cracker Jack's wild and crazy hair. It was snow white and thick, shoulder length, and looked as if each strand had a mind of its own. "Where do I know you from?" she asked, thinking.

"Well…."

"I know! You came to my high school and gave a talk on broadcasting. Gosh, how long ago was that?"

Cracker Jack smiled. "Was it just last year?"

Susie laughed. "Oh my gosh! We all talked about you for days."

Cracker Jack poured himself a glass of iced tea from a pitcher. "Oh, and what did you all say?"

"We said how inspiring it was that you said life had its ups and downs, but it's the middles that keep you going. You had a little teeter-totter that you sat on the podium."

Cracker Jack glanced at Ben and smiled. "I still have that little teeter-totter. Zig Ziegler's got his pump; I have my see-saw."

"But the funny thing is," Susie said. "We could never quite agree about what you meant."

"That's the point," Cracker Jack said. "See, it's like this…."

"Oh geez," Ben said. "Is it time for dessert yet?"

Everyone laughed.

"I'll be here all week," Cracker Jack said. "I'll explain fully."

~ * ~

There was so much to talk about. Slots, the wedding, the banquet, updates on the ReHab and ReHome project, Ben's eye surgery, Matthew's accident, his current eye challenges, the Appalachian trip, Ben's semi-retirement, the old-timers, T-Bone's Place, claiming races.

Carol put the children to bed and the adults all sat around the dinner table talking well into the evening. "Good luck on the claiming races," Cracker Jack said. "That's not going to be easy."

"Perhaps we can borrow your little teeter-totter," Tom said.

Everyone laughed and then grew serious.

"They have a rule in California about a claimed horse that breaks down in the race. The problem I have with that," Randy said, "is the horse has to be put down on the track. It doesn't cover the horse that somehow makes it back to the barn. Horsemen can gripe and carry on all they want, but until there's a way to stop trainers from trying to unload a horse through a claim, it's going to continue to go on."

Cracker Jack nodded. "Probably at least sixty percent of the races run in this country are claiming races."

Mark took out his Smartphone, typed in a question, and got a quick answer. "Sixty one percent and growing due to slots." He paused, reading further down the page. "With the influx of higher purse monies, trainers are playing the odds as never before and putting their horses' lives on the line."

"I hate that," Dawn said.

They all nodded.

"The reality is on any given day a horse can go into a race perfectly sound and break down for any number of reasons. No one should profit from that, particularly the lowlifes who lead a sore horse over knowing he's likely to break down and hoping he gets claimed," Tom said.

Dusty nodded. "And if he does break down in the race, regardless of the situation, I believe that claim should be null and void. It's as simple as that. No one should have to underwrite the unscrupulous behavior of a few undesirables. That's fraud. That's criminal. You're endangering the horse and the jockey, and the horses and jockeys all around them. It's all for money. If an owner or trainer doesn't know what to do with the horse at the end of its racing career, that's what we're here for, that's what

ReHab and ReHome is for. If that horse hasn't made him any money up until that point, shame on them. And if it has, shame on them even more. Neither situation justifies trying to get the horse claimed or cash a bet with a horse's one last hurrah. Each owner and every trainer has to be held accountable."

Everyone sat quietly for a moment. "This is never going to happen without the veterinarians getting involved," Randy said, "Totally. Any horse shipping in here to run as a claimer has to be examined. Any horse dropping down in price has to be examined. That would be a start."

Ben nodded. "The bottom line, if a horse gets claimed and it breaks down, regardless of any situation leading up to it, that claim should be cancelled. Are we in agreement of that?"

There was a unanimous show of hands.

"All right then."

Cracker Jack looked at his old friend and smiled proudly. "I know you, Ben. I know where you stood on slots. I know you didn't want them, no matter what. But I think by bringing them in you can make an even bigger difference in horse racing. If you can get a change in claiming rules to fly, you just might make a change none of you ever thought possible. Everything happens for a reason. I'm just hoping I'm alive to see it. I hope we all are, because it's not going to be easy."

Chapter Thirty-Four

Jason stepped out of the guard shack and smiled. "Another morning, another newspaper; no mention of us at all today."

"Good. That'll make Ben happy."

"It did."

Dawn thanked him and walked on, thinking about what he'd just said, and the way he'd said it. "Us. No mention of us at all today." She smiled, tucking the newspaper under her arm. Ben, Tom, Dusty, and Junior looked up when she entered the tack room. "We really are a team here, you know that? We're all connected."

All four men just looked at her.

"It's really a little too early in the morning for gushing," Tom said.

Dawn chuckled and poured a cup of coffee. "It's nice to see Cracker Jack. Do you think he's okay?"

"Ah, gee," Ben said.

"What? I was just wondering."

"Well, wonder about this," Tom said. "The old man has charted one to pony, one to walk, two to gallop, and Morning Dew gets breezed a half mile - this after he kept us up all night talking."

They all laughed. "If I recall," Ben said, "I was the one that went to bed first."

Junior yawned. "The old-timers stayed up all night too. Good thing I'm a sound sleeper."

"All right," Tom said. "Let's hit it."

Cracker Jack showed up a little after seven and walked with Dusty as he made rounds. Most everyone stopped to talk to him. After all, he'd been a local sports talk-show host for so many years, not to mention his striking appearance. "How tall?"

"Six-foot seven. I'm shrinking a little."

His hair made him look about eight feet tall.

They stopped to talk to Jackson, who said he was, "On top of the world. My race went. We'll win, you mark my words."

"Well, I might have to place a wager then," Cracker Jack said, patting the horse on the neck. Cracker Jack's son was in the same barn as Jackson. He stayed to "hang out" with his son and Dusty walked back to check on the new horse in the ReHab barn. There was a note taped to his feed door.

It read: I need your help. Dee Dee Swaggert

Dusty checked on the horse and walked down to the woman's barn. He found her sitting in her tack room with her head in her hands. He sat down next to her. She was obviously experiencing a great deal of anguish. "What's the matter?"

"They repo'd my truck."

"Again?"

She nodded, head still in her hands. Two tear drops the size of quarters dropped to her lap. Dusty hesitated. "I'd like to help you, Dee Dee, but you still haven't paid back from the last time."

"I know. I had it, but then...."

"You spent it," he said. "You bet it."

"Not all of it. I have some left."

Dusty sighed. "How much do you need?"

Dee Dee looked at him. "I don't expect you to loan me more."

"Then what do you want me to do?"

"I don't know. I'm such a loser."

"Well, in the betting department, yes," Dusty said.

Dee Dee wiped snot from her nose and smiled.

"How much?" Dusty repeated.

"About two hundred and twenty dollars. I have the rest. I don't want Rico to find out. It'll just be one more thing to throw up in my face when he gets mad."

"Did you talk to Pastor Mitchell like I said?"

She started to nod but then shook her head. "Not really."

"What's that mean, not really?"

"I wave to him. I say hi."

"Well, at least you're not lying to me," Dusty said. "Not this time at least."

"I'm so sorry about that," Dee Dee said. "It was Rico…."

Dusty stared down Dee Dee's shedrow. "I'll see what I can do," he said.

"Does that mean yes?"

He nodded. "I'll be back in a little while."

~ * ~

Señor helped George finish chores in the main barn. Liz helped Glenda harvest vegetables from the garden. They washed and peeled them in Liz's kitchen and started on the potpies. First time Liz made potpie for everyone at the farm there was some confusion. Aside from Randy and his dad, no one had ever eaten it made her way before.

"This is chicken potpie?" George asked. It certainly looked delicious, but nothing like potpie he knew.

"We don't like it in pie crust," Liz said. "We prefer the biscuits on top."

One taste and everyone loved it.

"Wow. It's hard to imagine eating it any other way now," Glenda had said.

The plan was to make four baking dishes of it for their dinner tonight with the old-timers. "Maybe we should make five," Liz suggested, "with Cracker Jack and Charlie and Gloria in town."

Glenda chuckled. "But Gloria doesn't eat that much."

"Quit," Liz said, chuckling as well.

The chicken was cooked in broth then the vegetables added and simmered until almost tender. While one of them cut up the chicken into bite-size pieces, the other made a rue and thickened the broth. Then they spooned what looked like a thick soup into the 9"x13" pans and covered them in aluminum foil and went out to check on the progress in the barn. The men had it Spic-n-Span clean. "Come on, guys, we don't want it too clean," Glenda said. "It's supposed to smell like a barn."

Señor and George laughed.

"How many chairs did we say we needed?" Liz asked.

"Twenty-seven, twenty-eight," Glenda said, "Thirty to be safe. You never know who'll drop in?"

"Is Gordon going to make it?"

"He said he'll try."

"Oh no," Liz said. "Here comes Mim!"

"Go talk to her," George said.

"Good luck trying to pull the wool over her eyes."

Glenda and Liz nodded and in the end, decided not to even try. They made Mim part of the plan instead. "Dinner in the aisle way of the barn? What a wonderful idea!" Mim said. "Close up each end of the barn when we come up to watch the horses gallop. They won't even notice."

Glenda and Liz gathered chairs from all the houses except T-Bone's Place, waved to the old-timers in passing, and parked on the other side of the barn so no one could see where the chairs were being unloaded. By then Señor and George had the tables made. They'd used plywood for table tops and sawhorses for the bottoms. They'd put them together with screws so they could take them apart and use them again if this worked out well.

They placed the chairs all around, leaving spaces for Jeanne's and Clint's wheelchairs on each end so they each would have plenty of room. Then it was off to get tablecloths, plates, silverware, glasses, cups and saucers and lots of salt and pepper shakers. When the tables were set, they covered everything in sheets to keep the dust and bugs away.

"This is going to be so grand," Liz declared.

~ 428 ~

Off they went to cut flowers and greens to make centerpieces.

~ * ~

Ben and Cracker Jack rode the elevator up to the third floor and from there took the stairs to the announcer's booth. Bud Gipson turned and flashed a big welcoming grin. "I heard you were here! Word gets around fast when a celebrity comes to town!" He shook Cracker Jack's hand and shook Ben's hand.

The horses for the first race were just entering the paddock. "So what do you think about the Browns this year?" Bud asked.

Cracker Jack shook his head. "I don't know. At some point, we have to stop rebuilding and play like we mean it."

Ben reached for Bud's binoculars and looked down at the crowd as the two men talked about the never-ending Browns' quarterback controversy.

"Who'd have ever thought," Ben said to himself.

"What?" Bud asked, turning.

"That we could come back to life."

Bud smiled. "I don't mind telling you, I had my doubts in the beginning. I thought, how in the hell are we going to do this? I'd look out there and there'd only be a handful of people watching the live races. Look at it now."

Ben and Cracker Jack nodded. "Well, we'll let you get back to work," Ben said. "We just wanted to come up and say hello." As they walked back down to the third floor they could hear the bugle sound the first race.

"I never tire of hearing that," Cracker Jack said.

"Me neither." The two of them strolled through the empty third floor.

"You say the old-timers lived up here all those months?"

"Yep. They ate in Richard's old office. Course, they went down to the clubhouse too. There were beds in these offices. Chairs lined up over there so they could watch the races and watch the horses train in the morning. They'll miss it here, but…."

Cracker Jack nodded. "They sure love it at T-Bone's Place at Meg's Meadows."

Ben smiled. "So do I. Although I have no idea what they're cooking up for tonight."

"Well, I know what it is," Cracker Jack said. "But I ain't sayin'."

They walked to the end of the third floor and looked out the window. The horses were approaching the gate. Ben motioned to the stairs. "This'll take us to the clubhouse."

~ * ~

Junior came up the hill on Bo-T, the colt dancing and prancing, and Junior singing a song. "Ladies and gentlemen, you're in for one hell of a show today."

"You gonna two-minute lick him?" Mim asked.

"That's what Ben said."

"Good, he's ready. Today's the day."

Junior walked Bo-T up into the turn, though the colt was more dancing and jigging than walking. He stopped, let the horse look around, then turned him straight away and let him jog for about a sixteenth of a mile. He broke into a canter under a stranglehold, and when he stopped fighting the bit, Junior let the reins out a notch.

Mim pressed her hand to her chest, could almost feel the thunder of his hooves inside. "Easy, Bo-T," she said. "Easy."

At the top of the turn, Junior got down lower and let the colt gallop strong. The old-timers watched in complete silence. Vicky watched in complete silence. Lucy watched in complete silence. Matthew's feverish sketching sounded amplified and misguided him. He used his eraser and started drawing slower, softer.

"That boy's good," Mim said, as Junior and Bo-T passed in front of them first time around.

"Did you hear that?" Lucy whispered, placing her hand on her tummy. "That's Daddy she's talking about."

The old-timers all smiled.

Bo-T galloped at an even pace, ears laid back and wanting to flat out run, but was held under wraps by Junior. Coming into the turn the horse tried picking up the pace, but Junior hung tough, standing in his stirrups and talking to him. "No, no, no, Big Man. No, no, no."

Mim nodded. "That's a good gallop."

"You think he win Saturday?" Miguel asked.

"If we stop talking about it, yes."

They all laughed.

By the time Junior pulled Bo-T up on the backstretch and walked him back, nice and slow, the horse's breathing was practically back to normal. He did a little dance coming off the track and tossed his head.

"Arrogance," Mim said.

"You talkin' to me?" Junior said, laughing.

"Yes, you too."

While the old-timers waited for Junior to come back with B-Bo, they played a racetrack version of trivia. Vicky kept score. Steven won.

"You always win," Clint said.

Here came B-Bo and Junior up the hill.

"You're just galloping, right?" Mim asked, watching the way the horse picked up and put down that leg with the old injury.

"Yep."

"How many times around? Three?"

"Yep." Junior smiled. "I think I'll take a nap while I'm at it."

~ 431 ~

The old-timers laughed. B-Bo was one of the most laid-back Thoroughbreds most of them had ever seen, which made the fact that he was such a great racehorse that much more amazing. Matthew had switched pages in his sketch book and was determined today to capture the look and feel in B-Bo's eyes.

"I would suggest that I could take a picture of him," Vicky said. "But I'm sure it wouldn't be the same."

Mim agreed with the second part. "It would be a moment in time, not a life, not living."

Lucy smiled. "How did you get to be so wise, Mim? Can I hold onto you and have some of it rub off on me?" She put her arms around Mim's neck. "I love you."

Mim smiled and patted Lucy on the shoulder, her eyes misting over.

B-Bo galloped around the track the first time nice and quiet, a second time nice and quiet, and a third and final time nice and quiet. He had his head slightly bowed and looked as if he was out for an afternoon hack in a field. No muss, no fuss, just galloping along and appearing happy to just be alive, to be a horse. He pulled up easily down the backstretch and moseyed back as if he hadn't a care in the world.

"That is the life," Clint said.

"Can you draw a butterfly landing on his forehead?" Mim asked.

Matthew smiled. He knew what she meant. He was trying to capture that same essence, minus the butterfly. When they all heard the rooster crow, they laughed, gathered themselves up and followed B-Bo and Junior down the hill.

Mim glanced ahead to make sure the back door on this side of the barn was closed. It was. As soon the entourage passed the barn, George opened it up and Señor closed the other side. No one was the wiser. No one even looked, but for Mim, and with big grin on her face.

~ * ~

The pie part of the potpie was done last. Liz peeled back the paper cover on the canned biscuits and popped them open on the edge of the counter. She'd put the potpies in the oven to warm, not too hot; just starting to bubble. Then she took them out, placed the biscuits all round the top, close to one another but not crammed together, and put the potpies back into the oven until the biscuits were golden brown on top. She tilted one of the biscuits up to see the soft bottom. "Perfect."

Carol had made three Jello salads; one sugar-free for the old-timers with diabetes. Dawn made a large tossed salad, the dressing a mixture of Italian and Ranch. By the time the old-timers came down and everyone assembled outside the barn, the food was all set out on the tables and looked like a holiday feast. George opened the barn doors and everyone filed in, amazed. There was even soft music playing.

Just after everyone was seated, Gordon arrived. "Dude!" he said. "Wow! This is awesome!" Pastor Mitchell arrived right behind him. Everyone held hands, a circle of friends and family as he said the grace.

"Lord, I never cease to be amazed by your abundance of love, by your stewards of humanity, of bountiful harvests, of the smell of potpie. Amen."

"Amen," everyone echoed. Food was dished out, plates passed, salad, Jello, coffee poured for one another, water, milk, salt and pepper was passed, Tabasco.

Dawn took several photos and when they all insisted she had to be in the photos too, she placed the camera on one of the stall fronts, set the timer and then hurried to her seat. "Say cheese," she said, "On three. One, two, three."

"Cheese!"

"All right! Let's eat!"

"Wait a minute! What's going on here?" someone said, standing just inside the barn door.

"Irene! Boots!" Ben smiled. "Come! Sit! Join us!"

"Well, we wouldn't want to intrude," Irene said, headed right for an empty chair. "Do you do this often out here?" Her husband Boots sat down next to Mark.

"Evening."

The table was full, everyone talking, laughing and eating. Ben looked around. "If the world was going to end tomorrow and you couldn't do a damned thing about it, how would you live your life today?" He looked around at everyone. "I can't think of a better way. Friends, family, horses, dogs…." The dogs were stretched out on the floor all around them. "I'd take a day just like today."

D.R. looked up at George, sitting next to him. "Is the world going to end tomorrow, Uncle George?"

"No," George said. "I have stalls to do."

Everyone laughed.

"You know what I wonder about?" Glenda said. "Why do people worry about things they can't change? I mean ever. Ever, ever, ever."

"How do you really feel, Glenda?" Señor asked.

They all laughed again. Pastor Mitchell motioned to Jeanne. "Next?"

Jeanne hesitated. "I wonder why people are so offended by tattoos. I hate it when they say oh but when they're old and in a nursing home that tattoo won't look the same. What's their point? Nothing will look the same."

Again, everyone laughed.

Dawn was next and had to think. "Well, this is just anything we want to say, right?"

Pastor Mitchell nodded.

"Okay. I told Biscuit today that we all loved him and I'm going to try and tell him every day."

"Oh, so that's why he was doing the moon walk out in the pasture earlier?" Junior said.

They all laughed.

"Does that count for my turn?" Junior asked.

"No."

Junior finished chewing, swallowed, and took a drink of water. "All right."

"Oh Lord," Tom said.

Junior laughed. "No, this is going to be serious. Come on, I'm a married man now. I'm going to be a daddy." He paused. "I think living is what life is all about." He looked around at everyone seated at the table. "Does that make sense?"

Everyone nodded.

Lucy was next. "Well, I think life is all about family. Friends and family."

They all smiled. It was Maeve's turn. "I want a bunny rabbit."

Everyone chuckled.

"You mean for dinner?" Tom asked.

"No. Uncle Tom, you're so silly. For my bedroom."

Carol shook her head. "I'm thankful there are no bunnies in your bedroom because I would find it in your bed for sure."

Maeve giggled.

D.R. was next in line. "I want a bunk bed so Jimmy can spend the night."

Randy looked at Dawn. Jimmy was D.R.'s imaginary friend. "Is he back?"

Dawn nodded with a raised eyebrow for emphasis. "But he can't stay. There's *no place* for him to sleep."

Everyone turned to Randy. "I see. Well, we'll look into that. Meanwhile, I wonder if we could just move along. I'm happy."

That elicited smiles all around. "I would like to do this more often," Wendy said. "This is just too nice."

Tom agreed. "What a nice surprise and us all here together."

Clint nodded. "When you opened the barn doors, I couldn't even do anything. I just...."

Vicky touched him gently on the shoulder. "I felt the same way."

Clint smiled and swiped a tear trickling down his cheek.

"I knew," Mim said. "And it still made me feel the same way. This is us. This is what we do, what we did. This is marvelous."

George helped himself to more potpie. "I don't know what was more fun. Setting this up today or delivering the cake to the wedding."

Señor laughed and gave a brief summation of the cake delivery, complete with how he rode to the banquet hall in the back of the pickup bracing the box and saying prayers for safe passage the entire way.

"Ask and ye shall receive," Pastor Mitchell said.

"The cake was delicious," Lucy said, and everyone agreed.

"Just like wedding cake in Mexico," Miguel said.

"I'm so sorry we missed the wedding," Gloria said. "I love wedding cake, though I only eat a small piece."

"I usually eat two," Charlie said. "I always say one for me and one for my wife. Then I tell Gloria to go get her own."

Everyone laughed. "It's true," Gloria said.

Boots helped himself to more potpie. "This is delicious. Irene, get the recipe."

"I'll write it up for you," Liz said. "It's so easy to make."

"The biscuits on top is so unique. I like it so much more than just crust," Irene said, as she put another spoonful on her plate.

"I ate so much of it the last time, my stomach swelled up like a balloon," Matthew said.

"Don't eat so much this time," Tom said.

"Are you kidding me?" Matthew passed Tom his plate for more.

"I'm eating for a week," Gordon said. "My thanks to you all."

Wendy looked at him. "Are you kidding?"

"About eating for a week? No. Yes."

Wendy shook her head. "I am thankful for sons who never cause their mother a worry in the world."

They all laughed.

Dusty spooned out another serving of Jello salad, more potpie, and more salad greens. Everyone looked at him. It was his turn. He paused, fork in hand. "I am grateful for my home, my family and friends. I am thankful for my job. I'm thankful for little Bonnie Bee. I'm thankful for *good* food to eat!"

"Amen," Pastor Mitchell said.

"I'm thankful for T-Bone's Place," Steven said, "For a roof over my head, caring people, horses, and for all of you. You *are* my family."

Bill hesitated. "Mine too. You are all I have. If I could I would give you all the world, but I really think all the world is right here, in this place, this farm…this barn."

Jack looked at him. "Since when did you become a poet?"

Bill laughed. "I am multi-faceted."

"Oh, you're faceted all right."

Bill chucked him with his elbow. "Shut up. It's your turn."

Jack nodded. "Well, no poetry from me. But I too am grateful. Being here with you all, on this farm, with everyone caring so much, and loving life. Living life to the fullest. These *are* happy days."

Cracker Jack drew a breath and sighed. "What can I say? Can I put my reservation in now? I can't think of any other place I'd rather be down the road."

Frank was next. "In my wildest imaginations, I never thought I could feel so loved." His voice cracked. "So cared about. We are *truly* family."

Mim drew a breath and sighed. "I would like to live here forever. Do you think you all can arrange that?"

Ben smiled. "We'll see what we can do." He looked around at everyone, cherishing the moment. "I am so thankful for each and every one of you all here. You have made my life worth living."

Everyone at the dinner table fell quiet.

"When Meg died, there didn't seem much point in living anymore," Ben said. "I went through the motions. Tom held me up many a day."

Tom looked at him, swallowing hard.

"Then this one morning," Ben's voice quivered, "this young reporter showed up at barn fourteen and said, 'Tell me everything you know about horse racing.'"

Dawn bit at her trembling bottom lip.

"Well, I had a lifetime to share and I thank you," he said, looking at Dawn. "I thank all of you."

"Amen," Pastor Mitchell said. "Amen."

Chapter Thirty-Five

Jason greeted Dawn with a big smile and handed her the paper. "Nothing. Nothing, nothing, nothing." Dawn thanked him as if he'd personally arranged the good news and walked to the barn, reading the comics. Ben, Tom, Dusty, and Junior looked up when she walked into the tack room. They were all on their second cup of coffee.

"All right, so I'm late," she said.

Ben shrugged. "We didn't notice. Did we notice?"

"Yes," Tom said. "We did."

Dawn shook her head, smiling. "It's nice to be noticed." She poured herself a cup of coffee and looked at the training chart. Batgirl, breeze 3/8ths. Whinny, race. Wee Born, work a half mile, Alley, gallop, Morning Dew, walk. "What race are we in?"

"Third," Ben said, handing her the Overnight.

"Bold Gamer is going to be scratched," Dusty said.

Dawn looked at the names of the other seven horses. "Wait a minute. Do I smell donuts?"

Tom had the box hidden behind him and brought it out slowly.

"There had better be a custard one in there for me." There was. Dawn wolfed it down, and the morning training began. Batgirl was first. She breezed 3/8^{ths} in 40 flat. Wee Born worked the half in 47.2/5ths. Junior galloped Alley. She tried to run off on him as soon as Tom cut them loose, but Junior held her tight. Pleased with how Batgirl and Wee Born trained this morning, Ben walked over to the Secretary's office to enter them both for Friday. Joe nodded, greeting him. There were five trainers already in line.

Ben decided to go check in with Wendy and come back in a few minutes. Richard was at his desk on the phone. Ben walked to the window and watched the horses training. He chuckled. Cracker Jack was standing by the rail. He could spot him a mile away being so tall and with that wild hair.

Richard hung up the phone. "Morning, Ben."

"Good Morning. Where are you off to today?"

"Believe it or not, my presence has been requested at the ITHA. Apparently, they want to hear firsthand how our zero tolerance on drugs and soft whips are working out. They also want to discuss our "aggressive" goal to reorganize claiming. The rep said they have a mega-corporation here in the states that might possibly want to be a pilot program using the same policies."

"Where?"

"They weren't at liberty to say. My bet they're in New York or Kentucky."

"Good luck," Ben said.

Richard nodded and studied the look in Ben's eyes as he watched the horses galloping. "The Thoroughbred industry is lucky to have someone like you, Ben, to set an example from experience."

"Thank you," Ben said. "I appreciate that. Meg would appreciate it too. A lot of the man I am is because of her. She could give a person hell."

Richard smiled. "What do you want me to tell the ITHA for you?"

Ben paused. "Tell them it's time to change and that it's long overdue. It's time."

~ * ~

Ben entered his two horses and heard the news from Joe: "Crimson Count is shipping in for the Burgundy Blue. They just called to apply for a stall in the receiving barn."

Ben signed his name on the entry forms and looked up at him.

"He'll pull in a crowd, that's for sure," Joe said.

Ben nodded. "How are these two races looking?"

"Good. They'll both fill."

Ben thanked him and walked away. Crimson Count? He took out his cellphone and dialed Randy. "Give me Mark's phone number. I need him to Google something for me."

Randy gave him the number. Ben programmed it in and dialed. "Mark?"

"Yes,"

"I need you to get me the form on Crimson Count."

"Give me a minute. I'll call you back."

Ben had certainly heard of the horse. Who hadn't? He'd run in the Kentucky Derby five or six years back and had performed consistently in stakes and allowance races ever since. Ben walked on to the barn, thinking out loud, "If I hadn't said we'd run the colt I wouldn't be dealing with this right now. I knew better than to second-guess myself. He loses to Crimson Count, that's a mark against him in breeding."

When Mark called him right back, Ben sat down on the bumper of a truck parked in the horsemen's lot and listened to the information. "Speed rating 101. Last time out he win going a mile by three lengths in 1:36 and 2/5ths. He's run seven times this year, three wins, two seconds, a fourth and a fifth, all allowance or stakes."

Ben thanked him and continued on to the barn. Dawn had just finished doing up Alley's legs and was brushing her off and fussing over her. Tom was raking the gravel under the walking machine. "What's the matter?" Tom asked, from the look on Ben's face.

"Crimson Count is shipping in for the Burgundy Blue."

"The derby horse?"

Ben nodded.

"And so now you're having a cow?"

Ben sighed and sat down on the bench outside the barn. "Last I heard, he was going to Breezeway Farm too. The press is going to have a field day with this."

Dawn listened from the stall. "Maybe they'll make him the favorite."

"Well," Ben stared at the ground, "That would be nice, though I don't know that I'd wish that on anyone, even someone competing against us. I mean, don't get me wrong, I want Bo-T to win, but…."

Ben's cellphone rang. It was Mark. "He's going to Breezeway Farm for stud after this race."

"That's what I thought," Ben said. "Somebody's setting this up as a match race."

"You think?"

"Well, I hope not, but…." Ben thanked him for the information and hung up and rubbed his eyes. "Oh, Jesus, I'm not supposed to do that." He blinked several times and looked at Tom.

When Tom swayed back and forth on purpose, Ben laughed. Junior came down through the barn area, helmet tucked under his arm, and looking dumbfounded. "What?" Tom said.

"Tony Guciano just said hi to me."

Ben smiled. "Are you heading out to the farm?"

Junior nodded. "B-Bo gallops, Bo-T walks. Right?"

Ben hesitated. Why? He had no idea. But here he was, second-guessing himself again. "He two-minute licked yesterday. Yes, he walks today. B-Bo gallops, a mile and half."

Ben stared down the road between the barns after Junior left. Tom went back to raking. "So what are you thinking, old man?"

Ben looked at him. "I'm thinking I want to win that race."

Tom smiled. "Now that's the Ben Miller I know."

It was a fun-filled afternoon for the old-timers. They got to watch B-Bo gallop. He galloped nice and even, nice and strong. Though worried initially about getting back to the house in time to watch the televised Daily Double at Nottingham Downs, but it turned out Lucy knew how to record the telecast. They could watch those two races in the evening. They all got situated back home and watched the running of the third race. Whinny was in the fourth.

"She got a good shot," Miguel said, studying the form.

"She's got to beat that Majestic horse."

Miguel nodded.

Lucy went upstairs for a nap. She thought about what it meant or might mean, her father greeting Junior. Was he just being polite? "No, dad's not the type to just be polite." She wondered if somehow, someway the wedding changed his feelings about Junior. She entertained that possibility and woke to screaming and yelling downstairs.

"Go Whinny! Go Whinny!"

"Go!!!!"

"Come on, Whinny!!"

"Come on, girl!"

Lucy walked down the stairs, sat on the bottom step, and watched the end of the race.

"Did she win?"

"Did she get up?"

"Did she win?"

"Oh look, there's Dawn."

"Ben too."

"It's almost like being there," Mim said.

Whinny ran second, beaten by a nose. Dawn held her as Juan dismounted, handed her over to Tom and Red, and walked behind them to the spit barn. Ben and Dusty walked with Juan a short ways.

"She run so good," Juan said. "She should win."

"That's about as close to a win as you can get," Ben said, patting the man on the back. "Thank you for a great ride."

Whinny cooled out well, drank her share of water, obliged when it came time for a urine sample and walked alongside Dawn to their barn, tired, but bright-eyed and proud, head held high and looking all around.

Tom smiled. "She's saying, did you see that? Did you see me run? Good Momma," he said, patting her. "Good girl." He had her stall done, haynet hung, water bucket filled. He felt her chest and patted her on the neck. "She's good."

Dawn shook her head. "Wow, I didn't know that. Thank you."

Tom laughed. "I'm going to go watch a couple of races up in the office."

"Where's Ben?"

"He went home."

"Again? Boy, he's serious about this semi-retirement thing."

"He said he was going home to take a walk. I told him he could walk here and he said it's not the same. He said when he walks here, he's walking some place. Home, he's simply walking."

"I like that," Dawn said.

Tom watched her lead Whinny down the shedrow past her stall. "What are you doing?" he asked, razzing her again.

She smiled. It was a habit of hers to walk a horse around their own shedrow after a race. They seemed to enjoy it and so did she. All the horses would come to the front of their stalls, nicker, their horse would nicker back. She imagined what they might be saying. How'd you do? Did you win? Looking good! And some even breaking into song. "Isn't she lovely, isn't she wonderful…."

Manny, the groom on the backside smiled. "You have lovely voice, Dawn. She run big, huh?"

Dawn nodded. "She run good. Just got beat by a nose."

"Teach her next time to stick tongue out."

Dawn laughed. "I wonder if that's ever been done?"

She put the mare in her stall and watched her for a moment. After turning a few circles, Whinny laid down and rolled, stood up and shook off, and then laid down and rolled on the other side. Randy pulled up next to the barn, got out, and walked down the shedrow. The mare was back up and eating hay.

"Did you miss the race?"

He nodded. "Sorry. Jason said she ran second."

"Just got beat," Dawn said. "You okay?"

"Yeah, I just had to put a horse down. He broke a leg in the pasture." He wrapped her in his arms and held her tight. "I stayed with him until the renderer came. The owner was hysterical, no one else there with her…."

"Thank you," Dawn said.

"For what?"

"For being you. For caring."

Randy sighed, kissed her on the forehead and looked at her. "And then, I stopped at Shifting Gears."

"Is everything all right?"

"Oh yeah. Hillary's talking to all the horses. They're all happy or in the process of getting happy, Veronica said. She showed up before I left. She's such a strange girl. Karen said she does some kind of ritual when she leaves every day, like imaginary wiping herself down, clearing the energy or something."

"It makes sense to me. She did that here too. She says otherwise it all comes at her at one time and doesn't leave."

"I don't know if that's a burden or a blessing," Randy said.

~ 445 ~

"Both probably."

"So where's dinner?"

"At your mom and dad's I think."

Randy nodded, and ducked under Whinny's webbing, ran his hands down her legs, felt her chest and looked at her eyes. "Remember the day she was born?" he asked, smiling and smoothing the mare's mane. "Such a cute little thing."

"Ben wants to retire her at the end of the year."

"She'll make a nice broodmare."

"He's really into this retirement thing lately."

"I don't think it's that," Randy said. "I think that's our hang-up. He's never hesitated stopping on a horse before."

"I guess you're right. I just hope that's all it is."

"What else could it be?"

"I don't know, like maybe he's trying to tie up loose ends."

"You mean before he dies? Dawn, we're all going to die sooner or later."

"That's uplifting."

Randy ducked out of the mare's stall, gave Dawn a kiss and walked to his truck. "I'll see you at dinner. Do you know what we're having?"

"Spaghetti and meatballs."

"Mom's sauce?"

Dawn nodded. The official winner of the sixth race was announced and with the wind blowing just the right way, she could hear perfectly clear. Sunrise Sam, Jackson's horse, was the winner. She walked out to the road and watched as Jackson led the horse into the spit barn. He gave her a thumbs up. The horse was dancing and prancing.

Ben walked down the street and at the crossroad, decided to keep right on walking. There was a big farm just up the way. He could see the cupolas on the barn. Meg loved cupolas. They had one on each barn. The closer he got, he could see that these were copper, and the farm, very grandiose. Judging from the horse and rider insignia on the sign, it was a dressage barn. He stopped to look at the outdoor riding ring with a gazebo at one end.

"Private" the sign read. "Horse boarded by appointment." He chuckled to himself, imagining a phone conversation. "I'd like to board my horse at four o'clock today, please."

He walked on, came to another crossroad, and decided to head on back. He didn't walk fast. He didn't walk slow. He just moseyed along, taking in the sights, watching the birds fly from tree to tree. He thought about winter, wondered about how he'd walk in the ice and the snow, but decided it was best not to think too far ahead. He'd cross that bridge when he came to it. He glanced ahead when he got close to Meg's Meadows and saw Dawn pull in the drive first, then Tom, then Dusty. He waved, kept walking, and stopped for a visit with the old-timers.

"I thought she win," Miguel said, of Whinny's race. They all nodded.

"Me too," Ben said. "She just got nosed out."

"She come back okay?" Mim asked.

"She came back good," Ben said. "How'd Bo-T go?"

"Strong," Mim said. "Two minute licking him a half-mile today after yesterday was good. I feared Junior might lose him at one point but he didn't."

"Shhh…." Lucy said. "Don't let the baby hear you say that."

Mim laughed and leaned down to talk to Lucy's tummy. "Your daddy did good. If he can't hold them, no one can."

Everyone laughed.

"Where is Junior?"

"He's stopping for ice cream. We're out," Lucy said.

Everyone pointed a finger at her.

"She hasn't added pickles yet, but…" Jeanne said.

They all grinned and smiled. Having Lucy there and pregnant was having the same effect on them that bringing home a puppy would to an aging dog.

"Junior say Crimson Count come in for the Burgundy Blue," Miguel said.

Ben nodded and looked at Mim.

"Stay the course," she said. "It'll be a horse race, but my bet's on Bo-T."

Ben was the last to arrive for dinner at Señor and Liz's. They were all getting concerned. Dawn watched for him out the window. "Here he comes. He was in the main barn." She sat down quickly.

Ben walked in, all smiles, went to the head of the table and sat down. Cracker Jack was having dinner with his family this evening and Gloria and Charlie had left for home, but everyone else was there except for Gordon. Liz was bursting with excitement. "We have a date. We leave three weeks from today for Appalachia. We're all set and will be there for two weeks."

Wendy cast a concerned glance at Matthew. The pleased look on his face confirmed that he'd already heard the news. "I feel like packing already."

She didn't want to put a damper on his enthusiasm and forced herself to smile. "This is so exciting for all of you."

Señor nodded. "It's all we can talk about."

Mark's girlfriend Susie was brought up to date on the trip and had lots of questions about the particulars. Ben enjoyed his meal, just listening, had second helpings, and then sat back and yawned. "Ah, tell me we're having Boston cream pie.

"We are."

Everyone passed plates down and the table was cleared of dishes and serving bowls. Coffee tureens were refilled, poured into cups, and dessert dished out. "I hear B-Bo galloped strong," Ben said, savoring each bite of dessert. "I think I'll sleep in tomorrow morning and see you all in the afternoon."

"What?" Tom and Dawn said together.

Ben smiled. "Gotcha! Just kidding."

Chapter Thirty Six

The Sports page lead story in the *Morning Banter* was all about Crimson Count shipping in for the race on Saturday. Dawn read the article as she walked along. "Representative of the fact that only male horses are allowed to run in the Burgundy Blue Stake, it is traditionally a field comprised of horses targeted for stud careers. It was rumored that Beau Together, known better as Bo-T to the home crowd, was sent home after his impressive come-from-behind win last week for rest. His short-lived retirement will have him challenging Crimson Count not only for the win in the Burgundy Blue but for sire options at Breezeway Farm this upcoming breeding season. Though the race is expected to draw an eight or nine-horse field, it would appear this will be a match race between stallion prospects Crimson Count and Bo-T. May the best man win."

No one was sitting in the tack room. They were all on their feet. Ben, Tom, Dusty, Junior. No one said the word jinx. No one would dare to say the word jinx, as that in itself at this stage would be just cause for a jinx. Dawn looked for a silver lining. "Are there any donuts?"

Tom shook his head and reached for Red's bridle. "Alley gallops. Morning Dew gallops. The rest walk. Let's hit it."

Dawn glanced at the Overnight. Batgirl was in the third tomorrow, Wee Born, the fifth. This was a good thing, keeping busy, less time to think. If one of them should win tomorrow, they'd go to The Rib to celebrate. That would take their minds off Saturday maybe. "Who am I kidding?" she said to herself. "We'll all be sweating bullets and I'll be living in the bathroom."

She wished her cousin Linda, Uncle Matt's daughter, was in town. She'd meet her at the club. She and her husband Harland and their children had gone to Italy for two months. She wouldn't be back for several more weeks. Dawn missed her.

"Loose horse!"

Dawn instinctively tucked back against the wall, just in time as the horse came barreling down the shedrow behind her.

"Shit!" Tom said, dropping Red's saddle and bridle. "Whoa, whoa….whoa…." He spread his arms, talking softly. "Whoa…."

The horse trotted right up to him and just stood there, wide-eyed. Tom took hold of the horse's lead shank, and again, the horse just stood there. A second ago, it was tearing down the shedrow, and now. "It's a sign," Tom said. "Thank you, Big Guy! Who do you belong to?"

Dawn laughed.

"Hey, it works for Hillary. Why can't it work for me? Who do you belong to?" he asked the horse. "Who's your daddy?"

"He ain't got no daddy," Chrissy Palmer said, walking toward them.

Tom laughed. "Oh no! It's yo' Momma! Hey, Chrissy."

"Thanks, Tom. You silly boy," she said to the horse, shaking her head. "Just think if you'd have hurt yourself." She took hold of his lead shank and led him back down the shedrow and around the backside to her barn.

Alley Beau galloped first. She galloped strong and came back playing. There was a race for her on Saturday. Morning Dew galloped next. There was a race for her next Wednesday. Dawn and Tom split cleaning the stalls. Dawn filled all the haynets. Tom did all the water buckets. With the other horses in the barn walking today, all the horses were back in their stalls and done up by nine o'clock.

Ben had walked over to the Secretary's office to enter Bo-T and Alley Beau and was accosted by a sports reporter and cameraman from Channel 8 news. "And here we have Mr. Ben Miller, owner of Nottingham Downs and owner of Beau Together."

Ben made an attempt to not look like a deer caught in headlights. The fact that he was the owner of the racetrack and also a horse owner had been met with negative press when the racetrack purchase was first made. "Morning."

"Much has been said about Beau Together this past week. He was rumored to have been shipped to Mountaineer, rumored to have been sent home to rest, rumored to be coming back."

"Seems like that's a lot of rumors," Ben said.

Wendy came out of the office, took one glance, and tried to come up with a distraction. Ben shook his head.

"You do know that Crimson Count is shipping in for the Burgundy Blue?" the reporter asked.

"So I've heard," Ben said.

"Have these two horses raced against each other before?"

Ben hesitated. That seemed like a pretty silly question coming from a sports reporter who should know the answer already. Wendy widened her eyes. Don't correct him, don't correct him, she seemed to be saying with her expression. "No, they haven't," Ben said. "But I just entered Bo-T and it'll be a horse race."

"Does that mean you think your horse has a chance to win?"

Ben flashed Wendy a look that surely conveyed where is Richard? She waved her arms discreetly and then pressed her fingers to her cheeks to make a big smile.

"Yes, I think he can win it," Ben said. "Now if you'll excuse me…."

"Just one more question, Mr. Miller. How do you feel about slots coming to Nottingham Downs?"

Wendy pressed her hands solid to her face, mouth open. She reminded Ben of that little kid in the movie "Home Alone." He smiled. "Well, I understand there are a lot of people excited about slots coming to Nottingham Downs. And I think that's a good thing." Thus said, he touched the rim of his hat and walked away.

"Well, there you have it," the reporter said looking into the camera. "Straight from the horse's mouth."

Ben walked back to the barn in dismay. "I just sold my soul," he told Tom and Dawn.

Tom smiled. "Not according to what I heard." He held up his cellphone. "Wendy said you were a master of discretion."

"I don't know why they couldn't talk to Richard."

"Because apparently he was in the men's room."

~ 452 ~

Ben just looked at him.

"I know," Tom said. "He picked a fine time to take a shit."

Ben laughed. Even Dawn laughed.

"I'm going home," Ben said. "Am I needed here?"

"Nope."

"Good, I'll see you both at the farm." He stopped by the ReHab barn on his way out. Dusty was doing up the Gulliver horse's injured leg. "I remember the day this horse broke his maiden."

"So do I," Dusty said. "He win by five lengths."

Ben nodded, leaning on the stall webbing and watching the horse eat hay. "Is he going to make a riding horse?"

"No. Pasture buddy Randy thinks. But he says there's always a possibility. He's going to Shifting Gears tomorrow."

"That's good," Ben said. "They doing okay?"

"Yeah, they're doing good. They're getting more donations. Those articles Dawn wrote helped. And now that they have Hillary."

Ben smiled. "Maybe I should have the girl come talk to Bo-T."

"Matthew said she talked to him the other day and everything was x-rated."

"Well, that's Bo-T," Ben said, and paused. "I'd really like to see him bred to some good mares. This is a first for me, you know, sending one away."

"Well, it'll just be for breeding season. Right?"

Ben nodded. "I'll miss him. They'll take good care of him though. I don't know what I'm worried about. I'm fine. He'll be fine. Meanwhile, we have a race to win, and nobody had better talk me into running him again, because this is it."

Dusty smiled when Ben walked away. Coming from a man who repeatedly cautioned others not to fall in love with their horses, he never knew a man who loved his horses more than Ben. That's probably why he and Ben got along so well.

~ * ~

Ben sat on the bleachers next to Vicky, Lucy, and some of the old-timers and watched Junior ride Bo-T up the path to the training track. Miguel, Steven, and Jack sat with Mim on the golf cart. They looked like a foursome on a golf course.

"Two miles," Ben said.

Junior looked at him, Bo-T bouncing and prancing. "Two?"

"Yep." Ben smiled, swirling his hand. "Four times around."

Junior laughed. "I can count."

Matthew, George and Glenda followed them up the hill at a safe distance. Señor and Liz climbed up the grass path from their backyard. Junior walked the horse onto the track, talking to him, singing to him, and jogged him up into the turn. He let him stand a minute and then straightened him around, a little trotting, a canter, and then into a gallop.

"Hold him," Ben said. "I want him finishing just as strong as he starts out. Make him think."

"Make him laugh," Miguel said.

Everyone looked at him. "John Balushi," he said. "I so love that movie."

They all chuckled.

Ben looked at Mim. "I got cornered by the press this morning."

"So I heard," she said.

"Who?"

"Wendy told Tom, Tom told Junior, Junior told Lucy, Lucy told us."

Ben looked at Lucy. She shrugged. "George and Glenda already knew."

George and Glenda both nodded. "We saw it on the noon news."

"We saw it too," Señor said.

They all watched Bo-T gallop into the far turn and start down the backstretch, galloping strong, nice and even. But then he ducked and they all collectively held their breath. "What happened?" Ben said. "Can you see what happened?"

Lucy probably had the best eyesight of all of them. "He looks fine now. I don't know what happened."

They watched Bo-T gallop into the near turn and down the stretch. Ben held up his hands. "What happened?"

"He heard the rooster!"

"What?"

"He heard the rooster crow!"

"Damn rooster," Ben said. "Is he all right?"

Junior looked back over his shoulder at them. "He's fine. He's fine," he sang. "He's so fine."

Ben shook his head.

"You know, I've been thinking," Mim said.

Ben glanced at her.

"I think a star or an asterisk next to the horse's name in the racing form could indicate a horse being an only horse. On the program too."

Ben looked at her and smiled. She was obviously trying to get him to think of something else besides the fact that the horse he'd entered in the Burgundy Blue just bobbled.

They all laughed when they heard Junior singing really loud as he galloped Bo-T down the backstretch so he could drown out the rooster should it crow again. Galloping down the stretch the second time, Bo-T looked strong and focused. The third time he looked just as good. Fourth time, he looked like he was getting a little bored.

"Click to him" Ben said.

Bo-T responded by bowing his head tighter and started snorting with each stride.

"Ah, I love that sound," Mim said.

They all did. Junior pulled Bo-T up going into the backstretch and walked him back on loose rein. "He's never felt better," Junior said, when they came around. Bo-T picked up his head, paying attention to something in one of the pastures.

Beau Born had come up to the water trough with Hurry Sandy and had raised his head high at the sight of Bo-T coming off the training track. He bellowed his stallion whinny and Bo-T whinnied back. Beau Born stomped. Bo-T stomped. Adding to this, All Together, two pastures over, whinnied.

Everyone looked from one to the other and then back at Bo-T, wide-eyed and with his head held high. Beau Born whinnied again. All Together whinnied again. Bo-T whinnied again.

"They're never done that before," Ben said.

"Wow!" Junior said.

Hurry Sandy turned and walked back down the hill in the pasture. Beau Born followed. All Together went back to grazing.

"I wish I knew what that meant," Ben said.

Mim looked at him. "Do you think they forget? They don't forget."

When Bo-T started dancing, George took hold of his rein and led him and Junior down the hill with Glenda right behind them. Junior returned a few minutes later on B-Bo. "Second verse, same as the first?" he asked Ben.

Ben nodded. Watching B-Bo gallop was a relaxing experience. The old-timers talked amongst themselves.

The rooster crowed. B-Bo galloped right on by. He galloped at the same pace all four laps and pulled up like a gentleman. He walked back with his neck and back all stretched out. He looked like he was scoping out the grass on the other side of the fence. When Junior stopped him and turned him toward the inside rail, the horse kicked lazily at a fly buzzing his belly and heaved a sigh.

The entourage followed him down the hill, went their separate ways, and Ben took to the road. It wasn't long before he was singing, "Ain't no mountain high enough, ain't no valley low enough." And then, "I'm Henry the Eighth I am, Hen-e-ry the Eighth I am, I am...." He sang both parts, high and low, and changed the words slightly. "Hen-e-ry! Hen-e-rey! Hen-e-ry! Hen-e-ry! Hen-e-ry the Eighth I am! Ain't no marrying the widow next door; she's been married seven times before...."

~ * ~

Dinner was meatloaf and mashed potatoes and peas at Dawn and Randy's. Carol made the meatloaf and two extra for the old-timers. Randy and Mark arrived a little late. Both washed up and sat down to eat. Richard arrived halfway through the meal. "No thank you. I had a late lunch," he said. "And then I had to eat again."

He'd been to two benefit events.

"How'd it go with the IHRA? " Ben asked.

"Well, that's why I'm here." He sat down, looked at the meatloaf and mashed potatoes and helped himself to a small serving of each. "Ah," he said, tasting both. "Delicious." He poured a glass of water. "They want to do a documentary on Nottingham Downs. Well, not them per se, but a Hollywood production company associated with the racing industry."

"Don't look at me," Ben said. "I did my part this morning. Last time I was featured on the news, I got kicked in the ribs."

"Maybe they can get an actor to play you," Tom said. "Course I don't know where they'll find one to fit those fancy walking shoes of yours."

Everyone laughed.

"See, that's the point. Ben. You're the draw. You're the old school embracing the new," Richard said.

Ben waved his fork. "I'm not exactly embracing it."

"I'm not even talking about slots, though that will be a part of it I'm sure."

"Didn't they try a documentary already?" Glenda asked.

Dusty nodded. "They did one on the jockeys too."

"So why do they want to do another one."

'I don't know," Richard said, "Maybe because those didn't work."

Ben looked at him. "When do they need to know?"

"Know what?" Richard asked, helping himself to more meatloaf and mashed potatoes.

Ben sat back.

Richard looked at him. "Come on, Ben. There's no way you can say no."

Ben shook his head. "I need to get through this weekend."

"Understandably," Richard said. "It'll take them at least a week to get started on it anyway."

Ben sighed.

Taking that as a yes, Richard finished eating and took his plate to the sink. "This was delicious! Thank you. I've got one more stop at the Hunt Club. I'll see you all tomorrow."

Maeve swirled her mashed potatoes. "We tell Biscuit we love him today."

"You did?" Randy asked.

"Yes!" D.R. said. "Mommy took us to the fence."

"Did Biscuit say I love you too?"

"Daddy!" Maeve said. "Horses don't talk."

"They go like this," D.R. said, making a motor boat sound. "And they do this with their head." He bobbed his head up and down.

"They do this with their foot," Maeve said, patting the table with her hand.

Randy smiled. "Well, then I guess that's how they talk."

"Grandma said the horses talked to each other today. All of them," D.R. said.

"It was amazing," Liz said.

Ben nodded. "Beau Born called to Bo-T, Bo-T called back, and then All Together started. It was the damnedest thing."

"Bo-T got a little worked up over it," George said. "It's like they really were saying something father, mother, son, to one another."

"I think we all need to learn to talk to the horses," Ben said.

"Linda called today," Dawn said. "She says it's official. She told them she wouldn't be back next year."

"Who's Linda?" Susie asked.

"One of the family," Ben said. "She's a clocker up at Erie."

"It'll be good having her here," Tom said.

"Not to mention little Maria," Liz added.

"I love Maria," Maeve said.

"I love her more," D.R. insisted.

Everyone laughed at this ongoing game of theirs, who loved who the most.

Ben looked around the table. All in all this had been a good day. Now if we can just get through the weekend, he thought.

"Does Bo-T gallop tomorrow?" Matthew asked.

Ben shook his head. "No, he'll walk."

"I'm almost finished with his drawing."

"You'll have to finish it in the barn, Son. The next time he leaves that stall, it'll be to load on the van for the Burgundy Blue."

"Are you taking him tomorrow or Saturday?" Tom asked.

Ben hesitated. Think long, think wrong. Stay the course. Don't change the plan now. All these thoughts ran through his mind. "Saturday," Ben said. "Matthew needs to finish his drawing."

Chapter Thirty-Seven

The *Morning Banter* had nothing written about the Burgundy Blue, nothing about Crimson Count, nothing about slots, nothing about Nottingham Downs at all aside from today's entries. It was a good start to the day. Ben was pleased. "Let's breeze Alley first." She was scheduled to go 3/16ths of a mile. Batgirl was in the third race. Wee Born was running in the fifth. Everyone went to work.

"Open for entries," Joe Feigler announced a short time later over the p.a. "Come on over."

Ben smiled, trailing along behind Alley Beau. She'd breezed good and was walking back to the barn in her typical stretched-out Cadillac limousine style. Lucy's dad, Tony Guciano, walked toward them following one of his horses.

"Hey, Junior," he said.

"Hey."

"Do you have time to get on one for me?"

"What time?" Junior said.

"Around nine."

Junior nodded.

Morning Dew was next. She galloped a mile and a half. Batgirl was handwalked. Wee Born was handwalked. Whinny was put on the walking machine. The horses were all back in their stalls by nine-thirty. Randy stopped by the barn around ten o'clock with a box of donuts and they all sat down in the tack room to take a break.

"Are you going to be here for the races this afternoon?" Dawn asked.

"I'm going to try. It's gelding day at the Russo farm." He knew better than to say "castration" day. Dawn hated that word. "If all goes well, I should be back at least for Wee Born's."

"Is Mark going with you?"

"Yes. He's going to meet me there." He gave her a kiss, grabbed another donut, and turned to leave. He didn't say anything. He tried not to even think of anything. Superstition ran deep in all of them.

Dawn smiled. "If we don't see you before then, we'll see you for dinner, wherever it might be." A win, they'd all go to The Rib. If not, they'd all gather at the farm. That was understood.

~ * ~

Cracker Jack Henderson sat in with announcer Bud Gipson for the calling of the Daily Double. The two were old friends and always "talked it up" as Ben would say. Ben looked at the announcer's booth and waved as he entered the paddock for the third race. Tom on Red, leading Batgirl, had just stepped onto the racetrack at the gap by the track kitchen.

Back at T-Bone's Place, the old-timers sat glued to their television.

"She such a pretty mare," Miguel said, when Tom dismounted Red and led Batgirl into the paddock. "She have good odds." She was 5-2. George and Glenda arrived to watch the race with them.

"Where's Matthew?" Vicky asked.

"Drawing. He says he's not leaving till he's done."

"It's hard watching him sometimes," Vicky said. "Especially when he holds his head to the side tying to visualize something he can't see facing head on."

"How he going to go hike a trail?" Miguel asked.

"I don't know," Glenda said, sitting down on the floor and making sure she wasn't in anybody's way.

"Oh, look, there's Cracker Jack!" Steven said.

"He come live here some day," Miguel said. "That what he say."

The bugle sounded and the horses were led out onto the racetrack.

"Whiskey City will be the one to beat," Mim said.

"Traitor," Clint said.

Mim shrugged. "I call 'em like I see 'em."

"So what are you doing in town?" Bud Gipson asked Cracker Jack.

"Well, I'm here to see some old friends, watch a few races, raise a little Cain."

Bud laughed. "Cracker Jack, as all of you may remember had the number one sports-talk show here in this city for well over thirty years. I remember you even more though for the charity marathons you used to run. What was that you used to say?"

"Winning isn't everything. It's how you run the race."

"All kidding aside, ladies and gentlemen, this man was one heck of a marathon runner. He never won…."

"But I always ran my race," Cracker Jack said.

"Look at the line at the hotdog stand," Bud said, "Looks like they're giving something away."

Everyone waiting for a hotdog waved up at them.

"Think you can throw us one? No, don't!" Bud said, he and Cracker Jack laughing.

"I could go for a hotdog," Clint said.

"The horses are approaching the gate."

Randy phoned Dawn. "I'm not going to make it. Four down and two to go, no pun intended."

"What about for Wee Born?"

"I don't know. We're trying."

Dawn hung up and walked out to the road between barns. The starting gate bell rang. "And they're off!"

She heard a loud truck noise behind her and turned to see a semi horse van pull up outside the receiving barn. The driver climbed down out of the cab, the engine still idling, and walked to the guard shack. He handed Jason some papers. Jason looked through them, signed one, and handed it back to the man.

With the big truck's diesel engine idling, there was no way Dawn could even hear herself think, let alone hear the call of the race. She looked down the road to the gap. She'd have to rely on seeing the horses pull up and hope Batgirl was one of the first ones to appear.

The driver of the van climbed up a metal ladder, looked inside, and then opened the doors. He pulled out the ramp and attached the wood panels on both sides to ensure the horse would walk down the ramp and not try to jump off. The horse's groom was inside the van with him.

When Dawn heard a loud whinny, she turned from watching the gap and got a glimpse of Crimson Count, standing in the van's center stall in crossties and bobbing his head. He was a gray horse. She hadn't realized that. The groom put a lead-shank on the horse, chain over his nose, and led him down the ramp. The horse stopped at the bottom, looked around for few seconds, and then walked with the man into the receiving barn and into the stall prepared for him. From this vantage point, Dawn could see him sniff all around the stall, then lie down and roll and stand up and shake off. He came to the front of his stall, leaned into the webbing and whinnied.

Dawn smiled. He was gorgeous! By the time she turned back around, the horses from the fourth race had already pulled up and were heading back to the grandstand. She couldn't make out Batgirl. "I must have missed her."

She glanced in at Wee Born. The mare was standing quietly in the back of her stall. The plan, if Batgirl went to the spit barn, was for Dusty to follow her back and help Tom. Dawn would need to do Wee Born's legs up in Vetwrap soon. If Batgirl didn't go to the spit barn, Tom would bring her back, Dawn would bath her at the wash rack and Tom would do Wee Born's legs. They didn't like doing a horse up too soon before it was time to leave the barn for the race, particularly the fillies and mares. They already had an inkling they were going to race today with having no hay in front of them.

Tom came around the corner at the gap on Red, leading Batgirl. Dawn looked for Dusty, looked and looked, walked way out into the road to try and spot him, and then here he came. Tom saw her and held up two fingers. She'd run second.

Dawn waved and walked down the shedrow to wrap Wee Born's legs. She was such a sweet mare, just stood there, looking around. Dawn told her all about Crimson Count. "Maybe you'll get to meet him someday. Who knows." By the time she got all four legs done and the mare's bridle on, mouth rinsed out and her tongue tied, the fourth race was just about to run. Tom called to her from outside the barn. She led the mare down the shedrow, handed her over, and followed them as far as the spit barn.

"Bring her back safe," she said.

Tom nodded. "That filly's game," Tom said, glancing over his shoulder. "She got knocked all over the place coming out of the gate, but none of the horses hit the board, so...."

"Who win it?"

"Whiskey City."

Dawn took Dusty's place in the spit barn. "Is she still drinking?"

"No, she's done." Dusty followed Tom and Wee Born to the paddock. After a few more laps around the spit barn, Dawn led Batgirl into the stall. She promptly squatted and "peed like a racehorse" as Tom would say and they walked back to their barn.

Dawn had the mare's stall already set up and did the ceremonial lap around their shedrow. Batgirl strutted her stuff, looking so proud. Horses nickered, came out to say hello and ooh and aah and watch her walking along. As soon as Dawn put her in her stall, she rolled, and then rolled again, stood and went right for her hay; behavior a horseman wants most to see in a horse after a race.

"And they're off!" she heard.

She walked down to the far end of the barn to try to hear better, stood up on the side of the muck bin and listened as hard as she could. "Wee Born. Wee Born." She cupped her ears. "Wee Born! Wee Born! Wee Born!" She distinctly heard Bud Gipson say the mare's name three times in a row. And then a final, "Weeeee Borrrrnnnn!"

"Yes! Yes! Yes!" she said. "Yes!"

The old-timers all cheered and clapped.

"Yes!"

Tom helped pull the mare up, patted her on the neck, and congratulated Johnny.

"Look, there's Tom," Jeannie said. "There's Ben."

"Hot damn!" Miguel said.

Tom dismounted Red and led the mare into the winner's circle. Ben, Dusty, and Cracker Jack Henderson stood at his side, all smiles. The race was posted official. The photographer snapped the photo.

~ * ~

The celebration at The Rib was a loud affair. Randy and Mark arrived late. There had been some concern over one of the "geldings" today, but all was well now. The horse came around and was up and eating when they left.

"I saw the replays," Mark said. "Both horses run big!"

Ben nodded. "That Batgirl's a gamer. She tried her hardest."

"Wee Born win easy," Tom said.

"That reminds me," Glenda said. "The old-timers would like to host dinner tomorrow night, no matter what uh…kind of weather we have."

Everyone laughed. Superstitions. She was referring to Bo-T and Alley Beau racing tomorrow. "They said they have enough chairs for an army. Miguel's going to make his famous chili and promised we'd all be able to eat it without the need of a fire extinguisher."

"Jeanne's going to make Johnnycake bread to go with it," Junior said.

"Mim's going to bake pies," Lucy said.

"They're all excited," Glenda added.

Ben smiled and raised his glass. "Then T-Bone's Place it is. Here's to tomorrow, to friends and family, to horses. Salud!"

"Salud!"

Chapter Thirty-Eight
The Burgundy Blue

Jason handed Dawn a copy of the *Morning Banter* and ducked back inside the guard shack out of the rain. Judging from his expression, she wasn't so sure she wanted to read it. "Match Race for Fame and Future. Stallion Careers on the Line." She tucked the paper inside her rain slicker and walked to the barn.

"This is bullshit!" Tom said.

"It's just all publicity," Dusty said.

"None of this would even be happening if it weren't for…."

Richard walked into the tack room.

"Oh, Jesus," Ben said. The last time this man showed up at the barn this early in the morning, his job was on the line. "What are you doing here?"

"Uh…." Richard paused, started for the coffee, and Ben stopped him.

"What?"

Richard cleared his throat. "How do you feel about Bo-T going to the receiving barn?"

"He has a stall here. This is his barn," Ben said. "Why would I take him there?"

"For publicity."

Ben turned. "I hate that word! Don't anyone ever say it again! Not in my presence! None of you!"

Richard hesitated. "It would be on the noon news. It might draw an even bigger crowd. The rivalry. The suspense. The anticipation."

"You know, Richard," Ben said. "Sometimes I don't even like you."

"I know." Richard said. "But that's okay. It's the times that you do that keep me going. You've entrusted me with a job to do, Ben, and that's what I'm doing. I'm doing my job."

Ben looked at him and glanced around the room at Tom, Dusty, Junior, and Dawn. This was his decision. "I don't have a crystal ball, Richard. And this being the first I've heard of this…. It's not about publicity for me. It's about what's right for the horse. I've half a mind to just scratch."

"Well, that's another thing," Richard said. "Two horses have already scratched this morning. Whether it's because of the rain or the match race, I don't know, but we're down to a seven-horse field."

Ben sighed. Bo-T liked the mud. According to Crimson Count's form, so did he. "You know, being the owner of a racetrack and having to make these kinds of decisions, when for me, it's still all about the horse…."

"But that's just it, Ben. If you weren't the owner, you'd have no choice. I wouldn't be here right now. You'd go where we tell you."

Ben looked at him and shook his head. "Let's just get one thing straight. Had I known I was shipping him into the receiving barn, I'd have brought him back yesterday. He'd have had the night to settle in. We're shipping him into a barn he's never seen, with horses on both sides he's never seen."

"We could put him by himself," Richard suggested.

"Which is worse, Richard. Come on!" Ben said. "Damn it!"

"Ben…." Dawn said. She hated seeing him upset. She worried, she feared. In the blink of an eye, she could see him slumped over his desk, another stroke.

"Dawn, don't," Ben said. "Don't say anything. Please. You don't think I know what you're thinking. I'm fine.

I'm a horse trainer, and I'm thinking about my horse! He belongs here in this barn," he said emphatically. "You want to throw the race? You want to ruin his stud career?" He shook his head and looked around at each and every one of them. "You're not thinking about the horse."

"Por favor, Meester Dusty," they all heard a small voice say. A man stood in the doorway, a stranger. "They say you here. My horse do no good. Barn empty. I ask mission so move."

Dusty spoke to him in Spanish and sat back. "Oh, Lord."

"What?" Tom asked.

"This is Crimson Count's groom. He says the horse is starting to worry."

Ben looked at Richard. "How's this for publicity?" He motioned at Dusty. "Tell him to bring him here. He can put him in B-Bo's stall. Junior, go help him."

Richard watched Junior and Dusty leave with the man and stood staring for a moment. "This'll work, I think. This'll work." He looked at Ben and started down the shedrow. "This'll work."

"No cameras down here all afternoon," Ben said. "You hear me?"

Richard waved. "I hear you."

Ben looked at Tom and Dawn. "Does he understand?"

They both nodded. It wasn't often it was just the three of them sitting here in this tack room. All the memories of their years together, the conversations, the laughter, the tears, it was all there between them, swirling around them, and deep inside. They just looked at one another for a moment. The heart of Nottingham Downs, past, present, and future.

"You make me proud, old man," Tom said, clearing his throat, his voice trembling. "You make me proud."

Dawn gave them both a hug and wiped her eyes. "I want you to know, no matter what happens, today or tomorrow or whenever, I love you," she said. "I love you both and I couldn't love you more."

~ * ~

Crimson Count made himself right at home in barn fourteen as did his groom Luis. "I be with horse all years," he said to Tom. Alley Beau, in the stall next to him, appeared rather enamored with the colt. The two horses seemed to have a calming effect on one another. Wendy had called in one of the backside security guards that was off duty today to watch over the barn. When Crimson Count's trainer Bill Maxwell arrived, somewhat unnerved as to why his horse was in this barn and not the receiving barn, Tom was on hand to explain the situation.

Bo-T was due to arrive any minute. Training was over for the morning. The horses were all back in their stalls and done up. Ben walked down the shedrow just as George pulled the van up outside the barn. Glenda had ridden with him. The two were planning to stay for the races. Bill Maxwell introduced himself to Ben. The two men shook hands, and Ben walked down to oversee Bo-T unload off the van. Bill Maxwell walked up beside him.

"So this is Bo-T."

The colt let out a whinny.

"I saw his sire race once," the man said. "Nice horse."

Ben nodded.

"He travel okay?" Ben asked George.

"He traveled good. You wouldn't even know he was there."

George pulled the ramp down and climbed in and put a lead shank on Bo-T. The colt whinnied again, rocking the van. Ben noticed several people out of the corner of his eye standing just behind the van. He shook his head. It was a reporter and photographer. "I got an okay for a few photos," the photographer said. "Do you want me to stand behind the truck?"

"No, "Ben said. "I want you to come over and stand next to me where he can see you."

The photographer took his place next to Ben and snapped several shots of Bo-T walking down the ramp off the van, another one from the side as George led him into the barn, and another from behind as George walked Bo-T down the shedrow to his stall.

"Mr. Miller, do you have time for a few questions?" the reporter asked.

"A few." Ben motioned for both him and the photographer to step into the tack room, and nodded at Bill Maxwell to follow.

"Do you mind?" The photographer pointed to the bridle with Bo-T's name above it. Ben shrugged. It was hanging next to the bridle with Beau Born's name above it. "This is nice." He switched to his video camera.

At that moment Bill Maxwell realized that Beau Born had been Ben Miller's. He listened as the reporter asked the question. "What's it like to have a champion in your barn again?"

"Well," Ben said. "I'd have to say it feels pretty good."

"I understand there's a possibility Beau Together, Bo-T, if you will, is targeted toward a stallion career."

"Yes, that's true. His first year of breeding will be Breezeway Farm. The fact is so will Crimson Count." He nudged the woman toward Bill, who smiled a million-dollar smile, quite used to being in the limelight. "This is Bill Maxwell, Crimson Count's trainer."

"Well, lucky timing," the reporter said. "Maybe I ought to go place a wager today."

Tom started into the tack room and backed out, but not before catching the woman's eye. He looked like the Marlboro man, she thought, in the flesh. "So, Mr, uh, Mr.

Maxwell. What do you think your horse's chance is today to beat Bo-T? I mean, after all, he is the track-record holder for 6 ½ furlongs."

"I think it's going to be a horse race. We're going a mile. My colt's fit. He's coming off two wins."

Ben gave him a thumbs up. Good answer.

"So, since this basically is a match race between these two horses, where will you be putting your money, Mr. Miller?"

Ben smiled. "I never bet against my own horse."

"Well, there you have it," the reporter said. "Ben Miller thinks he's going to win. Bill Maxwell thinks his horse will win. It'll be a race to watch."

Right after the reporter and photographer left, the blacksmith showed up. He checked both Alley Beau and Bo-T and said they were good to go. Ben looked at Bill Maxwell. "You want him to…?"

"Sure. Thank you."

Brownie checked Crimson Count. "Everything's good. He looks like he was done about a week ago."

"Precisely," Bill Maxwell said.

Randy walked down the shedrow, made his greetings and asked about Dawn. "Where is she?"

"She's over with Wendy. They're working on a video. She'll be back soon."

"She's not answering her cellphone."

"She left it in her rain slicker," Tom said. "It's been ringing off the hook."

It had stopped raining around nine this morning. Randy retrieved the phone, said he'd take it to her, and phoned Wendy to let her know. He looked back at Ben and Tom. He didn't say anything. He just looked back.

They both nodded.

Bill Maxwell looked at them.

"We're all superstitious," Tom said. "We don't…."

Bill laughed. "I understand, totally. I'm the same way. Just so you know when it happens, this one time I was leaving the barn for a race and I thought I forgot something. I turned around, realized I hadn't, and turned back around. We win that day. I haven't gone over for a race since without turning around in a circle before I leave the barn."

~ * ~

Tom tacked Red and led him down the shedrow. Alley had been done up all fours in Vetwrap, rundown patches applied. Because of the rain this morning, the track condition had been listed as slow for the first two races, but was drying and now cupping out a little. Dawn put Alley's bridle on, rinsed her mouth, and tied her tongue.

"Let's go," Tom said, mounting Red.

Dawn led the filly down the shedrow and around back so she wouldn't pass in front of Bo-T or Crimson Count and handed her over to Tom. "Bring her back safe."

Tom nodded. Even though there was a racetrack guard on watch, Dawn still remained at the barn to keep an eye on Bo-T. The guard was there to prevent wrong-doing, not to watch out for a horse's well-being. She looked in at the horse, didn't dwell, grabbed the muck basket, and started cleaning Alley's stall.

Crimson Count's groom was sitting on a bench outside his stall, whittling. "What are you making?" she asked, as she passed him on the way to dump the muck basket.

He looked up and shrugged.

On the way back she stopped and watched him for a moment. It looked like it could be the handle on a cane. She imitated walking with a cane and he nodded. "El abuelo."

"Ah, your grandfather." Dawn smiled and walked on, thinking about the old-timers. They were probably all in their living room lined up in front of the TV anxiously awaiting the race. She heard Bud Gipson announce, "Don't get shut out."

It must be getting close to post time, she thought. "Run good, Alley. Run good." It was over two weeks since she'd run last, a win. Dawn walked out to the road to hear the sound of the starting gate bell.

"And they're off!" There was no sound after that so she went back to finish cleaning the stall, bed it nice and deep, filled the haynet, did the filly's water bucket, and hung one in the shedrow. She walked back out onto the road, looked, listened, looked some more, and saw the horses canter past the kitchen. Their racing colors of green and white were never easy to spot this time of day against the backdrop of the infield grass.

She glanced over her shoulder at Bo-T, and then glanced again. What was he doing? Was he going to roll? She walked back to check on him. He'd laid down. This was a first, his laying down the day of a race, his laying down much at all during the day. She watched him for a moment, watched his breathing, watched his eyes, watched his bottom lip as it started to droop.

She heard a noise behind her and turned to see Tom leading Alley up to the barn. "She run fourth," he said. "She never got ahold of the track. She fought it the whole way."

Dawn walked out and took hold of her. Tom dismounted Red, loosened his girth and tapped Red on the butt. He walked down the shedrow into his stall. The filly was covered in dirt from head to toe; she even had dirt in her eyes. "This ain't nothing. You should've seen Jenny." The filly was still breathing hard and was all corded-up. Dawn took her bridle off. Tom put her halter on.

"I'll get her. Go check on Bo-T."

Tom looked at her. "Why?"

"I don't know. He's laying down."

"What? Bo-T?" Tom walked slowly down the shedrow, leaned, and peeked inside Bo-T's stall. The horse was not only laying down, but snoring. Tom looked at Dawn.

She motioned, whispering, "Is he okay?"

He peeked in again and walked back. "That's weird. If it were B-Bo, it'd be normal, but not Bo-T."

They gave Alley a drink and took her to the wash rack in clear sight of the barn, clear sight of Bo-T's stall. She got a good suds bath. Tom scraped her off, wiped her down and blew the dirt and mud out of her eyes. Back at the barn, they put a cooler on her and gave her another drink. Tom decided to walk her up and down the road, rather than in the shedrow in front of Bo-T and Crimson Count's stalls. Dawn hauled the water bucket out and hung it on the screw eye on the back of the barn facing the road.

The filly took a drink at each pass. Tom put her into her stall after about fifteen minutes, let her pee, and brought her back out. Dawn was just finishing up cleaning her bridle. "Did you think she was tying up?"

"A little. She seems fine now though."

"How's Ben?"

"He's good. He's in a good mood. Not her fault she's so big and lanky and the track's cupping out."

Dawn nodded. "Is he coming back to the barn?"

"He says no. He's going up to the clubhouse with Dusty and Cracker Jack."

Dawn smiled. The filly was watching a calico cat meandering down the road between the barns. She lowered her head for a better look and snorted. Tom patted her on the neck, felt her chest, walked her a little while longer, and then put her in her stall. Dawn crept down the shedrow to check on Bo-T. He was still all stretched out with eyes closed and sound asleep.

Alley Beau rolled in her stall, stood up and shook off, then rolled again. Another good body shake. With a mouthful of hay, she walked to the front of her stall and looked out as if she hadn't a care in the world and had never even left the barn.

Tom's cellphone rang. It was Mim.

"She okay?"

"Yeah, she's fine. She couldn't get a hold of the track."

"That's what I figured. All right, just checking. We're all with you."

"Thanks, Mim," Tom said.

"By the way," she said. "Matthew finished the painting of Bo-T."

Tom hesitated, just listening. Mim's voice had cracked.

"He has the eyes and heart of a champion. That boy does too."

Tom swallowed hard and couldn't speak. Just this morning, he'd seen Matthew reach for the remote and miss it entirely.

"Wish him well when he leaves and don't worry. He'll find his way."

~ * ~

With each race that afternoon, the track condition became faster and faster. The eighth race going a mile and 70 yards was won in a blistering pace of 1:41 and 2/5ths seconds.

"Let's go!" Tom said. "The race is over." George had walked back over to the barn in case he was needed. Dawn led Bo-T out of his stall, down the shedrow, and handed him over to Tom. Crimson Count followed their lead. His trainer did a complete circle before leaving the barn. He and the groom walked on both sides of the horse derby-style. Danno, the pony boy Bill Maxwell lined up for the race, rode his horse alongside. Dawn noticed several photographers along the way in the barn area. One stood at the gap leading onto the racetrack.

When Bo-T made a stallion kind of hrummph hrummph sound at a filly being led off the racetrack, Tom jiggled his rein and patted him on the head to divert his attention. "How can he smell her with all that Vicks up his nose? You be the man, Bo-T!"

George laughed.

"Did Dawn tell you he napped all afternoon?"

George nodded. 'He's been napping in the afternoons at the farm too, all stretched out and snoring. Just like B-Bo."

Dawn walked next to him, her stomach cramping. She couldn't remember the last time she'd gotten this nervous over a race. Another photographer was stationed just inside the paddock entrance.

"Ladies and gentlemen," Bud Gipson announced, "The horses for the fifteenth running of the Burgundy Blue Stake are entering the paddock. This race will be contested at a flat mile. For those of you who are visiting Nottingham Downs for the first time today, Beau Together also known as Bo-T, is the track record holder for six and a half furlongs here at Nottingham Downs."

The old-timers were all glued to the television at T-Bone's Place.

George took Bo-T from Tom, led him in, and Dawn headed for the ladies room. By the time she came back out, the horses were all tacked and being paraded around the paddock in front of the fans.

"He looks like a million bucks," Dusty said.

Ben nodded. Bo-T was strutting his stuff.

Dawn walked up next to him.

Crimson Count was right behind Bo-T, putting on a show as well. "If we breed one of our mares to him," Dawn asked, "would we get a gray?"

Ben smiled. "You'd have a good chance."

"I like him. Don't get me wrong, I want them to finish just the way they are now." Crimson Count was behind Bo-T. "But I like him. I think things happen for a reason. If we weren't running today, I'd have never even seen him."

The jockeys came out of the room and walked toward their horse's owners and trainers. "Hey, Bo-T," Johnny said, when the colt was led past him.

Bo-T pricked his ears and gave a little buck.

Crimson Count reacted by stomping.

The fans loved it!

Bo-T was coming out of the three hole. Crimson Count, the four. Both were at even odds. Ben pulled Johnny close and looked him in the eye. "I want a win. But I also want him coming back even more."

"I know," Johnny said. "I know what's at stake."

"Riders up!"

The bugle sounded.

George gave Johnny a leg-up and led Bo-T out to the racetrack and handed him over to Tom. "You ready, Big Man?" Tom asked. "You ready?"

"He's ready," Johnny said.

As the horses paraded in front of the crowd, Bud Gipson announced the horses' breeding and record of wins, places and shows. "These are all future sires. That's the legacy of the Burgundy Blue. Place your wagers. Don't get shut out."

Dawn, Ben, Dusty, George, Glenda, and Cracker Jack all took their places at the fence. Dawn glanced up at Wendy. Richard was standing next to her. When they both waved, Dawn covered her heart. It was beating a thousand times a minute.

"The horses are approaching the starting gate."

Going a flat mile, the horses were right in front of the grandstand. Dawn pressed her head against the fence and took a deep breath.

Ben smiled at her. "He'll be fine."

She nodded and glanced in the direction of the track kitchen. Randy's truck was parked next to the Ginny stand. Mark's truck was parked right behind it. She took another deep breath.

"Crimson Count is the last horse to load," Bud announced. "They're at the post for the running of the Burgundy Blue Stake. They're off!"

Dawn's heart skipped a beat. This was her baby. This was his last race.

"Away cleanly, it's Dunkirk Dave with an early lead. A length back is Rapid Essential with Top Banjo on his shoulder. Another length back it is Beau Together and Crimson Count running head to head. Then it's Neighbor Newton, Hathaway Tam trailing the field into the first turn."

Ben looked at the tote board, could see it fairly well. The first quarter was run in 23 and 2/5ths.

"Dunkirk Dave still leads by a length as they start down the backstretch. Rapid Essential is running second, Top Banjo third. Finding their stride and closing it's Beau Together and Crimson Count. Hathaway Tom continues to trail the field by six lengths."

Dawn strained to see over the tote board.

"He's making a move," Cracker Jack said, as tall as a mountain. "He's making his move."

"Dunkirk Dave reaches the half-mile mark in forty-six flat. Rapid Essential, Beau Together and Crimson Count are closing on the leader. As they start into the clubhouse turn, it's Rapid Essential now taking over the lead with Beau Together and Crimson Count right on his shoulder, followed by Neighbor Newton, and Hathaway Tam."

Dawn climbed up onto the fence.

"At the head of the stretch, Dunkirk Dave is dropping back. Rapid Essential is on the lead. But here comes Beau Together and Crimson Count, and making a big move out in the middle of the racetrack is Hathaway Tam."

"Come on, Bo-T," Dawn said.

Mim scooched to the edge of her seat. "Come on, Bo-T."

"Rapid Essential is on the rail, barely holding on to his lead as here comes Beau Together and Crimson Count. It is Beau Together taking over the lead.

"Come on, Bo-T," Ben said.

"Think of all those mares," George said. "Come on, Bo-T!"

"With an eighth of a mile left to go, it is Beau Together and Crimson Count, a two horse race out in front by two. Hathaway Tam is now third."

"Come, Bo-T. Come Bo-T," Miguel said, slapping his leg with the racing form. "Come, Bo-T!"

"Come on, Bo-T!" Junior yelled, leaning over the fence. "Come on, Bo-T!"

"Beau Together, Count Crimson! Beau Together by a nose, by a head!"

"Come on, Bo-T," Randy said. "Come on! Win it big!!"

"It's Beau Together by a neck. Crimson Count is running second. Hathaway Tam is third, followed by Dunkirk Dave, Rapid Essential, Neighbor Newton and Top Banjo!"

Dawn held her breath, gripped Ben's shoulder hard.

"It's Beau Together by half a length!"

"Come on, Bo-T," the crowd yelled.

"Come on, Bo-T!"

"Come on, Big Man," Junior said."Come on, Big Man! We're gonna be daddies!!"

"At the wire, maintaining his lead is Beau Together! Bo-T in complete command!"

Dawn flashed back to the day Bo-T broke his maiden, the day Ben said without a doubt in the world, "He's going to be a champion!"

"He's going to make you proud, Ben," Johnny had said. "He's going to make you proud."

"Ladies and gentlemen. It's not often history repeats itself. There is a new track record for the mile. Beau Together, track record holder for 6 ½ furlongs has just broken the track record for the mile by one-fifth of a second. Crimson Count equaled the track record. May we see their offspring for many years to come here at Nottingham Downs!"

Tom helped Johnny pull up Bo-T, congratulated the jockey, and patted the horse on the neck. "They be standing in line now, Big Man! You can dream fillies and mares tonight." Both Johnny and Tom congratulated Ramone Diaz, the jockey on Crimson Count and the two pony boys led the horses back to the grandstand, side by side.

The crowd was on their feet, cheering. Next to the Ohio Derby, this was the biggest race of the year at Nottingham Downs.

Dawn waved to Wendy and Richard, waved to Randy and Mark. Tom dismounted Red and led Bo-T and Johnny into the winner's circle. Everyone took their places for the win picture. The photographer snapped the photo, the sun shining bright, the horse gleaming with sweat and wide-eyed.

"Wait," Tom said. "Snap another one." He clicked to Red, who stepped into the winner's circle and sidled up next to Bo-T. Everyone in the winner's circle knew what this meant. It was pride in the pony horse's job all these years, a good-bye of sorts to Bo-T. "Well done," Tom said to both horses. "Well done."

"Ladies and gentlemen, the fifteenth running of the Burgundy Blue Stake is official. Beau Together, Bo-T, retired as of this moment in history is in the winner's circle. The Burgundy Blue Stakes winner! Let's hear it for Bo-T! Let's hear it for his pony, Red!"

Wendy wiped her eyes.

Tom mounted right at that moment and waved as he and Red led Bo-T out of the winner's circle to the roar of the crowd. Dawn walked along with George and Glenda behind the two horses, the three of them all smiles. Dusty and Cracker Jack walked with Ben and Johnny toward the jocks' room.

"He win easy, Ben," Johnny said. "Running off the farm agrees with him. You sure you want to retire him?"

Ben smiled. "I've never been surer of anything in my life." A reporter stood up ahead with a cameraman. Ben patted Johnny on the back and walked on.

"Mr. Miller?"

Ben stopped. Dusty and Cracker Jack at his side.

"If I might get a quote?"

"Well," Ben said, scratching his head and thinking for a moment. "I just got a great ride and I've had a great ride. I've had a great life. Don't get me wrong, I'm not done yet. We have babies at the farm. We have a good meal waiting for us with friends and family at home. I'm a lucky man."

"I'll say," Bill Maxwell said, walking with his jockey. He shook Ben's hand. "Congratulations!"

"You too," Ben said. "Your horse run big." He motioned for the reporter to talk with Bill and he and Dusty and Cracker Jack walked on. "I'll see you back at the barn."

~ * ~

The celebration dinner at T-Bone's Place was a jovial affair. They all sat eating Miguel's chili seasoned and simmered to perfection along with buttered chunks of Jeanne's Johnnycake bread, all looking forward to Mim's blackberry pie al a mode.

There was so much to talk about, so much to celebrate. Bo-T's win, his retirement, his future as a sire. "Today reminded me of the day he broke his maiden," Dawn said. "That was the day I think I decided to…."

"Commit yourself?" Ben said.

Dawn smiled. "Yes. Good word. At times, I've felt like I should be committed."

Everyone laughed. Some were seated at the table, some in the living room. The dogs were keeping vigil outside the screen door on the front porch.

"What you do with him now?" Miguel asked.

"Well," Ben said. "We'll bring him home tomorrow and in a couple of days start getting him used to pasture again."

"So he stay here?"

"Till breeding season. Then he'll be back. That's the way I set it up."

Dawn smiled. She liked that arrangement. "What about breeding one of the mares to Crimson Count?" Batgirl, Whinny, and Wee Born were all going to be six this coming year.

"We'll see," Ben said. He already had a stallion picked out for Whinny. "Maybe Wee Born."

"What about B-Bo?" Steven asked. "Will he go in to the track tomorrow?"

"No," Ben said, glancing at Randy. "I think I'm going to give him a little more time here. I just may run him off the farm," he said, thinking about the old-timers and how much they enjoyed watching the horses gallop. "It sure worked like a charm for Bo-T." They all smiled. "Not to mention the two-year olds. They'll be starting up soon."

Junior nodded, as did Tom and George. This was about the time of year they started getting the two-year olds used to being under saddle and depending on the horses' knees, start light training. "There will be lots going on here. Which reminds me," Ben said. "I think I'm going to sleep in tomorrow."

Everyone looked at him.

"Seriously," he said. "That's if I can. Old habits are hard to break."

"You're not coming to the track?" Tom asked.

"Nope. Not tomorrow. The horses all walk. There's no one to enter. I'm going to take it easy for a day. I'm looking forward to it."

Matthew unveiled his drawing of Bo-T after dinner. "Hillary came by to visit," he said. "She says I captured his thoughts." He looked at Mim. "Mim says I captured his eyes and his heart. I still have a little more to do on B-Bo's."

He'd captured it all, the beauty of a Thoroughbred racehorse galloping, proud, happy, strong, living in the moment and yet seeing into the future, a lifetime. Bo-T. A champion.

From far off in the starry distance, one could see T-Bone's Place lit up in the night. They could hear the sounds of laughter. A refuge: a place to lay one's head in the final years surrounded by friends and family. Look closer and you can see Lucy press her hand gently against the movement of her unborn child. Listen carefully and you can almost hear whispers of the hopes and dreams of everyone at Meg's Meadows. It is a welcome place. It's home.

~ * ~

Two weeks after the Burgundy Blue, Mim passed away. Vicky walked out onto the back porch and saw her sitting on her golf cart by the main pasture watching the horses graze as she'd done so many times. When she turned to go back inside, she noticed Mim's cane leaning against the porch.

She looked at Mim again and pressed her hand to her heart. "Oh, Mim, you knew," she said, tears of sadness mixing with tears of happiness welling up in her eyes. "You knew."

No one dressed in black. They wore the bright colors of the rainbow. They cried. They laughed. They remembered. Mim's golf cart remains in the same spot to this day, her ashes spread all around and flowers planted everywhere. It is a living memorial to one of the greatest horsewomen that ever lived.

May You Rest in Peace, Mim

May You Rest in Peace

Manufactured by Amazon.ca
Bolton, ON